495 h
S0-BON-220

MEDIEVAL RUSSIA

A Source Book, 900–1700

MEDIEVAL RUSSIA

A SOURCE BOOK, 900–1700

EDITED BY

BASIL DMYTRYSHYN
PORTLAND STATE COLLEGE

Holt, Rinehart and Winston, Inc.
NEW YORK, CHICAGO, SAN FRANCISCO,
TORONTO, LONDON

TO
VIRGINIA

DK
3
D57

WRM

Copyright © 1967 by Holt, Rinehart and Winston, Inc.
All Rights Reserved
Library of Congress Catalog Card Number: 66–24391
21870–0217
Printed in the United States of America

PREFACE

Medieval Russia: A Source Book is a collection of basic sources on political, social, economic, and cultural life in medieval Russia, and is designed for the student, the general reader, and the scholar who is not a specialist. It is neither a text nor a substitute for a text, but an attempt to furnish what a more formal volume cannot offer— extensive, illustrative source material to amplify and enrich the text.

The sections fall into two main categories: excerpts from chronicles, letters, and official instructions written or issued by medieval Russians; and observations of, or commentaries on, the customs, habits, and ideas of the Russian people as recorded by their European con- temporaries. Each of the forty-one selections is preceded by a brief introduction aimed at making the article more meaningful by placing it in its proper historical perspective.

The task of selecting representative documents that would con- tribute to a greater understanding of Russian medieval history was not an easy one, especially when dealing with such a complex and un- wieldy subject. Some readers may feel that their areas of interest have been under-represented, but, this is unavoidable in any effort to survey some eight hundred years of history in one volume. Space, too, was a problem, for complete documents (or documents as nearly complete as practicable) were preferred to brief excerpts so that the reader might achieve greater insight into the important events of the coun- try's past.

Wherever possible existing translations of documents were used; some of these appeared in rare or expensive editions and are now out of print or not readily available. Such translations are repro- duced here in their original form. Because there is no uniform way to transliterate from Cyrillic to Roman characters, the selections translated by different scholars show a diversity in the spellings of certain Russian names.

Many documents of this collection, however, appear here in English for the first time. Because of considerable difference in syntax and style, translation of these documents presented several technical diffi-

D11604— GEN. LIB. UNIVERSITY OF WASHINGTON LIBRARY SEATTLE

v

culties and many passages required some adaptation to modern English. The same solution, regarding spelling and transliteration, was applied to a number of documents written in sixteenth-century English. In all my own translations I have aimed for accuracy instead of poetic or elegant rendition, and I have adhered to the system of transliteration used by the Library of Congress, with only minor exceptions. Thus all Russian proper names ending in ий have been rendered as -ii- (Shuiskii); the Russian ю has been rendered throughout as -iu- (Iurii); and the Russian я has been rendered as -ia- (Iaroslav). An exception to this rule is the word бояр which, because of the widely used English spelling, has been rendered as boyar. All apostrophes have been excluded and plurals of all untranslatable Russian words (*voevodas, dengas*) have been anglicized. A glossary listing unfamiliar expressions and terms not readily translatable has been appended, as well as three genealogical tables of Russian princes and tsars from 862 to 1917 and a chronological table.

It is a pleasant custom among scholars to thank all those who have made possible the appearance of a work. I acknowledge my indebtedness to the following institutions and individuals: the Research Committee of Portland State College for financial assistance that helped defray travel expenses for the selection of material from the Russian collection at the University of California Library at Berkeley; the University of Illinois Research Board for providing a research assistant, Barry Hoffman, who assisted me in the preparation of the bibliography; the publishers who kindly permitted me to reprint selections from previously translated material (individually acknowledged under each item); my colleagues at Portland State College for their interest and encouragement; and Mrs. Elizabeth Phelps, Mrs. Deanna Bozeman, and Miss Doris Jamison, who volunteered their typing services.

Lastly, I owe more than I can express to my wife Virginia, who has read this manuscript with a keen eye, and whose critical judgment has helped to improve it. It is for this and many other reasons that this volume is dedicated to her.

Basil Dmytryshyn

Portland, Oregon
June 1966

CONTENTS

part 1

KIEVAN RUS

1

The Distribution
of Medieval Slavs

Our knowledge of the original home of the Slavs, like that of most people in their preliterary development, is nebulous. One of the most vital sources of the early history of eastern Slavs is *Povest Vremennykh Let* (*The Tale of Bygone Years*), also known as *Nachalnaia Letopis* or the *Primary Chronicle*. Modern scholarship has established that the *Primary Chronicle* was compiled between 1037 and 1118 by monks of the Kievan Crypt Monastery. Among its many contributors were Nikon, who recorded events from 1060 to 1073, some of which were eyewitness accounts; and Nestor, who in the year 1113 gave the *Primary Chronicle* its present form. Since Nestor's version was subsequently used by other Russian chroniclers, until the nineteenth century the *Primary Chronicle* was known as the *Chronicle of Nestor*. Although Nestor's original edition has not been preserved we have two later editions of his work: the *Lavrentian Chronicle*, prepared in 1377 for a prince in Suzdal, and the *Hypatian Chronicle*, which dates from the middle of the fifteenth century and was discovered in the Hypatian Monastery at Kostroma.

The *Primary Chronicle*, as well as similar medieval records of Russian history, is a mixture of re-

Reprinted by permission of the publishers from Samuel H. Cross, "The Russian Primary Chronicle," *Harvard Studies and Notes in Philology and Literature* (Cambridge, Mass., Harvard University Press, 1930), vol. 12, pp. 136–142.

ligious writings, legend, fact, and fiction. Except for
the introduction, it is organized on a yearly basis
beginning with the year 852 (or 6360 according to
the old Byzantine calendar used in Russia until
1699). The *Chronicle* contains many brief entries
as well as lengthy and colorful accounts of wars,
feuds, agreements, and other developments.

These are the narratives of bygone years regarding the origin of
the land of Rus, who first began to rule in Kiev, and from what source
the land Rus had its beginning. . . .

For many years the Slavs lived beside the Danube, where the Hungarian and Bulgarian lands now lie. From among these Slavs, parties
scattered throughout the country and were known by appropriate
names, according to the places where they settled. Thus some came
and settled by the river Morava, and were named Moravians, while others
were called Czechs. Among these same Slavs are included the White
Croats, the Serbs, and the Khorutanians. For when the Vlakhs attacked
the Danubian Slavs, settled among them, and did them violence, the
latter came and made their homes by the Vistula, and were then called
Lyakhs. Of these same Lyakhs some were called Polyanians, some Lutich-
ians, some Mazovians, and still others Pomorians. Certain Slavs settled
also on the Dnieper, and were likewise called Polyanians. Still others
were named Derevlians, because they lived in the forests. Some also
lived between the Pripet and the Dvina, and were known as Dregovichians. Other tribes resided along the Dvina and were called Polotians on
account of a small stream called the Polota, which flows into the Dvina.
It was from this same stream that they were named Polotians. The Slavs
also dwelt about Lake Ilmen, and were known there by their appropriate
name. They built a city which they called Novgorod. Still others had
their homes along the Desna, the Sem, and the Sula, and were called
Severians. Thus the Slavic race was divided, and its language was known
as Slavic.

When the Polyanians lived by themselves among the hills, a trade-
route connected the Varangians with the Greeks. Starting from Greece,
this route proceeds along the Dnieper, above which a portage leads to
the Lovat. By following the Lovat, the great lake Ilmen is reached. The
river Volkhov flows out of this lake and enters the great lake Nevo. The
mouth of this lake opens into the Varangian Sea. Over this sea goes the
route to Rome, and on from Rome overseas to Tsargrad. The Pontus,
into which flows the river Dnieper, may be reached from that point. The
Dnieper itself rises in the upland forest, and flows southward. The Dvina
has its source in the same forest, but flows northward and empties into
the Varangian Sea. The Volga rises in the same forest, but flows to the

east, and discharges through seventeen mouths into the Caspian Sea. It is possible by this route to the eastward to reach the Bulgars and the Caspians, and thus attain the region of Shem. Along the Dvina runs the route to the Varangians, whence one may reach Rome, and go on from there to the race of Ham. But the Dnieper flows through various mouths into the Pontus. This sea, beside which taught St. Andrew, Peter's brother, is called the Russian Sea. . . .

The Polyanians lived apart and governed their families, for thus far they were brethren, and each one lived with his gens on his own lands, ruling over his kinsfolk. There were three brothers, Kii, Shchek, and Khoriv, and their sister was named Lybed. Kii lived upon the hill where the Borich trail now is, and Shchek dwelt upon the hill now named Shchekovitza, while on the third resided Khoriv, after whom this hill is named Khorevitza. They built a town and named it Kiev after their oldest brother. Around the town lay a wood and a great pine-forest in which they used to catch wild beasts. These men were wise and prudent;

they were called Polyanians, and there are Polyanians descended from them living in Kiev to this day.

Some ignorant persons have claimed that Kii was a ferryman, for near Kiev there was at that time a ferry from the other side of the river, in consequence of which people used to say, "To Kii's ferry." Now if Kii had been a mere ferryman, he would never have gone to Tsargrad. He was then the chief of his kin, and it is related what great honor he received from the Emperor when he went to visit him. On his homeward journey, he arrived at the Danube. The place pleased him, and he built a small town, wishing to dwell there with his kinsfolk. But those who lived near by would not grant him this privilege. Yet even now the dwellers by the Danube call this town Kievetz. When Kii returned to Kiev, his native city, he ended his life there; and his brothers Shchek and Khoriv, as well as their sister Lybed, died there also.

After the death of these three brothers, their gens assumed the supremacy among the Polyanians. The Derevlians possessed a principality of their own, as did also the Dregovichians, while the Slavs had their own authority in Novgorod, and another principality existed on the Polota, where the Polotians dwell. Beyond them reside the Krivichians, who live at the head waters of the Volga, the Dvina, and the Dnieper, and whose city is Smolensk. It is there that the Krivichians dwell; and beyond them are the Severians. At Byelo-Ozero are situated the Ves, and on the lake of Rostov, the Merya, and on Lake Kleshchino the Merya also. Along the river Oka (which flows into the Volga), Muroma, the Cheremisians, and Mordva preserve their native languages. For the Slavic race in Rus includes only the Polyanians, the Derevlians, the people of Novgorod, the Polotians, the Dregovichians, the Severians, and the Buzhians, who live along the River Bug and were later called Volhynians. The following are other tribes which pay tribute to Rus: Chud, Merya, Ves, Muroma, Cheremis, Mordva, Perm, Pechera, Yam, Litva, Zimegola, Kors, Narva, and Liv. These tribes have their own languages and belong to the race of Japheth, which inhabits the lands of the north.

Now while the Slavs dwelt along the Danube, as we have said, there came from among the Scythians, that is, from the Khazars, a people called Bulgars, who settled on the Danube and oppressed the Slavs. Afterward came the White Huns, who inherited the Slavic country. For these Huns first appeared in the reign of the Emperor Heraclius, who campaigned against Chosroes, the Emperor of Persia. The Avars who attacked Heraclius the Emperor and nearly captured him, also lived at this period. They made war upon the Slavs, and harassed the Dulebians, who were themselves Slavs. They even did violence to the Dulebian women. . . . The Avars were large in stature and proud of spirit, and God destroyed them. They all perished, and not one Avar survived. There is to this day a proverb in Rus which runs, "They perished like the Avars."

Neither race nor heir of them remains. The Pechenegs came after them; and the Black Huns passed by Kiev later during the time of Olga.

Thus the Polyanians, who belong to the Slavic race, lived apart, as we have said, and called themselves Polyanians. The Derevlians, who are likewise Slavs, lived by themselves and adopted this tribal name. But the Radimichians and the Vyatichians sprang from the Lyakhs. There were in fact among the Lyakhs two brothers, one named Radim and the other Vyatko. Radim settled on the Sozh, where the people are known as Radimichians, and Vyatko with his family settled on the Oka. The people there were named Vyatichians after him. Thus the Polyanians, the Derevlians, the Severians, the Radimichians, the Vyatichians, and the Croats lived at peace. The Dulebians dwelt along the Bug, where the Volhynians now are found, but the Ulichians and the Tivercians lived by the Dniester, and extended as far as the Danube. There was a multitude of them, for they inhabited the banks of the Dniester almost down to the sea, and to this day there are cities in that locality which still belong to them. Hence they are called Great Scythia by the Greeks.

These Slavic tribes preserved their own customs, the law of their fore-fathers, and their traditions, each observing their individual usages. For the Polyanians retained the mild and peaceful customs of their ancestors, and showed respect for their daughters-in-law and their sisters, as well as for their mothers and fathers. For their mothers-in-law and their brothers-in-law they also entertained great reverence. They observed a fixed marriage custom, under which the groom's brother did not fetch the bride, but she was brought to the bridegroom in the evening, and on the next morning his gifts were presented.

The Derevlians, on the other hand, existed in bestial fashion, and lived like cattle. They killed one another, ate every impure thing, and there was no marriage among them, but instead they seized upon maidens by capture. The Radimichians, the Vyatichians, and the Severians had the same customs. They lived in the forest like any wild beast, and ate every unclean thing. They spoke obscenely before their fathers and their daughters-in-law. There were no marriages among them, but simply festivals among the villages. When the people gathered together for games, for dancing, and for all other devilish amusements, the men on these occasions carried off wives for themselves, and each took any woman with whom he had arrived at an understanding. Whenever a death occurred, a feast was held over the corpse, and then a great pyre was constructed, on which the deceased was laid and burned. After the bones were collected, they were placed in a small urn and set upon a post by the roadside, even as the Vyatichians do to this day. Such customs were observed by the Krivichians and the other pagans, since they did not know the law of God, but made a law unto themselves.

2

The Coming
of the Varangians

The political history of the early Kievan state began
with the Normans, or Vikings, whom the Greeks
called Varangians. According to the *Primary Chronicle,* the Varangians established a firm foothold in
northeastern Europe (Novgorod) about 862 A.D.
From here, under the leadership of Riurik, they
gradually brought other areas under their control,
and by 880 the entire Dnieper Basin, including the
city of Kiev, was Varangian-dominated. The dynasty
that Riurik established controlled the destiny of
Kiev, and subsequently of Moscow, until 1598 when
Feodor, the son of Ivan the Terrible, died without
leaving an heir.

In the eighteenth century the Norman origin of
the Kievan state gave rise to the so-called Normanist
theory, which argued that the Normans gave Kiev
not only its government but its culture as well. This
view was soon challenged by anti-Normanist scholars
who emphasized the Slavic origins of the Kievan
state. During the past two hundred years both
camps have produced many scholarly works in support of their positions. As a result of this investigation, both views have undergone considerable modi-
fication, but the two theories still attract avid followers.

6367 (859). The Varangians from beyond the sea imposed
tribute upon the Chuds, the Slavs, the Merians, the Ves, and the
Krivichians. But the Khazars imposed it upon the Polyanians, the Sever-

Reprinted by permission of the publishers from Samuel H. Cross, "The Russian
Primary Chronicle," *Harvard Studies and Notes in Philology and Literature*
(Cambridge, Mass., Harvard University Press, 1930), vol. 12, pp. 144–147.

ians, and the Vyatichians, and collected a squirrel-skin and a beaver-skin from each hearth.

6368–6370 (860–862). The tributaries of the Varangians drove them back beyond the sea and, refusing them further tribute, set out to govern themselves. There was no law among them, but tribe arose against tribe. Discord thus ensued among them, and they began to war one against another. They said to themselves, "Let us seek a prince who may rule over us, and judge us according to the law." They accordingly went overseas to the Varangian Russes: these particular Varangians were known as Russes, just as some are called Swedes, and others Normans, Angles, and Goths, for they were thus named. The Chuds, the Slavs, and the Krivichians then said to the people of Rus, "Our whole land is great and rich, but there is no order in it. Come to rule and reign over us." They thus selected three brothers, with their kinsfolk, who took with them all the Russes and migrated. The oldest, Rurik, located himself in Novgorod; the second, Sineus, in Byeloozero; and the third, Truvor, in Izborsk. On account of these Varangians, the district of Novgorod became known as the land of Rus. The present inhabitants of Novgorod are descended from the Varangian race, but aforetime they were Slavs.

After two years, Sineus and his brother Truvor died, and Rurik assumed the sole authority. He assigned cities to his followers, Polotzk to one, Rostov to another, and to another, Byeloozero. In these cities there are thus Varangian colonists, but the first settlers were, in Novgorod, Slavs; in Polotzk, Krivichians; at Byeloozero, Ves; in Rostov, Merians; and in Murom, Muromians. Rurik had dominion over all these districts.

With Rurik there were two men who did not belong to his kin, but were boyars. They obtained permission to go to Tsargrad with their families. They thus sailed down the Dnieper, and in the course of their journey they saw a small city on a hill. Upon their inquiry as to whose town it was, they were informed that three brothers, Kii, Shchek, and Khoriv, had once built the city, but that since their deaths, their descendants were living there as tributaries of the Khazars. Oskold and Dir remained in this city, and after gathering together many Varangians, they established their domination over the country of the Polyanians at the same time that Rurik was ruling at Novgorod. . . .

6378–6387 (870–879). On his deathbed, Rurik bequeathed his realm to Oleg, who belonged to his kin, and entrusted to Oleg's hands his son Igor, for he was very young.

6388–6390 (880–882). Oleg set forth, taking with him many warriors from among the Varangians, the Chuds, the Slavs, the Merians, and the Krivichians. He thus arrived with his Krivichians before Smolensk, took the city, and set up a garrison there. Thence he went on and captured Lyubech, where he also established a garrison. He then came to the hills of Kiev, and saw how Oskold and Dir reigned there. He hid his warriors in the boats, left some others behind, and went forward himself bearing the child Igor. He thus came to the foot of the Hunnish hill, and after concealing his troops, he sent messengers to Oskold and Dir, representing himself as a stranger on his way to Greece on an errand for Oleg and for Igor, the Prince's son, and requesting that they should come forth to greet them as members of their race. Oskold and Dir straightway came forth. Then all the soldiery jumped out of the boats, and Oleg said to Oskold and Dir, "You are not princes nor even of princely stock, but I am of princely birth." Igor was then brought forward, and Oleg announced that he was the son of Rurik. They killed Oskold and Dir, and after carrying them to the hill, they buried them there, on the hill now known as Hunnish, where the castle of Olma stands. Over that tomb Olma built a church dedicated to St. Nicholas, but Dir's tomb is behind St. Irene's. Oleg set himself up as prince in Kiev, and declared that it should be the mother of Russian cities. Varangians and Slavs accompanied him and his retainers were called Russes. Oleg began to build stockaded towns, and imposed tribute on the Slavs, the Krivichians, and the Merians. He commanded that Novgorod should pay the Varangians tribute to the amount of 300 *grivni* a year for the preservation of peace. This tribute was paid to the Varangians until the death of Yaroslav.

6391 (883). Oleg began military operations against the Derevlians, and after conquering them, he imposed upon them the tribute of a black marten-skin apiece.

6392 (884). Oleg attacked the Severians, and conquered them. He imposed a light tribute upon them and forbade their further payment of tribute to the Khazars, on the ground that there was no reason for them to pay it as long as the Khazars were his enemies.

6393 (885). Oleg sent messengers to the Radimichians to inquire to whom they paid tribute. Upon their reply that they paid tribute to the Khazars, he directed them to render it to himself instead, and they accordingly paid him a shilling apiece, the same amount that they had paid the Khazars. Thus Oleg established his authority over the Polyanians, the Derevlians, the Severians, and the Radimichians, but he waged war with the Uluchians and the Tivercians.

3

Byzantine-Kievan Relations

Following their conquest of the Dnieper Basin, the Varangians established lively relations with Constantinople which was the center of Byzantine civilization. They gained some concessions from the Greeks through trade and treaties; others through military conquests and destruction. The *Primary Chronicle* gives vivid and detailed accounts of both approaches. Regardless of the means employed, Kiev's relations with Constantinople before the middle of the tenth century grew and became one of the basic foundations of Kievan economic prosperity and cultural greatness. In addition to war booty, the Kievans returned from Constantinople with an alphabet, calendar, Christian concepts—in short, culture. Because of these strong ties the subsequent decline of Constantinople (in the twelfth and thirteenth centuries) exerted a powerful influence on the decline of Kiev.

6371–6374 (863–866). Oskold and Dir attacked the Greeks during the fourteenth year of the reign of the Emperor Michael. When the Emperor had set forth against the Saracens and had arrived at the Black River, the eparch sent him word that the Russes were approaching Tsargrad, and the Emperor turned back. Upon arriving inside the strait, the Russes made a great massacre of the Christians, and attacked Tsargrad in two hundred boats. The Emperor succeeded with difficulty in entering the city. The people prayed all night with the Patriarch Photius at the Church of the Holy Virgin in Blachernae. They also sang hymns and carried the sacred vestment of the Virgin to dip it in the sea. The weather was still, and the sea was calm, but a storm of wind came up,

Reprinted by permission of the publishers from Samuel H. Cross, "The Russian Primary Chronicle," *Harvard Studies and Notes in Philology and Literature* (Cambridge, Mass., Harvard University Press, 1930), vol. 12, pp. 145–146, 149–155, 157–159, 160–164.

and when great waves straightway rose, confusing the boats of the godless Russes, it threw them upon the shore and broke them up, so that
few escaped such destruction. The survivors then returned to their native
land. . . .

6412–6415 (904–907). Leaving Igor in Kiev, Oleg attacked the
Greeks. He took with him a multitude of Varangians, Slavs, Chuds,
Krivichians, Merians, Polyanians, Severians, Derevlians, Radimichians,
Croats, Dulebians, and Tivercians, who are Torks. All these tribes are
known as Great Scythia by the Greeks. With this entire force, Oleg
sallied forth by horse and by ship, and the number of his vessels was two
thousand. He arrived before Tsargrad, but the Greeks fortified the
strait and closed up the city. Oleg disembarked upon the shore, and
ordered his soldiery to beach the ships. They waged war around the city,
and accomplished much slaughter of the Greeks. They also destroyed
many palaces and burned the churches. Of the prisoners they captured,
some they beheaded, some they tortured, some they shot, and still
others they cast into the sea. The Russes inflicted many other woes upon
the Greeks after the usual manner of soldiers. Oleg commanded his
warriors to make wheels which they attached to the ships, and when
the wind was favorable, they spread the sails and bore down upon the
city from the open country. When the Greeks beheld this, they were
afraid, and sending messengers to Oleg, they implored him not to destroy the city and offered to submit to such tribute as he should desire.
Thus Oleg halted his troops. The Greeks then brought out to him food
and wine, but he would not accept it, for it was mixed with poison.
Then the Greeks were terrified, and exclaimed, "This is not Oleg, but
St. Demetrius, whom God has sent upon us." So Oleg demanded that
they pay tribute for his two thousand ships at the rate of twelve *grivni*
per man, with forty men reckoned to a ship.

The Greeks assented to these terms and prayed for peace lest Oleg
should conquer the land of Greece. Retiring thus a short distance from
the city, Oleg concluded a peace with the Greek Emperors Leo and
Alexander, and sent into the city to them Karl, Farulf, Vermund, Hrollaf, and Steinvith, with instructions to receive the tribute. The Greeks
promised to satisfy their requirements. Oleg demanded that they should
give to the troops on the two thousand ships twelve *grivni* per bench,
and pay in addition the sums required for the various Russian cities:
first Kiev, then Chernigov, Pereyaslavl, Polotzk, Rostov, Lyubech, and
the other towns. In these cities lived princes subject to Oleg.

The Russes proposed the following terms: "The Russes who come
hither shall receive as much grain as they require. Whosoever come as
merchants shall receive supplies for six months, including bread, wine,
meat, fish, and fruit. Baths shall be prepared for them in any volume
they require. When the Russes return homeward, they shall receive from

your Emperor food, anchors, cordage, and sails, and whatever else is needful for the journey." The Greeks accepted these stipulations, and the Emperors and all the courtiers declared: "If Russes come hither without merchandise, they shall receive no provisions. Your prince shall personally lay injunction upon such Russes as journey hither that they shall do no violence in the towns and throughout our territory. Such Russes as arrive here shall dwell in the St. Mamas quarter. Our government will send officers to record their names, and they shall then receive their monthly allowance, first the natives of Kiev, then those from Chernigov, Pereyaslavl, and the other cities. They shall not enter the city save through one gate, unarmed and fifty at a time, escorted by soldiers of the Emperor. They may purchase wares according to their requirements and tax-free."

Thus the Emperors Leo and Alexander made peace with Oleg, and after agreeing upon the tribute and mutually binding themselves by oath, they kissed the cross, and invited Oleg and his men to swear an oath likewise. According to the religion of the Russes, the latter swore by their weapons and by their god Perun, as well as by Volos, the god of cattle, and thus confirmed the treaty.

Oleg gave orders that silken sails should be made for the Russes and linen ones for the Slavs, and his demand was satisfied. The Russes hung their shields upon the gates as a sign of victory, and Oleg then departed from Tsargrad. The Russes unfurled their silken sails and the Slavs their sails of linen, but the wind tore them. Then the Slavs said, "Let us keep our canvas ones; linen sails are not made for the Slavs." So Oleg came to Kiev, bearing palls, gold, fruit, and wine, along with every sort of adornment. The people called Oleg "the Sage," for they were but pagans, and therefore ignorant. . . .

6420 (912).   Oleg despatched his vassals to make peace and to draw up a treaty between the Greeks and the Russes. His envoys thus made declaration:

"We of the Rus nation: Karl, Ingjald, Farulf, Vermund, Hrollaf, Gunnar, Harold, Karni, Frithleif, Hroarr, Angantyr, Throand, Leithulf, Fast, and Steinvith, are sent by Oleg, Great Prince of Rus, and by all the glorious boyars under his sway, unto you, Leo and Alexander and Constantine, great Autocrats in God, Emperors of the Greeks, for the maintenance and proclamation of the long-standing amity which joins Greeks and Russes, in accordance with the desire of our Great Princes and at their command, and in behalf of all those Russes who are subject to the hand of our Prince.

"Our serenity, above all desirous, through God's help, of maintaining and proclaiming such amicable relations as now exist between Christians and Russians, has often deemed it proper to publish and confirm this amity not merely in words but also in writing and under a firm oath sworn upon our weapons according to our religion and our law. As we previously agreed in the name of God's peace and amity, the articles of this convention are as follows:

"First, that we shall conclude a peace with you Greeks, and love each other with all our heart and will, and as far as lies in our power, prevent any subject of our serene Princes from committing any crime or misdemeanor. Rather shall we exert ourselves as far as possible to maintain as irrevocable and immutable henceforth and forever the amity thus proclaimed by our agreement with you Greeks and ratified by signature and oath. May you Greeks on your part maintain as irrevocable and immutable henceforth and forever the same amity toward our serene Princes of Rus and toward all the subjects of our serene Prince.

"In the matter of stipulations concerning damage, we subscribe to the following provisions:

"If clear proofs exist, there shall be a true declaration of such proofs. But if no credence attach to such declaration, the dissenting party shall take oath to this effect, and after he shall have taken oath according to his faith, a penalty shall be assessed in proportion to the trespass committed.

"Whatsoever Russ kills a Christian, or whatsoever Christian kills a Russ shall die, since he has committed murder. If any man flee after committing a murder, in the case that he is well-to-do, the nearest relative of the victim shall receive a legal portion of the culprit's property, while the wife of the victim shall receive a like amount, which is legally due her. But if the defendant is poor and has escaped, he shall be under distress until he returns or until he dies.

"If any man strike another with a sword or assault him with any other sort of weapon, he shall, according to Russian law, pay five pounds of silver for such blow or assault. If the defendant is poor he shall pay as much as he is able, and be deprived even of the very clothes he wears, and he shall also declare upon oath that he has no one to aid him. Thereafter the case against him shall be withdrawn.

"If any Russ commit a theft against a Christian, or vice versa, and should the transgressor be caught in the act by the victim of the loss, in case the culprit is killed in the process of committing the theft, no penalty shall be exacted for his death by either Greeks or Russes. The victim of the loss shall recover the stolen property. If the thief surrenders, he shall be taken and bound by the one upon whom the theft was committed, and the culprit shall return whatever he has dared to appropriate, making at the same time threefold restitution for it.

"If on the pretext of instituting a search, any person, whether Greek or Russ, employs abusive treatment or violence and appropriates some article by force, he shall repay three times its value.

"If a ship is detained by high winds upon a foreign shore, and one of us Russes is near by, the ship with its cargo shall be revictualed and sent on to Christian territory. We will pilot it through every dangerous passage until it arrives at a place of safety. But if any such ship thus detained by storm or by some terrestrial obstacle cannot possibly reach its destination, we Russes will extend aid to the crew of this ship, and conduct them with their merchandise in all security, in case such an event takes place near Greek territory. But if such an accident befalls near the Russian shore, the ship's cargo shall be disposed of, and we Russes will remove whatever can be disposed of for the account of the owners. Then, when we proceed to Greece with merchandise or upon an embassy to your Emperor, we shall render up honorably the price of the sold cargo of the ship. But if anyone on that ship is killed or maltreated by us Russes, or if any object is stolen, then those who have committed such acts shall be subject to the aforesaid penalty.

"From this time forth, if a prisoner of either nation is in durance either of the Russes or of the Greeks, and then sold into another country, any Russ or Greek who happens to be in that locality shall purchase the prisoner and return the person thus purchased to his own native country. The purchaser shall be indemnified for the amount thus expended, or else the value of the prisoner's daily labor shall be reckoned toward the purchase money. If any Russ be taken prisoner by the Greeks, he shall likewise be sent back to his native land, and his purchase price shall be repaid, as has been stipulated, according to his value.

"Whenever you find it necessary to declare war, or when you are conducting a campaign, providing any Russes desirous of honoring your Emperor come at any time and wish to remain in his service, they shall be permitted in this respect to act according to their desire.

"If a Russian prisoner from any region is sold among the Christians, or if any Christian prisoner is sold among the Russes, he shall be ransomed for twenty bezants and returned to his native land.

"In case a Russian slave is stolen or escapes or is sold under compulsion, and if a Russ institutes a claim to this effect which is substantiated, the slave shall be returned to Rus. If a merchant loses a slave and institutes a complaint, he shall search for this slave until he is found, but if any person refuses to allow him to make this search, the local officer shall forfeit his right of perquisition.

"With respect to the Russes professionally engaged in Greece under the orders of the Christian Emperor, if any one of them dies without setting his property in order and has no kinsfolk there, his estate shall be returned to his surviving relatives in Rus. But if he makes some disposition of his goods, the person whom he has designated in writing as his heir shall receive the property of which he thus disposed. This shall be the due process of inheritance in the cases of Russes engaging in trade, of casual travelers in Greece, and of those having debts outstanding there.

"If a criminal takes refuge in Greece, the Russes shall make complaint to the Christian Empire, and such criminal shall be arrested and returned to Rus regardless of his protests. The Russes shall perform the same service for the Greeks whenever the occasion arises.

"As a convention and an inviolable pledge binding equally upon you Greeks and upon us Russes, we have caused the present treaty to be transcribed in the handwriting of Ivan upon a double parchment, bearing your Emperor's and our own signatures, to be promulgated and handed to our envoys in the name of the Holy Cross and the Holy and Indivisible Trinity of your one true God. According to our own faith and the custom of our nation, we have sworn to your Emperor, who rules over you by the grace of God, that we will neither violate ourselves, nor allow any of our subjects to violate the peace and amity assured by the articles thus concluded between us. We have also given to your government an identic document for the mutual ratification of the same convention in order to confirm and promulgate the treaty thus concluded between us this second of September, in the year of Creation 6420 (912)."

The Emperor Leo honored the Russian envoys with gifts of gold, palls, and robes, and placed his vassals at their disposition to show them the beauties of the churches, the golden palace, and the riches contained therein. They thus showed the Russes much gold and many palls and jewels, together with the relics of our Lord's Passion: the crown, the nails, and the purple robe, as well as the bones of the Saints. They also instructed the Russes in their faith, and expounded to them the true belief. Thus the Emperor dismissed them to their native land with great honor. The envoys sent by Oleg returned to Kiev, and reported to him all the utterances of both Emperors. They recounted how they had made peace and established a covenant between Greece and Rus, confirmed by oaths inviolable for the subjects of both countries.

Thus Oleg ruled in Kiev, and dwelt at peace with all nations. . . .

6421 (913). Igor succeeded Oleg and began his reign. At the same time began the reign of Constantine, son of Leo and son-in-law of Romanus. . . .

6443–6449 (935–941). Igor attacked the Greeks, and the Bulgarians sent word to the Emperor that the Russes were advancing upon Tsargrad with ten thousand vessels. The Russes set out across the sea, and began to ravage Bithynia. They waged war along the Pontus as far as Heraclea and Paphlagonia, and laid waste the entire region of Nicomedia, burning everything along the gulf. Of the people they captured, some they butchered, others they set up as targets and shot at, some they seized upon, and after binding their hands behind their backs, they drove iron nails through their heads. Many sacred churches they gave to the flames, while they burned many monasteries and villages, and took no little booty on both sides of the sea. Then, when the army came out of the east, Pamphilus the Domestic with forty thousand men, Phocas the Patrician with the Macedonians, and Theodore the General with the Thracians, supported by other illustrious nobles, surrounded the Russes. After taking counsel, the latter threw themselves upon the Greeks, and as the conflict between them was desperate, the Greeks experienced difficulty in winning the upper hand. The Russes returned at evening to their companions, embarked at night upon their vessels, and fled away. Theophanes pursued them in boats with Greek fire, and dropped it through pipes upon the Russian ships, so that a strange miracle was offered to view.

The Russes upon seeing the flames, cast themselves into the seawater, being anxious to escape, but the survivors returned home. When they came once more to their native land, where each one recounted to his kinsfolk the course of events and described the fire launched from the ships, they related that the Greeks had in their possession the lightning from heaven, and had set them on fire by pouring it forth, so that the Russes could not conquer them. Upon his return, Igor began to collect a great army, and sent many messengers after the Varangians beyond the sea, inviting them to attack the Greeks, for he desired to make war upon them. . . .

6452 (944).   After collecting many warriors among the Varangians, the Russes, the Polyanians, the Slavs, the Krivichians, the Tivercians, and the Pechenegs, and receiving hostages from them, Igor advanced upon the Greeks by ship and by horse, thirsting for revenge. The Khersonians, upon hearing of this expedition, reported to Romanus that the Russes were advancing with innumerable ships and covered the sea with their vessels. Likewise the Bulgarians sent tidings to the effect that the Russes were on the way, and that they had won the Pechenegs for their allies. When the Emperor heard this news, he sent to Igor his best boyars to entreat him to come no nearer, but rather to accept the tribute which Oleg had received, and to the amount of which something should even be added. He likewise sent palls and much gold to the Pechenegs.

Now Igor, when he came to the Danube, called together his retinue, and after some reflection communicated to them the Emperor's offer. Igor's retinue then replied, "If the Emperor speaks thus, what do we desire beyond receiving gold, silver, and palls without having to fight for them? Who knows who will be victorious, we or he? Who has the sea for his ally? For we are not marching by land, but through the depths of the sea. Death lies in wait for us all." Igor heeded them, and bade the Pechenegs ravage Bulgaria. He himself, after receiving from the Greeks gold and palls sufficient for his whole army, returned again and came to Kiev in his native land.

6453 (945). Romanus, Constantine, and Stephen sent envoys to Igor to renew the previous treaty, and Igor discussed the matter with them. Igor sent his own envoys to Romanus, and the Emperor called together his boyars and his nobles. The Russian envoys were introduced and bidden to speak, and it was commanded that the remarks of both parties should be inscribed upon parchment like the previous agreement existing under Romanus, Constantine, and Stephen, the most Christian princes. . . .

[*The Greeks stipulated:*] "The Great Prince of Rus and his boyars shall send to Greece to the great Greek Emperors as many ships as they desire with their agents and merchants, according to the prevailing usage. The agents have hitherto carried gold seals, and the merchants silver ones. But your Prince has now made known that he will forward a certificate to our government, and any agents or merchants thus sent by the Russians shall be provided with such a certificate to the effect that a given number of ships has been despatched. By this means we shall be assured that they come with peaceful intent.

"But if such persons come uncertificated and are surrendered to us, we shall detain and hold them until we notify your Prince. If they do not surrender, but offer resistance, they shall be killed, and indemnity for their death shall not be exacted by your Prince. If, however, they flee to Rus, we shall so inform your Prince, and he shall deal with them as he sees fit.

"If Russes come without merchandise, they shall not be entitled to receive monthly allowances. Your Prince shall moreover prohibit his agents and such other Russes as come hither from the commission of violence in our villages and territory. Such Russes as come hither shall dwell by St. Mamas's Church. Our authorities shall note their names, and they shall then receive their monthly allowance, the agents the amount proper to their position, and the merchants the usual amount: first, those from the city of Kiev, then those from Chernigov and Pereyaslavl. They shall enter the city through one gate in groups of fifty without weapons, and shall dispose of their merchandise as they require, after which they shall depart. An officer of our government shall guard them, in order that, if any Russ or Greek does wrong, he may redress it.

"When the Russes enter the city, they shall not have the right to buy silk above the value of fifty bezants. Whoever purchases such silks shall exhibit them to the imperial officer, who will stamp and return them. When the Russes depart hence, they shall receive from us as many provisions as they require for the journey, and what they need for their ships (as has been previously determined), and they shall return home in safety. They shall not have the privilege of wintering in the St. Mamas quarter.

"If any slave runs away from Rus and flees into the territory of our Empire or escapes from the St. Mamas quarter, he shall be apprehended if he be in Greek territory. If he is not found, the Christian Russes shall so swear according to their faith, and the non-Christians after their custom, and they shall then receive from us their due, two pieces of silk per slave, according to previous stipulations. If, among the people of our Empire, whether from our city or elsewhere, any slave of ours escapes among you and takes anything with him, the Russes shall send him back again. If what he has appropriated is intact, the finder shall receive two bezants from its value.

"If any Russ attempts to commit theft upon subjects of our Empire, he who so acts shall be severely punished, and he shall pay double the value of what he has stolen. If a Greek so transgress against a Russ, he shall receive the same punishment that the latter would suffer for a like offence. If a Russ commits a theft upon a Greek, or a Greek upon a Russ, he must return not only the stolen article, but also its value. If the stolen article is found to have been sold, he shall return double the price, and also shall be punished both by Greek law and custom and by the law of the Russes.

"If the Russes bring in young men or grown girls who have been taken as prisoners from our dominions, the Greeks shall pay a ransom of ten bezants each and recover the captives. If the latter are of middle age, the Greeks shall recover them on payment of eight bezants each. But in the case that the captives are old persons or young children, the ransom shall be five bezants. If any Russes are found laboring as slaves in Greece, providing they are prisoners of war, the Russes shall ransom them for ten bezants each. But if a Greek has actually purchased any such prisoner, and so declares under oath, he shall receive in return the full purchase price paid for the prisoner.

"In the matter of the country of Kherson and all the cities in that region, the Prince of Rus shall not have the right to harass these localities, nor shall that district be subject to you. If the Prince of Rus calls on us for soldiers wherewith to wage war, we agree to supply him with any number required.

"In case the Russes find a Greek ship cast ashore, they shall not harm it, and if any person remove any object therefrom, or enslave a member of the crew, or kill him, he shall be amenable to both Russian and Greek law. If Russian subjects meet with Khersonian fishermen at the mouth of the Dnieper, they shall not harm them in any wise. The Russes shall, moreover, not have the right to winter at the mouth of the Dnieper, either at Byeloberg or by St. Eleutherius, but when autumn comes, they shall return home to Rus. Regarding the Black Bulgarians, who come and ravage the Kherson district, we enjoin the prince of Rus not to allow them to injure that region.

"If any crime is committed by a Greek subject to our Empire, the Russes shall not have the right to punish him, but according to the legislation of our Empire, he shall suffer in proportion to his misdeed.

"If a Christian kill a Russ, or a Russ a Christian, he who has committed the murder shall be held by the relatives of the deceased that they may kill him. If he who has committed murder runs away and escapes, the relatives of the murdered man shall receive the murderer's property in the case that he is wealthy. But if the escaped culprit is poor, he shall be pursued till found, and when he is found, he shall be executed.

"If a Russ assault a Greek, or a Greek a Russ, with sword, spear, or any other weapon, he who has committed this crime shall pay five pounds of silver according to the Russian law, but if he is poor, all his available property shall be sold, even to the garments he walks in, and these too shall be taken from him. Finally he shall swear upon his faith that he has no possessions, and then he shall be released.

"If our government shall desire of you military assistance for use against our adversaries, they shall communicate with your Great Prince, and he shall send us as many soldiers as we require. From this fact, other countries shall learn what amity the Greeks and the Russes entertain toward each other. . . ."

The agents sent by Igor returned to him with the Greek envoys, and reported all the words of the Emperor Romanus. Then Igor called the Greek envoys before him, and bade them report what injunction the Emperor had laid upon them. The Emperor's envoys replied, "The Emperor has sent us. He loves peace, and desires to maintain concord and amity with the Prince of Rus. Your envoys have received the pledge of our Emperors, and they have sent us to receive your oath and that of your followers." Igor promised to comply with their request.

In the morning, Igor summoned the envoys, and went to a hill on which there was a statue of Perun. The Russes laid down their weapons, their shields, and their gold ornaments, and Igor and his people took oath (at least such as were pagans), while the Christian Russes took oath in the Church of St. Elias, which is by the stream, in the vicinity of the place Pasynetz and of the Khazars. This was, in fact, a cathedral church, since many of the Varangians were Christians.

Igor, after confirming the treaty with the Greeks, dismissed their envoys, bestowing upon them furs, slaves, and wax, and sent them away. The envoys then returned to the Emperor, and reported all the words of Igor and his affection for the Greeks. Thus Igor began to rule in Kiev, enjoying peaceful relations with all nations.

4

Porphyrogenitus' Description of the Voyage Down the Dnieper River

The commercial and military expeditions to the Black Sea and Constantinople via the Dnieper River represented a test of endurance for the Varangians, and later the Kievans. The most hazardous part of the journey was the passage through the treacherous cataracts on the lower Dnieper which were usually surrounded by hostile nomads such as the Pechenegs.

The following account by Byzantine Emperor Constantine Porphyrogenitus (911–959) also includes additional information about the Kievan state in the tenth century, the Pechenegs, the Bulgars, and other peoples.

The single-straked *ships* which come down from outer Russia to Constantinople are from Novgorod, where Sviatoslav, son of Igor, prince of Russia, had his seat, and others from the city of Smolensk and from Teliutza [Liubech] and Chernigov and from Busegrad [Vyshegrad]. All these come down the river Dnieper, and are collected together at the city of Kiev, also called Sambatas. Their Slav tributaries, the so-called Krivichians and the Lenzanines and the rest of the Slavonic regions, cut the single strakers on their mountains in time of winter, and when they have fastened them together, as spring approaches, and the ice melts, they bring them on to the neighbouring lakes. And since these *lakes* debouch into the river Dnieper, they enter thence on to this same

From *Constantine Porphyrogenitus de Administrando Imperio* (*Constantine Porphyrogenitus on Administration of the Empire*). Greek text edited by Gy Moravesik. Translated by R. J. H. Jenkins (Budapest, 1949), pp. 57–63, alternate. Items in brackets are mine.

river, and come down to Kiev, and draw *the ships* along to be fitted out, and sell them to the Russians. The Russians buy these bottoms only, furnishing them with oars and rowlocks and other tackle from their old single-strakers, which they dismantle; and so they fit them out. And in the month of June they move off down the river Dnieper and come to Vitichev, which is a tributary city of the Russians, and there they gather during two or three days; and when all the single-strakers are collected together, then they set out, and come down the said Dnieper river. And first they come to the first barrage, called Essoupi, which means in Russian and Slavonic "Do not sleep!"; the barrage itself is as narrow as the width of the Polo-ground; in the middle of it are rooted high rocks, which stand out like islands. Against these, then, comes the water and wells up and dashes down over the other side, with a mighty and terrific din. Therefore the Russians do not venture to pass between them, but put in to the bank hard by, disembarking the men on to dry land but leaving the rest of the goods on board the single-strakers; they then strip and, feeling with their feet to avoid striking on a rock, . . . This they do, some at the prow, some amidship, while others again, in the stern, punt with poles; and with all this careful procedure they pass this first barrage, edging round under the river-bank. When they have passed this barrage, they re-embark the others from the dry land and sail away, and come down to the second barrage, called in Russian Oulvorsi, and in Slavonic Ostrovouniprach, which means "the Island of the Barrage." This one is like the first, awkward and not to be passed through. Once again they disembark the men and convey the single-strakers past, as on the first occasion. Similarly they pass the third barrage also, called Gelandri, which means in Slavonic "Noise of the Barrage," and then the fourth barrage, the big one, called in Russian Aeifor, and in Slavonic Neasit, because the pelicans nest in the stones of the barrage. At this barrage all put into land prow foremost, and those who are deputed to keep the watch with them get out, and off they go, these men, and keep vigilant watch for the Pechenegs. The remainder, taking up the goods which they have on board the single-strakers, conduct the slaves in their chains past by land, six miles, until they are through the barrage. Then, partly dragging their single-strakers, partly porting them on their shoulders, they convey them to the far side of the barrage; and then, putting them on the river and loading up their baggage, they embark themselves, and again sail off in them. When they come to the fifth barrage, called in Russian Varouforos, and in Slavonic Voulniprach, because it forms a large lake, they again convey their single-strakers through at the edges of the river, as at the first and second barrages, and arrive at the sixth barrage, called in Russian Leanti, and in Slavonic Veroutzi, that is "the Boiling of the Water," and this too they pass similarly. And thence they sail away to the seventh barrage, called in Russian Stroukoun, and in Slavonic Naprezi, which means "Little Barrage." This they pass at the so-called ford of Krarion, where the Chersonites cross over from Russia and the Pechenegs to Cherson; which ford is as wide as the Hippodrome, and is as high from below up to where the friends of the Pechenegs survey the scene as an arrow might reach of one shooting from bottom to top. It is at this point, therefore, that the Pechenegs come down and attack the Russians. After traversing this place, they reach the island called St. Gregory, on which island they perform their sacrifices because a gigantic oak-tree stands there; and they sacrifice live cocks. Arrows, too, they peg in round about, and others bread and meat, or something of whatever each may have, as is their custom. They also throw lots regarding the cocks, whether to slaughter them, or to eat them as well, or to leave them alive. From this island onwards the Russians do not fear the Pechenegs until they reach the river Selinas. So then they start off thence and sail for four days, until they reach the lake which forms the mouth of the river, on which is the island of St. Aitherios. Arrived at this island, they rest themselves there for two or three days. And they re-equip their single-strakers with such tackle as is needed, sails and masts and rudders, which they bring with them. Since this lake is the mouth of this river, as has been said, and carries on down to the sea, and the island of St. Aitherios lies on the sea, they come thence to the Dniester river, and having got safely there they rest again. But when the weather is propitious, they put to sea and come to the river called Aspros, and after resting there too in like manner, they again set out and come to the Selinas, to the so-called branch of the Danube river. And until they are past the river Selinas, the Pechenegs keep pace with them. And if it happens that the sea cast a single-straker on shore, they all put in to land, in order to present a united opposition to the Pechenegs. But after the Selinas they fear nobody, but, entering the territory of Bulgaria, they come to the mouth of the Danube. From the Danube they proceed to the Konopas, and from the Konopas to Constantia, and from Constantia to the river Varna, and from Varna they come to the river Ditzina, all of which are Bulgarian territory. From the Ditzina they reach the district of Mesembria, and there at last their voyage, fraught with such travail and terror, such difficulty and danger, is at an end. The severe manner of life of these same Russians in winter-time is as follows. When the month of November begins, their chiefs together with all the Russians at once leave Kiev and go off on the "poliudie," which means "rounds," that is, to the Slavonic regions of the Vervians and Drugovichians and Krivichians and Severians and the rest of the Slavs who are tributaries of the Russians. There they are maintained throughout the winter, but then once more, starting from the month of April, when the ice of the Dnieper river melts, they come back to Kiev. They then pick up their single-strakers, as has been said above, and fit them out, and come down to Romania [i.e., the Byzantine Empire].

5

Olga's Vengeance

Varangian conquest of the Dnieper Basin had positive as well as negative features. For instance, it brought political unity to the area, but it also imposed increased tribute. The *Primary Chronicle* records frequent complaints and even open rebellions against the excessive tribute demanded by the new masters, the most interesting of which occurred in 945 when the Derevlians killed Prince Igor (912–945). Igor's wife, Olga (945–957), avenged the death of her husband by killing the important men of the Derevlians and then destroying their cities. Because of her subsequent acceptance of Christianity, Olga was canonized by the Orthodox Church. It is to be noted that her punishment of the Derevlians reflected little saintliness.

6453 (945). In this year, Igor's retinue said to him, "The servants of Sveinald are adorned with weapons and fine raiment, but we are naked. Go forth with us, oh Prince, after tribute, that both you and we may profit thereby." Igor heeded their words, and he attacked Dereva in search of tribute. He demanded the previous tribute, and collected it by violence from the people with the assistance of his followers. After thus gathering the tribute, he returned to his city. On his homeward way, he said to his followers, after some reflection, "Go forward with the tribute. I shall turn back, and rejoin you later." He dismissed his retainers on their journey homeward, but being desirous of still greater booty, he returned on his tracks with a few of his vassals.

The Derevlians heard that he was again approaching, and consulted with Mal, their prince, saying, "If a wolf comes among the sheep, he will take away the whole flock one by one, unless he be killed. If we do not thus kill him now, he will destroy us all." They then sent forward

Reprinted by permission of the publishers from Samuel H. Cross, "The Russian Primary Chronicle," *Harvard Studies and Notes in Philology and Literature* (Cambridge, Mass., Harvard University Press, 1930), vol. 12, pp. 164–168.

to Igor inquiring why he had returned, since he had collected all the tribute. But Igor did not heed them, and the Derevlians came forth from the city of Izkorosten, and slew Igor and his company, for the number of the latter were few. So Igor was buried, and his tomb is near the city of Izkorosten in Dereva even to this day.

But Olga [Igor's wife] was in Kiev with her son, the boy Svyatoslav. . . . The Derevlians then said, "See, we have killed the Prince of Rus. Let us take his wife Olga for our Prince Mal, and then we shall obtain possession of Svyatoslav, and work our will upon him." So they sent their best men, twenty in number, to Olga by boat, and they arrived below Borichev in their boat. At that time, the water flowed below the heights of Kiev, and the inhabitants did not live in the valley, but upon the heights. The city of Kiev was on the present site of the palace of Gordiat and Nicephorus, and the prince's palace was in the city where the palace of Vratislav and Chud now stands, while the ferry was outside the city. Without the city there stood another palace, where the palace of the Cantors is now situated, behind the Church of the Holy Virgin upon the heights. This was a palace with a stone hall.

Olga was informed that the Derevlians had arrived, and summoned them to her presence with a gracious welcome. When the Derevlians had thus announced their arrival, Olga replied with an inquiry as to the reason of their coming. The Derevlians then announced that their tribe had sent them to report that they had slain her husband, because he was like a wolf, crafty and ravening, but that their princes, who had thus preserved the land of Dereva, were good and that Olga should come and marry their Prince Mal. For the name of the Prince of Dereva was Mal.

Olga made this reply, "Your proposal is pleasing to me; indeed, my husband cannot rise again from the dead. But I desire to honor you tomorrow in the presence of my people. Return now to your boat, and remain there with an aspect of arrogance. I shall send for you on the morrow, and you shall say, 'We will not ride on horses nor go on foot; carry us in our boat.' And you shall be carried in your boat." Thus she dismissed them to their vessel.

Now Olga gave command that a large deep ditch should be dug in the castle with the hall, outside the city. Thus, on the morrow, Olga, as she sat in the hall, sent for the strangers, and her messengers approached them and said, "Olga summons you to great honor." But they replied, "We will not ride on horseback nor in wagons, nor go on foot; carry us in our boat." The people of Kiev then lamented, "Slavery is our lot. Our Prince is killed, and our Princess intends to marry their prince." So they carried the Derevlians in their boat. The latter sat on the cross-benches in great robes, puffed up with pride. They thus were borne

into the court before Olga, and when the men had brought the Derevlians in, they dropped them into the trench along with the boat. Olga
bent over and inquired whether they found the honor to their taste.
They answered that it was worse than the death of Igor. She then commanded that they should be buried alive, and they were thus buried.

Olga then sent messages to the Derevlians to the effect that, if they
really required her presence, they should send after her their distinguished
men, so that she might go to their Prince with due honor, for otherwise
her people in Kiev would not let her go. When the Derevlians heard
this message, they gathered together the best men who governed the
land of Dereva, and sent them to her. When the Derevlians arrived, Olga
commanded that a bath should be made ready, and invited them to
appear before her after they had bathed. The bathhouse was then heated,
and the Derevlians entered in to bathe. Olga's men closed up the bathhouse behind them, and she gave orders to set it on fire from the doors,
so that the Derevlians were all burned to death.

Olga then sent to the Derevlians the following message: "I am now
coming to you, so prepare great quantities of mead in the city where you
killed my husband, that I may weep over his grave and hold a funeral
feast for him." When they heard these words, they gathered great quantities of honey, and brewed mead. Taking a small escort, Olga made the
journey with ease, and upon her arrival at Igor's tomb, she wept for her
husband. She bade her followers pile up a great mound, and when they
had piled it up, she also gave command that a funeral feast should be
held. Thereupon the Derevlians sat down to drink, and Olga bade her
followers wait upon them.

The Derevlians inquired of Olga where the retinue was which they
had sent to meet her. She replied that they were following with her
husband's bodyguard. When the Derevlians were drunk, she bade her
followers fall upon them, and went about herself egging on her retinue
to the massacre of the Derevlians. So they cut down five thousand of
them; but Olga returned to Kiev and prepared an army to attack the
survivors.

6454 (946). Olga, together with her son Svyatoslav, gathered a large
and valiant army, and proceeded to attack the land of the Derevlians.
The latter came out to meet her troops, and when both forces were
ready for combat, Svyatoslav cast his spear against the Derevlians. But
the spear pierced the ears of the horse, and struck the horse's foot, for the
prince was but a child. Then Sveinald and Asmund said, "The prince has
already begun battle; press on, vassals, after the prince." Thus they
conquered the Derevlians, with the result that the latter fled, and shut
themselves up in their cities.

Olga hastened with her son to the city of Izkorosten, for it was there
that her husband had been slain, and they laid siege to the city. The

Derevlians barricaded themselves within the city, and fought valiantly from it, for they realized that they had killed the prince, and to what fate they would in consequence surrender.

Olga remained there a year without being able to take the city, and then she thought out this plan. She sent into the town the following message: "Why do you persist in holding out? All your cities have surrendered to me and submitted to tribute, so that the inhabitants now cultivate their fields and their lands in peace. But you had rather die of hunger, without submitting to tribute." The Derevlians replied that they would be glad to submit to tribute, but that she was still bent on avenging her husband. Olga then answered, "Since I have already avenged the misfortune of my husband twice on the occasions when your messengers came to Kiev, and a third time when I held a funeral feast for him, I do not desire further revenge, but am anxious to receive a small tribute. After I have made peace with you, I shall return home again."

The Derevlians then inquired what she desired of them, and expressed their readiness to pay honey and furs. Olga retorted that at the moment they had neither honey nor furs, but that she had one small request to make. "Give me three pigeons," she said, "and three sparrows from each house. I do not desire to impose a heavy tribute, like my husband, but I require only this small gift from you, for you are impoverished by the siege." The Derevlians rejoiced, and collected from each house three pigeons and three sparrows, which they sent to Olga with their greetings. Olga then instructed them, in view of their submission, to return to their city, promising that on the morrow she would depart and return to her own capital. The Derevlians reentered their city with gladness, and when they reported to the inhabitants, the people of the town rejoiced.

Now Olga gave to each soldier in her army a pigeon or a sparrow, and ordered them to attach by a thread to each pigeon and sparrow a match bound with small pieces of cloth. When night fell, Olga bade her soldiers release the pigeons and the sparrows. So the birds flew to their nests, the pigeons to the cotes, and the sparrows under the eaves. Thus the dove-cotes, the coops, the porches, and the haymows were set on fire. There was not a house that was not consumed, and it was impossible to extinguish the flames, because all the houses caught fire at once. The people fled from the city, and Olga ordered her soldiers to catch them. Thus she took the city and burned it, and captured the elders of the city. Some of the other captives she killed, while she gave others as slaves to her followers. The remnant she left to pay tribute.

She imposed upon them a heavy tribute, two parts of which went to Kiev, and the third to Olga in Vyshegorod; for Vyshegorod was Olga's city. She then passed through the land of Dereva, accompanied by her

son and her retinue, establishing laws and tribute. Her residences and
hunting-preserves are there still. Then she returned with her son to Kiev,
her city, where she remained one year.

6

Sviatoslav's Conquests

The early Varangian princes of Kiev were brave and
colorful conquerors. None, however, matched the
qualities of Prince Sviatoslav (957–972). In search
of spoils and glory, he enlisted the aid of other bold
adventurers and, moving with extraordinary speed,
destroyed the Empire of the Khazars along the
Volga before turning against the Bulgars and the
Greeks to seek more fortunes in the Balkans. As a
result of these military exploits, Sviatoslav elevated
Kiev's power to unprecedented heights. The triumph was short-lived, for the downfall of the
Khazar Empire in the East created a political
vacuum and attracted the nomadic Pechenegs who
overran the area north of the Black Sea, disrupted
Kievan-Byzantine trade and, in 972, ambushed and
killed Sviatoslav.

6464–6472 (956–964). When Prince Svyatoslav had grown
up and matured, he began to collect a numerous and valiant army. Step-
ping light as a leopard, he undertook many campaigns. Upon his expeditions he carried with him neither wagons nor kettles, and boiled no
meat, but cut off small strips of horseflesh, game, or beef, and ate it after

Reprinted by permission of the publishers from Samuel H. Cross, "The Russian
Primary Chronicle," *Harvard Studies and Notes in Philology and Literature*
(Cambridge, Mass., Harvard University Press, 1930), vol. 12, pp. 170–177.

roasting it on the coals. Nor did he have a tent, but he spread out a garment under him, and set his saddle under his head; and all his retinue did likewise. He sent messengers to the other lands announcing his intention to attack them. He went to the Oka and the Volga, and on coming in contact with the Vyatichians, he inquired of them to whom they paid tribute. They made answer that they paid a' silverpiece per plough-share to the Khazars.

6473 (965). Svyatoslav sallied forth against the Khazars. When they heard of his approach, they went out to meet him with their Prince, the Kagan, and the armies came to blows. When the battle thus took place, Svyatoslav defeated the Khazars and took their city of Byelavyezha. He also conquered the Yasians and the Kassogians.

6474 (966). Svyatoslav conquered the Vyatichians and made them his tributaries.

6475 (967). Svyatoslav marched to the Danube to attack the Bulgarians. When they fought together, Svyatoslav overcame the Bulgarians, and captured eighty towns along the Danube. He took up his residence there, and ruled in Pereyaslavetz, receiving tribute from the Greeks.

6476 (968). While Svyatoslav was at Pereyaslavetz, the Pechenegs invaded Rus for the first time. So Olga shut herself up in the city of Kiev with her grandsons, Yaropolk, Oleg, and Vladimir. The nomads besieged the city with a great force. They surrounded it with an innumerable multitude, so that it was impossible to escape or send messages from the city, and the inhabitants were weak from hunger and thirst. Those who had gathered on the other side of the Dnieper in their boats remained on that side, and not one of them could enter Kiev, while no one could cross over to them from the city itself. . . .

But the people of Kiev sent to Svyatoslav, saying, "Oh Prince, you visit and observe foreign lands. But while you neglect your own country, the Pechenegs have all but taken us captive, along with your mother and your children as well. Unless you return to protect us, they will attack us again, if you have no pity on your native land, on your mother in her old age, and on your children." When Svyatoslav heard these words, he quickly bestrode his charger, and returned to Kiev with his retinue. He kissed his mother and his children, and regretted what they had suffered at the hands of the Pechenegs. He therefore collected an army, and drove the Pechenegs out into the steppes. Thus there was peace.

6477 (969). Svyatoslav announced to his mother and his boyars, "I do not care to remain in Kiev, but should prefer to live in Pereyaslavetz on the Danube, since that is the centre of my realm, where all riches are concentrated: gold, silks, wine, and various fruits from Greece, silver and horses from Hungary and Bohemia, and from Rus furs, wax, honey, and slaves. . . ."

6478 (970). Svyatoslav set up Yaroslav in Kiev and Oleg in Dereva.

At this time came the people of Novgorod asking for themselves a prince. "If you will not come to us," said they, "then we will choose a prince of our own." So Svyatoslav promised them that a prince should be designated, but Yaropolk and Oleg both refused, so that Dobrynya suggested that the post should be offered to Vladimir . . . The citizens of Novgorod thus requested Svyatoslav to designate Vladimir, and he granted their request. The Novgorodians took Vladimir to be their prince, and he went forth to Novgorod with Dobrynya his uncle. But Svyatoslav departed thence to Pereyaslavetz.

6479 (971). Svyatoslav arrived before Pereyaslavetz, and the Bulgarians fortified themselves in the city. They made one sally against Svyatoslav; there was great carnage, and the Bulgarians came off victors. But Svyatoslav cried to his soldiery, "We seem to be conquered here already. Let us fight bravely, brothers and companions!" Toward evening, Svyatoslav finally gained the upper hand, and took the city by storm. He then sent messages to the Greeks, announcing his intention to march against them and capture their city, as he had taken Pereyaslavetz. The Greeks replied that they were in no position to offer resistance, and therefore begged him to accept tribute instead for himself and his soldiery, requesting him to notify them how many Russes there were, so that they might pay so much per head. The Greeks made this proposition to deceive the Russes, for the Greeks are crafty even to the present day. Svyatoslav replied that his force numbered twenty thousand, adding ten thousand to the actual number, for there were really but ten thousand Russes. So the Greeks armed one hundred thousand men to attack Svyatoslav, and paid no tribute.

Svyatoslav advanced against the Greeks, who came out to meet the Russes. When the Russes perceived their approach, they were terrified at the multitude of the Greek soldiery, and Svyatoslav remarked, "Now we have no place whither we may flee. Whether we will or no, we must give battle. Let us not disgrace Rus, but rather sacrifice our lives, lest we be dishonored. For if we flee, we shall be disgraced. We must not take to flight, but we will resist boldly, and I will march before you. If my head falls, then look to yourselves." Then his vassals replied, "Wherever your head falls, there we too will lay down our own." So the Russes went into battle, and the carnage was great. Svyatoslav came out victor, but the Greeks fled. Then Svyatoslav advanced toward the capital fighting as he went, and destroying towns that stand deserted even to the present time.

The Emperor summoned his boyars to the palace, and inquired what they should do, for they could not withstand Svyatoslav's onslaught. The boyars advised that he should be tempted with gifts, to discover whether Svyatoslav liked gold and silks. So they sent to Svyatoslav gold and silks, carried by a clever envoy. To the latter they gave command to look well upon his eyes, his face, and his spirit. The envoy took the gifts, and went out to Svyatoslav. It was reported to the Prince that Greeks had come bringing greetings, and he ordered that they should be introduced. They then came near and greeted him, laying before him the gold and silks. Svyatoslav, without noticing the presents, bade his servants keep them. So the envoys returned before the Emperor; and the Emperor summoned his boyars. Then the envoys reported that when they had come before Svyatoslav and offered their gifts, he had taken no notice of them, but had ordered them to be retained. Then another courtier said, "Try him a second time; send him arms."

This suggestion was adopted, and they sent to Svyatoslav a sword and other accoutrements which were duly brought before him. The Prince accepted these gifts, which he praised and admired, and returned his greetings to the Emperor. The envoys went back to the Emperor and reported what had occurred. Then the boyars remarked, "This man must be fierce, since he pays no heed to riches, but accepts arms. Submit to tribute." The Emperor accordingly requested Svyatoslav to approach no nearer, but to accept tribute instead. For Svyatoslav had indeed almost reached Tsargrad. So the Greeks paid him tribute, and he took also the share of those Russes who had been slain, promising that their families should receive it. He accepted many gifts besides, and returned to Pereyaslavetz with great acclaim.

Upon observing the small number of his troops, Svyatoslav reflected that if haply the Greeks attacked him by surprise, they would kill his retinue and himself. For many warriors had perished on the expedition. So he resolved to return to Rus for reinforcements. He then sent envoys to the Emperor in Silistria (for the Emperor was then at that place) indicating his intention to maintain peaceful and friendly relations. When the Emperor heard this message, he rejoiced, and sent to Svyatoslav gifts even more valuable than the former ones. Svyatoslav accepted these gifts, and on taking counsel with his retinue declared, "If we do not make peace with the Emperor, and he discovers how few of us there are, the Greeks will come and besiege us in our city. Rus is far away, and the Pechenegs are hostile to us. So who will give us aid? Let us rather make peace with the Emperor, for the Greeks have offered tribute; let that suffice. But if the Emperor stops paying tribute, we shall once more collect troops in Rus in still greater numbers, and march again on Tsargrad." His speech pleased his followers, and they sent their chief men to the Emperor. The envoys arrived in Silistria, and reported to the Emperor. He summoned them before him on the following day, and gave them permission to state their errand. They then replied, "Thus says our Prince: 'I desire to maintain true amity with the Greek Emperor henceforth and forever.'" The Emperor rejoiced, and commanded his scribe to set down on parchment the words of Svyatoslav. One envoy recited all his words, and the scribe wrote them down. . . .

After making peace with the Greeks, Svyatoslav journeyed by boat to the cataracts of the Dnieper, and the general, Sveinald, advised him to ride around the falls on horseback, for the Pechenegs were encamped in the vicinity. The Prince did not heed him, but went on by boat. The people of Pereyaslavetz informed the Pechenegs that Svyatoslav was returning to Rus after seizing from the Greeks great riches and immense booty, but that his troop was small. When the Pechenegs heard this news, they ambuscaded the cataracts, so that when Svyatoslav arrived it was impossible to pass them. So the Prince decided to winter in Byeloberg, but the Russes had no rations, so that there was a severe famine, and they paid as much as half a grivna* for a horse's head. But Svyatoslav wintered there nevertheless.

When spring came, in 6480 (972), Svyatoslav approached the cataracts, where Kurya, Prince of the Pechenegs, attacked him; and Svyatoslav was killed. The nomads took his head, and made a cup out of his skull, overlaying it with gold, and they drank from it.

7

The Acceptance of Christianity

Christianity was introduced into Kievan Rus long before Prince Vladimir (980–1015) adopted it as the official religion of the state. There was, for instance, a Christian church in Kiev during the reign of Igor. As noted earlier, Igor's wife Olga, by em-

Reprinted by permission of the publishers from Samuel H. Cross, "The Russian Primary Chronicle," *Harvard Studies and Notes in Philology and Literature* (Cambridge, Mass., Harvard University Press, 1930), vol. 12, pp. 183–184, 197–201, 204–205, 210–211, 213.

* See the glossary.

bracing Christianity, became a saint of the Orthodox Church and many merchants, as well as warriors of Kievan princes, were either converts to or
had an acquaintance with the new faith.

The *Primary Chronicle* reports, in one narrative,
many different legends concerning the adoption of
Christianity, as well as several traditional accounts
of the baptism of Prince Vladimir. It is ironic that
no one knows exactly where or even when Vladimir
was baptized, whether in 988 or 989. Following his
conversion, Vladimir imposed the new faith on his
subjects. In some places this imposition was peaceful; in others, force had to be used. The adoption of
Christianity from Constantinople opened Kiev to
widespread Byzantine cultural influence.

6494 (986). Vladimir was visited by Bulgarians of Mohammedan faith. . . . Then came the Germans, asserting that they were come
as emissaries of the Pope. . . . The Jewish Khazars heard of these mis-
sions, and came themselves. . . . Then the Greeks sent to Vladimir a
scholar. . . .

6495 (987). Vladimir summoned together his vassals and the city
elders, and said to them, "Behold, the Bulgarians came before me urging me to accept their religion. Then came the Germans and praised
their own faith; and after them came the Jews. Finally the Greeks appeared, criticizing all other faiths but commending their own, and they
spoke at length, telling the history of the whole world from its beginning. Their words were artful, and it was wondrous to listen and pleasant
to hear them. They preach the existence of another world. 'Whoever
adopts our religion and then dies shall arise and live forever. But whosoever embraces another faith, shall be consumed with fire in the next
world.' What is your opinion on this subject, and what do you answer?"
The vassals and the elders replied, "You know, oh Prince, that no man
condemns his own possessions, but praises them instead. If you desire
to make certain, you have servants at your disposal. Send them to inquire about the ritual of each and how he worships God."

Their counsel pleased the prince and all the people, so that they chose
good and wise men to the number of ten, and directed them to go first
among the Bulgarians and inspect their faith. The emissaries went their
way, and when they arrived at their destination they beheld the disgraceful actions of the Bulgarians and their worship in the mosque; then they
returned to their own country. Vladimir then instructed them to go
likewise among the Germans, and examine their faith, and finally to visit
the Greeks. They thus went into Germany, and after viewing the Ger-

man ceremonial, they proceeded to Tsargrad, where they appeared before the Emperor. He inquired on what mission they had come, and they reported to him all that had occurred. When the Emperor heard their words, he rejoiced, and did them great honor on that very day.

On the morrow, the Emperor sent a message to the Patriarch to inform him that a Russian delegation had arrived to examine the Greek faith, and directed him to prepare the church and the clergy, and to array himself in his sacerdotal robes, so that the Russes might behold the glory of the God of the Greeks. When the Patriarch received these commands, he bade the clergy assemble, and they performed the customary rites. They burned incense, and the choirs sang hymns. The Emperor accompanied the Russes to the church, and placed them in a wide space, calling their attention to the beauty of the edifice, the chanting, and the offices of the archpriest and the ministry of the deacons, while he explained to them the worship of his God. The Russes were astonished and in their wonder praised the Greek ceremonial. Then the Emperors Basil and Constantine invited the envoys to their presence, and said, "Go hence to your native country," and thus dismissed them with valuable presents and great honor.

Thus they returned to their own country, and the Prince called together his vassals and the elders. Vladimir then announced the return of the envoys who had been sent out, and suggested that their report be heard. He thus commanded them to speak out before his vassals. The envoys reported, "When we journeyed among the Bulgarians, we beheld how they worship in their temple, called a mosque, while they stand ungirt. The Bulgarian bows, sits down, looks hither and thither like one possessed, and there is no happiness among them, but instead only sorrow and a dreadful stench. Their religion is not good. Then we went among the Germans, and saw them performing many ceremonies in their temples; but we beheld no glory there. Then we went on to Greece, and the Greeks led us to the edifices where they worship their God, and we knew not whether we were in heaven or on earth. For on earth there is no such splendor or such beauty, and we are at a loss how to describe it. We only know that God dwells there among men, and their service is fairer than the ceremonies of other nations. For we cannot forget that beauty. Every man, after tasting something sweet, is afterward unwilling to accept that which is bitter, and therefore we cannot dwell longer here." Then the vassals spoke and said, "If the Greek faith were evil, it would not have been adopted by your grandmother Olga, who was wiser than all other men." Vladimir then inquired where they should all accept baptism, and they replied that the decision rested with him.

After a year had passed, in 6496 (988), Vladimir marched with an armed force against Kherson, a Greek city. . . . Vladimir and his retinue entered the city, and he sent messages to the Emperors Basil and Con-

stantine, saying, "Behold, I have captured your glorious city. I have also
heard that you have an unwedded sister. Unless you give her to me to
wife, I shall deal with your own city as I have with Kherson." When the
Emperors heard this message, they were troubled, and replied, "It is not
meet for Christians to give in marriage to pagans. If you are baptized,
you shall have her to wife, inherit the kingdom of God, and be our
companion in the faith. Unless you do so, however, we cannot give you
our sister in marriage." When Vladimir learned their response, he
directed the envoys of the Emperors to report to the latter that he was
willing to accept baptism, having already given some study to their religion, and that the Greek faith and ritual, as described by the emissaries sent to examine it, had pleased him well. When the Emperors
heard this report, they rejoiced, and persuaded their sister Anna to consent to the match. They then requested Vladimir to submit to baptism
before they should send their sister to him, but Vladimir desired that the
princess should herself bring priests to baptize him. The Emperors complied with his request, and sent forth their sister, accompanied by some
dignitaries and priests. Anna, however, departed with reluctance. "It is
as if I were setting out into captivity," she lamented; "better were it
for me to die here." But her brothers protested, "Through your agency
God turns the land of Rus to repentance, and you will relieve Greece
from the danger of grievous war. Do you not see how much evil the
Russes have already brought upon the Greeks? If you do not set out,
they may bring on us the same misfortunes." It was thus that they overcame her hesitation only with great difficulty. The Princess embarked upon
a ship, and after tearfully embracing her kinsfolk, she set forth across the
sea and arrived at Kherson. The natives came forth to greet her, and
conducted her into the city, where they settled her in the palace.

By divine agency, Vladimir was suffering at that moment from a
disease of the eyes, and could see nothing, being in great distress. The
Princess declared to him that if he desired to be relieved of this disease,
he should be baptized with all speed, otherwise it could not be cured.
When Vladimir heard her message, he said, "If this proves true, then of
a surety is the God of the Christians great," and gave orders that he
should be baptized. The Bishop of Kherson, together with the Princess's
priests, after announcing the tidings, baptized Vladimir, and as the
Bishop laid his hand upon him, he straightway received his sight. Upon
experiencing this miraculous cure, Vladimir glorified God, saying, "I
have now perceived the one true God." When his followers beheld this
miracle, many of them were also baptized.

Vladimir was baptized in the Church of St. Basil, which stands at
Kherson upon a square in the center of the city, where the Khersonians
trade. The palace of Vladimir stands beside this church to this day, and
the palace of the Princess is behind the altar. After his baptism, Vladimir

took the Princess in marriage. Those who do not know the truth say he was baptized in Kiev, while others assert this event took place in Vasiliev, while still others mention other places.

After Vladimir was baptized, the priests explained to him the tenets of the Christian faith, urging him to avoid the deceit of heretics. . . .

Hereupon Vladimir took the Princess and Anastasius and the priests of Kherson, together with the relics of St. Clement and of Phoebus his disciple, and selected also sacred vessels and images for the service. In Kherson he thus founded a church on the mound which had been heaped up in the midst of the city with the earth removed from his embankment; this church is standing at the present day. Vladimir also found and appropriated two bronze statues and four bronze horses, which now stand behind the Church of the Holy Virgin, and which the ignorant think are made of marble. As a wedding present for the Princess, he gave Kherson over to the Greeks again and then departed for Kiev.

When the Prince arrived at his capital, he directed that the idols should be overthrown, and that some should be cut to pieces and others burned with fire. He thus ordered that Perun should be bound to a horse's tail and dragged along Borichev to the river. He appointed twelve men to beat the idol with sticks, not because he thought the wood was sensitive, but to affront the demon who had deceived man in this guise, that he might receive chastisement at the hands of men. . . . While the idol was being dragged along the stream to the Dnieper, the unbelievers wept over it, for they had not yet received holy baptism. After they had thus dragged the idol along, they cast it into the Dnieper. But Vladimir had given this injunction, "If it halts anywhere, then push it out from the bank, until it goes over the falls. Then let it loose." His command was duly obeyed. . . .

Thereafter Vladimir sent heralds throughout the whole city to proclaim that if any inhabitant, rich or poor, did not betake himself to the river, he would risk the Prince's displeasure. When the people heard these words, they wept for joy, and exclaimed in their enthusiasm, "If this were not good, the Prince and his boyars would not have accepted it." On the morrow, the Prince went forth to the Dnieper with the priests of the Princess and those from Kherson, and a countless multitude assembled. They all went into the water; some stood up to their necks, others to their breasts, the younger near the bank, some of them holding children in their arms, while the adults waded farther out. The priests stood by and offered prayers. . . .

When the people were baptized, they returned each to his own abode. Vladimir, rejoicing that he and his subjects now knew God himself, . . . ordained that churches should be built and established where pagan idols had previously stood. He thus founded the Church of St. Basil on the hill where the idol of Perun and the other images had been set, and where the Prince and the people had offered their sacrifices. He began to found churches and to assign priests throughout the cities, and to invite the people to accept baptism in all the cities and towns.

He took the children of the best families, and sent them to schools for instruction in book-learning. The mothers of these children wept bitterly over them, for they were not yet strong in faith, but mourned as for the dead. . . . Vladimir was enlightened, and his sons and his country with him. . . .

6497 (989). After these events, Vladimir lived in the Christian faith. With the intention of building a church dedicated to the Holy Virgin, he sent and imported artisans from Greece. After he had begun to build, and the structure was completed, he adorned it with images, and entrusted it to Anastasius of Kherson. He appointed Khersonian priests to serve in it, and bestowed upon this church all the images, vessels, and crosses which he had taken in that city. . . .

[6502–6504 (994–996)] . . . [Vladimir] invited each beggar and poor man to come to the Prince's palace and receive whatever he needed, both food and drink, and marten-skins from the treasury.

With the thought that the weak and the sick could not easily reach his palace, he arranged that wagons should be brought in, and after having them loaded with bread, meat, fish, various fruits, mead in casks, and kvass, he ordered them driven out through the city. The drivers were under instruction to call out, "Where is there a poor man or a beggar who cannot walk?" To such they distributed according to their necessities. Moreover, he caused a feast to be prepared each week in his palace for his subjects, and invited the boyars, the court officers, the centurians, the decurions, and the distinguished citizens, either in the presence of the Prince or in his absence. There was much meat, beef, and game, and an abundance of all victuals. On one occasion, however, after the guests were drunk, they began to grumble against the prince, complaining that they were mistreated because he allowed them to eat with wooden spoons instead of silver ones. When Vladimir heard of their complaint, he ordered that silver spoons should be moulded for his retinue to eat with, remarking that with silver and gold he could not secure a retinue, but that with a retinue he was in a position to win these treasures, even as his grandfather and his father had sought riches with their followers. For Vladimir was fond of his followers, and consulted them concerning matters of administration, wars, and government. He lived at peace with the neighboring Princes, Boleslav of Poland, Stephen of Hungary and Udalrich of Bohemia, and there was amity and friendship among them.

While Vladimir was thus dwelling in the fear of God, the number of bandits increased, and the bishops, calling to his attention the multiplication of robbers, inquired why he did not punish them. The Prince answered that he feared the sin entailed. They replied that he was appointed of God for the chastisement of malefactors and for the practice of mercy toward the righteous, so that it was entirely fitting for him to punish a robber condignly, but only after due process of law. Vladimir accordingly abolished wergild and set out to punish the brigands. The bishops and the elders then suggested that as wars were frequent, the wergild might be properly spent for the purchase of arms and horses, to which Vladimir assented. Thus Vladimir lived according to the prescriptions of his father and his grandfather. . . .

When the people heard of this [Vladimir's death on July 15, 1015], they assembled in multitudes and mourned him, the boyars as the defender of their country, the poor as their protector and benefactor. They laid him in a marble coffin, and preserved the body of the blessed Prince amid their mourning.

He is the new Constantine of mighty Rome, who baptized himself and his subjects; for the Prince of Rus imitated the acts of Constantine himself. . . . Vladimir died in the orthodox faith. He effaced his sins by repentance and by almsgiving, which is better than all things else.

8

Russian Justice: The Short Version

One of the most important legal sources on Kievan history is a document called *Russkaia Pravda*, or *Russian Justice*. There are two basic versions of this document—short and expanded. The short version

From M. N. Tikhomirov, *Posobie dlia izucheniia Russkoi Pravdy* (An Aid for the Study of Russian Justice) (Moscow, Izdatelstvo Moskovskogo Universiteta, 1953), pp. 75–86. Translation mine. Items in brackets are mine.

includes the old *Pravda* of Iaroslav, which appeared
in the 1030s, and the *Pravda* of Iaroslav's sons,
which appeared in the 1070s. The expanded version,
which includes many of the points of the short version plus additional items, appeared at the end of
the twelfth or early in the thirteenth century. In
reading the document, note that economic questions and problems of property relationships occupy
a prominent place.

Article 1

If a man kills a man, the brother is to avenge his brother; the son, his
father; or the father, his son; or nephews, their uncles; and if there is
no avenger [the murderer pays] forty *grivnas* fine; if [the killed man]
is a [Kievan] Russian, or a member of the *druzhina* [retinue], or a
merchant, or a sheriff, or an agent of the prince, or even an *izgoi*
[serf], or a [Novgorodian] Slav, the fine is forty *grivnas*.

Article 2

If a man is bleeding or is blue from bruises, he does not need any eyewitness; if he has no sign [of injury] he is to produce an eyewitness; if
he cannot, the matter ends there; if he cannot avenge himself he is to
receive three *grivnas*, while the physician is to get an honorarium.

Article 3

If a person hits another with a stick, or a rod, or a fist, or a bowl, or a
[drinking] horn, or the dull side of a sword, he is to pay twelve *grivnas*
fine; if the offender is not hit back [by his victim], he must pay, and
there the matter ends.

Article 4

If a person strikes another with an unsheathed sword, or with the hilt
of a sword, he pays twelve *grivnas* for the offense.

Article 5

If a person hits [another's] arm and the arm is severed or shrinks, he pays
forty *grivnas* fine. And if he hits the leg [but does not sever it], and then
he [the victim] becomes lame, let both [parties] reach an agreement.

Article 6

And if a finger is cut off, three grivnas for the offense.

Article 7

For the mustache twelve grivnas; and for the beard twelve grivnas.

Article 8

If anyone unsheathes his sword, but does not hit, he pays one grivna fine.

Article 9

If a man pulls another man toward himself or pushes him away and [the offended] brings two witnesses, the fine is three grivnas; if he should be a Varangian or a Kolbiag, an oath is to be taken.

Article 10

If anyone conceals a runaway slave of a Varangian or a Kolbiag for three days, and if it is discovered on the third day, the original owner gets back his slave and three grivnas for the offense.

Article 11

If anyone rides another's horse without the owner's permission, he has to pay three grivnas.

Article 12

If anyone steals another's horse, or weapon, or clothes, and the owner recognizes it within his township, he gets back his property and three grivnas for the offense.

Article 13

If anyone should recognize his stolen property, he should neither take it nor say to a person, "This is mine"; he should say as follows: "Let us go to the place where you got it"; if he will not go immediately, he must post bond within five days.

Article 14

If a business partner should demand money from his associate and the latter should demur, he must be brought to a court of twelve men; and if it should be established that he [the associate] cheated, the partner shall receive his share and three *grivnas* for the offense.

Article 15

If the original owner should recognize his [runaway] slave and should want him back, the present owner shall lead him to the party from whom he purchased the slave, and he may go to the second party; and should the matter go to the third party, the third party should be told: "Give me back my slave, and try to get your money back [from the fourth party] with the aid of an eyewitness."

Article 16

If a slave should hit a free man and then hide in the house of his master, and the master should be unwilling to give him up, the slave must be seized and his master must pay twelve *grivnas* fine; and the offended free man may beat that slave wherever he finds him.

Article 17

And if anyone should break [someone's] spear, or shield, or damage his clothes, and then should want to keep [these items], he must pay for them; and if he should insist on returning the damaged article he must pay for the value of that article.

The Law of the Russian Land enacted at a meeting of Princes Iziaslav, Vsevolod, and Sviatoslav, and their advisors Kosniachko, Pereneg, Nikifov of Kiev, Chudin, and Mikula.

Article 18

Should a bailiff be killed deliberately, the killer must pay eighty *grivnas* fine; the people are not to pay; and for [the murder of] a prince's adjutant, eighty *grivnas*.

Article 19

And if a bailiff is killed in a highway attack and the people do not search for the killer, the fine will be paid by that locality where the killed official is found.

Article 20

Should a bailiff be killed near a barn, or near a horse [stable], or a livestock [shed], or [trying to prevent] rustling of cattle, the murderer

should be killed like a dog; the same law is applicable to the murderer
of a steward.

Article 21

And for a prince's steward, eighty *grivnas*; and for a master of the stable
[killed] near his livestock, also eighty *grivnas*, as decreed by Iziaslav when
the Dorogobuzhians killed his master of the stable.

Article 22

For [the murder of] an elder of a prince's village, or for a field overseer,
twelve *grivnas*; and for the helper of a steward, five *grivnas*.

Article 23

And for the killing of a peasant or a slave, five *grivnas*.

Article 24

And if a slave-nurse or her son is killed, twelve *grivnas*.

Article 25

And for [the killing of] a prince's horse, if the latter has a brand, three
grivnas, and for a peasant's horse, two *grivnas*.

Article 26

And for a mare, sixty *rezanas*;* for an ox, one *grivna*; for a cow, forty
rezanas; for a three-year-old cow, fifteen *kunas*;* for a yearling [heifer],
one-half *grivna*; for a calf, five *rezanas*; for a yearling ewe, one *nogata*;*
and for a yearling ram, one *nogata*.

Article 27

If anyone should abduct someone's male or female slave, he has to pay
twelve *grivnas* for the offense.

Article 28

If a man should come bleeding or bruised, he needs no witness.

----

* See the glossary.

Article 29

And whoever steals either a horse or an ox, or robs a barn, if he is alone he has to pay one grivna and thirty rezanas; if there were as many as eighteen thieves, each pays three grivnas and thirty rezanas.

Article 30

And if anyone damages or burns a prince's bee hive, three grivnas.

Article 31

And if anyone should torture a peasant, without the prince's order, three grivnas for the offense.

Article 32

And [for the torture of] a bailiff, a steward, or a sheriff, twelve grivnas.

Article 33

And whoever should plow over the property line or destroy a property mark, twelve grivnas for the offense.

Article 34

And whoever steals a boat, he has to pay [the owner] thirty rezanas for the boat, and sixty rezanas fine.

Article 35

And for [the theft of] a dove or a chicken, nine kunas.

Article 36

And for [the theft of] a duck, a goose, a crane, or a swan, thirty rezanas and a fine of sixty rezanas.

Article 37

And if anyone steals someone's hunting dog, or a hawk, or a falcon, three grivnas for the offense.

Article 38

If anyone should kill a thief in his own yard, or at the barn, or at the stable, he is [justly] killed; if, however, anyone detains the thief till daylight, he must bring him to the prince's court; and should he [the thief] be killed, and should people see that the thief was bound, the killer must pay for him.

Article 39

If anyone should steal hay, nine *kunas;* and for wood, nine *kunas.*

Article 40

If a gang of ten thieves should steal an ewe, or a goat, or a pig, each must pay a fine of sixty *rezanas.*

Article 41

And whoever should apprehend a thief receives ten *rezanas;* and a sheriff receives fifteen *kunas* from three *grivnas* [of fines collected]; fifteen *kunas* go [to the Church] as tithe; and the prince receives three *grivnas.* And from twelve *grivnas* of theft, the apprehender of the thief will receive seventy *kunas;* [the Church] two *grivnas* as tithe; and the prince ten *grivnas.*

Article 42

The following is the tax collecting custom: the collectors [during their journey] should receive seven buckets of malt, a ram or some other meat or two *nogatas;* and on Wednesday one *rezana* or cheese; the same on Friday; and as much bread and millet as they can eat; and two chickens per day; and shelter for four of their horses and feed for them, as much as they can eat; the collectors should [collect] sixty *grivnas,* ten *rezanas,* twelve *veveritsas,* and a *grivna* in advance; and during Lent collectors should receive fish and should get seven *rezanas* for fish; during a week they should receive fifteen *kunas* and food as much as they can eat; tax collectors should complete their task in one week; such is Iaroslav's decree.

Article 43

The following is the code of bridge builders: when they complete a bridge, they should receive for their work one *nogata;* also one *nogata* for every span; and if an old bridge needs repair of several planks, three, or four, or five, the same payment.

9

The Struggle
for Succession

The Varangians introduced many innovations to Kievan Rus—constructive as well as destructive. Of the latter, the most famed was the struggle for succession. Following the death of each Grand Prince, beginning with Sviatoslav in 972, the country experienced prolonged and bitter quarreling and fighting among the princes until one victor emerged. These feuds exhausted the country's resources, disrupted trade, forced people to flee certain areas, invited foreign intrusions, and contributed in innumerable ways to the downfall of the Kievan state.

6484–6485 (976–977). Yaropolk marched against his brother Oleg into the district of Dereva. Oleg sallied out to meet him, and they came to blows. When the companies fought, Yaropolk overcame Oleg. Where Oleg fled with his warriors into the town called Vruchi, there was a bridge across a moat to the city gates, and as the soldiery pressed hard on each other's heels, they fell into the moat. Oleg also was pushed from the bridge into the ditch; many men fell in, and the horses crushed the soldiers.

When Yaropolk entered his brother's city, he seized the latter's property, and sent in search of him. Upon looking for Oleg, Yaropolk's men were unable to find him, until one native of Dereva reported that he had seen Oleg pushed off the bridge the night before. So Yaropolk sent men to look for his brother. They dragged bodies from the moat from morning till noon, and found Oleg also under the other corpses. They carried him away and laid him upon a rug. Then Yaropolk came and wept

Reprinted by permission of the publishers from Samuel H. Cross, "The Russian Primary Chronicle," *Harvard Studies and Notes in Philology and Literature* (Cambridge, Mass., Harvard University Press, 1930), vol. 12, pp. 177–180, 214–225, 231–232, 235, 238–239, 245, 255.

over him. . . . So they buried Oleg in the city of Vruchi, and his tomb is there to this day. Yaropolk seized his property. . . . When Vladimir in Novgorod heard that Yaropolk had killed Oleg, he was afraid, and fled abroad. Then Yaropolk sent his viceroys to Novgorod, and was thus the sole ruler in Rus.

6686–6688 (978–980). Vladimir returned to Novgorod with Varangian allies, and instructed the viceroys of Yaropolk to return to the latter and inform him that Vladimir was advancing against him prepared to fight. . . .

Vladimir came to Kiev with a large force. Yaropolk could not resist him, but shut himself up in Kiev with his people and with Blud. Vladimir came to a halt at Dorogozhichi, and entrenched himself between there and Kapichi; his earthwork is there to this day. Vladimir then sent treacherous proposals to Blud, Yaropolk's general, saying, "Be my friend; if I kill my brother, I will regard you as my father, and you shall have much honor from me. It was not I who began to fight with my brother, but he, and I was for that reason overcome by fear, and therefore have come against him." Blud replied to the messengers of Vladimir that he would join with him in sincere friendship. . . .

Blud shut himself up with Yaropolk with the intention of betraying him, and he sent frequent messages to Vladimir, urging him to storm the city while he himself planned how he might kill Yaropolk. But on account of the citizens, it was not possible to kill him. So Blud, not being able to destroy him thus, contrived it by means of a ruse, while he urged the prince not to go forth from the city to fight. Thus he craftily suggested to Yaropolk that the people of Kiev were sending messages to invite Vladimir to approach the town so that they might betray Yaropolk into his hands, and advised him to flee from the city. Yaropolk heeded his suggestion, and he fled from Vladimir. He then shut himself up in the city of Rodnya at the mouth of the Ros, while Vladimir entered the city of Kiev, and then laid siege to Yaropolk at Rodnya. There was great famine there, and we have to this day a proverb which speaks of famine as in Rodnya.

Blud then said to Yaropolk, "Do you see what a large force your brother has? We cannot overcome them. Make peace with your brother." He spoke thus plotting treachery against him. But Yaropolk assented. Blud then sent word to Vladimir that he would bring Yaropolk before him in accordance with his wishes. Vladimir, upon hearing these tidings, went to his father's castle with the hall . . . and settled there with his retinue. Blud next induced Yaropolk to appear before his brother and express his readiness to accept any terms he might offer. Yaropolk thus went in person to Vladimir, though he had been previously warned by Varyazhko not to go. "My prince," said he, "they will kill you. Flee rather to the Pechenegs and collect an army." But the

Prince heeded him not. Yaropolk came accordingly before Vladimir, and when he entered the door, two Varangians stabbed him under the arms with their swords, while Blud shut the doors and would not allow his men to follow him. Thus Yaropolk was slain. . . . Vladimir then began to reign alone in Kiev. . . .

[Vladimir had twelve sons: Izyaslav, Mstislav, Yaroslav, Sudislav, Vsevolod, Svyatopolk, Vysheslav, Svyatoslav, Stanislav, Boris, Pozvizd, and Gleb. In 1015, following Vladimir's death] Svyatopolk settled in Kiev . . . and after calling together all the inhabitants of Kiev, he began to distribute largess among them. They accepted it, but their hearts were not with him, because their brethren were with Boris. When Boris returned with the army, after meeting the Pechenegs, he received the news that his father was dead. He mourned deeply for him, for he was beloved of his father before all the rest.

When he came to the Alta, he halted. His father's retainers then urged him to take his place in Kiev on his father's throne, since he had at his disposal the latter's retainers and troops. But Boris protested, "Be it not for me to raise my hand against my elder brother. Now that my father has passed away, let him take the place of my father in my heart." When the soldiery heard these words, they departed from him, and Boris remained with his servants.

But Svyatopolk was filled with lawlessness. Adopting the device of Cain, he sent messages to Boris that he desired to live at peace with him, and would increase the territory he had received from his father. But he plotted against him how he might kill him. So Svyatopolk came by night to Vyshegorod. After secretly summoning to his presence Putsha and the boyars of the town, he inquired of them whether they were wholeheartedly devoted to him. Putsha and the men of Vyshegorod replied, "We are ready to lay down our lives for you." He then commanded them to say nothing to any man, but to go and kill his brother Boris. They straightway promised to execute his order. . . .

These emissaries came to the Alta . . . fell upon him [Boris] like wild beasts about the tent, and overcame him by piercing him with lances. They also overpowered his servant, who cast himself upon his body. . . .

The desperados, after attacking Boris, wrapped him in a canvas, loaded him upon a wagon, and dragged him off, though he was still alive. When the impious Svyatopolk saw that he was still breathing, he sent two Varangians to finish him. When they came and saw that he was still alive, one of them drew his sword and plunged it into his heart. . . .

The desperate murderers, godless wretches that they were, returned to Svyatopolk in hope of commendation. The names of these contemners of the law are Putsha, Taletz, Elovit, and Lyashko. . . .

The impious Svyatopolk then reflected, "Behold, I have killed Boris; now how can I kill Gleb?" Adopting once more Cain's device, he craftily sent messages to Gleb to the effect that he should come quickly, because his father was very ill and desired his presence. Gleb quickly mounted his horse, and set out with a small company, for he was obedient to his father. When he came to the Volga, his horse stumbled in a ditch on the plain, and broke his leg. He arrived at Smolensk, and setting out thence at dawn, he embarked in a boat on the Smyadyn. At this time Yaroslav received from Predslava the tidings of their father's death, and he sent word to Gleb that he should not set out, because his father was dead and his brother had been murdered by Svyatopolk. Upon receiving these tidings, Gleb burst into tears, and mourned for his father, but still more deeply for his brother. . . .

While he was thus praying amid his tears, there suddenly arrived those sent by Svyatopolk for Gleb's destruction. These emissaries seized Gleb's boat, and drew their weapons. The servants of Gleb were terrified, and the impious messenger, Goryaser, gave orders that they should slay Gleb with despatch. Then Gleb's cook, Torchin by name, seized a knife, and stabbed Gleb. . . .

After Gleb had been slain, his body was thrown upon the shore between two tree-trunks, but afterward they took him and carried him away, to bury him beside his brother Boris in the Church of St. Basil. . . .

Now the impious and evil Svyatopolk killed Svyatoslav in the Hungarian mountains, after causing him to be pursued as he fled into Hungary. Then he began to reflect how he would kill all his brethren and rule alone in Rus. . . .

The impious Svyatopolk thus began his reign in Kiev. Assembling the people, he began to distribute skins to some and furs to others, and thus dissipated a large sum.

When Yaroslav heard of his father's death, he had many Varangians under his command, and they offered violence to the inhabitants of Novgorod and to their wives. The men of Novgorod then rose and killed the Varangians in their market place. Yaroslav was angry, and departing to Rakom, he took up his abode in the castle. Then he sent messengers to Novgorod with the comment that the death of his retainers was beyond remedy, but at the same time he summoned before him the chief men of the city who had massacred the Varangians, and craftily killed them. The same night news came from Kiev sent by his sister, Predslava, to the effect that his father was dead, that Svyatopolk had settled in Kiev after killing Boris, and was now endeavoring to compass the death of Gleb, and she warned Yaroslav to be exceedingly on his guard against Svyatopolk. When Yaroslav heard these tidings, he grieved for his father and his retainers.

On the morrow, he collected the remnant of the men of Novgorod and regretfully lamented, "Alas for my beloved retainers, whom I yesterday

caused to be killed! You would indeed be useful in the present crisis."
He wiped away his tears, and informed his subjects in the assembly that
his father was dead, and that Svyatopolk had settled in Kiev after killing
his brethren. Then the men of Novgorod said, "We can still fight for
you, oh Prince, even though our brethren are slain." So Yaroslav collected one thousand Varangians and forty thousand other soldiers, and
marched against Svyatopolk. . . . When Svyatopolk learned that Yaroslav
was on his way, he prepared an innumerable army of Russes and Pechenegs, and marched out toward Lyubech on one side of the Dnieper,
while Yaroslav was on the opposite bank.

6524 (1016). Yaroslav arrived before Kiev, and the brothers stood
over against each other on both banks of the Dnieper, but neither party
dared attack. They remained thus face to face for three months. Then
Svyatopolk's general rode out along the shore and scoffed at the men of
Novgorod, shouting, "Why did you come hither with this crooked-
shanks, you carpenters? We shall put you to work on our houses." When
the men of Novgorod heard this taunt, they declared to Yaroslav, "Tomorrow we will cross over to them, and whoever will not go with us
we will kill." Now it was already beginning to freeze. Svyatopolk was
stationed between two lakes, and caroused with his retinue the whole
night through. Yaroslav on the morrow marshaled his troops, and crossed
over toward dawn. His forces disembarked on the shore and pushed the
boats out from the bank. The two armies advanced to the attack, and
met upon the field. The carnage was terrible. Because of the lake, the
Pechenegs could bring no aid, and Yaroslav's troops drove Svyatopolk
with his followers toward it. When the latter went out upon the ice, it
broke under them, and Yaroslav began to win the upper hand. Svyatopolk then fled among the Lyakhs, while Yaroslav established himself in
Kiev upon the throne of his father and his grandfather. . . .

6526 (1018). Boleslav attacked Yaroslav with Svyatopolk and his
Lyakhs. After collecting Russes, Varangians, and Slavs, Yaroslav marched
forth against Boleslav and Svyatopolk, and upon arriving at Volyn, they
camped on both sides of the river Bug. . . .

Then Yaroslav fled with four men to Novgorod, and Boleslav entered
Kiev in company with Svyatopolk. Boleslav ordered that his force should
be dispersed to forage throughout the cities, and so it was done. When
Yaroslav arrived at Novgorod in his flight, he planned to escape overseas,
but the viceroy Constantine, son of Dobrynya, together with the men
of Novgorod, destroyed his boats, protesting that they wished to fight
once more against Boleslav and Svyatopolk. They set out to gather funds
at the rate of four skins per man, ten *grivni* from each elder, and eighteen
grivni from each boyar. With these funds they recruited Varangians
whom they imported, and thus collected for Yaroslav a large army.

While Boleslav was settled in Kiev, the impious Svyatopolk ordered that any Lyakhs found in the city should be killed, and so the Lyakhs were slain. Then Boleslav fled from Kiev, taking with him the property and the boyars of Yaroslav, as well as the latter's two sisters, and made Anastasius steward of the property, for the latter had won his confidence by his flattery. He took with him a large company, and having appropriated to himself the cities of Cherven, he returned to his native land. Svyatopolk thus reigned alone in Kiev, but Yaroslav attacked him again, and Svyatopolk fled among the Pechenegs.

6527 (1019). Svyatopolk advanced with a large force of Pecheneg supporters, and Yaroslav collected a multitude of soldiery, and went forth against him to the Alta River. . . . The two armies attacked, and the plain of the Alta was covered with the multitudinous soldiery of both forces. It was then Friday. As the sun rose, they met in battle, and the carnage was terrible, such as had never before occurred in Rus. The soldiers fought hand to hand and slaughtered each other. Three times they clashed, so that blood flowed in the valley. Toward evening Yaroslav conquered, and Svyatopolk fled. . . . He could not endure to stay in one place, but fled through the land of the Lyakhs, pursued by the wrath of God. Upon reaching the wilderness between Poland and Bohemia, he ended his life in an evil fashion. . . .

6529 (1021). Bryachislav, son of Izyaslav, grandson of Vladimir, came and captured Novgorod, and having taken the people of Novgorod and their property, he returned to Polotzk. When he arrived at the Sudomir River, Yaroslav came thither from Kiev on the seventh day. He conquered Bryachislav, and returned the people of Novgorod to their city, while Bryachislav fled to Polotzk.

6530 (1022). Yaroslav came to Brest. At this time Mstislav, who was in Tmutorakan, attacked the Kassogians. . . .

6531 (1023). Mstislav marched against Yaroslav with a force of Khazars and Kassogians.

6532 (1024). While Yaroslav was at Novgorod, Mstislav arrived before Kiev from Tmutorakan, but the inhabitants of Kiev would not admit him. He thus departed thence and established himself upon the throne of Chernigov, while Yaroslav was at Novgorod. In this year, magicians appeared in Suzdal, and killed old people by satanic inspiration and devil worship, saying that they would spoil the harvest. There was great confusion and famine throughout all that country. The whole population went along the Volga to the Bulgarians, from whom they bought grain and thus sustained themselves. . . . Then Mstislav proposed to Yaroslav that the latter, as the eldest brother, should remain in Kiev, while the Chernigov district should belong to Mstislav. But Yaroslav did not dare to return to Kiev until they were properly reconciled. So Mstislav settled in Chernigov, and Yaroslav in Novgorod, though Kiev was occupied by subjects of Yaroslav.

6534 (1026). Yaroslav recruited many soldiers and arrived at Kiev, where he made peace with his brother Mstislav near Gorodetz. They divided Rus according to the course of the Dnieper. Yaroslav took the Kiev side, and Mstislav the other. They thus began to live in peace and fraternal amity. Strife and tumult ceased, and there was a great calm in the land. . . .

[In 1036 Mstislav died and] Yaroslav assumed the entire sovereignty, and was the sole ruler in the land of Rus. . . .

6562 (1054). Yaroslav, Great Prince of Rus, passed away. While he was yet alive, he admonished his sons [Izyaslav, Svyatoslav, Vsevolod, Viacheslav, Vysheslav and Igor] with these words: "My sons, I am about to quit this world. Love one another, since ye are brothers by one father and mother. If ye dwell in amity with one another, God will dwell among you, and will subject your enemies to you, and ye will live at peace. But if ye dwell in envy and dissension, quarreling with one another, then ye will perish yourselves and bring to ruin the land of your ancestors, which they won at the price of great effort. Wherefore remain rather at peace, brother heeding brother. The throne of Kiev I bequeath to my eldest son, your brother Izyaslav. Heed him as ye have heeded me, that he may take my place among you. To Svyatoslav I give Chernigov, to Vsevolod Pereyaslavl, to Igor the city of Vladimir, and to Vyacheslav Smolensk." Thus he divided the cities among them, commanding them not to violate one another's boundaries, not to despoil one another. He laid upon Izyaslav the injunction to aid the party wronged, in case one brother should attack another. Thus he admonished his sons to dwell in amity. . . .

[Following Yaroslav's death in February, 1054] Izyaslav then took up his abode at Kiev, with Svyatoslav in Chernigov, Vsevolod at Pereyaslavl, Igor in Vladimir, and Vyacheslav at Smolensk. . . .

6564–6565 (1056–1057). Vyacheslav, ˙ son of Yaroslav, died at Smolensk, and Igor took up his abode in Smolensk, moving over from Vladimir. . . .

6567 (1059). Izyaslav, Svyatoslav, and Vsevolod liberated their uncle Sudislav from the prison where he had been confined for twenty-four years, and after they had obtained his oath of fealty, he took the monastic habit. . . .

6575 (1067). Vseslav, the son of Bryacheslav of Polotzk, undertook a campaign and captured Novgorod. Izyaslav, Svyatoslav, and Vsevolod, the three sons of Yaroslav, though it was the dead of winter, collected a force and set forth against him. They arrived before Minsk, but the citizens barricaded themselves in the city. Then the brethren captured it, put the men to the sword, sold the women and children into slavery, and proceeded to the Nemiga. Vseslav came forward to meet them. The two forces thus collided at the Nemiga, on March 3, with heavy snow on the ground. They thus attacked and the carnage was severe. The casualties were numerous, but Izyaslav, Svyatoslav, and Vsevolod won the day, while Vseslav sought safety in flight. On July 10 following, Izyaslav, Svyatoslav, and Vsevolod took oath as to their peaceful intentions and offered Vseslav safe-conduct if he would join them. He put his confidence in their sworn oath, and crossed the Dnieper by boat. Izyaslav preceded Vseslav into their tent, and contrary to their oath, the brethren thus took Vseslav captive at Rsha near Smolensk. Izyaslav then brought Vseslav to Kiev and there threw him and his two sons into prison. . . .

[In 1068 a general discontent occurred in Kiev]. The mob then gave a shout and went off to Vseslav's prison. When Izyaslav beheld their action, he fled with Vsevolod from the palace. But on September 15, the people thus haled Vseslav from his dungeon, and set him up in the midst of the Prince's palace. They then pillaged the palace, seizing a huge amount of gold and silver, furs, and marten-skins. Izyaslav made his escape to Poland. . . .

6577 (1069).   Reinforced by Boleslav [of Poland], Izyaslav marched to attack Vseslav, who went forth to meet them, and arrived at Byelgorod. But during the night he hid himself from the men of Kiev, and fled from Byelgorod to Polotzk. Then the men of Kiev saw on the morrow that their prince had fled, they returned to Kiev, and after calling an assembly, they sent messages to Svyatoslav and Vsevolod saying, "We did wrong in expelling our Prince, and now he leads the Poles against us. Return to your father's city. If you refuse to return, then we have no alternative but to burn our city and depart to Greece." Svyatoslav replied, "We shall communicate with our brother. If he marches upon you with the Poles to destroy you, we shall fight against him, and not allow him to destroy our father's city. If his intentions are peaceful, then he shall approach with a small troop." Then the people of Kiev were pacified.

Svyatoslav and Vsevolod then sent messengers to Izyaslav, announcing that Vseslav had fled, and requesting him accordingly not to lead his Poles in attack upon Kiev, because no one was really opposing him. They also let it be understood that if he intended to nurse his wrath and destroy the city, they would be properly concerned for the ancestral capital. When Izyaslav received these tidings, he left the Poles and came forward, accompanied only by Boleslav himself and a small Polish escort. He sent his son Mstislav ahead of him into Kiev, and upon the latter's arrival, he slew those who had freed Vseslav, to the number of seventy, blinded others, and executed without any investigation others, who were entirely innocent. When Izyaslav arrived at the city, the inhabitants went forth to welcome him, and the men of Kiev received him as their Prince. He scattered the Poles to forage, and then had them secretly killed. Boleslav then returned to his native country. Izyaslav transferred the market place to the hill, and drove Vseslav out of Polotzk, where he set up his own son Mstislav. But the latter soon died, and Izyaslav enthroned in his stead his brother Svyatopolk, since Vseslav was fled. . . .

6581 (1073). The devil stirred up strife among these brothers, the sons of Yaroslav. When disagreement thus ensued among them, Svyatoslav and Vsevolod united against Izyaslav. The latter left Kiev, but Svyatoslav and Vsevolod arrived there upon March 22 and established themselves on the throne at Berestovoye, though they thus transgressed against their father's injunction. Svyatoslav was the instigator of his brother's expulsion, for he desired more power. He misled Vsevolod by asserting that Izyaslav was entering into an alliance with Vseslav for the purpose of attacking them, and by this means he irritated Vsevolod against Izyaslav. Now Izyaslav took considerable treasure with him on his flight into Poland with the intention of recruiting supporters there. But the Poles robbed him of all his property, and expelled him from their boundaries. Svyatoslav thus ruled in Kiev after the expulsion of his brother, and thus broke the injunction of his father and of God. . . .

6585 (1077). Izyaslav advanced with Polish support, and Vsevolod went forth against him. Boris settled at Chernigov on May 4; his reign lasted eighty days until he fled to join Roman in Tmutorakan. Vsevolod went to Volyn to attack his brother Izyaslav. Peace was concluded, so that Izyaslav came and settled in Kiev on July 15. Oleg, the son of Svyatoslav, was with Vsevolod at Chernigov.

6586 (1078). Oleg, son of Svyatoslav, fled from Vsevolod to Tmutorakan on April 10. In this year, Gleb, the son of Svyatoslav, was killed in Zavolochye. . . .

While Svyatopolk, the son of Izyaslav, was ruling at Novgorod in his stead, and while Yaropolk was reigning in Vyshegorod and Vladimir at Smolensk, Oleg and Boris led the pagans to attack Rus, and fell upon Vsevolod with their Polovcian reinforcements. Vsevolod advanced to meet them as far as the Sozh. The Polovcians then vanquished the Russes, and many lost their lives. Ivan, son of Zhiroslav, and Tuki, the brother of Chud, along with Porei and many others, met their death there on August 28. Oleg and Boris arrived before Chernigov, thinking they had won, and they visited much harm upon the land of Rus.

10

The Struggle
with the Nomads

Next to the struggle for succession, the most important factor contributing to the downfall of Kiev was the struggle with intruding Asiatic nomads—the Pechenegs, the Torks, the Polovtsians, and others. The nomads were attracted to the area by its favorable climate and topography as well as its political disunity. Nomadic attacks disrupted trade with Constantinople, caused depopulation of the Kievan realm, exhausted resources of the country, and on many occasions played a significant role in internal feuds. In fact, between 1060 and 1210, the country was invaded by the Polovtsians over fifty times.

6476 (968). While Svyatoslav was at Pereyaslavetz, the Pechenegs invaded Rus for the first time. So Olga shut herself up in the city of Kiev with her grandsons, Yaropolk, Oleg, and Vladimir. The nomads besieged the city with a great force. They surrounded it with an innumerable multitude, so that it was impossible to escape or send messages from the city, and the inhabitants were weak from hunger and thirst. . . .

But the people of Kiev sent to Svyatoslav [nevertheless, a messenger], saying, "Oh Prince, you visit and observe foreign lands. But while you neglect your own country the Pechenegs have all but taken us captive, along with your mother and your children as well. Unless you return to

Reprinted by permission of the publishers from Samuel H. Cross, "The Russian Primary Chronicle," *Harvard Studies and Notes in Philology and Literature* (Cambridge, Mass., Harvard University Press, 1930), vol. 12, pp. 171–172, 177, 207–209, 211–212, 225–226, 233, 235, 239, 255, 258, 265–268, 270, 272–274, 292–296.

protect us, they will attack us again, if you have no pity on your native land, on your mother in her old age, and on your children." When Svyatoslav heard these words, he quickly bestrode his charger, and returned to Kiev with his retinue. He kissed his mother and his children, and regretted what they had suffered at the hands of the Pechenegs. He therefore collected an army, and drove the Pechenegs out into the Steppes. Thus there was peace. . . .

After making peace with the Greeks [in 971], Svyatoslav journeyed by boat to the cataracts of the Dnieper, and the general Sveinald, advised him to ride around the falls on horseback, for the Pechenegs were encamped in the vicinity. The Prince did not heed him, but went on by boat. The people of Pereyaslavetz informed the Pechenegs that Svyatoslav was returning to Rus after seizing from the Greeks great riches and immense booty, but that his troop was small. When the Pechenegs heard this news, they ambuscaded the cataracts, so that when Svyatoslav arrived it was impossible to pass them. So the Prince decided to winter in Byelobereg, but the Russes had no rations, so that there was a severe famine, and they paid as much as half a *grivna* for a horse's head. But Svyatoslav wintered there nevertheless.

When spring came, in 6480 (972), Svyatoslav approached the cataracts, where Kurya, Prince of the Pechenegs, attacked him; and Svyatoslav was killed. The nomads took his head, and made a cup out of his skull, overlaying it with gold, and they drank from it. . . .

6500 (992). Vladimir attacked the Croats. When he had returned from the Croatian War, the Pechenegs arrived on the opposite side of the Dnieper from the direction of the Sula. Vladimir set forth against them, and encountered them on the banks of the Trubezh, where Pereyaslavl now stands. Vladimir took up his position on the near side, and the Pechenegs theirs on the other, and the Russes did not venture to the farther shore any more than their foes did to this side of the river. The prince of the Pechenegs came down to the river bank, and calling to Vladimir, proposed to him, "Send one of your warriors, and I will detail one of mine, that they may do battle together. If your vassal conquers mine, let us not fight together for three years to come. But if our champion wins, let us fight three years in succession." Then each prince returned to his own force.

Vladimir returned to his camp, and sent heralds through it to inquire whether there was no man who would fight with the champion of the Pechenegs. But none was found anywhere. On the morrow, the Pechenegs arrived, bringing their champion; but on our side there was none. Vladimir now began to be concerned as he sought a champion throughout his whole army. Then there came to the Prince an old man who said to him, "Oh Prince, I have a younger son at home. I came forth with four others, but he abides by the hearth. Since his childhood, there has been no man who could vanquish him. One day, when I reprimanded him while he was tanning a hide, he flew into a rage at me and tore the leather to bits in his hands." When the Prince heard these words, he rejoiced, and summoned the youth. So he was brought before the Prince, and the Prince informed him of all that had occurred. Then the youth said, "Oh Prince, I know not whether I be capable of this feat; wherefore let them test me. Is there no large and strong bull hereabouts?" Such a bull was soon found, and he directed them to anger the animal. The men put hot irons on him, and then let him go. The bull ran past the youth, and he seized the beast's flank with his hand. He thus pulled off the skin along with as much flesh as he could grasp. Then Vladimir remarked, "You are well qualified to do combat with the champion."

On the morrow the Pechenegs approached, and began to shout, "Is there no champion available? See, ours is ready!" Vladimir had given orders that night to rest upon their arms, and at dawn the two champions went forth. The Pechenegs had sent out their man, who was gigantic and fearsome. Vladimir sent forward his champion, and when the Pecheneg saw him, he laughed, for he was of but moderate size. A space was duly measured off between the two armies, and the warriors were allowed to attack each other. They came to grips, and seized upon each other with violence. But the Russ crushed the Pecheneg to death in his arms, and cast him upon the ground. The Russes raised a cheer, and the Pechenegs took to flight. The Russes pursued them, cut them down, and drove them away. In his joy, Vladimir founded a city on this river bank, and called it Pereyaslavl, because this youth had won glory there. Vladimir made him and his father great men, and then returned to Kiev with victory and great renown. . . .

Then [between 994–996] the Pechenegs came to Vasiliev, and Vladimir went forth against them with a small company. When the troops met, he could not withstand the enemy, so he fled, and took position under a bridge, where he concealed himself with difficulty from the foe. . . .

6505 (997). When Vladimir went to Novgorod after upland troops with which to fight the Pechenegs (for there was desperate and constant conflict with them), the latter, on perceiving that for the moment there was no prince at hand, came and beset Byelgorod. They allowed no sally from the city, and great famine prevailed. Vladimir could not bring succor, for he had no troops with him, and the number of the Pechenegs was great. The siege was thus prolonged, and the famine grew increasingly severe. . . .

6523 (1015). . . . When Vladimir fell ill, Boris [his son] was with him at the time. Since the Pechenegs were attacking the Russes, he sent Boris out against them, for he himself was very sick. . . .

[1034–1036]. While Yaroslav was still at Novgorod, news came to him that the Pechenegs were besieging Kiev. He then collected a large army of Varangians and Slavs, returned to Kiev, and entered his city. The Pechenegs were innumerable. Yaroslav made a sally from the city and marshaled his forces, placing the Varangians in the center, the men of Kiev on the right flank, and the men of Novgorod on the left. When they had taken position before the city, the Pechenegs advanced, and they met on the spot where the metropolitan Church of St. Sophia now stands. At that time, as a matter of fact, there were fields outside the city. The combat was fierce, but toward evening Yaroslav with difficulty won the upper hand. The Pechenegs fled in various directions, but as they did not know in what quarter to flee, they were drowned, some in the Syetoml, some in other streams, while the remnant of them is fleeing yet. . . .

6569 (1061). The Polovcians invaded Rus for the first time. On February 2, Vsevolod went forth against them. When they met in battle, the Polovcians defeated Vsevolod, but after the combat they retired. This was the first evil done by these pagan and godless foes. Their prince was Iskal. . . .

6576 (1068). A multitude of those nomads known as the Polovcians attacked the land of Rus, and Izyaslav, Svyatoslav, and Vsevolod went forth against them as far as the Alta. They joined battle in the dead of night, but since God had let loose the pagans upon us because of our transgressions, the Russian princes fled and the Polovcians were victorious. . . .

6579 (1071). The Polovcians raided about Rostovetz and Neyatin. . . .

[6586 (1078)]. While Svyatopolk, the son of Izyaslav, was ruling at Novgorod in his stead, and while Yaropolk was reigning in Vyshegorod and Vladimir at Smolensk, Oleg and Boris led the pagans to attack Rus, and fell upon Vsevolod with their Polovcian reinforcements. Vsevolod advanced to meet them as far as the Sozh. The Polovcians then vanquished the Russes, and many lost their lives. . . .

6587 (1079). Roman advanced with Polovcian forces as far as Voin, but Vsevolod remained near Pereyaslavl and made peace with the Polovcians. . . .

6588 (1080). The Torks of Pereyaslavl made an attack upon Rus. Vsevolod sent forth his son Vladimir, who went out and conquered them. . . .

[In the spring of 1093] the Polovcians attacked Rus, but when they learned that Vsevolod was dead, they sent propositions for peace to Svyatopolk. Without consulting with the numerous adherents of his father and his uncle, but taking counsel only with those who had accompanied him to the capital, Svyatopolk seized the Polovcian envoys

and cast them into prison. When the Polovcians heard of this outrage,
they immediately declared war. A large force of them thus laid siege
to the city of Torchesk. Being desirous of peace Svyatopolk released
the Polovcian envoys.

The Polovcians, however, were not anxious for peace, and continued
their attacks. Svyatopolk then set out to recruit a force with the intention of attacking them. The wise men advised him not to oppose
the nomads, since his force was small. He replied that he had eight
hundred of his followers who could easily withstand them. Other rash
advisers urged him to pursue his project, but the wiser heads informed
him that even if he had a force of eight thousand, it would be none too
strong. They reminded him that the country was already impoverished
by war and taxes, and suggested that he should ask his cousin Vladimir
for aid. Svyatopolk followed their advice, and sent to Vladimir a request
for assistance. Vladimir assembled his troops, and requested his brother
Rostislav at Pereyaslavl to give Svyatopolk his support as well. When
Vladimir arrived at Kiev, the cousins met at St. Michael's, and composed
between them their quarrels and disagreements. They were thus reconciled, and kissed the Cross to seal their compact. While the Polovcians
were ravaging the countryside, the wise counsellors said to the princes,
"Why do you allow discord to part you? Behold, the pagans lay waste
the land of Rus. You may arrive at an understanding at some later time,
but for the present go out and meet the pagans either to conclude a
peace or to wage war." Vladimir favored a peace, but Svyatopolk was
for war.

Svyatopolk, Vladimir, and Rostislav thus proceeded to Trepol. They
arrived at the Stugna, and before crossing the river, they called their
followers into consultation and began to deliberate. Vladimir suggested
that in view of the present danger they had better remain on the near
side of the river and make peace with the Polovcians. Yan and the other
prudent men supported this opinion, but the men of Kiev were not in
accord with it, and urged the crossing of the river because they were
eager to fight. This counsel found favor, and they crossed the river
Stugna, which at the moment was considerably swollen. After marshaling
their troops, Svyatopolk, Vladimir, and Rostislav then moved forward.
Svyatopolk marched on the right wing, Vladimir on the left, and Rostislav led the centre. When they had passed Trepol, they passed the
rampart. Then the Polovcians advanced to the attack with their bowmen
in the van. When our men took position between the ramparts, the
pagans set up their standards, and the bowmen advanced from their en-
campment. The Polovcians reached the rampart, raised their standards,
and first attacked Svyatopolk, whose troop they broke up. Svyatopolk
made a firm stand, but his soldiers fled without resisting the pagan
onslaught, and he himself was obliged to flee also. The Polovcians then
attacked Vladimir. The battle was fierce, and Vladimir took to flight

with Rostislav. In their flight, they arrived at the river Stugna, and dived in. Rostislav straightway began to drown before Vladimir's very eyes. He was anxious to save his brother, and almost perished himself in the attempt. But Rostislav, the son of Vsevolod, thus met his death.

Vladimir swam the river with a small escort, for many of his troop and his boyars had fallen. When he arrived at the other bank of the Dnieper, he bewailed his brother and his vassals, and thus returned to Chernigov heavy with sorrow. Svyatopolk escaped to Trepol and there barricaded himself. He remained there till evening, and during the night departed for Kiev.

Upon perceiving their victory, the Polovcians scattered upon marauding expeditions throughout the countryside, while others returned to Torchesk. . . . While the Polovcians were besieging Torchesk, the inhabitants resisted and fought boldly from the town, so that they killed many of the enemy. The Polovcians then began to press them hard and cut off their water supply, so that the inhabitants weakened from hunger and thirst. They thus sent messages to Svyatopolk to inform him that unless he sent them food supplies they would be obliged to surrender. Svyatopolk despatched the supplies, but because of the multitude of the besiegers it was impossible to introduce them into the town. When the enemy had thus beleaguered the town for nine weeks, they divided into two parties, one of which remained near the city to prosecute the siege, while the rest marched toward Kiev and scattered on raiding parties between Kiev and Vyshegorod. Svyatopolk sallied forth as far as Zhelan, where the two forces advanced to the attack. When the battle-lines met, a fierce combat ensued, but our men fled before the pagans, and many perished, even a larger number than at Trepol. Svyatopolk arrived at Kiev with two companions, and the Polovcians returned to Torchesk. . . .

6602 (1094). Svyatopolk made peace with the Polovcians, and took to wife the daughter of their prince Tugortkan. In this same year, Oleg arrived from Tmutorakan before Chernigov with a force of Polovcians. Vladimir fortified himself in the city. Oleg then approached and burned the environs, including the monasteries. Vladimir made peace with Oleg, and departed from Chernigov to occupy his father's throne in Pereyaslavl, while Oleg took possession of the city that had been his own father's. The Polovcians committed many depredations in the vicinity of Chernigov, and Oleg made no attempt to restrain them for the reason that he himself had inspired their raids. This was, in fact, the third time that he had led a force of pagans to attack Rus. . . .

In this same year [1095], the Polovcians appeared before Yuryev. They besieged the city for a whole year, and had almost reduced it when Svyatopolk succeeded in pacifying them. The Polovcians returned beyond the Ros, and the citizens of Yuryev abandoned their town and fled to Kiev. Svyatopolk ordered that a town should be built on the hill of Vitichev, and he bade the Bishop Marinus settle there with the people from Yuryev, Sakov, and other refugees from various localities. The Polovcians then burned the deserted town of Yuryev. . . .

At this time [1096], Bonyak and his Polovcians appeared before Kiev on a Sunday evening, and while ravaging the environs, they burned the prince's palace at Berestovoye. Kurya and another band of Polovcians ravaged simultaneously the environs of Pereyaslavl, and burned Ustye on May 24. . . .

In this same month, Tugortkan, the father-in-law of Svyatopolk, came to Pereyaslavl and laid siege to the city. The inhabitants fortified themselves for resistance, while Svyatopolk and Vladimir advanced against him down the west bank of the Dnieper. They arrived at Zarub and crossed the river without being detected by the Polovcians, for God protected them. They then marshaled their forces and advanced toward the city. When the inhabitants observed their approach, they rejoiced, and came forth to meet them, while the Polovcians were standing on the other bank of the Trubezh in battle array. Svyatopolk and Vladimir immediately crossed the river to engage the Polovcians. Vladimir first intended to reform his troop, but they did not await his command, and instead spurred up their horses against their adversaries. When the Polovcians beheld their charge, they turned in flight, and our men pursued the foemen, cutting down their opponents. Upon this day the Lord performed a great deliverance. The aliens were thus conquered on July 19. Their prince Tugortkan was killed, and many others of our enemies fell. On the morrow, they found the dead body of Tugortkan, and Svyatopolk, respecting him as his father-in-law even though he was a foe, brought him to Kiev and buried him at Berestovoye, between the road to Berestovoye and the road to the monastery.

On Thursday, the twentieth of this same month, Bonyak, that godless, mangy thief and bandit, came suddenly to Kiev for the second time. The Polovcians almost entered the city, burned the suburbs about the town, and then attacked the monastery. After burning the monasteries of Stephen and Germanus together with the neighboring villages, they came to the Crypt Monastery while we were resting in our cells after matins, and they howled about the monastery. They planted two standards before the monastery gates, and we fled, some of us behind the building of the monastery, and others to its various rooms. The godless sons of Ishmael slew the brethren in the monastery and wandered about among the cells, breaking down the doors, and they carried off whatever they found in the various rooms. Then they set fire to the shrine of the Holy Virgin. Upon arriving before the church, they thus set fire to the south and the north doors, and upon making their way into the chapel near the grave of Theodosius, they seized the eikons, burned the doors, and blasphemed against God and our faith. . . .

[In 1102–1103 Svyatoslav and Vladimir] resolved to attack the Polovcians and invade their territory. . . . They then sent to Oleg and David and invited them to make a life-or-death stand against the Polovcians. David accepted, but Oleg opposed the campaign on the ground that he was unwell. Vladimir then embraced his cousin, and proceeded to Pereyaslavl, whither he was followed by Svyatopolk, David son of Svyatoslav, David son of Vseslav, Mstislav grandson of Igor, Vyacheslav son of Yaropolk, and Yaropolk son of Vladimir. They advanced on horseback and by boat, arrived below the cataracts, and halted by the rapids at the island of Khortich. They then mounted their horses, and when the footsoldiers had disembarked from the boats, they traveled across country for four days, and arrived at Suten.

When the Polovcians learned that the Russes were on their way, they collected innumerable forces and began to deliberate. Urusoba proposed that the Polovcians should make peace with the Russes, since the latter would offer the nomads a violent combat in view of the fact that the Polovcians had done much scathe to Rus. The younger chiefs replied to Urusoba that even if he was afraid of the Russes, they were not dismayed, for after conquering the Russes, they would invade their country and take their cities, and they wondered who would protect the Russes against them. . . .

The Polovcians advanced, and sent Altunapa in front as a vanguard, since he was celebrated among them for his courage. The Russian princes likewise sent forward their advance party. They thus surprised the vanguard of Altunapa, upon whom they fell, slaying him and his followers. Not one of them escaped, for the Russes slew them all. The nomad troops came on like the trees of the forest, and their mass was impenetrable. The Russes straightway advanced to meet them. Now God on high inspired an awful fear in the Polovcians, so that terror and trembling beset them at the sight of the Russian forces, and they wavered. Even their steeds possessed no more swiftness of foot. But our soldiery, both foot and horse, advanced joyously to the combat.

Upon beholding the effort of the Russes against them, the Polovcians fled before the Russian troops without even waiting to meet them, and our men gave chase and cut them down. On April 4, God thus performed a great salvation and bestowed upon us a mighty victory over our foes. Upon this expedition twenty Polovcian princes were slain: Urusoba, Kchi, Arslanapa, Kitanopa, Kuman, Asup, Kurtek, Chenegrepa, Surbar, and many other princes. Beldyuz was taken captive.

The kinsmen then rested since they had overcome their foes. They brought Beldyuz before Svyatopolk, and the Polovcian chief offered to pay gold and silver, horses and cattle as his ransom. Svyatoslav then sent him to Vladimir. When he stood before him, Vladimir inquired, "Have you noticed how your former oath has brought you to ruin? Though you often gave pledges, you continued to harass the land of Rus. Why did you not admonish your sons and your kinsfolk not to violate their oaths by the shedding of Christian blood? Your blood be upon your own head." He then directed that the Polovcian should be killed, and they cut him to pieces.

Thereafter all the kinsmen gathered together, and Vladimir exclaimed, "This is the day that the Lord hath made, let us rejoice and be glad in it. For the Lord hath freed us from our foes and put down our enemies, and crushed the serpents' heads. He hath given them as food to the men of Rus." They thus seized sheep and cattle, horses and camels, tents with booty and slaves, and with the tents they captured Pechenegs and Torks. They then returned to Rus carrying great spoil, with glory and a great victory won. . . .

6614 (1106). The Polovcians raided in the vicinity of Zarechesk, and Svyatopolk sent Yan son of Vyshata, his brother Putyata, and Ivan the Khazar, son of Zakhari, to pursue them. They drove off the Polovcians and took some spoil. . . .

[In May, 1107], Bonyak raided and seized many horses in the vicinity of Pereyaslavl. In the same year, Bonyak and old Sharukan and many other chieftains came and laid siege to Lubny. Svyatopolk, Vladimir, Oleg, Svyatoslav, Mstislav, Vycheslav, and Yaropolk marched out to attack them at this town. At the sixth hour of the day, they crossed the Sula and shouted at the foe. The Polovcians were terrified, and because of their fear could not even raise a standard, but seized their horses and fled, while their foot-soldiers took to flight also. Our men then began to cut them down as they pursued them, and took others captive. They drove them thus nearly to the Khorol. They thus slew Taz, Bonyak's brother, while Sharukan barely escaped. On August 12, the Polovcians abandoned their camp after the capture of which the Russian soldiery returned home with a great victory. . . .

6618 (1110). In the spring, Svyatopolk, Vladimir, and David marched forth to attack the Polovcians, but returned after reaching the Voin.

11

The Testament
of Vladimir Monomakh

Vladimir Monomakh (1113–1125) was one of the most energetic rulers of Kiev. He was greatly admired by the people, and feared by the feuding princes and nomadic raiders. His wise but firm policies curtailed lawlessness and civil strife, and his very strong impression on the Polovtsians during his adult life succeeded in reducing their attacks on Rus. Monomakh was also a true Christian prince. He advised his children to have faith in God, and to show this faith in good deeds, to love peace, to be humble, to protect the weak, to be hospitable and generous, to shun idleness, and to depend upon themselves.

I, wretched man that I am, named Vasili at my baptism by my pious and glorious grandsire Yaroslav, but commonly known by my Russian name Vladimir, and surnamed Monomakh by my beloved father and mother . . . and for the sake of Christian people, for I was many times saved from all distress through his mercy and through the prayers of my father.

As I sat upon my sledge, I meditated in my heart and praised God, who has led me, a sinner, even to this day. Let not my sons or anyone else who happens to read this brief discourse laugh at its contents. But rather let any one of my sons who takes my words to heart and is not disposed to laziness conduct himself according to my counsel. First, for the sake of God and your own souls, retain the fear of God in your hearts, and give alms generously, for such liberality is the root of all good. If this document displeases anyone, let him not be angry, but

Reprinted by permission of the publishers from Samuel H. Cross, "The Russian Primary Chronicle," *Harvard Studies and Notes in Philology and Literature* (Cambridge, Mass., Harvard University Press, 1930), vol. 12, pp. 301–309.

rather let him believe that, in my old age, I talked nonsense as I sat upon my sledge. For emissaries from my kinsmen met me on the Volga with the message, "Join with us quickly, that we may expel the sons of Rostislav, and seize their possessions. If you do not join us, we shall act for our own advantage, and you may conduct yourself as you deem best." I replied, "At the risk of your wrath, I cannot go with you or break my oath."

When I had dismissed the emissaries, in my sorrow I took up the Psalter, and when I opened it this passage struck my eye: "Why art thou cast down, my soul? Why dost thou disquiet me?" etc. (Ps. xliii, 5.) I collected these precious words and arranged them in order and copied them. If the last passage does not please you, then accept the first. "Why art thou sorrowful, my soul? Why dost thou disquiet me? Hope in God, for I will confess to him." . . .

It was thus that Basil, after gathering together young men who were pure in heart and untainted in body, inculcated in them a brief and a meek conversation and the word of God in right measure. He taught them to eat and to drink without unseemly noise; to be silent in the presence of the aged; to listen with profit to the wise; to humble themselves before their elders; to live in charity with their equals and their inferiors; to speak without guile, but to understand much; not to be immoderate in their language, nor to insult others in their conversation; not to laugh excessively; to respect the aged; to refrain from converse with shameless women; to cast their eyes downward and their souls upward; and to walk and not to leap. He taught them to respect all established authorities which are honored of all men. If any one of you can render a service to another, let him expect his recompense from God, and he shall thus enjoy eternal blessing.

Oh sovereign Mother of God! Take away pride and presumption from my poor heart, lest I be exalted in this empty life by the vanity of this world. Let the faithful learn to strive with pious effort. According to the word of the Gospel, learn to govern your eyes, to curb your tongue, to moderate your temper, to subdue your body, to restrain your wrath; and to cherish pure thoughts, exerting yourself in good works for the Lord's sake. When robbed, avenge not; when hated or persecuted, endure; when affronted, pray. Destroy sin, render justice to the orphan, protect the widow. "Come let us reason together, saith the Lord; if your sins be as scarlet, I will make them white as snow." (Is. i, 18.)

The dayspring of fasting shall shine forth, and likewise the light of repentance. Let us purify ourselves, my brethren, from every corporal and spiritual blemish, and, as we call upon our Creator, let us say, "Glory to thee, lover of mankind!" In truth, my children, understand how merciful, yea, how supremely merciful is God, the lover of mankind. Being of human stock, we are so sinful and mortal that, when anyone does us evil, we desire to destroy him and to shed his blood speedily. But our Lord, the ruler of life and death, suffers our sins to be higher than our heads, and yet he loves us all our lives as a father loves his son whom he chastens and then summons once more to his embrace.

Thus our Lord has promised us the victory over our enemies through three means of conquering and overcoming them: repentance, tears, and almsgiving. My children, the commandment of God to conquer your sins by these three means is not severe. But I implore you for God's sake, be not lazy, nor forget these three means. For they are not difficult of attainment. Not through solitude nor an ascetic life, nor by such fasting as other good men endure, but through easy efforts may you thus obtain the mercy of God. . . .

As you read these words, my sons, praise God who has shown us his mercy and admonished you through the medium of my poor wit. Give heed to me, and accept an half of my instruction if you are not disposed to adopt it all. When God softens your hearts, shed tears for your sins, and pray, "As thou hast taken pity upon the adultress, the robber, and the publican, have pity also upon us sinners," and utter these words both in the church and before you retire to rest. If it is in any way possible, fail not one single night to kneel to the ground three times, in the case that you cannot do so more often. Forget not nor be remiss in this observance, for by his nightly worship and hymn man conquers the devil, and by this means expiates what sins he has committed during the day. When you are riding forth upon your horse, if you have no special subject of conversation with a companion and cannot utter some other prayer, then exclaim without ceasing "Kyrie eleison!" within yourselves. This is the best prayer of all, and infinitely better than thinking evil thoughts. Above all things, forget not the poor, but support them to the extent of your means. Give to the orphan, protect the widow, and permit the mighty to destroy no man. Take not the life of the just or the unjust, nor permit him to be killed. Destroy no Christian soul even though he be guilty of murder.

When you speak either good or evil, swear not by the name of God, nor cross yourselves, for that is unnecessary. Whenever you kiss the Cross to confirm an oath made to your brethren or to any other man, first test your heart as to whether you can abide by your word, then kiss the Cross, and after once having given your oath, abide by it, lest you destroy your souls by its violation.

Receive with affection the blessing of bishops, priests, and priors, and shun them not, but rather, according to your means, love and help them, that you may receive from them their intercession in the presence of God. Above all things, admit no pride in your hearts and minds, but say, "We are but mortal; today we live and tomorrow we shall be in the grave. All that thou hast given us is not ours, but thine, and thou hast but lent it to us for a few days." Hoard not the treasures of earth, for therein lies great sin. Honor the ancient as your father, and the youth as your brother.

Be not lax in the discipline of your homes, but rather attend to all matters yourselves. Rely not upon your steward or your servant, lest they who visit you ridicule your house or your table. When you set out to war, be not inactive, depend not upon your captains, nor waste your time in drinking, eating, or sleeping. Set the sentries yourselves, and take your rest only after you have posted them at night at every important point about your troops; then take your rest, but arise early. Do not put off your accoutrements without a quick glance about you, for a man may thus perish suddenly through his own carelessness. Guard against lying, drunkenness, and vice, for therein perish soul and body. When journeying anywhere by road through your domain, do not permit your followers or another's company to visit violence upon the villages or upon the dwellings, lest men revile you. Wherever you go, as often as you halt, give the beggar to eat and to drink. Furthermore, honor the stranger, if not with a gift, at least with food and drink, whencesoever he comes to you, be he simple, or noble, or an emissary. For travelers give a man a universal reputation as generous or niggardly.

Visit the sick, and accompany the dead, for we are all but mortal. Pass no man without a greeting; give him a kindly word. Love your wives, but grant them no power over you. This is the end of all things: to hold the fear of God above all else. If you forget all my admonition, read this counsel frequently. Then I shall be without disgrace, and you shall profit thereby.

Forget not what useful knowledge you possess, and acquire that with which you are not acquainted, even as my father, though he remained at home in his own country, still understood five languages. For by this means honor is acquired in other lands. Laziness is the mother of all evil; what a man knows, he forgets, and what he does not know he does not learn. In the practice of good works, you cannot neglect any item of good conduct.

First of all, go to church; let not the rising sun find you in your bed. For this was my father's habit, and it is likewise the custom of all good and perfect men. After rendering praise to God at matins, as you look upon the rising sun, render praise to God with gladness once again, saying, "Thou hast lightened my eyes, oh Christ my God, thou hast given me thy bright light. Grant me increase, oh Lord, in the years to come, so that, as I repent my sins and order my life righteously, I may thus continue to praise God." Then sit and deliberate with your retainers, or render justice to the people, or ride out for hunting or for pleasure, or else lie down to sleep. Sleep is established by God for noonday repose, since birds and beasts and men then rest from their labors.

I now narrate to you, my sons, the fatigue I have endured on journeys and hunts for fifty-three years. First I rode to Rostov through the Vyatichians, whither my father had sent me while he himself went to Kursk. (1073) Second, to Smolensk with Stavko the son of Skordyata; he then went to Brest with Izyaslav, and sent me to Smolensk. From Smolensk, I rode on to Vladimir.

In that same winter, my brethren sent me to Brest to the place which they had burned, and there I watched their city. Then I went to my father in Pereyaslavl, and after Easter, from Pereyaslavl to Vladimir to make peace with the Poles at Suteiska. Thence back to Vladimir again in the summer.

Then Svyatoslav sent me to Poland; after going beyond Glogau to the Czechish forest, I traveled four months in that country. (1076) In this year, my oldest child was born in Novgorod. Thence I went to Turov, in the spring to Pereyaslavl again, and then back to Turov. Svyatoslav then died, and I again went to Smolensk, and thence during the same winter to Novgorod, and in the spring to help Gleb. In the summer, I went with my father to Polotzk, and during the second winter before Polotzk the city was burned. He then went to Novgorod, while I, supported by Polovcians, marched against Odresk, carrying on constant warfare, and thence traveled to Chernigov. (1077) Then, on my return from Smolensk, I rejoined my father in Chernigov a second time.

Then Oleg came from Vladimir, and I invited him to dinner with my father at the Red Palace in Chernigov, and I gave my father three hundred *grivni* of gold. Upon leaving Smolensk, I fought my way through the Polovcian forces, and arrived at Pereyaslavl, where I found my father newly arrived from a raid. Then I rode with my father and Izyaslav to Chernigov to fight with Boris, and we conquered Boris and Oleg. (1078) Then we went to Pereyaslavl, and remained in Obrov. Vseslav at that juncture fired Smolensk. I set forth with men from Chernigov and two horses, but we did not catch Vseslav at Smolensk. On this pursuit of Vseslav, I burned the countryside and ravaged as far as Lukaml and Logozhsk, then attacked Dryutesk, and returned to Chernigov.

In the winter of that year, the Polovcians devastated the whole of Starodub. I marched with men of Chernigov against the Polovcians. At the Desna, we seized the princes Asaduk and Sauk, and killed their followers. The next day, behind Novgorod, we scattered the powerful force of Belkatgin, and took their swords and all their booty. We then went for two winters among the Vyatichians to attack Khodota and his son. The first winter, I went to Korden, and then to Mikulen in pursuit of the sons of Izyaslav, whom we did not catch. In that spring we joined with Yaropolk at Brody.

The following summer, we chased the Polovcians beyond the Khorol, after they had captured Goroshin. During the autumn, in company with

men of Chernigov, as well as Polovcians and Chityeyeviches, we captured
the city and left in it neither slaves nor cattle. (1084) In that winter,
we went to Brody to join Yaropolk, and concluded an important pact of
friendship. In that winter, my father set me up to rule in Pereyaslavl,
and we crossed the Supoi.

While we were on our way to the town of Priluk, we suddenly encountered the Polovcian chieftains with eight thousand men. We were
ready and willing to fight with them, but we had sent our equipment
ahead with the baggage train, and we therefore entered the town. They
thus captured alive only Semtsya and a few peasants. Our men, on the
other hand, killed or captured a large number of them. They did not
even dare to lead away their mounts, and during the night fled to the
Sula. On the following day, which was Sunday, we arrived at Byela
Vyezha. With the aid of God and of the Holy Virgin, our troops killed
nine hundred Polovcians, and captured the two princes Asin and Sakza,
the brothers of Bagubars, and only two men of their force escaped. We
then pursued the Polovcians to Svyatoslavl, thence to Torchesk, and
still further to Yuryev. (1086) Then again, on the east bank of the
Dnieper, we once more defeated the Polovcians at Krasnoye. In company with Rostislav, we subsequently captured their camp at Varin. I
then went to Vladimir and set up Yaropolk as prince, but he soon died.

(1093)   After the death of my father, Svyatopolk and I together
fought until evening with the Polovcians at the Sula in the vicinity of
Khalep, and then made peace with Tugortkan and other Polovcian
chiefs. We took from Gleb's followers all their troops. (1094) Oleg
subsequently attacked me in Chernigov with Polovcian support; my
troops fought with him for eight days by the small entrenchment and
would not let him inside the outworks. I took pity on the souls of our
Christian subjects, and upon the burned villages and monasteries, and
said, "It is not for the pagans to boast." I therefore gave my kinsman my
father's place, and retired myself to my father's domain of Pereyaslavl.
We left Chernigov on the day of St. Boris, and rode through the Polovcians in a company of not more than a hundred together with the women
and children. The Polovcians showed their teeth at us, as they stood like
wolves at the fords and in the hills. But God and St. Boris did not deliver
us up to them as their prey, so that we arrived at Pereyaslavl unscathed.

I remained in Pereyaslavl three summers and winters with my retainers, and endured great distress through war and famine. We attacked the
Polovcian forces behind Rimov, and God stood by us, so that we defeated them and took many captives. We overthrew the troops of Itlar,
and after marching beyond Goltav, we captured their camp. We now
attacked Oleg at Starodub, because he had made common cause with the
Polovcians. In pursuit of Bonyak, we advanced to the Bug and later

beyond the Ros in company with Svyatoslav. (1095) After reaching Smolensk, we became reconciled with David.

We set out a second time from Voronitza. At this juncture, the Torks and the Chityeyeviches came from among the Polovcians to attack us, so that we advanced against them to the Sula. We then returned again to Rostov for the winter, and three winters later I returned to Smolensk. Thence I went to Rostov.

A second time, Svyatopolk and I pursued Bonyak, but the nomads escaped and we did not catch them. Thereupon we again followed Bonyak beyond the Ros, yet did not overtake him. During the winter, I traveled to Smolensk, but left there on Easter Day. George's mother passed away. In the summer, I went to Pereyaslavl, and assembled my kinsmen together. Bonyak with his entire force of Polovcians approached Kosnyatin, and we sallied forth from Pereyaslavl to meet them as far as the Sula. By God's help, we were able to make peace with Ayepa, and after receiving his daughter as hostage, we proceeded to Smolensk. Thence we journeyed to Rostov. On departing thence, I again attacked the Polovcians under Urusoba in company with Svyatopolk, and God aided us. Then I again attacked Bonyak at Lubno, and God again vouchsafed us his aid. In company with Svyatopolk, I set out once more upon a campaign. With Svyatopolk and David, I later went as far as the Don, and God granted us his aid.

Ayepa and Bonyak had approached Vyrev with the intention of capturing it. I advanced to meet them as far as Romny with Oleg and my sons. When the nomads learned of our coming, they fled. Then we marched to attack Gleb at Smolensk, because he had captured our retainers. (1116) God aided us, and we accomplished our purpose. Thereupon we marched to attack Yaroslav son of Svyatopolk at Vladimir, since we were no longer disposed to endure his malice. (1117) On one occasion, I rode at full speed in one day from Chernigov to join my father in Kiev. Among all my campaigns, there are eighty-three long ones, and I do not count the minor adventures.

I concluded nineteen peace treaties with the Polovcians with or without my father's aid, and dispensed much of my cattle and my garments. I freed from their captivity the best Polovcian princes, including two brothers of Sharukan, three brothers of Bagubars, four brothers of Ovchin, and one hundred of their foremost leaders. Of other chieftains whom God delivered alive into my hands, I took captive, killed, and had cast into the river Slavlya Koxus and his son, Aklan, Burchevich, Azgului prince of Tarev, and fifteen other young chieftains, and at the same time not less than two hundred of the leading prisoners were likewise killed, and cast into the same river.

I devoted much energy to hunting as long as I reigned in Chernigov and made excursions from that city. Until the present year, in fact, I without difficulty used all my strength in hunting, not to mention other hunting expeditions around Turov, since I had been accustomed to chase every sort of game while in my father's company.

At Chernigov, I even bound wild horses with my bare hands or captured ten or twenty live horses with the lasso, and besides that, while riding along the Rus, I caught these same wild horses barehanded. Two bisons tossed me and my horse on their horns, a stag once gored me, one elk stamped upon me, while another gored me, a boar once tore my sword from my thigh, a bear on one occasion bit my kneecap, and another wild beast jumped on my flank and threw my horse with me. But God preserved me unharmed.

I often fell from my horse, fractured my skull twice, and in my youth injured my arms and legs when I did not reck of my life or spare my head. In war and at the hunt, by night and by day, in heat and in cold, I did whatever my servant had to do, and gave myself no rest. Without relying on lieutenants or messengers, I did whatever was necessary; I looked to every disposition in my household. At the hunt, I posted the hunters, and I looked after the stables, the falcons, and the hawks. I did not allow the mighty to distress the common peasant or the poverty-stricken widow, and interested myself in the church administration and service.

Let not my sons or whoever else reads this document criticize me. I do not commend my own boldness, but I praise God and glorify his memory because he guarded me, a sinful and a wretched man, for so many years in these dangerous vicissitudes, and did not make me inactive or useless for all the necessary works of man. As you read this screed, prepare yourselves for all good works, and glorify God among his saints. Without fear of death, of war, or of wild beasts, do a man's work, my sons, as God sets it before you. If I suffered no ill from war, from wild beasts, from flood, or from falling from my horse, then surely no one can harm you and destroy you, unless that too be destined of God. But if death comes from God, then neither father, nor mother, nor brethren can hinder it, and though it is prudent to be constantly upon one's guard, the protection of God is fairer than the protection of man.

12

The Tale
of the Host of Igor

It was during the Kievan period of Russian history that lay literature, in addition to chronicles and church literature, made a formal appearance. Of this lay literature, the most important representative, which subsequently became a national classic, is *Slovo o polku Igoreve*, or *The Tale of the Host of Igor*. This poetic description of an unsuccessful campaign against the Polovtsians in 1185 by Prince Igor of Novgorod-Seversk (1180–1202) was composed by an anonymous author at the end of the twelfth century. The original copy of this classic has not been preserved. In 1795 Count A. I. Musin-Pushkin discovered a sixteenth century manuscript of the *Slovo*, but that manuscript was destroyed in the great Moscow fire of 1812. Fortunately, a copy which had been prepared for Catherine II survived, and the present translation, aiming more for accuracy than for poetic rendition, was made from that copy.

Brothers, might it not be proper for us
To begin in ancient diction
A mournful tale of the campaign of Igor,
Igor, son of Sviatoslav?[1]
Let us begin this song, however,
As told in contemporary epics
And not as conceived by Boian.[2]

From *Slovo o polku Igoreve, Igoria syna Sviatoslavlia vnuka Olgova* (*The Tale of the Host of Igor, Igor Son of Sviatoslav, Oleg's Grandson*) (Moscow, Gosudarstvennoe Izdatelstvo Khudozhestvennoi Literatury, 1954). Translation mine.

[1] Prince of Novgorod-Seversk, 1180–1198; later, Prince of Chernigov; died in 1202.

[2] An ancient bard.

For the prophetic Boian,
Whenever he wished to compose a song for someone,
He wandered in his thoughts
[Like a nightingale] over the tree,
Like a gray wolf across the land
And like a blue eagle beneath the clouds.

You know how they [determined] to sing of wars of early times;
They released ten falcons upon a flock of swans;
And whose falcon was first, his song was sung first!
Be it to Iaroslav the Elder[3] or Mstislav the Brave,[4]
Who slew Rededia[5] before the Kasog troops,
Or to Roman the Fair,[6] son of Sviatoslav.
Brothers, Boian really did not release ten falcons upon a flock of swans,
He only placed his prophetic fingers on the living strings
And they themselves murmured glory to the princes.

Brothers, let us begin this tale
From Vladimir the Elder[7] to our Igor,
Who tightened his mind with firmness,
Sharpened his heart with manliness,
And imbued with fighting spirit
Led his brave troops against the land of the Polovtsians
For the sake of the Russian land.
Then Igor looked up at the bright sun
And saw his warriors covered with darkness.
And Igor spoke to his troops:
"Brothers and soldiers!
It would be better for us to perish than to surrender.
Brothers, let us mount our swift horses
And gaze at the blue Don!"
The Prince was inclined to visit the Great Don
But an ominous sign blocked his desire.
"I wish," he said, "to break my spear
With you, Russian people, at the frontier of the Polovtsian land!
I want either to die or be able to drink a helmetful of the Don!"

O Boian, nightingale of old times!
If you could sing of those wars

---

3 Also known as Iaroslav the Wise; Prince of Kiev, 1019–1054.
4 Brother of Iaroslav; Prince of Tmutorokan, a principality located between the Black and Azov Seas.
5 Prince of the Kasogs (Cherkess); slain by Mstislav in 1022.
6 Prince of Tmutorokan; killed in 1079.
7 Apparently Vladimir the Great; Prince of Kiev, 980–1015.

Hopping like a nightingale over the tree of thought,
Flying in thought beneath the clouds,
Weaving all glories of those times,
And racing along the Troian Trail[8] across the plains to the mountains!
You should sing the song of Igor, the grandson of Oleg!
The storm did not carry falcons across the wide fields!
Flocks of daws fly toward the Great Don!
You prophetic Boian, grandson of Veles,[9] should sing of this.

Horses neigh beyond the Sula [River]
Glory rings in Kiev,
Trumpets call in Novgorod [Seversk],
Banners stand in Putivl,[10]
Igor awaits his dear brother Vsevolod.[11]

And the Wild Bull Vsevolod told him:
"Igor, you are my only brother, my bright light!
We both are sons of Sviatoslav!
Brother, saddle your swift horses
For mine have already been saddled
And are waiting for you near Kursk!
My men of Kursk are famous fighters!
They were swaddled under the trumpets,
They were brought up under helmets,
They were nourished by the point of the spear,
They are familiar with all the roads,
They know all the ravines,
Their bows are strung tight,
Their quivers are open,
Their sabres are sharpened,
They lope like gray wolves in the field,
Seeking honor for themselves and glory for their prince!"
Then Prince Igor set his foot in the golden stirrup
And rode out into the open field.
The sun covered his way with darkness
The night, ominously moaning unto him, awakened the birds.
The herds of animals howl.

---

[8] Apparently a reference to Roman Emperor Trajan (98–117), during whose reign present-day Rumania was brought under Roman influence.
[9] A Kievan pagan deity; a protector of artists and singers.
[10] A city on the Seim River.
[11] Brother of Igor; Prince of Kursk.

The Deva[12] calls from atop the trees
And commands the unknown land to listen:
The Volga, the [Azov] Seashore and the Sula land,
And Surozh and Korsun,[13]
And you, idol of Tmutorokan.
But meanwhile, the Polovtsians run over untrodden roads to the Great
            Don,
Their wagons squeak at midnight like dispersed swans.

Igor leads his warriors to the Don.
The birds in oak trees portend his misfortunes
The wolves howl of the menace in the ravines
The eagles with their clatter summon beasts to a bony feast,
The foxes yelp at the crimson shields.
O Russian land! You are so far behind the mountains.
Darkness of the night came!
The dawn began to break!
The mist has covered the fields,
The nightingales have stopped their chatter,
The daws have silenced their sounds.
With their shields the Russians have divided the great field
Seeking honor for themselves and glory for their prince.

At dawn Friday they trampled the pagan troops of the Polovtsians
And dispersing themselves like arrows over the field
They seized the fair Polovtsian maidens,
And with them also gold, and brocades, and precious samites.
Using Polovtsian caparisons, mantles, fur coats, and other items
They made bridges over bogs and marshes.
But the crimson flag with a white banner
And a crimson forelock with a silver hilt
Went to the Brave [Igor], son of Sviatoslav.
Oleg's brave family slumbers in the field
It has flown too far!
It was born to be insulted
Neither by a falcon nor by a hawk
Nor by you, black raven, pagan Polovtsian!
Gzak runs like a gray wolf
And Konchak[14] prepares a track for him to the Great Don.
Next day, early in the morning, red stars herald the dawn.

---

[12] A demon bird of Oriental mythology; a cross between an owl and a peacock.
[13] Greek cities in Crimea.
[14] Gzak and Konchak were Polovtsian khans.

From the sea come black clouds
In an attempt to cover the four suns.
They flicker with blue lightning
And a great thunder can be heard.
The rain of arrows comes from the Great Don.
Here spears shall break
Here too sabres shall blunt
Against the Polovtsian helmets,
At the Kaiala River near the Great Don.
O Russian land, you are so far beyond the mountains!

Now the winds, Stribog's[15] grandsons
Blow arrows from the sea
Against the brave troops of Igor!
The earth trembles
The rivers flow turbidly
Dust covers the fields
The banners proclaim:
Polovtsians are coming from the Don, from the Sea,
And from all sides!
Russian forces retreated!
The sons of demons divided the field with their [war] cries
While the brave Russians [divided it] with their crimson shields.
Fierce Bull Vsevolod!
Stand your ground
Dart your arrows at [enemy] soldiers
Crash through their helmets with the sword of steel!
You, Bull, wherever you charge, gleaming with your golden helmet
There lie pagan heads of the Polovtsians.
You, fierce Bull Vsevolod
Cut Avar helmets[16] with tempered sabres!
Brothers, will any injury matter to one
Who has forgotten about life and honors,
The city of Chernigov and the golden throne of his fathers
And the wants and habits of Gleb's daughter, his beautiful wife?

There have been Troian's ages
Gone are the years of Iaroslav
There have been wars of Oleg
Oleg,[17] son of Sviatoslav.

---

[15] The ancient Kievan god of the wind.

[16] Made by the Avars in East Caucasus and had a sharp apical point.

[17] Prince of Chernigov, 1075–1115; often responsible for the Polovtsian invasions of Kiev territories.

That Oleg forged sedition with a sword
And dispersed arrows over the land.
He set his foot in the golden stirrup in the city of Tmutorokan,
Old Great Iaroslav,[18] and the son of Vsevolod,[19] heard of his fame!
While prince Vladimir every morning stopped his ears in Chernigov.
Lust for glory brought to judgment Boris, son of Viacheslav.[20]
They buried him in a green horse blanket
For an offense against Oleg, the brave young prince.
From the Kaiala River after the beating
Supported by Hungarian cavalry
Sviatopolk[21] brought his father to the Church of St. Sophia in Kiev.
Then, during the reign of Boris, son of Gorislav
Feuds started and intensified
And grandsons of Dazhbog[22] lost their lives.
Princely feuds killed a whole generation!
Across the Russian land seldom were then heard songs of ploughmen
But often did the ravens croak
While dividing corpses among themselves,
And while jackdaws chattered in their tongue:
"Let us fly to a feast!"

Thus it was in those battles and in those wars.
But no one has heard of this kind of war.
From morning till evening
From evening till dawn
Fly tempered arrows
Clang sabres against the helmets
Crack steel spears
In an unknown field
Amidst the Polovtsian land!
Under [horses] hooves the black soil
Was covered with bones
And saturated with blood
And trouble came to the Russian land!
Do I seem to hear a noise and ringing
Early before the dawn?
Igor is turning his troops back!
He is sorry for his dear brother Vsevolod!
They fought one day,

---

[18] Prince of Kiev, 1019–1054.
[19] Apparently Vladimir Monomakh; Prince of Kiev, 1113–1125.
[20] Prince of Smolensk; killed in 1078 near Chernigov.
[21] Prince of Kiev, 1093–1113.
[22] A Kievan pagan deity; sun god.

They fought another,
And on the third day around noon
Igor's banners fell!
Here the brothers parted on the banks of the swift Kaiala
Here too the bloody wine ran out
And here the brave Russians finished the feast.
(They got their guests drunk)
And themselves fell in defense of the Russian land!
The grass wilts because of the sorrow
And the tree bends down because of grief!
Brothers, a sad time has descended!
A wilderness has covered our strength.
Forces of Dazhbog's grandsons have been wounded!
Misfortune has descended on the land of Troian like a maiden
Who flapped her swan wings
Over the blue sea and by the Don.
Gone are the days of abundance,
Over are princely wars against the infidel!
Now brother said to brother:
This is mine and that is mine also!
And the princes began to argue about trifles
As if they were great things.
And they began to create discord among themselves!
And from all sides the pagans invaded the Russian land victoriously.
Oh, falcon, you have gone too far to the sea in slaying birds!
Igor's brave troops cannot be resurrected!
The mourners began to weep
And sorrow spread throughout the Russian land
Spreading among the Russian people embers in a glowing horn!
Russian women wept, saying:
"We shall never be able to visualize our dear husbands
Nor to think of them nor even to see them!
Much gold and silver has been lost!"
Brothers, Kiev groaned from sorrow,
Chernigov from disaster,
Anguish engulfed the Russian land.
Deep sorrow spread over Russian lands.
Princes brought the discord upon themselves
While the pagans made victorious inroads into the Russian land
Collecting from each household a tribute of one squirrel's skin.

Thus those two brave sons of Sviatoslav
Igor and Vsevolod started the feud,
Which their mighty father,

Sviatoslav the Dread,[23] the Grand Prince of Kiev, stopped.
Sviatoslav was a terror!
He defeated enemies with his mighty forces
And with swords of steel!
He invaded the Polovtsian land
Trampled [their] hills and ravines
Muddled [their] rivers and lakes
And drained their creeks and marshes.
Like a hurricane he seized
The pagan Kobiak[24] on the shore of the sea
From amidst the mighty Polovtsian forces!
Kobiak found himself in the city of Kiev
[Prisoner] in the Court of Sviatoslav!

Germans and Wends,
Greeks and Moravians,
Sing glory to Sviatoslav,
But reproach Prince Igor,
Who lost an army at the bottom of the Kaiala, the Polovtsian River,
Now filled with the Russian gold.
There Prince Igor exchanged his golden saddle for a slave's saddle.
They removed the ramparts in the cities,
And all joy came to an end.

Sviatoslav had a sad dream:
"This night," he said, "in the Kievan hills early in the evening
You dressed me up in a black cloth on a bed of yew.
You gave me [to drink] blue wine mixed with bitters
And from hollow quivers you poured out
Into my lap a great treasure of the pagans
And then you flattered me.
My gold-plated throne was empty—without a prince!
And on the outskirts of Plesensk the ill-boding crows
Chattered from dusk through the night.
They flew into the Kisan Forest
And I could not drive them away to the blue sea."
And the boyars said to the prince:
"Prince, grief has captivated your mind
Because two falcons have flown off the golden
Ancestral throne in search of the city of Tmutorokan,
Or perhaps to drink a helmetful of the Don.
But the pagan sabers have clipped the falcons' wings

---

23 Prince of Kiev, 1177–1194.
24 A Polovtsian khan; taken prisoner by Prince Sviatoslav of Kiev in 1184.

And the birds themselves are now entangled in an iron mesh.
Darkness came on the third day.
Two suns faded out.
Two crimson pillars were extinguished
And with them two young moons, Oleg and Sviatoslav,
Were covered with darkness.
On the Kaiala River darkness covered the world!
Polovtsians spread over the Russian land like a brood of panthers
And submerged it into the sea [of blood],
And a great uproar went up in the Khan's [camp]!
Disgrace transcended glory,
Slavery crashed down upon freedom,
Deva burst back to earth.
Beautiful Gothic maidens
Burst into a song on the shore of the blue sea,
Tinkling with the Russian gold
They sing of the time of Bus!
They glorify the vengeance of Shurokan![25]
While our troops are thirsty after joy."

Then, mingled with tears, the Great Sviatoslav spoke a golden word:
"Oh, my sons, Igor and Vsevolod," he said,
"Too early you started to harass the land of the Polovtsians
In search of personal glory!
You have conquered ingloriously!
Ingloriously, too, you have shed pagan blood!
Your brave hearts were forged of hard steel
And tempered in violence!
But what have you done to my silver gray hair?
I see no more the might of my powerful,
Rich and war-experienced brother Iaroslav[26]
With his forces of Chernigov
And with his [mercenaries] Moguts, Tatrans, and Shilberans,
And Topchaks, Revugas, and Olbers![27]
[In the past] they conquered enemy forces without shields
Using only swords and war cries,
All for the glory of their ancestors!
But you have said: 'Let us be our own heroes!
Let us capture the glory of the future
And divide the glory of the past!'

---

[25] A Polovtsian khan; grandfather of Konchak; defeated by Kievan forces in 1107.

[26] Prince of Chernigov; died in 1198.

[27] Turkic tribes who settled in the principality of Chernigov.

Brothers, is there any wonder when an old man feels young again?
When a falcon molts
He chases the birds on high
And permits no harm to befall his nest.
But there is great trouble! [Other] princes will not aid me."
Gloomy times have arrived.
Inhabitants of Romen[28] cry under the Polovtsian swords
While Prince Vladimir is wounded.
Grief and misfortune has befallen Gleb's sons.
Where are you Great Prince Vsevolod?[29]
Do you intend to come from far away
To defend the golden throne of your ancestors?
You are strong enough to scatter the Volga with the oars [of your fleet]
And empty the Don with the helmets [of your soldiers].
If you were here with us then a female slave would go for one *nogata*
And a male slave for one *rezana*.[30]
With [the help of] the courageous sons of Gleb [Prince of Riazan]
You can shoot live arrows over dry land.
And you valiant Riurik and David![31]
Did not your golden helmets float in blood?
Do not your brave warriors roar like wild bulls
When wounded by steel swords in a unknown praire?
Lords, set your feet in the golden stirrups
To avenge the outrage of our time, for the Russian land,
For the wounds of Igor, the brave son of Sviatoslav!
You Iaroslav Osmomysl [Eight-minded] of Galicia![32]
You sit high on your throne wrought of gold!
With your strong forces you defend the Hungarian mountains,
You block the path to the [Hungarian] king,
Close the gates on the Danube River,
And toss stones over the clouds.
Your rule extends all the way to the Danube.
All lands stand in fear of you.
You can open the gates of Kiev,
And from your ancestral golden throne
You can shoot at the sultans beyond the [Russian] land.
Lord, shoot at Konchak, the pagan slave,

---

28 A city in the principality of Pereiaslavl; besieged by Konchak.
29 Prince of Vladimir, 1176–1212; also known as "Big Nest" because of his large family.
30 *Nogata* and *rezana* were monetary units in Medieval Russia.
31 Riurik, Prince of Belgorod, died in 1215; David, Prince of Smolensk died in 1198.
32 Prince of Galicia, 1152–1187; apparently spoke eight languages.

For Russian land, for the wounds of Igor, the brave son of Sviatoslav!
And you brave Roman and Mstislav![33]
[In the past] your courage has led you to great deeds.
To accomplish a vital task you fly on high,
Literally like a falcon that rides the winds
As he tries to overcome the bird!
Under your Latin [i.e., West European] helmets you have iron breast
            plates!
Your forces have shaken the earth,
Including many countries ruled by the Khan.
Lithuanians, Iatvigians, Deremelians[34]
And Polovtsians have dropped their spears
And bowed their heads under your swords of steel!

For Prince Igor, however, the sun has stopped shining.
And the tree has ominously shed its foliage.
[The enemy] has divided cities along the Ros and Sula Rivers
While Igor's brave forces cannot be resurrected.
Princes, the Don calls you!
The Don calls princes to victory!
Brave princes, descendants of Oleg, are ready for war!
You Ingvar and Vsevolod[35] and you three sons of Mstislav,
You are six-winged falcons of good family
Did you not gain your power through a [military] victory?
Where are your golden helmets
And Polish lances and shields?
Close the prairie gates with your sharp arrows
For Russian land, for the wounds of Igor, the brave son of Sviatoslav!

The silver stream of the Sula River
Flows no more [and does not protect] the city of Pereiaslavl.
And even the Dvina flows muddily
Towards the stern men of Polotsk
As a result of the pagans' war cries.
Only Iziaslav,[36] son of Vasilko
Clanged his sharp swords against Lithuanian helmets
Only to defame the glory of his grandfather Vseslav,[37]
And to fall on the bloody grass beneath the crimson shields

---

[33] Roman, Prince of Volyn, 1172–1205; Mstislav, brother of Roman, died in 1226.
[34] Lithuanian tribes.
[35] Sons of the Prince of Lutsk.
[36] A Prince of Polotsk; killed by the Lithuanians in 1162.
[37] Prince of Polotsk, 1044–1101.

Cut down by Lithuanian swords.
And from his death bed he said:
"Prince, the wings of birds have covered your warriors
And the beasts have begun to lick their blood."
Neither brothers Briachislav[38] nor Vsevolod were there.
[Iziaslav] alone released his precious soul
From a brave body through a golden gorget!
All voices became silent!
All joy came to an end!
[Only] the trumpets of Gorodets resounded!
You Iaroslav,[39] and all your grandsons of Vseslav,[40]
The time has come to lower your banners
And to sheathe your dented swords.
You have deviated from the glory of your ancestors.
By your feuds you have enticed the pagans
Against the Russian land, against the possessions of Vseslav.
Your feuds, indeed, brought violence from the Polovtsian land.

During the seventh age of Troian
Vseslav casts lots for a maiden he loved.
With the aid of crutches he mounted a horse
And galloped to the city of Kiev,
Where with his lance he touched the golden throne of Kiev.
[Then] like a wild beast under cover of blue mist,
He galloped at midnight from Belgorod.
Clinging to a horse, by morning he opened the gates of Novgorod.[41]
He destroyed Iaroslav's glory!
And like a wolf he leaped from Dudutki to the Nemiga River.
On the Nemiga they spread sheaves of heads
And threshed them with flails of steel.[42]
They sacrificed lives on the threshing floor
And winnowed souls from their bodies.
The bloody banks of the Nemiga
Were not planted with grain
But with bones of Russia's sons!
Prince Vseslav judged the people
And sold cities of [other] princes.
But at night he prowled like a werewolf.

---

[38] Prince of Iziaslavl, near Polotsk.
[39] Prince of Turov.
[40] A Prince of Polotsk and Kiev; died in 1101; was considered a sorcerer.
[41] Vseslav attacked Novgorod in 1069.
[42] Vseslav was defeated in 1067 on the Nemiga River by Iziaslav, Sviatoslav, and Vsevolod.

He reached Tmutorokan from Kiev
Before the cock could crow.
Like a werewolf he crossed the path of the Great Hors.[43]
The bells of St. Sophia of Polotsk tolled matins for him
And he could hear these bells ringing in Kiev!
Though a wise soul lived in his mighty body,
He often suffered misfortunes.
The prophetic Boian once wisely foretold of him:
"Neither a crafty, nor a clever man
Though he be swifter than a bird
Can escape divine judgment."
Oh, Russian land, you must mourn
And recall your early times and your early princes!
The Old Vladimir should not have been nailed to the Kievan hills.
Some of his banners now belong to Riurik,
And others to David!
They are worn now by oxen as they plow the soil
While the lances sing their song at the Danube River.

One can hear the voice of Iaroslavna.[44]
Like a cuckoo she sings early in the morning:
"Like a cuckoo," she says, "I will fly along the Danube
I will dip my beaver sleeve in the Kaiala River
And will cleanse the bleeding wounds of the prince
On his mighty body."
In the morning Iaroslavna cries again
Along the walls of Putivl, saying:
"Oh, wind, great wind!
Why lord do you blow so fiercely?
Why do you carry on your light wings
Khan's arrows against the forces of my beloved?
Are you not satisfied with blowing the clouds up high
Or with rocking ships upon the blue sea?
Why, lord, did you scatter my happiness
Over the feather grass [of the prairie]?"

In the morning Iaroslavna cries again
Along the walls of Putivl, saying:
"Oh, Dnieper, famed river!
You have pierced the stone mountains
Of the Polovtsian land!

---

[43] Great Hors was a pagan deity, perhaps a sun god.
[44] Wife of Prince Igor.

You have carried Sviatoslav's boats against Kobiak's forces.
Bring, oh lord, my beloved to me
So that I might stop sending tears every morning to the sea."
In the morning Iaroslavna cries again
Along the city walls of Putivl, saying:
"You bright, you beautiful sun!
You warm everyone equally,
You are beautiful equally to all.
Why did you, oh lord, spread your burning rays
On the forces of my beloved?
Why did your rays increase their thirst in a waterless prairie
And thereby close their quivers with misfortune?"
The sea splashed [with fury] at midnight
Hurricanes advance through the mist.
Gods shows the road to Igor,
From the Polovtsian to the Russian land,
To the ancestral golden throne.
The evening glow now has faded.
Igor sleeps, Igor keeps vigil.
In his thought Igor surveys the land
From the Great Don to the Little Donets.
At midnight the horse was ready.
Across the river Ovlur[45] whistled
A warning for the prince to get ready.
Prince Igor will not remain a prisoner!
As he called, the earth trembled,
The grass rustled,
And the Polovtsian tents began to stir.
Like an ermine Prince Igor sped to the reeds
And like a white duck he swam across the water.
Then he leaped on a swift horse,
Jumped off it like a roaming wolf,
Sped towards the valley of the Donets,
Flew like a falcon under the clouds
Killing geese and swans for breakfast, lunch, and dinner.
When Igor flew like a falcon
Ovlur followed him like a wolf,
Shaking off the cold dew.
They both exhausted their horses.
The Donets said: "Prince Igor!
Great glory awaits you,

---

[45] Ovlur, a Polovtsian guard who aided Igor in his escape.

[Great] disappointment awaits Konchak,
While happiness is in store for the Russian land."
And Igor replied: "Oh, Donets!
Great glory awaits you, too,
For rocking a prince on your waves,
For spreading for him green grass
Along your silver banks,
For covering him with warm haze
Under the shadow of a green tree,
For disguising him on water as a white duck,
As a seagull on the stream,
And as a black duck in the air."
"Entirely different," he said, "is the Stugna River.[46]
Its stream is weak.
Because it has swallowed up other rivers
Its mouth is also wide.
The Dnieper imprisoned young prince Rostislav[47]
On the bottom of its banks.
And Rostislav's mother mourns the young prince.
Flowers have withered from sorrow,
While trees have bent to the ground in grief."

This is not the chattering of the magpies,
It is Gzak and Konchak following Igor's trail.
Crows did not caw at that time,
The daws became silent
And even magpies stopped chattering.
Everything crawled on all fours,
And with their noise the woodpeckers showed the way to the river,
And nightingales with their gay song announced the dawn.
Said Gzak to Konchak:
"If the falcon should reach the nest
We will shoot the falconet[48] with our gilded arrows."
And Konchak replied to Gzak:
"If the falcon should reach the nest
We will enmesh the falconet with [the charms of] a beautiful girl."
And said Gzak again to Konchak:
"If we enmesh him with [the charms of] a beautiful girl,
We will lose both the falconet and the beautiful girl,
And the birds will start fighting us in the Polovtsian land."

---

[46] A tributary of the Dnieper; located south of Kiev.
[47] Brother of Vladimir Monomakh, drowned in 1093 in the Stugna River.
[48] Refers to Igor's son Vladimir, who remained a prisoner of the Polovtsians.

Boian, the song-maker of old times,
Said the following of the wars of Sviatoslav,
The grandson of Iaroslav, son of Oleg:
"It is difficult for a head to be without shoulders
It is equally difficult for a body to be without the head."
It is difficult for the Russian land to be without Igor.
The sun shines in the sky.
Prince Igor has returned to the Russian land.
Maidens sing on the Danube
Their voices reach Kiev across the sea.
Igor rides along the Borichev[49]
[To the church of] the Holy Virgin of Pirogoshch.[50]
The countryside is rejoicing,
Cities are jubilant,
Singing songs first to the old princes
And then to the young.
Let us sing glory to Igor, son of Sviatoslav,
To Wild Bull Vsevolod,
To Vladimir, son of Igor.
Hail to the princes and their troops
Who fight against pagan forces for Christendom.
Glory to the princes and to their troops—Amen.

---

[49] The Dnieper River.
[50] A church built in 1136 to house an icon brought to Kiev from Constantinople.

13

Mongol Conquest
of Northern Rus
in 1237–1238

The Mongol conquest of Northern Rus in 1237–
1238 was part of a larger scheme—the conquest of
Europe—devised by Genghis Khan's successors at a
Great *Kuriltai*, or Council, in 1235. Led by Batu
Khan, the Mongols, using Chinese technicians and
Turkic manpower, encountered little or no opposition from the feuding princes of Rus. They captured
and devastated the cities of Riazan, Moscow, Suzdal,
Vladimir, and Tver. They took some of the inhabitants captive, massacred others, and forced those
who survived to pay tribute. This conquest inaugurated a period in Russian history known as the
"Mongol Yoke" that technically was to last until
1480.

It happened in 1237. That winter, the godless Tartars, under
the leadership of Batu, came to the Riazan principality from the East
through the forests. Upon arriving they encamped at Onuza, which they
took and burned. From here they despatched their emissaries—a woman
witch and two men—to the princes of Riazan demanding a tithe from
the princes and complete armor and horses from the people. The princes
of Riazan, Iurii Igorevich and his brother Oleg, did not allow the
emissaries to enter the city, and [together with] the Murom and Pronsk
princes [they] moved against the Tartars in the direction of Voronezh.
The princes replied: "When we are gone, everything will be yours." . . .
The princes of Riazan sent a plea to Prince Iurii of Vladimir, begging
him to send aid or to come in person. Prince Iurii, however, did not go;

From *Polnoe Sobranie Russkikh Letopisei* (*Complete Collection of Russian
Chronicles*) (St. Petersburg), 1885, vol. 10, pp. 105–115. Translation mine.

neither did he listen to the plea of the princes of Riazan, as he wanted
to fight the Tartars alone. . . .

The princes of Riazan, Murom, and Pronsk moved against the godless
and engaged them in a battle. The struggle was fierce, but the godless
Mohammedans* emerged victorious with each prince fleeing toward
his own city. Thus angered, the Tartars now began the conquest of the
Riazan land with great fury. They destroyed cities, killed people, burned
and took [people] into slavery. On December 6, [1237] the cursed
strangers approached the capital city of Riazan, besieged it, and surrounded it with a stockade. The princes of Riazan shut themselves up
with the people in the city, fought bravely, but succumbed. On December
21, [1237] the Tartars took the city of Riazan, burned it completely,
killed Prince Iurii Igorevich, his wife, slaughtered other princes, and of
the captured men, women, and children, some they killed with their
swords, others they killed with arrows and [then] threw them into the
fire; while some of the captured they bound, cut and disemboweled their
bodies. The Tartars burned many holy churches, monasteries, and villages, and took their property.

Then the Tartars went toward Kolomna. From Vladimir, Grand
Prince Iurii Vsevolodovich sent his son, Prince Vsevolod, against them;
with him also went Prince Roman Igorevich of Riazan with his armies.
Grand Prince Iurii sent his military commander, Eremei Glebovich,
ahead with a patrol. This group joined Vsevolod's and Roman Igorevich's forces at Kolomna. There they were surrounded by the Tartar's.
The struggle was very fierce and the Russians were driven away to a hill.
And there they [the Tartars] killed Prince Roman Igorevich Riazanskii,
and Eremei Glebovich, the military commander of Vsevolod Iurievich,
and they slaughtered many other men. Prince Vsevolod, with a small
detachment, fled to Vladimir. The Tartars [then] went toward Moscow.
They took Moscow and killed the military commander Philip Nianka,
and captured Vladimir, the son of Prince Iurii; they slaughtered people
old and young alike, some they took with them into captivity; they
departed with a great amount of wealth.

When Grand Prince Iurii Vsevolodovich heard about this . . . he entrusted the rule of Vladimir to a bishop, Princes Vsevolod and Mstislav,
and his own military leader Peter Osliadiukovich, while he himself went
toward the Volga with his nephews—Vasilko Konstantinovich, Vsevolod
Konstantinovich, and Vladimir Konstantinovich. They made their camp
on the Siti. There the Grand Prince awaited the arrival of his brothers—
Prince Iaroslav Vsevolodovich and Prince Sviatoslav Vsevolodovich—
with their soldiers, and he himself began to collect an army; while he
appointed Zhiroslav Mikhailovich his military commander.

---

* Russian medieval sources refer to all non-Christian believers as "godless."

On Tuesday February 3, [1238] . . . the Tartars approached Vladimir. The inhabitants of Vladimir, with their princes and military commander, Peter Osliadiukovich, shut themselves up in the city. The Tartars came to the Golden Gates, brought with them Prince Vladimir, the son of the Grand Prince Iurii Vsevolodovich, and inquired: "Is the Grand Prince Iurii in the city?" But the inhabitants of Vladimir began to shoot at them. They, however, shouted: "Do not shoot!" And, having approached very close to the gates, they showed the inhabitants of Vladimir their young Prince Vladimir, son of Iurii, and asked: "Do you recognize your young Prince?" As a result of privation and misfortune his face was sad and he looked weak. Vsevolod and Mstislav stood atop the Golden Gates and recognized their brother Vladimir. Oh, how sad and tearful it is to see one's brother in such a condition! Vsevolod and Mstislav, with their boyars and all the inhabitants, wept as they looked at Vladimir. And the Tartars departed from the Golden Gates, circled the entire city, examined it, and encamped at Zremany in front of the Golden Gates and about the entire city; and there were many of them. . . .

After they made camp around Vladimir, the Tartars went and occupied the city of Suzdal. . . . They brought a multitude of prisoners into their camp, approached the city of Vladimir on Saturday, and from early morning till evening they built scaffolds and set up rams, and during the night they surrounded the entire city with a fence. In the morning, the princes, Bishop Mitrophan, military leader Peter Osliadiukovich, and all the boyars and the people realized that their city would be taken and they all began to weep. . . . On Sunday, February 8, [1238] . . . early in the morning the Tartars approached the city from all sides and began to hit the city [walls] with rams, and began to pour great stones into the center of the city from far away, as if by God's will, as if it rained inside the city; many people were killed inside the city and all were greatly frightened and trembled. The Tartars broke through the wall at the Golden Gates, also from the Lybed [side] at the Orininy and the Copper Gates, and from the Kliazma [direction] at the Volga Gates, and in other places; they destroyed the whole city, threw stones inside and . . . entered it from all sides like demons. Before dinner they took the new city which they set on fire; and there they killed Prince Vsevolod with his brother, many boyars and people, while other princes and all the people fled into the middle city. Bishop Mitrophan and the Grand Duchess with her sons and daughters, daughters-in-law, grandchildren, boyars and their wives, and many people fled into a church, locked the church gates, and climbed inside the church to the choir loft. The Tartars took this city too, and began to search after the princes and their mother, and found that they were inside the church. . . . The Tartars broke the gates of the church and slaughtered those who were inside and resisted. And they began to ask the whereabouts of the princes and their mother and found they were in the choir loft. They began to entice them to come down. But they did not listen to them. The Tartars then brought many fire logs inside the church and set it on fire. Those present in the choir loft, praying, gave their souls to God; they were burned and joined the list of martyrs. And the Tartars pillaged the holy church, and they tore the miracle-making icon of the Mother of God.

From here the Tartars advanced against Grand Prince Iurii; some went toward Rostov, while others went toward Iaroslavl, which they took; some went along the Volga and toward Gorodets and burned everything along the Volga up to Merski Golich. Some went toward Pereiaslavl and took that city and slaughtered the people. And from there they set the entire countryside and many cities on fire: Iuriev, Dmitrov, Volok, Tver, where they also killed Iaroslav's son; and there was not a town till Torzhok which was not occupied by the Tartars. In February [1238], in the Rostov and Suzdal principalities alone, they took fourteen cities in addition to villages and churchyards.

At the end of February [1238], a messenger brought the news to Grand Prince Iurii Vsevolodovich, his brother Sviatoslav Vsevolodovich, and their nephews Vasilko, Vsevolod, and Vladimir Konstantinovich, that the city of Vladimir had been captured, the bishop, grand dukes, princes, and all the inhabitants had been burned and some slaughtered. "And they killed your eldest son Vsevolod, and his brothers, inside the city and now they go toward you." . . . Iurii waited for his brother Iaroslav, but he did not come. And the prince ordered that his military leader strengthen his people and prepare them to fight, and sent a brave man, Dorofei Semenovich, with 3000 men, to gather information about the Tartars. But hardly had he left when he returned with these words: "Lord! The Tartars have surrounded us."

When he heard this, Prince Iurii with his brother Sviatoslav and his nephews—Vasilko, Vsevolod, and Vladimir—and with their men, mounted their horses and advanced against the heathens. Grand Prince Iurii Vsevolodovich began to organize his regiments when suddenly the Tartars arrived at Siti. Prince Iurii forgot all about fear and advanced to meet them. Regiments met and there ensued a major battle and fierce slaughter; blood flowed like water. Because of God's will, the Tartars defeated the Russian princes. Grand Prince of Vladimir, Iurii Vsevolodovich, was killed then as were many of his military leaders and boyars and soldiers. The Tartars took his nephew, Vasilko Konstantinovich of Rostov, into captivity and brought him to the Sherenskii Forest. They also encamped there.

THE MONGOL–TARTAR INVASIONS
OF THE THIRTEENTH CENTURY

Area of Russian principalities
paying tribute to the Golden Horde

Boundaries of Russian principalities

1237 Routes and dates of Mongol–Tartar conquests

Domain of the Golden Horde

0   200
Miles

CASPIAN SEA

GOLDEN HORDE

1237

1239

SEA OF AZOV

Sarai

Galich

Beloozero

Suzdal
Vladimir
Tver
Moscow
Rostov
Riazan

Novgorod

Pskov

Smolensk

Novgorod-
Seversk

Chernigov

Kiev

Minsk

LITHUANIA

LIVONIAN ORDER

TEUTONIC ORDER

Vladimir

Lvov

Galich

POLAND

Cracow

1241

1241

HUNGARY

Budapest

Liegnitz

HOLY
ROMAN
EMPIRE

ADRIATIC SEA

14

Mongol Capture of Kiev in 1240

The Mongol conquest of Northern Rus removed a possible threat to their westward progress. In 1240, after two years of rest, Batu Khan ordered his forces west. Employing tactics of siege and massive assault, the Mongols overran Pereiaslavl and Chernigov and took Kiev in December of 1240. Mongol capture of Kiev was important for two basic reasons: it cleared the road through Galicia and Poland to central and western Europe, though actually they reached only the city of Liegnitz, near Breslau; and it symbolized the end of the Kievan state which had been on the decline for quite some time.

In this year [1240] Batu Khan approached and surrounded the city of Kiev with a great multitude of soldiers. The Tartar force besieged it and it was impossible for any one either to leave the city or to enter it. Squeaking of wagons, bellowing of camels, sounds of trumpets and organs, neighing of horses, and cry and sobs of an innumerable multitude of people made it impossible to hear one another in the city. The entire country was overflowing with the Tartars. The Kievans then captured a Tartar by the name of Tavrul, and he named all the great princes who were with Batu, and spoke of his innumerable strength. And he had with him the following of his brothers and of his strong military leaders: Urdiuy, Baydar, Biriuy, Kaydar, Bechar, Mengay, Kailug, [and] Kuiuk; but he [Kuiuk] returned [to Mongolia] when he learned of the death of the [Great] Khan. [The Great] Khan did not belong to the Batu family, but was his first and great leader. Batu Khan mourned him because the latter liked him very much. Other military leaders [of Batu Khan at

From *Polnoe Sobranie Russkikh Letopisei* (*Complete Collection of Russian Chronicles*) (St. Petersburg, 1885), vol. 10, pp. 115–117. Translation mine. Items in brackets are mine.

Kiev] and great princes included: Butar, Aydar, Kilemet, Burunday, Batyr, who captured the Bulgar and Suzdal lands, and a great number, countless, other military leaders. Batu ordered that many wall-destroying rams be brought to Kiev and placed near the Polish Gate, because that part was wooded. Many rams hammered the walls without interruption day and night and the inhabitants were frightened, and there were many killed and blood flowed like water. And Batu sent the following message to the inhabitants of Kiev: "If you surrender to me, you will be forgiven; if, however, you are going to resist you will suffer greatly and will perish cruelly." The inhabitants of Kiev, however, did not listen to him, but calumniated and cursed him. This angered Batu very much and he ordered [his men] to attack the city with great fury. And thus with the aid of many rams they broke through the city walls and entered the city, and the inhabitants ran to meet them. It was possible to hear and see a great crash of lances and clatter of shields; the arrows obscured the light and because of this it was impossible to see the sky, but there was darkness from the multitude of Tartar arrows, and there were dead everywhere and everywhere blood flowed like water. [Kiev's] military leader Dmitri was severely wounded and many strong men were killed. The inhabitants [of Kiev] were defeated, and the Tartars climbed on the walls and because of great exhaustion they remained there. The night came. During the night the inhabitants [of Kiev] built a new fortification around the Church of the Virgin Mary. When morning came the Tartars attacked them and there was a bitter slaughter. Some people fainted and [some] fled to the church steeple with their possessions; and the church walls collapsed from the weight and the Tartars took the city of Kiev on St. Nicholas Day, December 6, [1240]. They brought the wounded military leader Dmitri before Batu, and Batu ordered that he not be killed because of his bravery. And Batu began to inquire about Prince Daniel [of Galicia], and they told him that the Prince had fled to Hungary. Batu left his own military leader in Kiev and he himself went toward Vladimir in Volyn.

15

John of Pian de Carpine's Journey to Mongolia in 1246

The Mongol conquest of all of northern and central Asia and of eastern Europe made a very strong impression in western Europe. In 1245 Pope Innocent IV sent a monk, John of Pian de Carpine, on a mission to Mongolia to determine whether the Mongols could be converted to Christianity. Brother John set out from Lyons on April 16, 1245 via Prague, Galicia, and Kiev, and delivered the Pope's letter to Emperor Kuiuk Khan near the Mongol capital of Karakorum. Although the mission failed to accomplish its main purpose, Brother John left an interesting description of his efforts to reach his destination. As the first west European to travel to the capital of the Mongol Empire at its peak, unfamiliar with the language and geography of the area, Brother John's account is vague and unclear in several places. Taken as a whole, however, the story of his journey is rich in description of medieval travel hazards, of the vastness of the Mongol Empire, and of customs and practices of Mongol officials. Some of these practices were later adopted by Russian princes and thus became an integral part of Russia's cultural heritage.

Reprinted with permission of the Cambridge University Press from *The Journey of William Rubruck to the Eastern Parts of the World, 1253–55, as Narrated by Himself, With Two Accounts of the Earlier Journey of John of Pian de Carpine.* Translated from the Latin, and Edited, with an Introductory Notice by William Woodville Rockhill (London, Published for the Hakluyt Society, 1900), pp. 1–32. See original source for footnote references. Spellings of certain proper names have been modernized. Items in brackets are mine.

When therefore we had arranged, as has been already stated elsewhere, to set out for the (land of the) Tartars we (left Lyons on the 16th April, 1245, and after travelling through Germany) came to the King of Bohemia. And having asked his advice, for we were personally acquainted with this lord [Wenceslaw I] from of old, which was the best road for us to go by, he answered that it were best, it seemed to him, to go by Poland and Rus [Galicia]; for he had relatives in Poland, with whose aid we could enter Rus; so having given us his letters and a good escort to take us through Poland, he caused also money to be given us to defray our travelling expenses through his lands and cities as far as (the court of) Boleslaw, Duke of Silesia, his nephew, with whom also we were personally acquainted.

The latter also gave us his letters and an escort and money for our expenses in his towns and cities, as far as Conrad, Duke of Lenczy [Cracow]. At that time, through God's special grace, the Lord Vasilko, Duke of Rus [Volyn and Vladimir], had come there, from whom we learnt more accurately of the Tartars; for he had sent his ambassadors to them, who had come back to him and to his brother Daniel [Duke of Galicia], bearing to the lord Daniel a safe conduct to go to Batu. And he told us that if we wanted to go to them we must have rich presents to give them, for they were in the habit of asking for them most importunately, and if they were not given them (and this is quite true), an ambassador could not conduct his business satisfactorily with them; and that furthermore he was looked upon as a mere nothing. Not wishing that the affairs of the Lord Pope and of the Church should be obstructed on this account, with some of that which had been given us in charity, so that we should not be in want and for use on our journey, we bought some skins of beavers and of some other animals. Duke Conrad, the Duchess of Cracow, some knights and the Bishop of Cracow, hearing of this, gave us some more of these skins. Furthermore, Duke Conrad, his son, and the Bishop of Cracow besought most earnestly Duke Vasilko to help us as much as he could in reaching the Tartars; and he replied that he would do so willingly.

So he took us with him to his country; and as he kept us for some days as his guests that we might rest a little, and had called thither his bishops at our request, we read them the letters of the Lord Pope, in which he admonished them to return to the unity of holy mother Church; we also advised and urged them as much as we could, as well the Duke as the Bishops, and all those who had met there, to that same end. But as at the very time when this duke had come to Poland, his brother, Duke Daniel, had gone to Batu and was not present, they could not give a final answer, but must wait his return before being able to give a full reply.

After that the Duke sent one of his servants with us as far as Kiev.

Nevertheless we travelled ever in danger of our lives on account of the Lithuanians, who often committed undiscovered outrages as much as possible in the country of Rus [Volyn] and particularly in these places through which we had to pass; and·as the greater part of the men of Rus [Volyn] had been killed by the Tartars or taken off into captivity, they were unable to offer them the least resistance; we were safe, however, from the Ruthenians on account of this servant. Thence then, by the grace of God having been saved from the enemies of the Cross of Christ, we came to Kiev, which is the metropolis of Rus. And when we came there we took counsel with the Millenarius [Mongol official], and the other nobles who were there, as to our route. They told us that if we took into Tartary the horses which we had, they would all die, for the snows were deep, and they did not know how to dig out the grass from under the snow like Tartar horses, nor could anything else be found (on the way) for them to eat, for the Tartars had neither straw nor hay nor fodder. So, on their advice, we decided to leave our horses there with two servants to keep them; and we had to give the Millenarius presents, that he might be pleased to give us pack-horses and an escort. Before we reached Kiev, when in Danilov I was ill to the point of death; but I had myself carried along in a cart in the intense cold through the deep snow, so as not to interfere with the affairs of Christendom.

Having settled then all these matters at Kiev, on the second day after the feast of the Purification of Our Lady (February 4, 1246), we started out from Kiev for other barbarous peoples, with the horses of the Millenarius and an escort. We came to a certain town which was under the direct rule of the Tartars and is called Canov; the prefect of the town gave us horses and an escort as far as another town in which was a certain Alan prefect who was called Micheas, a man full of all malice and iniquity, for he had sent to us to Kiev some of his body-guard, who lyingly said to us, as from the part of Corenza, that we being ambassadors were to come to him; and this he did, though it was not true, in order that he might extort presents from us. When, however, we reached him, he made himself most disagreeable, and unless we promised him presents, would in no wise agree to help us. Seeing that we would not otherwise be able to go farther, we promised to give him some presents, but when we gave him what appeared to us suitable, he refused to receive them unless we gave more; and so we had to add to them according to his will, and something besides he subtracted from us deceitfully and maliciously.

After that we left with him on the second day of Quinquagesima (19th February), and he led us as far as the first camp of the Tartars, and on the first Friday after Ash Wednesday (23d February), while we were stopping for the night as the sun went down, the Tartars broke in on us in arms in horrible fashion asking who we were. We answered them that we were envoys of the Lord Pope, and then, having accepted some food from us, they left at once. Starting again at morn, we had only gone a little way when their chiefs who were in the camp came to us, and inquired of us why we came to them, and what was our business. We answered them that we were the envoys of the Lord Pope, who was the lord and father of Christians; that he had sent us to the King as well as to the princes and all the Tartars, because he desired that all Christians should be friends of the Tartars and at peace with them. Moreover, as he wished that they should be mighty with God in heaven, he, the Lord Pope, advised them as well through us as by his letters, that they should become Christians and receive the faith of Our Lord Jesus Christ, for otherwise they could not be saved. He told them furthermore that he was astonished at the slaying of human beings done by the Tartars, and especially of Christians and above all of Hungarians, Moravians and Poles, who were his subjects, when they had injured them in nothing nor attempted to injure them; and as the Lord God was gravely offended at this, he cautioned them to abstain henceforth from such acts, and to repent them of those they had done. Furthermore we said that the Lord Pope requested that they should write to him what they would do and what was their intention; and that they would give answer to him to all the above points in their letters. Having heard our motives, and understood and noted them down, they said that, in view of what we had said, they would give us pack-horses as far as Corenza [a Mongol general], and supply a guide; and at once they asked for presents, which we gave them, for we must needs to their will.

Having given them the presents, and taken as pack-horses some from which they got off, we started under their guidance for Corenza; but they sent ahead a swift messenger to this chief with what we had told them. This chief is lord of all those (Tartars) who are encamped facing the peoples of the West, lest they suddenly and unexpectedly attack them. This chief has under him, we were told, sixty-thousand armed men. When we reached him, he made us put our tents far from him, and sent us his slave stewards who asked us with what we wanted to bow to him, that is to say whether we would make him presents. We replied that the Lord Pope had not sent any presents, for he was not sure we could reach them; and that furthermore we had to pass through very dangerous places, exposed to the Lithuanians, who make raids along the roads from Poland to near the Tartars, over which we had had to travel; but nevertheless with what we were carrying with us, by the grace of God and of our Lord the Pope, and for our personal use, we would show him our respect as well as we could. But when we had given him a number of things, they were not enough for him, and he asked for more through intermediaries, promising to have us conducted most honourably if we complied with his request, which we had to do since we wished to live and carry out satisfactorily the order of the Lord Pope.

Having received the presents they led us to his *orda* or tent, and we were instructed to bend three times the left knee before the door of his dwelling, and to be very careful not to put our feet on the threshold of the door; and this we were attentive to observe, for sentence of death is on those who knowingly tread upon the threshold of a chief's dwelling. After we had entered we were obliged to repeat on bended knee before the chief and all the other nobles, who had specially been convened there for that purpose, what has been previously said. We presented to him also the letters of the Lord Pope; but as our interpreter, whom we had brought with us from Kiev, was not able to translate them for him, nor was there any one else competent to do so, they could not be interpreted. After this, horses were given us, and three Tartars, two of whom were chiefs over ten, and the other a man of Batu, guided us with all speed to that latter chief. This Batu is more powerful than all the other Tartar princes save the Emperor, whom he is held to obey.

We started (for Batu's camp) on the Monday after the first Sunday of Quadragesima (26th February), and riding as fast as horses could go trotting, for we had fresh horses three or four times nearly every day, we rode from morning to night, and very often even at night, and it was not before Wednesday in Holy Week (4th April) that we could get to him. We crossed the whole country of the Comans [*i.e.,* Polovtsians], which is all a plain, and has four great rivers. The first is called Dnieper, along which, on the side of Rus [Western side] roams Corenza, and on the other side through those plains, Mauci, who is mightier than Corenza. Secondly, the Don, along which roams a certain prince called Catan, who has as wife Batu's sister. The third is the Volga, a very big river, along which goes Batu. The fourth is called Yaik [Ural], along which go two Millenarii, one along one side of the river, the other along the other. All these (chiefs) descend in winter time to the sea, and in summer go up the courses of these rivers to the mountains. Now this sea is the Mare-Magnum from which goes out the arm of Saint George which goes to Constantinople. We went along for many days on the ice of the Dnieper. These rivers are big, very full of fish, especially the Volga, and they fall into the sea of Greece which is called Mare-Magnum [Black Sea]. We went for many days along the shore of this sea, which on account of the ice was very dangerous in several places; for it freezes along the coast quite three leagues out. But before we came to Batu, two of our Tartars went ahead to tell him all we had said at Corenza's.

When then we came to Batu on the borders of the Coman's country, we were made to camp a good league from their tents, and before we were taken to his court we were told we would have to pass between two fires, which we refused to do under any consideration. But they told us: "Fear not, we only make you pass between these two fires lest perchance you think something injurious to our lord, or if you carry some poison, for the fire will remove all harm." We answered them: "Since it is thus we will pass through, so that we may not be suspected of such things." When we came to the *orda* we were questioned by his procurator, who is called Eldegai, as to what we wanted to make our obeisance with, that is to say, what gifts we desired to give him; we answered him as we had previously answered Corenza, that the Lord Pope had sent no presents, but that we ourselves, of those things which we had by the grace of God and the Lord Pope for our expenses, desired to show him our respect as best we could. Presents having been given and accepted, the procurator called Eldegai questioned us as to our coming; and to him we gave the same reasons as we had previously given to Corenza.

Having been informed of our reasons, they led us into the dwelling, after having made a bow, and heard the caution about the threshold, which has been mentioned. Having entered then we said what we had to say on bended knees, and then we presented him the letters (of the Pope), and requested that interpreters be given us able to translate them. These were given us on Good Friday (6th April), and we carefully translated the letters into the Ruthenian, Saracenic, and Tartar languages, and this latter interpretation was given to Batu, who read it and noted it carefully. After that we were taken back to our dwelling, but no food was given us, save once on the night of our arrival a little millet in a bowl.

This Batu holds his court right magnificently, for he has door-keepers and all the other officials like unto their Emperor. He sits also in a raised place, as on a throne, with one of his wives; but every one else (of his family), as well his brothers and his sons as others of lesser degree, sit lower down on a bench in the middle (of the tent). All the other people sit behind them on the ground, the men to the right, the women to the left. He has tents made of linen. They are large and quite handsome, and used to belong to the King of Hungary. And no outsider save a servant dare enter the tent, no matter how great and mighty he may be, unless he is called, unless perchance he knows he is wanted. When we had stated our object, we took a seat to the left, for thus do all ambassadors in going, but on coming back from the Emperor they always placed us on the right. In the middle of the dwelling near the door is a table, on which is placed drink in gold and silver vases; and Batu never drinks, nor does any prince of the Tartars, especially when they are in public, without there being singing and guitar playing. And when he rides out, there is always carried over his head on a pole an umbrella or little awning; and all the very great princes of the Tartars do likewise. This Batu is kind enough to his own people, but he is greatly feared by them. He is, however, most cruel in fight; he is very shrewd and extremely crafty in warfare, for he has been waging war for a long time.

On Holy Saturday (7th April) we were called to his tent and that same procurator of Batu's came out to us and told us from him that we were to go to the Emperor Kuiuk in their country, and that some of our party would be kept there (with Batu) in the expectation that they would want to send them back to the Lord Pope. We gave them letters concerning all we had done to carry back (to the Pope), but when they had got as far as Mauci, he detained them until our return. As for ourselves, on the day of the Resurrection of the Lord (8th April), having said mass and settled everything, accompanied by the two Tartars who had been detailed to us at Corenza's, we started out most tearfully, not knowing whether we were going to life or death. We were furthermore so feeble that we could hardly ride; during the whole of that lent our only food had been millet with salt and water; and likewise on the other fast days; nor had we anything else to drink but snow melted in the kettle. . . .

After that we entered the country of the Cangitae, which in many places suffers from a great scarcity of water, and in which but few people remain on account of this deficiency of water. And so it happened that the men of Iaroslav, Duke of Rus, who were going to join him in the country of the Tartars, lost some of their number who died of thirst in this desert. In this country and also in Comania, we found many human skulls and bones scattered about on the ground like cattle-dung. We travelled through this country (of the Cangitae) from the eighth day after Easter to nearly the Ascension of our Lord (17th May). These people are pagans, and the Comans as well as the Cangitae do not till the soil, but only live on the produce of their animals; nor do they build houses, but live in tents. The tartars have also annihilated them, and now occupy their country; those of them who were left they have reduced to slavery.

Leaving the country of the Cangitae we entered that of the Bisermins. These people used to speak the Coman language, and do still speak it; but they hold the religion of the Saracens. We found in that country innumerable ruined cities, overthrown villages, and many deserted towns. There is a great river in that country whose name I do not know,* and on which stands a city called Ianckint, and also another called Barchin, and still another called Ornas [also known as Ortar], and many more whose names I do not know. This country used to have a lord who was called the Great Sultan, and he was put to death by the Tartars with all his progeny, but I am ignorant of his name. The country has very high mountains; to the south of it is Jerusalem, Baghdad, and the whole country of the Saracens. Near its borders are stationed the chiefs Burin and Cadan, who are uterine brothers. To the north of it is a part of the country of the Black Kitayans and an Ocean, and in that quarter is sta-

---

* Syr Daria.

tioned Sitan, a brother of Batu. We travelled through this country from
the feast of the Ascension (17th May) to about eight days before the
feast of Saint John the Baptist (24th June).

After that we entered the country of the Black Kitayans, in which they
(the Mongols) have built anew, as it were, a city called Omyl, in which
the Emperor has erected a house where we were invited to drink; and
he who was there on the part of the Emperor made the nobles of the
town and also his own two sons clap their hands before us (when we
drank). Leaving this place we found a not very large lake, and as we
did not ask its name, we do not know it. On the shore of this lake was
a little hill, in where there is said to be an opening, whence in winter
there issue out such great tempests of wind that people can barely and
at great danger pass by. In summer, however, though one always hears
the sound of the winds, but little comes out of the opening, according
to what the inhabitants told us. We travelled along the shore of this
lake for several days; it has several islands in it, and it lay upon our left
hand. This country has great abundance of streams, not large ones, however; on either bank of these rivers are woods, but of no great width.
Ordu lives in this country; he is older than Batu, in fact older than any
of the other chiefs of the Tartars, and the orda or court is that of one of
his wives who rules over it. For it is a custom among the Tartars that
the courts of their princes and nobles are not broken up (on their
death), but some women are always appointed who govern them, and
the same proportion of presents are given them that their lord had been
in the habit (during his life) of allowing them. After this we came to
the first orda of the Emperor [Ogodai], in which was one of his wives;
but as we had not yet seen the Emperor they would not invite us nor let
us come into her orda, though they had us well served in our own tent,
according to Tartar fashion; and they kept us there for a whole day, so
that we might rest.

Proceeding thence on the eve of the feast of Saint Peter (28th June),
we entered the country of the Naiman, who are pagans. On the day of
the feast of the apostles Peter and Paul (29th June) there fell in that
place a great snow, and we experienced great cold. This country is ex-
ceptionally mountainous and cold, and there is very little plain in it.
These two nations [Black Kitayans and Naimans] do not till the soil,
but like the Tartars live in tents. These latter have nearly exterminated
them. We travelled through this country many days.

After that we entered the country of the Mongols, whom we call
Tartars. And we journeyed through that country for three weeks, I think
riding hard, and on the day of the feast of blessed Mary Magdalen (22d
July) we arrived at Kuiuk's, the present Emperor. Along all this (part
of the) route we travelled very fast, for our Tartars had been ordered
to take us quickly to the solemn court which had already been convened

for several years for the election of an emperor, so that we might be present at it. So we had to rise at dawn and travel till night without a stop; often we arrived so late that we did not eat at night, but that which we should have eaten at night was given us in the morning; and we went as fast as the horses could trot, for there was no lack of horses, having usually fresh horses during the day, those which we left being sent back, as I have stated previously; and in this fashion we rode rapidly along without interruption.

When we reached Kuiuk's camp, he caused us to be given a tent and allowances such as the Tartars are in the habit of giving; but they treated us better than they did the other ambassadors. We were not called (before Kuiuk) however, for he had not yet been elected, nor had they settled about the succession; the translation of the letters of the Lord Pope, and what else we had said (to Corenza and Batu), had been sent him by Batu. And when we had been there five or six days, he sent us to his mother, where the solemn court was being held. When we got there they had already erected a great tent made of white purple, which in our opinion was large enough to hold more than two thousand persons; and around it a wooden paling had been made, and it was ornamented with divers designs.

On the second or third day we went with the Tartars who had been assigned to guard us (to this tent); and all the chiefs met there, and each one was riding around in a circle over hill and dale with his men. On the first day they were all dressed in white purple; on the second day, and then it was that Kuiuk came to the tent, they were dressed in red (purple); on the third day they were all in blue purple, and on the fourth day in the finest baldakins. In the paling near the tent were two big gates: one through which only the Emperor could pass, and at which there was no guard though it was open, for no one would dare to go in or out by it; and the other way by which all those who had admittance went in, and at this one were guards with swords, bows and arrows, and if anyone came near the tent outside of the set bounds, he was beaten if caught, or shot at with headless arrows if he ran away. The horses were kept at about two arrow-flights, I should say, from the tent. The chiefs went about everywhere with a number of their men all armed; but nobody, unless a chief, could go to the horses, without getting badly beaten for trying to do so. And many (of the horses) there were which had on their bits, breast-plates, saddles, and cruppers quite twenty marks worth of gold I should think. And so the chiefs held counsel beyond the tent, and discussed the election, while all the rest of the people were far away from the tent. And there they remained till about noon, when they began drinking mare's milk, and they drank till evening so plentifully that it was a rare sight.

They called us inside (the tent), and gave us mead, for we would not drink mare's milk at all; and this was a great honor they showed us; and they kept on urging us to drink, but not being in the habit of it, we could not do so, and we let them see that it was distasteful to us, so they stopped pressing us. In the great square was the Duke Iaroslav of Suzdal in Rus, and several princes of the Kitayans and Solanges, also two sons of the King of Georgia, a sultan, the ambassador of the Caliph of Baghdad, and more than ten other sultans of the Saracens, I believe, and as we were told by the procurators. For there were more than four thousand envoys, as well those bringing tribute as those offering presents, sultans and other chiefs who had come to present themselves in person, those who had been sent by their (rulers), and those who were governors of countries. All these were put together outside the paling, and drink was given to them at the same time; as for ourselves and the Duke Iaroslav, whenever we were outside with them they always gave us a higher place. I think, if I remember rightly, that we were at that place for a good four weeks; and I am under the impression that the election was made there, though it was not proclaimed. It was for the following reason that it was generally believed (that Kuiuk had been chosen): whenever Kuiuk came out of the tent, they sang to him, and as long as he remained outside of it they inclined before him certain fine staffs on the ends of which were (tufts of) red wool, which was done to no other chief. They call this tent or court the Sira-Orda.

Coming out of the tent, we all rode together to another place some three or four leagues distant, where there was a fine large plain near a river flowing between mountains, where another tent was set up, and it is called by them the Golden Orda: and here it was that Kuiuk was to have been placed on the throne on the day of the Assumption of our Lady (15th August); but it was deferred on account of the hail which fell, to which I have referred previously. This tent rested on pillars covered with gold plates, fastened with gold nails and other woods, and the top and sides of it were covered with baldakins; the outside, however, being of other kinds of stuff. Here we remained until the feast of Saint Bartholomew (24th August), when there assembled a great multitude, and they all stood with their faces turned to the south, some of them a stone's throw from others, going ever farther and farther away, making genuflexions towards the south. As for us, not knowing whether they were making incantations or bending their knees to God or what else, we would not make any genuflexions. After doing this for a long while they went back to the tent, and placed Kuiuk on the imperial seat, and the chiefs knelt before him; and after that the whole people did likewise, except ourselves who were not his subjects. Then they began drinking, and as is their custom, they kept on drinking till evening. After that they brought in carts of cooked meat, without salt, and to each four or five they gave a quarter. To those who were inside (the tent) they gave meat and salted broth for sauce; and in this fashion they passed days in feasting.

It was at this place (the Golden Orda) that we were called into the Emperor's presence; after that Chingay the prothonotary had written down our names and the names of those who had sent us, and also those of the chief of the Solanges and of the others, he repeated them all, shouting with a loud voice before the Emperor and all the chiefs. When this had been done each of us had to bend the left knee four times, and they cautioned us not to touch the threshold, and having searched us carefully for knives, and not having found any, we entered the door on the east side, for no one dare enter that on the west side save the Emperor; and the same rule applies if it is the tent of a chief; but those of low rank pay little attention to such matters. And when we entered his tent, it was the first occasion since he had been made Emperor (that he had given an audience). He received likewise the ambassadors, but very few persons entered his tent. Here also such great quantities of presents were given him by the ambassadors, silks, samites, purples, baldakins, silk girdles worked in gold, splendid furs, and other things, that it was a marvel to see. Here also it was that a kind of umbrella or awning that is carried over the Emperor's head was presented to him, and it was all covered with precious stones. Here also a certain governor of a province brought to him many camels covered with baldakin and with saddles on them, and a kind of arrangement inside of which people could sit, I think there were forty or fifty of them; and (he also gave him) many horses and mules covered with armour, some of hide, others of iron. They asked us if we wished to make any presents; but we had already used up nearly everything we had, so we had nothing at all to give him. It was while here that on a hill some distance from the tent there were more than five hundred carts, all full of gold and silver and silken gowns, all of which was divided up between the Emperor and the chiefs; and the various chiefs divided their shares among their men as they saw fit.

Leaving this place, we came to another where there was a wonderful tent, all of red purple, a present of the Kitayans. We were taken into it also, and here again when we entered they gave us mead or wine to drink, and offered us cooked meat, if we wanted it. There was a high platform of boards in it, on which was the Emperor's throne; and the throne was of ebony, wonderfully sculptured; and there were also (on it) gold, and precious stones, and, if I remember rightly, pearls; and one went up to it by steps, and it was rounded behind. There were benches placed around the throne, on which the ladies sat in rows on the left side; on the right side no one sat on raised seats, but the chiefs sat on seats of lesser height placed in the middle (of the tent), and the other people sat behind them, and the whole day there came there a great concourse of ladies. These three tents of which I have spoken were very big; but his wives had other tents of white felt, and they were quite large and handsome. It was here also that they separated: the mother of the Emperor went in one direction, the Emperor in another, for the purpose of rendering justice. The paternal aunt of the Emperor was in prison, for she had killed his father in the time when their army was in Hungary, and it was for this that the army had retreated from those countries. She and a number of others were tried for this, and put to death.

At this same time Iaroslav, Grand Duke in a part of Rus called Suzdal, died at the Emperor's orda. It happened that he was invited by the mother of the Emperor (to her tent), and she gave him to eat and drink with her own hand, as if to honor him; and he went back to his lodgings straightway and felt ill, and after seven days he was dead, and all his body became livid in strange fashion; so that everyone believed that he had been poisoned, that they might get free and full possession of his lands. As an argument in favor of this (supposition, the Empress) sent at once, without the knowledge of any of her people who were there, an envoy in all haste to his son Alexander in Rus to come to her, for she wished to give him his father's lands; but he would not go, but remained there (at home); in the meanwhile (the Empress) sent also letters for him to come and receive his father's lands. It was believed by all that he would be put to death if he should come, or imprisoned perpetually.

It was after this death (of Iaroslav) that our Tartars took us to the Emperor, if I remember correctly the time; and when the Emperor heard from our Tartars that we had come to him, he ordered us to go back to his mother, for he wanted two days after that to unfurl his standard against the whole of the western world, as was emphatically told us by those who knew, as has been previously stated, and he wished us not to know it. When we had returned (to the Empress), we remained there a few days, when we were sent back again to him; and we remained with him for quite a month, in such hunger and thirst that we were barely able to keep alive, for the allowances which they gave the four of us were scarcely enough for one; and we could find nothing to buy, the market being too far away. Had not the Lord sent us a certain Ruthenian called Kuzma, a goldsmith, and a great favorite of the Emperor, who helped us a little, I verily believe we should have died, unless the Lord had helped us in some other way. He showed us before putting it in place the throne of the Emperor which he himself had made, and also the seal he had manufactured for him, and he told us the superscription on his seal [God in Heaven, and Kuiuk Khan on Earth, Might of God. The Seal of the Emperor of All Men]. We also learned many private details about the Emperor, from those who had come with other chiefs, several Ruthenians and Hungarians who knew Latin and French, also Ruthenian clerks and others who had been with them, some as long as thirty years, in war and in other events, and who knew all about them as they understood the language, having been continually with them some twenty, others ten years, more or less. From these we were able to learn about everything: they told us most freely of all things without our having to question them, for they knew of our 'desire.

After these things had happened the Emperor sent his prothonotary Chingay to tell us to write down what we had to say and our business, and to give it to him; this we did, writing down all we had previously said at Batu's, as has been stated above. After an interval of several days, he had us again called, and told us, through Kadak, the procurator of the whole Empire, and in the presence of the prothonotaries Bala and Chingay, and of many others of his secretaries, to say all we had to say; and this we did right willingly. Our interpreter on that occasion as well as on the other, was Temer, a knight of Iaroslav's, now a clerk with him, and another clerk of the Emperor's. And he (Kadak) asked us on the latter occasion if there were any persons with the Lord Pope who understood the written languages of the Ruthenians or Saracens or Tartars. We replied that we did not use either the Ruthenian, Tartar, or Saracenic writing, and that though there were Saracens in the country, they were far distant from the Lord Pope. We added that it appeared to us the best plan for them to write in Tartar, and to have it translated to us, and that we would carefully write it down in our language, taking both the (original) letter and the translation to the Lord Pope. On this they left us and went back to the Emperor.

On the feast of Saint Martin (11th November) we were again summoned, and Kadak, Chingay, Bala and several others of the secretaries came to us, and the letter was translated to us word for word; and as we translated it into Latin they made us explain each phrase, wishing to ascertain if we had made a mistake in any word; and when the two letters were written they made us read them together and separately for fear we had left out anything, and they said to us: "Be sure you understand it all, for it must not be that you do not understand everything, when you have reached such very distant lands." And having told them: "We understand it all," they re-wrote the letter in Saracenic, so that it might be read to the Lord Pope if he could find any one in our part of the world able to do so.

It is the custom of the Emperor of the Tartars never to address in person a stranger, no matter how great he may be; he only listens, and then answers through the medium of someone, as I have explained. Whenever they explain any business to Kadak, or listen to an answer of the Emperor, those who are under him (i.e., his own subjects), remain on their knees until the end of the speech, no matter how great they may be. One may not, for it is not the custom, say anything more about any question after it is disposed of by the Emperor. This Emperor has a procurator, prothonotaries and secretaries, and also all the other officers for public as well as private affairs, except advocates, for they carry out without a murmur all judgments according to the Emperor's decision. The other princes of the Tartars do in like manner as regards those things which pertain to their offices.

This Emperor may be forty or forty-five years or more old; he is of medium stature, very prudent and extremely shrewd, and serious and sedate in his manners; and he has never been seen to laugh lightly or show any levity, and of this we were assured by Christians who were constantly with him. We were also assured by Christians who were of his household that they firmly believed that he was about to become a Christian. As signal evidence of this he keeps Christian clerks and gives them allowances, and he has always the chapel of the Christians in front of his great tent, and (these priests) chant publicly and openly and beat (a tablet) according to the fashion of the Greeks at appointed hours, just like other Christians, and though there may be ever so great a multitude of Tartars and of other people. And the other chiefs do not have this.

Our Tartars who were to come back with us told us that the Emperor proposed sending his ambassadors with us. He wished, however, I think, that we should ask him to do so, for one of our Tartars, the elder of the two, told us to ask it; but it not seeming to us good that they should come, we replied that it was not for us to ask it, but that if the Emperor of his own will sent them, we would with God's help guide them safely. There were various reasons, however, for which it seemed to us inexpedient that they should come. The first reason was that we feared they would see the dissensions and wars among us, and that it would encourage them to march against us. The second reason was that we feared they were intended to be spies. The third reason was that we feared lest they be put to death, as our people for the most part are arrogant and hasty: thus it was that when the servants who were with us at the request of the Cardinal Legate in Germany were going back to him in Tartar dress, they came near being stoned by the Germans on the road, and were forced to leave off that dress. And it is the custom of the Tartars never to make peace with those who have killed their envoys till they have wreaked vengeance upon them. The fourth reason was that we feared they would carry us off, as was once done with a Saracen prince, who is still a captive, unless he is dead. The fifth reason was that there was no need for their coming, for they had no other order or authority than to bring the letters of the Emperor to the Lord Pope and the other princes (of Christendom), which we (already) had, and we believed that evil might come of it. Therefore it pleased us not that they should come. The third day after this, which was the feast of Saint Brice (13th

November), they gave us permission to leave and a letter of the Emperor signed with his seal, and then they sent us to the Emperor's mother, who gave to each of us a fox-skin gown with the fur outside and wadding inside, and also a piece of purple—of which our Tartars stole a palm's length from each, and also more than half of another piece which was given to our servant; but though it was no secret to us, we did not choose to make any ado over it.

So we started on our way back, and we were travelling the whole winter, resting most of the time in the snow in the desert, save when in the open plain where there were no trees we could scrape a bare place with our feet; and often when the wind drifted it we would find (on waking) our bodies all covered with snow. And so we travelled along till we came to Batu, on the Ascension of our Lord (9th May, 1247), and to him we told what (the Emperor) had answered the Lord Pope. He replied that he had nothing to ask other than what the Emperor had written; but he said that we must carefully tell the Lord Pope and the other lords everything the Emperor had written. Safe conducts having been given us we left him, and reached Mauci on the Saturday after the octave of Pentecost (2d June), where were our companions and servants who had been detained, and whom we caused to be brought back to us. Thence we went to Corenza, who again begged presents of us, but not having (anything) we gave nothing. He gave us two Comans, who were accounted of the Tartars, as far as Kiev in Rus. Our own Tartar did not leave us till we had left the last Tartar camp. The others who had been given us by Corenza led us in six days from the last camp to Kiev.

We reached (Kiev) fifteen days before the feast of Saint John the Baptist (9th June). The Kievans who had heard of our arrival all came out to meet us rejoicing, and congratulated us as if we had risen from the dead, and so they did to us throughout Rus, Poland and Bohemia. Daniel and Vasilko his brother received us with great rejoicing, and kept us, against our will, for quite eight days; during which time they held counsel between themselves and the bishops and other notables about those things on which we had spoken to them when on our way to the Tartars. And they answered us jointly, saying, that they wished to have the Lord Pope for their particular lord and father, and the holy Roman Church as their lady and mistress, and confirming likewise all they had previously transmitted on the matter through their abbot; and after that they sent with us to the Lord Pope their letters and ambassadors.

16

The Court of Batu Khan in 1253

The Mongol appearance in eastern Europe aroused the interest of the political as well as the religious leaders of western Europe. In 1253, the French king, Louis IX, sent a Franciscan monk, William of Rubruck, on a mission to Mongolia to seek an alliance against the followers of Islam in the Near East and North Africa. The assignment took Brother William to the Mongol capital of Karakorum. This mission, like that of John of Pian de Carpine, was a failure in its main task, but Brother William left an interesting account of his impressions of the Court of Batu Khan and his audience with the ruler of the Golden Horde. The account of Brother William, like that of Brother John, ranks as high as Marco Polo's report in the literature of medieval travel.

When I saw the ordu of Batu, I was astonished, for it seemed like a great city stretched out about his dwelling, with people scattered all about for three or four leagues. And as among the people of Israel, where each one knew in which quarter from the tabernacle he had to pitch his tents, so these know on which side of the ordu they must place themselves when they set down their dwellings. A court is orda in their language, and it means "middle," for it is always in the middle of the people, with the exception, however, that no one places himself right to the south, for in that direction the doors of the court open. But to the right and left they may spread out as they wish, according to the lay

Reprinted with permission of the Cambridge University Press from *The Journey of William Rubruck to the Eastern Parts of the World, 1253–55, as Narrated by Himself, With Two Accounts of the Earlier Journey of John of Pian de Carpine*. Translated from the Latin, and Edited, with an Introductory Notice by William Woodville Rockhill (London, Published for the Hakluyt Society, 1900), pp. 122–126. See original source for footnote references. Spellings of certain proper names have been modernized. Items in brackets are mine.

of the land, so long as they do not bring the line of tents down right before or behind the court.

We were first taken to a certain Saracen, who gave us no food. The next day we were taken to the court, and they had a great awning spread, for the dwelling could not hold all the men and women who had come thither. Our guide cautioned us to say nothing until Batu should have bid us speak, and then to speak briefly. He asked also whether you had already sent ambassadors to the Tartars. I said that you had sent to Keu Khan [i.e., the mission of Friar Andrew in 1249], but that you would not even have sent envoys to him and letters to Sartach if you had not believed that they were Christians. Then they led us before the pavilion, and we were warned not to touch the ropes of the tent, for they are held to 'represent the threshold of the door. So we stood there in our robes and barefooted, with uncovered heads, and we were a great spectacle unto ourselves. (Friar John of Pian de Carpine) had been there; but he had changed his gown, fearing lest he should be slighted, being the envoy of the Lord Pope. Then we were led into the middle of the tent, and they did not require us to make any reverence by bending the knee, as they are used to do of envoys. We stood before him the time to say: "*Miserere mei, Deus*," and all kept profound silence. He was seated on a long seat as broad as a couch, all gilded, and with three steps leading up to it, and a lady was beside him. Men were seated about on his right, and ladies on his left; and where the room on the women's side was not taken up by them, for there were only present the wives of Batu, men occupied it. A bench with *cosmos* and big cups of gold and silver, ornamented with precious stones, was in the entry of the tent. He looked at us intently, and we at him, and he seemed to me to be about the height of my lord John de Beaumont, may his soul rest in peace. And his face was all covered at that time with reddish spots. Finally he bid me speak, and our guide told us to bend the knee and speak. I bent one knee as to a man, but he made sign to me to bend both, which I did, not wishing to dispute over it. Then he bid me speak, and I, thinking I was praying God, having both knees bent, began my speech by saying: "Oh lord, we pray God from whom proceedeth all good things, and who gave you these worldly goods, to give you hereafter celestial ones, for the former without the latter are vain." And as he listened attentively, I added: "You must know for certain that you shall not have the celestial goods unless you have been a Christian; for God saith: 'He who shall have believed and have been baptized, shall be saved, but he who shall not have believed shall be condemned!' " At this he quietly smiled, and the other Moal began clapping their hands, laughing at us, and my interpreter stood dumbfounded, and I had to reassure him that he be not afraid. Then silence being reestablished, I said: "I came to your son, because we had heard that he was a Christian, and I brought him letters from the lord King of the French. He (Sartach) it is who has sent me here to you. You must know the reason why." Then he caused me to rise, and he asked your name and mine, and that of my companion and of the interpreter, and he had it all written down, and he also asked against whom you were waging war, for he had heard that you had left your country with an army. I replied: "Against the Saracens who are profaning Jerusalem, the house of God." He also asked whether you had ever sent envoys to him. "To you," I said, "never." Then he made us sit down, and had us given of his milk to drink, and they hold it to be a great honor when anyone drinks *cosmos* with him in his dwelling. While sitting there I was looking down, but he bid me turn my face up, either wishing to see me better, or on account of their sorcery, for they hold it to be a bad omen or sign, or as portending evil, if one sits before them with face turned down as if in sorrow, and especially so if he rest his chin or his cheek in his hand. Then we went out, and after a little while our guide came to us, and while conducting us to our lodging said to me: "The lord King requests that you remain in this country, but Batu may not do this without the permission of Mangu Khan. So you and your interpreter must go to Mangu Khan. As to your companion and the other man, they will go back to Sartach, where they will await your return." Then the interpreter Homo Dei began to lament, deeming himself lost, and my companion to declare that they might sooner cut off his head than separate him from me; and I said that without a companion I could not go, and moreover that we really required two servants, for should one happen to fall ill, I could not be left alone. So he went back to the court and told Batu what I had said. Then he commanded: "Let the two priests and the interpreter go, and the clerk return to Sartach." He came back and told us the decision; but when I wanted to speak about the clerk, that he might come with us, he said: "Say no more about it, for Batu has settled it, and I dare not go again to the court." The clerk Gosset had twenty-six yperpera* of your alms and no more; of these he kept ten for himself and the boy [a slave boy called Nicholas, bought at Constantinople], and he gave the sixteen others to Homo Dei for us; and so we parted from each other with tears, he going back to Sartach, and we remaining there.

---

* According to Mr. Rockhill's calculations, 26 yperpera equalled £14 and 12s. in 1900.

17

A Treaty between Novgorod and the Hanseatic League, 1270

Next to Kiev, Novgorod was the most prosperous city along the route "from the Varangians to the Greeks." Its prosperity stemmed largely from both regional and international trade. Before the twelfth century Novgorod traded mainly with Constantinople, but also with the Scandinavian countries and with Central Asia and the Middle East via the Volga River. During the thirteenth and fourteenth centuries, Novgorod's commercial relations were closely tied to the fortunes of the Hanseatic League whose merchants had their own quarter, church, and guild in Novgorod. Relations with the Hanseatic merchants were based on treaties whose terms regulated the traffic, needs of merchants, claims, debts, loss of property, and similar problems.

I, Prince Iaroslav, the son of Prince Iaroslav, with *posadnik* [mayor] Pavlo, *tysiatsky* [police officer] *Gospodin* Ratibor, city elders, and all the Novgorodians [on the one hand], and German Ambassador Heinrich Wullenpund from Lübeck, and Ludolf Dobrücke and Jacob Kuring from Gottland [on the other hand], have reviewed, approved, and signed a treaty in your language, for you Germans and Gottlanders and for all the people of the Catholic faith.

Article 1

[We have approved] the old treaty concerning travel on the Neva River between Gottland and the island of Kotlin [in the Neva] and between

From Ivan Andreevsky, ed., *O dogovore Novagoroda s nemetskimi gorodami i Gotlandom zakliuchenom v 1270 godu* (On a Treaty Concluded in 1270 between Novgorod and German Cities and Gotland) (St. Petersburg, 1855), pp. 19–34. This edition includes Russian, Middle High German, and Modern German texts. Translation mine. Items in brackets are mine.

Kotlin and Novgorod; according to this [treaty], should anything happen to a merchant coming to Novgorod during the summer, the prince and the Novgorodians will be responsible for it; those merchants who come [to Novgorod] during the winter shall receive protection from the prince, the mayor, and all the Novgorodians in accordance with a previous treaty and without any hindrances, and they shall, in accordance with the previous treaty, receive a Novgorodian commissioner and Novgorodian merchants. And should they not accept a Novgorodian commissioner then, in case something develops [on the way] between Novgorod and Kotlin, neither the prince nor the Novgorodians will be responsible for it; should the Novgorodians fail to dispatch a commissioner and should their merchants fail to go, then the Germans will leave without a commissioner and in that case they will travel directly to Kotlin in accordance with the previous treaty. Should a German or a Gottlander leave on a business venture to Karelia, and should something happen to him, the Novgorodians will not be responsible for it. Should any Novgorodian [hired by a German to go to Karelia] refuse to return by boat, then he must pay a fine of one-half of a silver mark for the trip.

Article 2

Whenever a merchant enters the Neva River and has need for either wood or a mast he has the right to cut down the necessary trees along both banks of the river wherever he wants.

Article 3

If a thief should be apprehended between Ketlingen and Aldagen, he should be taken to Aldagen and sentenced there according to the laws [of Aldagen]; but if a thief should be apprehended between Aldagen and Novgorod, he should be sentenced in Novgorod, according to the latter's laws.

Article 4

Whenever the Germans or the Gottlanders enter the Volkhov Rapids they must request, without delay, rapid pilots and take passengers on their vessels and collect from them only as much as in the past and not more.

Article 5

And when a merchant arrives at Gesteveld he should pay a tax in the amount that was customarily paid in the past and no more.

Article 6

And the pilot who is hired for the journey up and down the Neva River should receive food and five marks of *kuna*, or one *okorok*; if he is hired [for a journey] from Novgorod to Ladoga and back, he should receive food, three marks of *kuna*, or half of one *okorok*.

Article 7

Should a bark sent after goods or [loaded] with goods be destroyed, there is no need to pay for it; however, one should pay for the rent of that bark.

Article 8

Should the above mentioned pilots disagree with the merchants during their voyage up and down the river and then reconcile, let it thus be; however, should there be no reconciliation during the voyage, the entire matter should then be taken to the merchant court at Novgorod where the *tysiatsky* and other Novgorodians will try to resolve it.

Article 9

Drivers in Novgorod should be paid for every bark [load] brought from the river to Novgorod—those going to the German warehouse [should be paid] fifteen *kunas*, those to the Gottland warehouse ten *kunas*, and those leaving [Novgorod] half of one mark per bark.

Article 10

Should a Novgorodian merchant contract a debt in Gottland he should not be arrested. Equally the same treatment should apply to German and Gottland merchants in Novgorod; likewise no bailiff should be sent to them, nor clothes be collected from them, but each side should demand the presence of a city official.

Article 11

Should there develop a disagreement between the Germans and the Novgorodians, it ought to be settled at the Court of St. John with the *posadnik*, *tysiatsky*, and merchants present.

Article 12

Should someone come to either the German or the Gottland warehouse armed and wound anyone with the intent to steal a commodity and then be apprehended, he should be turned over to the court and be sentenced according to custom.

Article 13

Should anyone break a gate or a fence, he should be sentenced according to custom; if the fence was old, a new one should be installed and no additional charges made.

Article 14

Meadows that belong either to Germans or Gottlanders should be their property wherever they should decide them to be so.

Article 15

Should there develop a disagreement during the summer journey, it should not affect the winter journey; equally, disagreements on winter journeys should not affect summer journeys.

Article 16

In case summer or winter merchants should have court cases pending against them, they should settle these with city officials, the elders, or Novgorodians, and depart without delay on their journey. Should a new case develop, it should be resolved on the spot.

Article 17

Should there develop a dispute over the sequestration of property, it should be reported during the first year, but commodities should not be seized; this rule is also applicable for the second year; when the dispute is not settled by the third year, then commodities should be seized and the owner arrested.

Article 18

In case a war should develop between Novgorod and its neighboring territories, merchants are allowed [to travel] without hindrance by water and overland [routes] as far as the sovereignty of Novgorod extends. Accordingly, a merchant who travels along the Neva River should be allowed to proceed on the Neva, and those coming overland should be allowed to move along.

Article 19

In case a German and a Novgorodian should both produce witnesses, and should they both agree on the same individual, that individual's testimony should be accepted as final. But should they disagree and fail to produce a witness, then they should draw lots and he who draws the lot is the winner.

Article 20

Anyone who enters into a business transaction with either a German or a Gottlander and then either dissipates or damages his goods, must first compensate those merchants and then all those to whom he is obligated.

Article 21

In case a wife vouches for her husband, she is personally responsible with him for the debt they are unable to repay. If a wife did not vouch for her husband then she is not responsible for his debt.

Article 22

In case a Novgorodian ambassador is killed abroad, twenty marks of silver should be paid for his death; the same sum of money is to be paid for the death of a German ambassador [killed] in Novgorod or its territories.

Article 23

The above sum of twenty marks of silver should also be paid for the killing of a priest as well as for an elderman, while for a merchant the sum of ten marks of silver is to be paid.

Article 24

Whoever wounds a man with a sharp weapon or a lance should pay him a fine of one and one-half marks of silver.

Article 25

If someone strikes another on his ear or on his neck, he should pay him a fine of three *verdings* [one-half mark of silver].

Article 26

Weights and measures for silver and other goods measured on scales should be kept accurate. A *kap* [a measure of some 417 kilograms] should contain eight Livonian pounds.

18

Life in Medieval Novgorod

Novgorod is a unique phenomenon in medieval Russian history. In theory it was a principality, however, the powers of the prince were greatly limited so that in reality both the city and its possessions were governed by a merchant oligarchy. Life in the city of Novgorod was crowded, busy, exciting, and dangerous. The danger stemmed from multiple causes, of which fire, famine, foreign invasions, and bloody street fights between feuding factions of the populace were the most common.

A.D. 1124.   On the 11th day of August before evening service the sun began to decrease and it totally perished; oh, there was great terror and darkness! there were stars and the moon; then it began to re-appear and came out quickly in full; then all the city rejoiced. . . .

A.D. 1128.   . . . This year it was cruel; one *osminka* of rye cost a

From *The Chronicle of Novgorod 1016–1471*. Translated from the Russian by Robert Michell and Nevill Forbes. With an Introduction by C. Raymond Beazley, and an account of the Text by A. A. Shakhmatov. (Camden Third Series, vol. 25) (London, Royal Historical Society, 1914), pp. 10–11, 18, 22–23, 27, 31, 34–35, 37, 42, 52, 54, 58, 72, 74, 79–80, 84–87, 92–97, 110, 117–118, 137, 143–145, 153, 186–188, 204. Reprinted with permission of the publishers. Items in brackets are mine.

grivna; the people ate lime tree leaves, birch bark, pounded wood pulp mixed with husks and straw; some ate buttercups, moss, horse flesh; and thus many dropping down from hunger, their corpses were in the streets, in the market place, and on the roads, and everywhere. They hired hirelings to carry the dead out of the town; the serfs could not go out; woe and misery on all! fathers and mothers would put their children into boats in gift to [foreign] merchants, or else put them to death; and others dispersed over foreign lands. Thus did our country perish on account of our sins. This year, the water was high in the Volkhov, and carried away many houses. . . .

A.D. 1145.   There were two whole weeks of great heat, like burning sparks, before harvest; then came rain, so that we saw not a clear day till winter; and a great quantity of corn and hay they were unable to harvest; and that autumn the water was higher than three years before; and in the winter there was not much snow, and no clear day, not till March. . . .

A.D. 1157.   There was a bad tumult in the people, and they rose against *Knyaz* [Prince] Mstislav Gyurgevits, and began to drive him out of Novgorod; but the Mercantile Half [Eastern Half] stood up in arms for him; and brother quarrelled with brother; they seized the bridge over the Volkhov, and guards took their stand at the town gates, and [so did] the others on the other side; and they were within a little of shedding blood between them. And then Svyatoslav Rostislavits and David entered, and that night Mstislav fled out of the town. After three days Rostislav himself entered, and the brothers came together, and there was no harm at all. . . .

A.D. 1161.   . . . The same year the sky stood clear all summer and all the corn was scorched, and in the autumn frost killed all the spring corn.

But furthermore for our sins the evil did not stop there, but again in the winter the whole winter stood with heat and rain, and there was thunder; and we bought a little barrel for seven *kunas*. Oh, there was great distress in the people and want! . . .

A.D. 1170.   There was dearness in Novgorod; and they bought a barrel of rye at four *grivnas*, and bread at two *nogatas*, honey at ten *kunas* a *pud*. The men of Novgorod having taken counsel showed *Knyaz* Roman the road [i.e., expelled him], and themselves sent to Andrew for peace with [guarantee of] full liberty. . . .

A.D. 1181.   . . . The same year the men of Novgorod went to Dryutsk with Svyatoslav, Oleg's grandson; and at that time came Vsevolod with his whole force and with men of Murom and of Ryazan against Novitorg; and the men of Novitorg shut themselves in the town with *Knyaz* Yaropolk, and they besieged the town, and sat [there] five weeks, and they became exhausted in the town: because there was no food for them, others of them ate even horse-flesh; and they shot at *Knyaz* Yaropolk in the town, and there was great distress among them; and the men of Novitorg surrendered, and he led away Yaropolk with him, having fettered [him], and all the men of Novitorg with wives and children, and set fire to the town; and the men of Novgorod returned from Dryutsk, having set fire to the town. . . .

A.D. 1188. . . . The same winter things were dear, they bought bread for two *nogatas*, and one barrel of rye for six *grivnas*; but by God's mercy there were no ill effects among the people. The same year the men of Novgorod were plundered by the Varangians in Gothland and by the *Nemtsy* [Germans], in Khoruzhk and in Novitorg, and in the spring they let no man of their own go beyond sea from Novgorod, and gave no envoy to the Varangians, but they sent them away without peace. . . .

A.D. 1191. The men of Novgorod went in sailing vessels with the Korel people against the Yem people, and made war on their land and burned it, and cut to pieces the cattle. . . .

The same year *Knyaz* Yaroslav went to Luki, summoned by the *Knyazes* and people of Polotsk, and took with him the foremost *druzhina* of the men of Novgorod, and they met on the border and put love between each other, how in the winter they would all meet either against the Lithuanians or the Chud people. And *Knyaz* Yaroslav came to Novgorod with gifts. . . And it was in the winter, *Knyaz* Yaroslav with the men of Novgorod, of Pleskov and of his own province went against the Chud people, took the town of Gyurgev, burned their country, and brought countless plunder; and themselves all came back well to Novgorod. . . .

A.D. 1194. A fire broke out in Novgorod on All Saints' Sunday during Fast, on going to early morning service; it started in Savko's Court in Yaryshev Street, and the fire was bad, three churches were burned; . . . and many good houses; and they subdued it at Luka Street. And for our sins evil did not stop here; but on the next day it started in Cheglov Lane, and about ten houses took fire. And then more arose; on Friday in the same week during market, it started from Khrevkov Street as far as the Stream in the Nerev end, and seven churches were burnt and large houses. Thence the evil grew: every day it would start unseen at six and more places, and people dared not feed in their houses, but lived a-field; and then the *Gorodishche* [Novgorod's suburb] took fire. The same year Ladoga took fire before Novgorod, and then, too, Russa took fire; and in the Lyudin end ten courts took fire; and thus wonders continued from All Saints up to Our Lady's Day. . . .

A.D. 1200. The Lithuanians took the Lovot [River] up to [the village of] Nalyuch from Belaya [village] as far as [the villages of] Svinort and Vorch and the men of Novgorod pursued them to [the village of]

Tsernyany and fought with them and killed eighty men of the Lithuanians, and of the men of Novgorod fifteen [were killed]: . . . they [Novgorodians] recovered all the plunder and the rest escaped. The same year Nezdila Pekhtsinits went as Voyevoda to Luki; he went with a small druzhina from Luki into Lotygola [Livonia], and they found them [Livonians] in their bedrooms, killed forty men of them, took their wives and children, and themselves came all well to Luki; and from those who had not followed them from Molbovich with some of the druzhina they took money, having beaten them. . . .

A.D. 1212. Mstislav went with the men of Novgorod against the Chud people called Torma, and made many captives and brought back countless cattle. Later, in the winter, Knyaz Mstislav went with the men of Novgorod against the Chud town called Medvezhya Golova, and ruined their villages; and they came up to the town and the Chud people bowed down to the Knyaz, and he took tribute from them; and all came [back] well. . . .

A.D. 1214. On February 1, on Quinquagesima Sunday, there was thunder after morning service, and all heard it; and then at the same time they saw a flying snake. On the same day Knyaz Mstislav marched with the men of Novgorod against the Chud people to Ereva, through the land of the Chud people towards the sea, he ruined their villages and captured their forest fortresses. And he stayed with the men of Novgorod by the town of Vorobino and the Chud people bowed down to him, and Knyaz Mstislav took tribute from them; and gave two parts of the tribute to the men of Novgorod, and the third part to the courtiers. . . .

A.D. 1215. . . . The same autumn much harm was done; frost killed the corn crops throughout the district; but at Torzhok all remained whole. The Knyaz seized all the corn in Torzhok, and would not let one cartload into the city; and they sent Semen Borisovits, Vyacheslav Klinyatits, for Zubets Yakun to fetch the Knyaz and he detained them; and he detained whomever you sent. And in Novgorod it was very bad, they bought one barrel of rye for ten grivnas, one of oats for three grivnas, a load of turnips for two grivnas; people ate pine bark and lime tree leaves and moss. O brothers, then was the trouble; they gave their children into slavery. They dug a public grave and filled it full. O, there was trouble! corpses in the market place, corpses in the street, corpses in the fields; the dogs could not eat up the men! The Vod people all died; the rest were scattered. And thus for our sins our power and our town went asunder. . . .

A.D. 1217. Mstislav went away to Kiev, leaving the Knyaginya [Princess] and his son Vasili in Novgorod. . . . Then, too, Volodimir went to Novgorod on his own business, and the Lithuanians made war in Shelon. The men of Novgorod went in pursuit of them but did not reach them; and they went with *Knyaz* Volodimir and *Posadnik* [Mayor] Tverdislav to Medvezhya-Golova, and halted before the town. And the Chud people began to send greetings deceitfully, but sent for the *Nemtsy*. And the men of Novgorod began to deliberate with the men of Pleskov about the message of the Chud people; going far away from their baggage, and the night guards had come in and the day guards had not gone out, and they [the Chud people] unexpectedly attacked the baggage, and the men of Novgorod ran from their *Veche* [meeting] to the baggage, and having taken up their arms, beat them off the baggage. And the *Nemtsy* fled to the town, and the men of Novgorod killed two *Voyevodas* [leaders] and took a third with their hands; and they took 700 horses, and returned all well. And *Knyaz* Mstislav came to Novgorod without them [while they were away], and took Stanimir Dirnovits with his son, Nezdila, and having put them in fetters, imprisoned them; and seized countless quantity of goods and let them go again. The same spring, on May 31, a bakery caught fire in the middle of the morning at Ivan Yarishevits's; by midday the whole side was burnt as far as the fishery, not a house was left; and all who had fled into the stone churches with their goods were all burnt there themselves together with their goods. And in the Varangian church all the countless Varangian merchandise was burnt; fifteen churches were burnt; and the tops and the porches of the stone churches were burned. . . .

A.D. 1229. *Knyaz* Mikhail came from Chernigov to Novgorod on Holy Day, at the close of St. Thomas's Week, and the men of Novgorod were glad at their choice; and he kissed the Cross [i.e., took the oath of office] on the whole liberty of Novgorod and on all the charters of Yaroslav, and he granted the serfs freedom not to pay taxes for five years, who ever had fled to other folk's land, and those who live here he ordered to pay taxes as former *Knyazes* had fixed. And the men of Novgorod took much money from Yaroslav's favourites and the people of *Gorodishche*; they did not plunder their houses but made them give towards the building of the great bridge. The same year they began the foundation of a great bridge above the old bridge. They then took the *Posadnik*-ship from Ivanko Dmitrovits and gave it to Vnezd Vodovik; and they gave Torzhok to Ivanko; he went to Torzhok but the Novitorg people would not receive him, and thence he went to Yaroslav. . . .

A.D. 1230. . . . The same year, Stepan Tverdislavits quarrelled with Vodovik, Ivanko Timoshkinits siding with Stepan, and the *Posadnik's* servants beat Ivanko; this happened in the *Gorodishche*. And the next morning he called a *Veche* in Yaroslav's Court against the *Posadnik*, and went against his Court, and they plundered it. The *Posadnik* and Simon Borisovich again roused up the whole town against Ivanko and Yakim Vlunkovits and Proksha Lashnev; they went from the *Veche* and plundered many houses and they killed Volos Blutkinits at the *Veche*. The

Posadnik said; "Thou didst try to set fire to my Court." Proksha's Court they set fire to, and Yakim fled to Yaroslav, while others hid themselves, but they made these take oath and then let them go. And Vodovik having caught Ivanko, later killed him, casting him into the Volkhov. . .

A.D. 1234. Knyaz Yaroslav with the men of Novgorod and with the whole district, and with his own forces, went against the Nemtsy towards Yurev, and the Knyaz halted before he had reached the town with his forces, and he let his people ravage the land. But the Nemtsy issued out of the town, some staying to guard Medvezhya Golova, and fought with them right up to the main force. And God helped Knyaz Yaroslav with the men of Novgorod; and they drove them down to the river, and several of the best Nemtsy fell there; and when the Nemtsy were crossing the river Omovyzh they broke through and many were drowned; and some of the wounded escaped to Yurev, others to Medvezhya Golova. And they laid much of their land waste, and destroyed many of their crops about Yurev and Medvezhya Golova. And the Nemtsy did obeisance to the Knyaz, and Yaroslav took peace with them on his own terms, and the men of Novgorod returned all well, but some men of the Low country [area southeast of Moscow] fell. . . .

The same year the Lithuanians drove the men of Russa nearly as far as the market place and the men of Russa halted; and [there was] an ambuscade; and the citizens and body-guard and some of the merchants and traders drove them out of the town again, fighting in the field, and here they killed several of the Lithuanians, and four of the men of Russa. . . And they pillaged the whole monastery of St. Saviour, and the whole church they stripped, the images and the altar, and four monks they killed, and retired to Klin. Then the news came to Novgorod to Knyaz Yaroslav, and the Knyaz with the men of Novgorod taking to the boats, and others on horse-back, went after them up the Lovot. And when they came to the village of Moravin the boatmen turned back thence to the town; and the Knyaz let them go because they had not enough bread, and he himself with the mounted men went after them and overtook them at Dubrovna, a village in the Toropets district, and there he fought with the accursed and godless [Lithuanians]. And there God and the Holy Cross and the Holy Sophia [Church], the Mighty Wisdom of God, helped Knyaz Yaroslav and the men of Novgorod over the pagans, and they took from them 300 of their horses with their goods and they fled into the woods, having thrown down their arms and shields and lances and everything from themselves; and others fell here dead. And of the men of Novgorod they killed there ten men. . . .

A.D. 1240. The Swedes came in great strength with the Murman, Sum, and Yem people in very many ships. The Swedes came with their Knyaz and with their bishops, and halted in the Neva at the mouth of the Izhera, wishing to take possession of Ladoga, or in one word, of Novgorod, and of the whole Novgorod province. But again the most kind and merciful God, lover of men, preserved and protected us from the foreigners since they laboured in vain without the command of God. For the news came to Novgorod that the Swedes were going towards Ladoga, and Knyaz Alexander [Nevsky] with the men of Novgorod and of Ladoga did not delay at all; he went against them and defeated them by the power of St. Sophia and the prayers of our Sovereign Lady the Holy Mother of God. . . . And there was a great slaughter of Swedes. Their Voyevoda, by name Spiridon, was killed, and some thought that their bishop was also killed there; and a very great number of them fell. And having loaded two vessels with their best men got away first to sea; and the rest of them having dug a pit they threw into it without number; and many others were wounded; and the same night without waiting for the light of Monday they went away in shame. . . . And Knyaz Alexander with the men of Novgorod and of Ladoga all came back in health to their own country, preserved by God and St. Sophia, and through the prayers of all the saints.

The same year the Nemtsy with the men of Medvezhya [Golova], of Yurev, and of Velyad with Knyaz Yaroslav Volodimirich took Izborsk. And the news came to Pleskov that the Nemtsy had taken Izborsk and all the men of Pleskov went out and fought with them and the Nemtsy beat them. And there they killed the Voyevoda Gavrilo Gorislavich, and pursuing the men of Pleskov, killed many of them and others they caught with their hands. And having driven them up under the town, they burned the whole place, and there was much damage, churches, honourable ikons, books, and Gospels were burnt, and they devastated many villages around Pleskov. And they stayed near the town a week, but they did not take the town. But the children of good men they took as hostages, and went away and so they were without peace. . . .

A.D. 1242. Knyaz Alexander with the men of Novgorod and with his brother Andrei and the men of the Lower country went in the winter in great strength against the land of the Chud people, against the Nemtsy, that they might not boast, saying: "We will humble the Sloven race under us," for Pskov was already taken, and its Tiuns in prison. And Knyaz Alexander occupied all the roads right up to Pleskov; and he cleared Pleskov, seized the Nemtsy and Chud men, and having bound them in chains, sent them to be imprisoned in Novgorod, and himself went against the Chud people. And when they came to their land, he let loose his whole force to provide for themselves. And Domash Tverdi- slavich and Kerbet were scouring [the country] and the Nemtsy and Chud men met them by a bridge; and they fought there, and there they killed Domash, brother of the Posadnik, an honest man, and others with him, and others again they took with their hands, and others escaped to the troops of the *Knyaz*. And the *Knyaz* turned back to the lake and the *Nemtsy* and Chud men went after them. Seeing this, *Knyaz* Alexander and all the men of Novgorod drew up their forces by Lake Chud at Uzmen by the Raven's Rock; and the *Nemtsy* and Chud men rode at them driving themselves like a wedge through their army; and there was a great slaughter of *Nemtsy* and Chud men. And God and St. Sophia and the Holy Martyrs Boris and Gleb, for whose sake the men of Novgorod shed their blood, by the great prayers of those Saints, God helped *Knyaz* Alexander. And the *Nemtsy* fell there and the Chud men gave shoulder, and pursuing them fought with them on the ice, seven *versts* short of the Subol shore. And there fell of the Chud men a countless number; and of the *Nemtsy* 400, and fifty they took with their hands and brought to Novgorod. . . . The same year the *Nemtsy* sent with greeting, in the absence of the *Knyaz:* "The land of the Vod people, of Luga, Pleskov, and Lotygola, which we invaded with the sword, from all this we withdraw, and those of your men whom we have taken we will exchange, we will let go yours, and you let go ours." And they let go the Pleskov hostages, and made peace. . . .

A.D. 1245. . . . The Lithuanians made ravages about Torzhok and Bezhitsy, and the men of Novitorg with *Knyaz* Yaroslav Volodimirovich chased and fought them; and they took the horses from the men of Novitorg, and beat the men themselves and went away with their plunder. And Yavid and Erbet with the men of Tver and of Dmitrov, and Yaroslav with the men of Novitorg, pursued them and beat them near Toropets, and the sons of their *Knyaz* took refuge in Toropets.

The next morning Alexander came up with men of Novogorod and took away all the plunder, and slew more than eight of their *Knyaz's* sons. And from there the men of Novgorod turned back; but the *Knyaz* pursued them [Lithuanians] with his own court and defeated them near [the village of] Zizech, and did not let a single man go, and there he killed the rest of the *Knyaz's* sons. And he himself took his own son from Vitebsk and went with a small company and met another force at lake Vosvyat; and there God helped him, and he destroyed those two and himself returned well and his company also. . . .

A.D. 1253. The Lithuanians ravaged the district of Novgorod and went off with captives, and the men of Novgorod with *Knyaz* Vasili overtook them at Toropets; and so Christian blood was avenged on them. And they defeated them and took back the captives from them, and returned well to Novgorod. The same year the *Nemtsy* came to Pleskov and burned the town, but the men of Pleskov killed many of them. And the men of Novgorod went out to them in arms from Novgorod, and they ran away; and the men of Novgorod having come to Novgorod, and having armed and prepared themselves, went beyond the Narova and laid waste their district; and the Korel people also did much harm to their districts. And the same year they went with the men of Pleskov to ravage them, and they put out a force against them; and the men of Novgorod with the men of Pleskov defeated them by the power of the honourable cross; for they began it against themselves, the accursed transgressors of right; and they sent to Pleskov and to Novgorod desiring peace on all the terms laid down by Novgorod and Pleskov. And so they made peace. . . .

A.D. 1257. Evil news came from Russia, that the Tartars desired the *tamga* [a customs tax] and tithe on Novgorod; and the people were agitated the whole year. And at Lady-day *Posadnik* Anani died, and in the winter the men of Novgorod killed *Posadnik* Mikhalko. If anyone does good to another, then good would come of it; but digging a pit under another, he falls into it himself.

The same winter Tartar envoys came with Alexander, and Vasili fled to Pleskov; and the envoys began to ask the tithe and the *tamga* and the men of Novgorod did not agree to this, and gave presents to the *Tsar* [the Tartar khan], and let the envoys go with peace.

And *Knyaz* Alexander drove his son out of Pleskov and sent him to the Low Country, and punished Alexander and his company. He cut off the noses of some, and took out the eyes of others, of those who had led Vasili to evil; for evil every man shall perish evilly!

The same winter they killed Misha. The same winter they gave the *Posadnik*-ship to Mikhail Fedorovich, having brought him out of Ladoga, and they gave the post of *Tysyatski* [commander of Novgorod's militia] to Zhirokha.

A.D. 1258. The Lithuanians with the men of Polotsk came to Smolensk and took [the town of] Voishchina by assault. The same autumn the Lithuanians came to Torzhok, and the men of Novitorg issued out. For our sins the Lithuanians ambushed them; some they killed, others they took with their hands, and others barely escaped; and there was much evil in Torzhok. The same winter the Tartars took the whole Lithuanian land, and killed the people.

A.D. 1259. There was a sign in the moon; such as no sign had ever been. The same winter Mikhail Pineshchinich came from the Low Country with a false mission, saying thus: "If you do not number yourselves for tribute there is already a force in the Low Country." And the men of Novgorod did number themselves for tribute. The same winter the accursed raw-eating Tartars, Berkai and Kasachik, came with their wives, and many others, and there was a great tumult in Novgorod, and they did much evil in the province, taking contribution for the accursed Tartars. And the accursed ones began to fear death; they said to Alexander: "Give us guards, lest they kill us." And the *Knyaz* ordered the son of the *Posadnik* and all the sons of the *Boyars* to protect them by night. The Tartars said: "Give us your numbers for tribute or we will run away [and return in greater strength]." And the common people would not give their numbers for tribute but said: "Let us die honourably for St. Sophia and for the angelic houses." Then the people were divided: who was good stood by St. Sophia and by the True Faith; and they made opposition; the greater men bade the lesser be counted for tribute. And the accursed ones wanted to escape, driven by the Holy Spirit, and they devised an evil counsel how to strike at the town at the other side, and the others at this side by the lake; and Christ's power evidently forbade them, and they durst not. And becoming frightened they began to crowd to one point to St. Sophia, saying: "Let us lay our heads by St. Sophia." And it was on the morrow, the *Knyaz* rode down from the *Gorodishche* and the accursed Tartars with him, and by the counsel of the evil they numbered themselves for tribute; for the *Boyars* thought it would be easy for themselves, but fall* hard on the lesser men. And the accursed ones began to ride through the streets, writing down the Christian houses; because for our sins God has brought wild beasts out of the desert to eat the flesh of the strong, and to drink the blood of *Boyars*. And having numbered them for tribute and taken it, the accursed ones went away, and *Knyaz* Alexander followed them, having set his son Dmitri on the throne. . . .

A.D. 1287. There was a great tumult in Novgorod against Semeon Mikhailovich; all Novgorod rose against him without just cause, they went out against him from all the quarters, like a strong army, every man armed, in great strength, a pitiful sight! and thus they went against his house and took his whole house with uproar. Semeon fled to the *Vladyka* [Bishop] and the *Vladyka* led him into St. Sophia; and thus God preserved him; and on the morrow they came together in love. . . .

A.D. 1311. The men of Novgorod went in war over sea to the country of the *Nemtsy* [in this case Finland], against the Yem people, with *Knyaz* Dmitri Romanovich, and having crossed the sea they first occupied the Kupets River, they burned villages, and captured people and destroyed the cattle. And there Konstantin, the son of Ilya Stanimirovich was killed by a column that went in pursuit. They then took the whole of the Black River, and thus following along the Black River they reached the town of Vanai and they took the town and burned it. And the *Nemtsy* fell back into the Detinets [citadel]: for the place was very strong and firm, on a high rock, not having access from any side. And they sent with greeting, asking for peace, but the men of Novgorod did not grant peace, and they stood three days and three nights, wasting the district. They burned the large villages, laid waste all the cornfields, and did not leave a single horn of cattle; and going thence, they took the Kavgola River and the Perna River, and they came out on the sea and returned all well to Novgorod.

The same spring, on May 19, a fire broke out at night in Yanev Street, and forty less three houses were burnt and seven people. Then in the night of June 28 Glebov's house in Rozvazha Street caught fire, and the Nerev quarter was burnt, on one side so far as the fosse, and on the other beyond Borkov Street; and the Church of SS. Kosma and Demyan was burnt, also that of St. Sava, and forty churches were damaged by fire and several good houses. Oh, woe, brethren, the conflagration was fierce, with wind and hurricane! And wicked and bad men having no fear of God, seeing people's ruin, plundered other men's property. Then on July 16 a fire broke out at night in the Ilya Street, and here likewise was a fierce conflagration with a high wind, and crashing noise; the market place was burnt, and houses up to Rogatitsa Street, and the churches burnt were—seven wooden churches. . . .

A.D. 1342. The same year the men of Pleskov gave themselves over to Lithuania, renouncing Novgorod, and the *Veliki Knyaz*. They fetched into their midst *Knyaz* Olgert from Lithuania, son of Gedymin, with the Lithuanians; they had first turned out Alexander Vsevolodits. And Olgert and his son baptised in the name of Andrei, and he set him in Pleskov, and himself departed to Lithuania.

The same year the men of Pleskov beat the *Nemtsy*, pursuing them up to their town Novogrodek on the border, killing about 300 of them. And the *Nemtsy* came in great strength to Izborsk with battering rams, and stood before the town eleven days and nearly took it; but they killed many *Nemtsy*, and there also they killed Voinev, son of the Lithuanian *Knyaz*, and several Lithuanians and men of Izborsk fell; and the *Nemtsy* withdrew.

The same year a fire broke out in Novgorod in Danislav Street, extending along the bank to the fosse, and up the hill to the Churches of the Forty Saints and SS. Kuzma and Damian, and three churches were burnt, St. Nikola and the stone Church of St. Yakov; and a watchman also was burnt there, and good man Esif Davidovich; the third was the Church of St. Georgi; and much evil was done. And the people took fright, and dared not dwell in the town, but over the fields, others settled on the water-meadows, others along the banks, in boats. And the whole town was to be seen in motion; the people wandered about for a week and longer; people endured much harm and loss at the hands of miscreants who fear not God. . . .

A.D. 1350. The men of Novgorod went to war against the *Nemtsy*, with Boris the son of the lieutenant, Ivan Fedorovich the *Tysyatski*, the *Voyevodas* Mikhail Danilovich, Yuri Ivanovich, and Yakov Khotov; and came to the town of Viborg on Monday the 21st day of March, and burned the whole of the town. On the next day the *Nemtsy* came out of the town and the men of Novgorod fell on them and the *Nemtsy* fled into the town, and there they killed several *Nemtsy*, and ravaged and burned the district near the town and killed many *Nemtsy*, both women and children, and took others alive; and they returned to Novgorod all well.

The same year the men of Novgorod went to Yurev, and made an exchange with the *Nemtsy* of the Swedish captives taken at Orekhov for Avraam and Kuzma, Alexander and Andrei and the company who had been over sea in the Swedish King Magnush's country. And they returned all well to Novgorod by the mercy of God, and by the power of the honourable Cross in which they trusted. . . .

The same year the men of Novgorod drove *Posadnik* Fedor out of Novgorod, together with his brother Mikhail, and Yuri and Ondreyan; their houses they pillaged, and they plundered the whole of Prussian Street. And Fedor, Mikhail, Yuri and Ondreyan fled to Pskov, and after being there a short while they went to Koporya. . . .

A.D. 1352. . . . There was a great plague in Pleskov. The same year envoys arrived in Novgorod from Pleskov calling the *Vladyka* to Pleskov to bless the people. And the *Vladyka* heard their prayer and went and blessed the people of Pleskov, and on his way back to Novgorod going from Pleskov he was seized with a severe illness, and died at the Uza River on the 3d day of July. . . .

The same year there was a great plague [the Black Death] in Novgorod; it came on us by God's loving kindness, and in His righteous judgment, death came upon people, painful and sudden, it began from Lady Day till Easter; a countless number of good people died then. These were the symptoms of that death: a man would spit blood and after three days he was dead. But this death did not visit Novgorod alone; I believe it passed over the face of all the land. . . .

A.D. 1372. The men of Novgorod went to Torzhok to build up the town [that was completely burnt in 1371]; and they sent Mikhail's lieutenants away from Torzhok. And *Knyaz* Mikhail came with a force to Torzhok, and burned the whole town, and the Christians suffered great distress: some were burnt with fire in their houses with their property, others took refuge in St. Saviour's, and were there suffocated; very many were burnt, others escaping from the fire were drowned in the Tvertsa River. And good women and girls foreseeing their violation at the hands of the men of Tver, for they were stripping them to utter nakedness, as even the pagans did not do, from shame and grief drowned themselves in the river; monks and nuns were all stripped. First of all Alexander Obakunovich met them in the open, and there laid his bones for St. Saviour and for the wrongs of Novgorod; and with him they killed Ivan Shakhovich and another Ivan Timofeich, and Grigori Shchebelkov; and several others fell there, but some escaped. Others again were taken, and were led away captives to Tver, men and women, a countless number. They also took a great deal of property, what was left from the fire, and many of the silver frames from off the pictures. And who, my brethren, can help grieving over this? Those who remained alive, seeing how those others suffered violent and bitter death, the churches burnt and the town utterly laid waste: for such wrongdoing had never been suffered even from the pagans. And they filled five pits with dead bodies of the killed, drowned and burnt; and others were burnt so that nothing was left, and others drowned without being heard of, and floated down the river Tvertsa. . . .

A.D. 1418. The same month [April] this happened in Novgorod at the instigation of the devil: a certain man Stepanko seized hold of the *Boyar* Danilo Ivanovich, Bozha's grandson, and, holding him, cried out to the people: "Here, sirs! help me against this miscreant." And seeing his cry folk dragged him like a miscreant to the people, beating him with wounds nearly to death, and they led him from the *Veche* and hurled him from the bridge. And a certain man from the people, Lichko's son, wishing him well, caught him up into his boat; but the people, enraged against that fisherman, plundered his house. And the aforesaid *Boyar*, wishing to avenge his dishonour, caught the impostor and put him to torture, and wishing to cure the evil raised up still greater trouble; I will not recall the spoken words: "Vengeance is mine." And the people learning that Stepanko had been seized, began to summon a *Veche* in Yaroslav's Court, and a multitude of people assembled, and they kept shouting and crying for many days: "Let us go against that *Boyar* and plunder his house." And they came armed and with a banner to Kuzma Demyan Street, sacked his house and many other houses, and ravaged the quay in Yanev Street. And the people of Kuzma Demyan Street became afraid at these robberies that worse would befall them, surrendered Stepanko, and coming to the *Vladyka* prayed him to send him to the meeting of the people. And the prelate heard their prayer and sent him with a priest and one of his own *Boyars*, and they received him. And again they became enraged like drunkards, against another *Boyar*, Ivan Yevlich, of Chudinets Street, and on his account pillaged a great many *Boyars*' houses, as well as the monastery of St. Nikola in the Field crying out: "Here is the treasure house of the *Boyars*." And again the same morning they plundered many houses in the Lyudgoshcha Street, calling out: "They are our enemies." And they came to Prussian Street, but there they beat them off successfully. And from that hour the mischief began to increase. Returning to their own, the commercial side, they said: "The Sophia side is going to arm against us, and to plunder our houses." And they began to ring throughout the whole town, and armed men began to pour out from both sides as for war, fully armed, to the great bridge. And there was loss of life too. Some fell by arrows, others by arms, they died as in war, the whole town trembled at this terrible storm and great rebellion and a dread fell on the people on both sides. And *Vladyka* Simeon shed tears from his eyes on hearing of the

internecine war between his children, and he ordered those under him
to gather his congregation; and the Vladyka, having entered the Church
of St. Sophia, began to pray with tears, and arraying himself in his vestments with his clergy he ordered them to take the Lord's Cross and the
image of the Holy Mother of God, and went to the bridge, and there
followed him the priests and servants of the church and all who called
themselves Christians, and a great multitude, shedding tears and saying:
"O Lord, make it to cease by the prayers of our lord." And God-fearing
people fell in tears at the feet of the prelate saying: "Go, lord, and may
the Lord cause this internecine war to cease, through thy blessing." And
others said: "May this evil be on the heads of those who began the fighting." And on reaching the middle of the bridge the prelate raised the
life-giving Cross and began to bless both sides. And those who looked
at the honourable Cross wept. The opposite side, hearing of the prelate's
arrival, Posadnik Fedor Timofeich came with other Posadniks and
Tysyatskis and bowed to the Vladyka; and the Vladyka heard their
prayer and sent the Archimandrite Varlam and his spiritual father, and
an archdeacon to Yaroslav's Court to bestow the blessing on the acting
Posadnik Vasili Esifovich and on the Tysyatski Kuzma Terenteyevich to
go to their homes; and they dispersed through the prayers of the Holy
Mother of God and with the blessing of Vladyka Simeon, and there was
peace in the town. . . .

A.D. 1446. Tsar Mahmed let the Veliki Knyas Vasili return to the
Russian Land, taking a ransom of two hundred thousand roubles; and
what else, God knows, and they.

That same year the people began to find fault with the silver coinage,
till all the men of Novgorod looked one at the other, there was tumult
and rebellion and animosity amongst them.

And the Posadnik and the Tysyatski and all Novgorod appointed five
minters, and they began to re-mould the old coins and to mint new coins
of the same value: of the same weight of four pochki, and half a denga
was taken off the new grivna. There was much distress and loss among
the Christians in the town and in the districts. And this will not be forgotten even in the last generations.

The same year, on January 3, there were heavy clouds with rain, and
wheat and rye and corn were beaten down altogether [the autumn-sown
crops], both in the fields, and in the forests, all round the town for five
versts from the Volkhovets [river], and as far as the Msta river, for fifteen
versts. The people bore into the town whatever they could gather up;
and the townspeople collected to see this curious marvel, whence and
how it came.

part 2

MOSCOVITE RUSSIA

19

Moscow's First Successful Challenge of the Mongols, 1380

The "Mongol Yoke," as the period from 1238 to 1480 is known in Russian history, was a bitter experience for the population and many attempts were made to terminate it. As long as the Golden Horde was united and powerful, successful revolts against the Mongols were impossible. In the second half of the fourteenth century, however, the Horde began to show signs of disintegration from within. This development offered an opportunity to throw off the "yoke." In 1380, Prince Dmitri Donskoi (1359–1389) defeated the Mongols at Kulikovo. It proved to be a short victory, for the Mongols recovered from the defeat, overwhelmed Moscow's forces in 1382, and it was only in 1480 that Mongol domination finally came to an end.

That year [1380] Prince Mamai of the [Golden] Horde, accompanied by other princes and all the Tartar and Polovtsi forces, and joined by such mercenaries as: the Turks, Armenians, Genoese, Cherkessians, Burtasians, and supported by [Grand Prince] of Lithuania Iagello and [Prince] Oleg of Riazan, advanced against Grand Prince Dmitri, and on September 1, made a camp on the bank of the Oka River. Oleg

From *Polnoe Sobranie Russkikh Letopisei* (*Complete* Collection of Russian Chronicles) (St. Petersburg, 1885), vol. 23, pp. 124–127. Translation mine. Items in brackets are mine.

supplied everything to Mamai and to Iagello through Epiphan Koreev. Grand Prince [Dmitri] was informed about all this in August [1380]. Following this, Oleg, like Judas, informed the Grand Prince about Mamai's preparation against him. Having learned this, the Grand Prince went to the Church of the Mother of God, where he prayed for a long time; after he had finished he sent for all the Russian princes, voevodas, and all the people, and having collected his own force of 100,000, excluding those of the Russian princes and local voevodas, he went to Kolomna. There never was such a mighty Russian army, for all forces combined numbered some 200,000. With him, [Dmitri] was Andrei Olgerdoyich [Prince of Pskov] with his people and [Andrei's brother] Dmitri [Prince of Briansk] with his people. Mamai's camp was in a meadow, not far from the Don where, with all of his forces he awaited for about three weeks the arrival of Iagello; to the Grand Prince, Mamai sent [a message] demanding the tribute which had existed during the reign of Dzhanibek Khan [1342–1357]; the Grand Prince wanted to give him a tribute from the Christian force, but this he did not want to accept. Oleg, however, paid him a tribute and also sent to him some of his forces; Grand Prince Dmitri offered a prayer at the Church of the Holy Virgin, received a blessing from Bishop Herasim, left Kolomna on August 20, and upon arriving at the mouth of the Lopastra River [left tributary of the Oka] he received information about the heathens. There at last he also received Prince Vladimir Andreevich [his half-brother] and Timofei [a voevoda from Vladimir]; here they crossed the river a week before St. Simeon's Day and a week later, on September 6, they reached the River Don. Then he [Dmitri] received a letter from the Reverend Abbot Sergei [founder of the Troitsk Monastery] urging him to fight the Tartars; Dmitri, however, ordered his troops to put on their native garments while he himself waited for a long time, contemplating. Some said, "Let us go beyond the Don"; but others opposed it say, "If we do, our enemies will increase, from the Tartars to the Lithuanians and to the people of Riazan." When Mamai learned of the arrival of the Grand Prince at the Don . . . he said, "Let us move toward the Don before Iagello arrives there." The Grand Prince ordered bridges built across the Don and a search by night for fords, and early Saturday morning, on September 8, he told his troops to cross the river and go to the meadow. At first there was a heavy fog but when it later disappeared everyone crossed the Don; there was a real multitude of troops as far as one could see, extending all the way to the mouth of the Nepriadva River. At six o'clock in the morning the godless Tartars appeared in the field and faced the Christians. There was a great multitude of both; and when these two great forces met they covered an area thirteen versts long. And there was a great massacre and bitter warfare and great noise, such as there never had been in Russian principalities; and they fought from six to nine, and blood flowed like a heavy rain and there were many killed on both sides. At nine o'clock God took mercy on the Christians; many saw an angel and saintly martyrs helping the Christians; even the godless [i.e., the Tartars] saw regiments moving in the air and hitting mercilessly. Shortly thereafter the godless fled and the Christians pursued them, hitting them until they reached the Mecha River; regiments of the Prince pursued the Tartars to their camp where they took all of their wealth and their cattle, killing many and trampling others. It was here that many Russians lost their lives. . . .

The Grand Prince himself was very fortunate, for, although he had fought the Tartars from the very beginning, he received no wounds to his body. His *voevodas* told the Prince, "Lord, do not stay at the front; go either to the rear or to the side, or to a safe place." He, however, replied: "I will neither protect my face nor hide in the rear, but let us all brothers fight together. I want to die for Christianity ahead of anyone else, with deed as well as word, so that all others who see it will become bold." He did what he said. He fought ahead of everyone else, striking to the right and to the left, killing many; he himself was surrounded by many [Tartars] and was hit many times on his head and his body but God protected him from everything. Lithuanian Prince Iagello came to Mamai's aid with all of his Lithuanian and Latvian forces one day too late; when he heard what had happened to the Tartars and that Mamai had fled, he [Iagello] fled back with all of his force. The Grand Prince remained overnight at the Tartar-deserted camp which was full of their bodies, where he, together with his troops, thanked God [for victory]; in the morning he departed for his land. There he was informed that Prince Oleg of Riazan had sent his force to aid Mamai, that he had destroyed bridges across the rivers and that he had robbed and stripped of everything all those subjects of the Grand Prince who crossed his land [Riazan]. The Grand Prince wanted to send an army [against Riazan]. But at about that time the *boyars* from Riazan came to him and told him that Prince Oleg had fled from his principality with his wife and children; and the *boyars* paid homage and prayed him not to attack them. He accepted them and sent his governors to Riazan.

Mamai, angered, arrived in his territory with his few remnants and began collecting a new force in an effort to undertake a new expedition against Rus. He received news, however, that Khan Tokhtamysh from the Ak-Orde was advancing against him from the east. Mamai went to meet him and both forces met at the River Kalka and began to fight. Mamai's princes dismounted from their horses and joined Tokhtamysh. When Mamai saw this he fled, but Tokhtamysh ordered a pursuit. He fled to Kafa [in Crimea] where he asked protection, which he received. He took much gold, wealth, and silver with him, and after a period of flattery ended, the people of Kafa killed him. Khan Tokhtamysh advanced, took his [Mamai's] camp and his wives, and divided his treasury among his troops. He sent his ambassadors to Rus, to the Grand Prince, and to all Russian princes, informing them that, having defeated Mamai, he had ascended the Khanate of the Golden Horde. They received his ambassadors with dignity, and in the spring they sent to him their own ambassadors with many gifts.

20

Restrictions
on Peasant Movement

In general, serfdom in Russia developed slowly from two basic sources: obligations which princes and nobles imposed upon free peasants; and government decrees which sought to limit free movement of the peasantry. The following two decrees, dating from about 1450 and 1463–1468, are the earliest known official documents which paved the way to serfdom in Russia. By the terms of these decrees, Russian peasants were allowed to leave or change their masters only during a designated time, that is, about November 26, after the harvest and the fulfillment of other annual obligations toward their masters. This freedom was of little real value, for by late November the full fury of the Russian winter would have a hampering effect.

From *Akty, sobrannye v arkhivakh Rossiiskoi imperii Arkheograficheskoiu ekspeditsieiu imp. Akademii nauk* (*Documents Collected in Libraries and Archives of the Russian Empire by the Archeographic Expedition of the Imperial Academy of Sciences*) (St. Petersburg, 1836), vol. 1, no. 48 and *Akty sotsialnoekonomicheskoi istorii Severo-Vostochnoi Rusi kontsa XIV i nachala XVI v.* (*Documents on Socio-Economic History of North Eastern Rus from the End of the 14th to the Beginning of the 16th Century*), Moscow: Akademiia Nauk, 1952, vol. 1, no. 338, p. 245. Translation mine. Items in brackets are mine.

[An instruction] from Prince Michael Aleksandrovich [1432–1486] of Beloozero to [my] governor, all *boyars*, lesser nobility, inhabitants of the region, administrators of my *votchinas*, and everyone without exception. My [spiritual] father, Abbot Kasian of the Kirilov Monastery, has petitioned me, and has informed me that you entice his financial debtors, sharecroppers, and persons hired for a given task as well as those hired for the entire year; [he has informed me that] you entice these people not during the period of St. George's Day [November 26], but around Christmas and some on St. Peter's Day [June 29]. Do not entice financial debtors, sharecroppers, and monastery peasants. You may entice financial debtors and sharecroppers on St. George's Day only if they have paid their debt; after St. George's Day do not entice financial debtors; when he pays his debt, yes. I have instructed the abbot not to release debtors after St. George's Day. Whoever shall disobey this decree shall be fined.

* * *

[An instruction] from Grand Prince Ivan Vasilevich to Prince Ivan Vasilevich, my *boyar* and *namestnik* in Iaroslavl, to your *volost* administrative assistants, and to your steward.

The abbot of the Troitsk-Sergeev Monastery, with his brothers, has informed me that you accept people from his villages of Fedorovsk and Nerekhta as well as other [villages] during the entire year and that you then dispatch them to my possessions in Iaroslavl. As his Grand Prince I have granted his petition [and am instructing you] not to accept [in the future] any people from his village of Fedorovsk as well as other villages into the Iaroslavl district during any other time than St. George's Day [November 26]. And whoever should leave [monastery estates] on other than St. George's Day, I am ordering you to return him. Do not accept any people during the rest of the year; whoever wants to come from monastery estates to my estate in Iaroslavl, you may accept him only during two weeks of the year—one week before and one week after St. George's Day. But do not, in accordance with this instruction, accept anyone during any other time of the year. Read this instruction [to the people who will come to you] and send them back and he [the abbot] will keep them thereafter.

Grand Prince

21

Ivan III's Conquest of Novgorod in 1471

One of the most startling successes of Ivan III's reign (1462–1505) was the relatively easy absorption of the city and territories of Novgorod. The underlying causes of Moscow's triumph were fourfold: the rise of Moscovy's ambition to "gather Russian lands"; Novgorod's lack of adequate defenses; constant feuds between the members of ·the ruling oligarchy; and Ivan's effective control of Novgorod's food supplies. However, the immediate factor was the decision of Novgorod's ruling group to seek aid and protection from a Catholic Lithuanian Prince. This action was interpreted as treason to Orthodox Christianity, both by Ivan and by the lower strata of Novgorod's population. Ivan conquered the city in 1471 and absorbed it fully into his state by 1475. The following account of the suppression of Novgorod's independence was edited by Ivan the Terrible in the sixteenth century.

A.D. 1471. The Veliki Knyaz Ioan Vasilievich marched with a force against Novgorod the Great because of its wrong doing and lapsing into Latinism.

Concerning these [people of Novgorod] this is a copy of the introductory words to the narrative of the first taking [of Novgorod] by the Veliki Knyaz Ioan Vasilievich of all Russia [Ivan III], the grandfather of the Veliki Knyaz Ioan Vasilievich [Ivan the Terrible] of all Russia, when there were dissensions in Great Novgorod.

Reprinted with permission of the Royal Historical Society from *The Chronicle of Novgorod, 1016–1471*, translated from the Russian by Robert Michell and Nevill Forbes. With an Introduction by C. Raymond Beazley, and an account of the Text by A. A. Shakhmatov. (Camden Third Series, vol. 25) (London, Royal Historical Society, 1914), pp. 205–220. Items in brackets are mine.

King of kings, and Lord of lords, God supreme and ruling and strong, Owner and Creator of all, our Lord Jesus Christ, keep everlasting kingdom, having neither beginning nor end. That one only is all powerful whom the Creator of Heaven and earth and all else may create of His own will; power and glory he is pleased to give to him, the sceptres of empire He entrusts him with, and by His mercifulness establishes all virtue, and pours his grace on all who fear him. It is written in the old books as it was said: "A country wishing to be ruled in the face of God sets up a prince who is pious and just, regardful of his kingdom and of the governing the land, and loving justice and truth." Of those, it is said, who in goodness build earthly [kingdoms] receive also a heavenly one. Truly has the Lord God of His unspeakable mercy with His life-bearing right hand raised a chief over the God-loved Russian Land, who maintains it in truth and piety, whose honourable head is filled with wisdom, who has organized it like to a lamp of illumination of piety, a promoter of truth, a guardian of godly law, a strong champion of Orthodoxy, the honourable, pious and trusty *Veliki Knyaz* Ioan Vasilievich [Ivan III] of all Russia. The Lord God and the most pure Mother of God by their unspeakable mercy have committed to him the prosperity and the strengthening of all; extending their godly mercy through shedding the light of religion over Russian Lands.

Likewise it is written. Length of days, and long life and peace shall be added to thee, and he found favour and was beloved for his righteous acts, the *Veliki Knyaz* of all Russia, Ioan Vasilievich; yet the deceitful people would not submit to him; stirred by a savage pride, the men of Novgorod would not obey their sovereign *Veliki Knyaz*, until they were reminded of the great piety of old times told to them. For that reason did their fame abate, and their face was covered with shame: by reason of the men of Novgorod leaving the light and giving themselves over in their pride to the darkness of ignorance, saying that they would draw away and attach themselves to the Latins.

Thus have these inclined away from their sovereign the *Veliki Knyaz*, wishing to give themselves over to the Latin king, bringing evil to all Orthodoxy. The pious sovereign and *Veliki Knyaz* of all Russia, Ioan Vasilievich, has frequently sent his messengers to them, calling on them to keep his patrimony from all harm, to improve themselves in all things within his ancestral estates, and to live according to old custom. He suffered much in these things from their vexatious ways and contumacy within his paternal domains, while he expected from them a thorough amendment of their conduct towards himself and a respectful submission.

And again when the Novgorod *Posadnik* Vasili Ananin came as envoy from Great Novgorod, the patrimony of the *Veliki Knyaz*, laying before him all the affairs of Novgorod, he did not say a single word of the ill-

behaviour of the men of Novgorod and of their failure to amend their
ways, but in reply to the *Boyars* of the *Veliki Knyaz* Vasili he said:
"Under that head I have no instructions from Great Novgorod, and I
have no orders to speak." The sovereign *Veliki Knyaz* was sorely aggrieved
by their churlishness, who, while sending to him men from his patrimonial domains to implore favours, bear themselves with insolence and
are unmindful of their misbehaviour. Therefore has the *Veliki Knyaz* laid
his anger upon them, upon the land of his inheritance, upon Great
Novgorod, and he has commanded Vasili, the Novgorod envoy, to tell
Great Novgorod: "Mend your ways towards me, my patrimony, and
recognize us; encroach not on my lands and my waters, and keep my
name of *Veliki Knyaz* in strictness and in honour as of old; and send to
me, the *Veliki Knyaz*, representatives to do homage and to make settlement. I desire to keep you, my patrimony, in good favour, on the old
conditions." With that he dismissed him, informing his patrimony
that his power of endurance was exhausted, and that he would not suffer
their misbehaviour and contumacy any longer.

The *Veliki Knyaz* sent also to Pskov, his patrimony, repeating the
same words and with commands to acquaint Pskov with the opposition
to him of his patrimony Great Novgorod, and to say: "If you send to
me, the *Veliki Knyaz*, with due homage, then I will hold them in my
favour; but if my patrimony, Great Novgorod, fails in so doing, then
must you be ready to act against them with me." And after this the
Vladyka [bishop] Ioan of Great Novgorod and of Pskov died amóngst
them, and the men of Novgorod chose the monk Feofil [Theophilus] as
their father to occupy his place, without reference to the *Veliki Knyaz*
Ivan Vasilievich of all Russia. And it was after this selection that they
sent their *Boyar*, Nikita Savin, to the *Veliki Knyaz* Ivan Vasilievich of
all Russia to ask on behalf of Great Novgorod, the patrimony of the
Veliki Knyaz, for letters of safe conduct; and Nikita in the name also of
all Great Novgorod prayed Filip the Metropolitan of all Russia and the
spiritual father of the *Veliki Knyaz*, as well as the *Knyaginya* Marya, the
mother of the *Veliki Knyaz*, to intercede for them with the *Veliki
Knyaz*, in obtaining guarantee of security in submitting their petition
for Feofil whom the men of Novgorod had nominated, for the *Posadniks*
and *Tysyatskis* and *Boyars* who would come to Moscow to do homage
to the *Veliki Knyaz* and to obtain confirmation of Feofil as *Vladyka* of
Novgorod the Great and of Pskov, with the white hood, that they might
all depart again in freedom. The *Veliki Knyaz* acceeding to the solicita-
tions of his spiritual father the Metropolitan and of his mother the
Knyaginya Marya, granted letters of security and withdrew his displeasure
from his patrimony Great Novgorod. Yet the men of Novgorod, gone
mentally astray, and forgetful of this, went not in fear of God's words
spoken to the whole congregation of the children of Israel.

Those ancient Israelites hearkened not to the words of God, and they did not obey his commandments; they were therefore deprived of the promised land and were scattered over many countries. Thus also the people of Novgorod, enraged by the pride in them, followed in the ways of the old desertion and have been false to their sovereign the *Veliki Knyaz*, choosing to have a Latin ruler as their sovereign, and having before that accepted from him in Great Novgorod the *Knyaz* Mikhail Alexandrovich of Kiev, keeping him a long time in Novgorod, doing offence in this wise to their sovereign Ivan Vasilievich the *Veliki Knyaz* of all Russia. By their artful devices they won over evilly inclined men, who were thus caught in the nets of the snarer and destroyer of the soul of man, the many-headed beast and cunning enemy, the devil; like a living hell has he devoured them by his evil counsel.

That tempter the devil entered in their midst into the wily Marfa [Martha] Boretskaya, widow of Isaak Boretski, and that accursed [woman] entangled herself in words of guile with the Lithuanian *Knyaz* Mikhail. On his persuasion she intended to marry a Lithuanian *Boyar*, to become Queen, meaning to bring him to Great Novgorod and to rule with him under the suzerainty of the King over the whole of the Novgorod region.

This accursed Marfa like to them beguiled the people, diverting them from the right way to Latinism, for the dark deceits of Latinism blinded her soul's eyes through the wiles of the cunning devil and the wicked imaginings of the Lithuanian *Knyaz*. And being of one mind with her, prompted to evil by the proud devil Satan, Pimin the monk and the almoner of the old *Vladyka*, the cunning [man], engaged with her in secret whispering and helped her in every wickedness, seeking to take the place of his lord as *Vladyka* of Great Novgorod during his life, having suffered much punishment for his rogueries; his desire had not been gratified, inasmuch as the Lord God had not favoured him in the drawing of the lot, and he was not, therefore, accepted by the people for the high office. That wicked man is like Peter the Stammerer, the first perverter of the faith, or like the ancient *Farmos*, those originators of the Latin heresies; and they were followed in our time by the apostate Metropolitan Isidor who attended the eighth *Veche* of Rome at Florence [i.e., Council of Florence, 1438–1439], tempted by the Pope's gold and coveting a cardinalship, seceding to Latinism. Among these is also Grigori, his apostate pupil, who is now in Kiev called Metropolitan; but he is not received into our great Orthodox church of the Russian Land, but excluded.

This cunning monk Pimin sought his appointment by the apostate Grigori, spreading it among the people that he should be sent to Kiev where he would receive his confirmation, being unmindful of the words in the Holy Gospels spoken by the lips of our Lord: "He that entereth not by the door into the sheep-fold, but climbeth up some other way, the same is a thief and a robber." Now this cunning man not only sought like a wolf to climb over the fence into the sheep-fold of the house of Israel, but to scatter and to destroy God's church; and he in this wise ruined the whole of the Novgorod land, the accursed one. According to the Prophet: "He made not God his strength, but trusted in the abundance of his riches and strengthened himself in his wickedness." This Pimin did similarly trust in the abundance of his riches, giving of them also to the crafty woman Marfa, and ordering many people to give money to her to buy over the people to their will; and this accursed wicked serpent fearing not God and having no shame before man, has spread destruction throughout all the Novgorod land and destroyed many souls.

The most venerable priest-monk Feofil, their spiritual father, nominated to the *Vladyka*-ship, exhorted them to refrain from their wicked ways, but they would not hearken to him, and he tried many times to withdraw to his cell in his own monastery, but they would not let him go, while they persevered in their wicked design.

The *Veliki Knyaz* Ioan Vasilievich, hearing of what was doing in his patrimony, Novgorod the Great, of the uncurbed outrages of his people who were like the waves of the sea, bethought him of these occurrences in the goodness of his heart, yet he did not hasten to show his wrath, but quieted his most honest soul with a goodly patience, filled, like the Apostle, with the fear of God, and in remembrance of the holy light of the righteous Son, of Christ's merciful long-suffering, when the word of God came down from heaven and humbling himself, he descended to the earth, taking the form of a servant for the salvation of mankind; the *Veliki Knyaz* allowed them sufficient time, saying to himself: "Thou art just, O Lord, and thy judgments are correct; and as the Lord is just, so may I, loving justice, be just in His sight." Thinking thus, being favourably inclined towards his patrimony, and not being desirous of witnessing the shedding of Christian blood, he said to himself: "Even as the waves dash into foam against the rocks and come to naught, so also our people the men of Novgorod have more than once acted treasonably towards us, and the Lord God will subdue them." With this view he commanded his [spiritual] father Filip, the Metropolitan of all Russia, to write to them in his name, admonishing them, and instructing them not to draw away from the light of piety, to abandon their evil designs, and to withstand the darkness of the Latin allurements. The Metropolitan of all Russia did repeatedly write to Novgorod the Great, sending his blessing and writing instructions from the sacred Book: "It has come to my hearing, my sons, that some among you are endeavouring to cause a great rebellion and to produce dissent in God's holy church, to renounce the Orthodox Christian faith, and to pass over to the Latins. You must disadvise those wicked people among you from their evil inclinations, for, my sons, theirs is false and godless work; for by abandoning the light of piety they will unwittingly bring down upon themselves the future judgment of God and many eternal torments; let them be guided by a godly wisdom and by God's commandments. Stand in fear of the wrath of God, and in dread of the awful scythe which was seen by the great prophet Zachariah descending from heaven upon the unruly; you must punish those who make tumult and sow dissension among you, and teach them to walk in the old ways of their fathers and to dwell in the former ways of peace and piety. Cruel and irremediable will be the effects of these beginnings, if you neglect the new law of piety and salvation of the testament of the living God, and adhere to Latinism. The Lord God will call to account all the godless perverters of the faithful, so that you must restrain the evil-doers according to the words: 'Fly from sin as from a foe; fly from deceit as from the face of a serpent, that it may not sting thy soul with the barb of eternal perdition.' You know, my sons, how many cities, countries and places of mighty kingdoms have been ruined and desolated in former times for breaking the law and for disobeying the Prophets and for not following the teachings of the Apostles and the holy Fathers; that countries and cities which did not submit to God and to their sovereign were destroyed. The once pious and great Imperial city of Constantinople perished because of that same Latinism; it fell through impiety, and is now possessed by the heathen Turk. Fear the wrath of God, ye sons of God's world, it is not only one or two among you who are working to depart from the truth and to turn from the right way, forgetting your past greatness and the laws of your fore-fathers; but the whole multitude of your people are in commotion. Submit yourselves, my sons, to him under whose strong arm God has placed you and the God-serving land of Russia, the Veliki Knyaz Ioan Vasilievich our hereditary ruler, according to the direction of Christ's Apostle Paul the teacher of the universe, who said: 'Whosoever submits to the power of God, obeys His ordinances, but whosoever resisteth the power, resisteth the ordinance of God;' and again: 'Fear God and obey the king.' The minister of God beareth not the sword in vain as an avenger, but also in defence of the godly. Ponder, therefore, my children, over these things, and humble yourselves, and may the God of peace be with you."

They remained, however, not only implacable, but also stone-hearted, and gave no attention to the above writing, and were as deaf as adders, closing their ears to the voice, as it were, of the charmers. So these men of Novgorod giving no heed to the writing, nor accepting the benediction, and continuing in their evil courses, could not be compacted [in the right]. The pious sovereign and Veliki Knyaz of all Russia Ioan Vasilievich being still gracious to them, sent to Great Novgorod, his patrimony, his servant Ioan Fedorovich Tovarkov with fair words, saying: "His

patrimony should not abandon the Orthodox faith, but cast the evil
thought from off their hearts, and should not adhere to Latinism; that
the great sovereign holds the men of Novgorod in favour and in his
regards as of old." But the wicked people minded him not, and clung
to the intention of abandoning Orthodoxy and giving themselves over
to the king. We will state the accusation against them.

The *Veliki Knyaz* being informed of the unceasing evil doings of the
men of Novgorod, dispatched to Novgorod the Great a challenge in writing exposing the malpractices of the people and their treason, and announcing that he was himself marching with a force against them. The
Veliki Knyaz had first sent his *Voyevodas* Vasili Fedorovich Obrazets and
Boris Matveyevich Tyushtev with his men of Ustyug, of Vyatka and of the
Vologda district, to the Dvina and the country beyond the *Volok*, and
into all the territories of Novgorod in those parts. In advance of his
own force the *Veliki Knyaz* sent an army under his *Voyevodas*, *Knyaz*

NORTHEASTERN RUS,
LATE FOURTEENTH CENTURY

Lake Ladoga

THE GREAT

Novgorod

LANDS OF NOVGOROD

Volkhov R.

PRINCIPALITY OF
IAROSLAVL

Iaroslavl

Volga R.

GRAND DUCHY OF TVER

Tver

Rostov

GRAND DUCHY OF SUZDAL
AND NIZHNII–NOVGOROD

Nizhnii Novgorod

Oka R.

Volga R.

Moscow

PRINCIPALITY OF MUROM

Murom

GRAND DUCHY OF LITHUANIA

Smolensk

LAND OF SMOLENSK

Dnieper R.

Gorodets-Meshcherskii

UPPER PRINCIPALITIES

Pereiaslavl-
Riazanskii

GOLDEN
HORDE

Oka R.

GRAND DUCHY OF
RIAZAN

Don R.

0   150
Miles

Boundary of
Northeastern Rus

Territory of the Grand Duchy
of Moscovy

Other frontiers

● Capitol cities of the grand duchies

○ Autonomous principalities

Danilo Dmitrievich Kholmski and his Boyar Fedor Davidovich, accompanied by many others of his court; they were ordered to scour the country around Novgorod, towards Russa beyond the Ilmen lake and to burn all places of habitation. To his patrimony Pskov the *Veliki Knyaz* sent to say that the men of Pskov should release themselves from their engagement on oath to Great Novgorod, and take to horse in his service against Novgorod which had abjured Orthodoxy and was giving itself to the Latin king. They issued forth at once with all the men of the country of Pskov, and at the instance of the *Veliki Knyaz* they revoked their oath on the Cross to Novgorod the Great.

The pious sovereign and *Veliki Knyaz* Ioan Vasilievich prayed to God and to the most pure Mother of God, shedding many tears before them, beseeching their mercy for the pacification of the world, and for the well-being of God's holy churches and the Orthodox faith. His heart filled with sorrow, he said to himself: "It is known to Thee, Almighty God and everlasting King, who knowest the secrets of all men's hearts, it is not of my own desire and will that I dare to do this which may cause much shedding of Christian blood upon this earth. I stand by the godly laws of the holy Apostles and holy Fathers and for the true Orthodox faith of the Russian Land, also for my patrimony and against their renunciation of the true faith and adoption of Latinism." And praying thus, the pious worker invoked to his aid the great defender and speedy helper in war, the *Voyevoda* of the celestial forces, the *Archistrategos* Mikhail, and the great unconquerable sufferers for Christ, Dmitri of Selun [Salonika], Georgi the Brave and Feodor Stratilat [Theodore *Stratelates*,], also his saintly and Orthodox ancestors St. Vladimir and his two sons Boris and Gleb; and putting his trust in the prayers of the Saints, of the great sanctifier Ioan Zlatoust [John Chrysostom], the Bishop of Tsargrad [Constantinople], the miracle-worker Nikola, Peter the Russian Metropolitan, Alexis the miracle-worker and Russian Metropolitan, St. Leonti the miracle-worker and Bishop of Rostov, and the Saints and miracle-workers Sergei, Varlam, and Kiril, and Nikita the almoner of the miracle-worker of Pereyaslavl. By their prayers might he be strengthened and established for many years by the Lord God with His help from on high.

And so putting his trust in God, the *Veliki Knyaz* mounted his horse; and in the house of the Most Pure Mother of God and of the great Sanctifier Peter the miracle-worker, he left his son the faithful and pious *Veliki Knyaz* Ioan Ioanovich to sit in his throne in Moscow in guard of his patrimony and to govern the land of Russia; he left his younger brother *Knyaz* Andrei Vasilievich with him, and he commanded his son to retain by him the *Tsarevich* Murtasa, the son of *Tsar* Mustafa, with his *Knyazes* and *Kazaks* [Bodyguard], to serve him on any emergency.

The Veliki Knyaz took along with him his younger brother Knyaz Yuri Vasilievich and his youngest brothers Andrei and Boris Vasilievich, also Knyaz Mikhail Andreyevich with his son Vasili, with a large number of other Knyazes in his service, and Boyars and Voyevodas; he took with him also the son of Tsar Aldayaras Kasimovich of the Meshcher country with his Kazaks and retinue. The men of Pskov joined their forces from the borders of their country.

Thus did the Veliki Knyaz advance with all his host against his patrimonial domain Novgorod the Great because of the rebellious spirit of the people, their pride and their conversion to Latinism. With a numerous and overpowering force he occupied the entire Novgorod country from border to border, visiting every part of it with the dread powers of his fire and sword. As in ancient times Jeremiah prophesied of Nebuchadnezzar, King of Jerusalem: "From the rumbling and thunder of his chariots and from the neighing of his horses the earth shall tremble"; and so by the mercy and aid of God shall the same prophecy be fulfilled in our time over the wicked men of the Novgorod country, through the pious sovereign Veliki Knyaz Ioan Vasilievich of all Russia, for their abjuration of the faith and for their wrong-doing.

The Novgorod country is filled with lakes and swamps, for which reason mounted forces were never employed against Novgorod by former Veliki Knyazes and the wicked people in their wonted contumacy dwelled in security during the summer after, following their own evil ways from the autumn to the winter, and even up to spring time, by reason of the inundation of the lands.

By the beneficence of God, vouchsafed by God from on high to the Veliki Knyaz Ioan Vasilievich of all Russia to the detriment of the Novgorod land, not a drop of rain had fallen during the summer, from the month of May to the month of September the land was dry and the heart of the sun had dried up all the swamps. The troops of the Veliki Knyaz found no impediments and could ride in every direction over the country, driving the cattle over dried ground; thus did the Lord God through this desiccation punish the men of Novgorod for their evil-doing and subject them to the strong hand of the pious sovereign and Veliki Knyaz Ioan Vasilievich of all Russia. When the men of Novgorod heard that the Veliki Knyaz was marching upon them with a large army, those cunning men sent to him professions of duty and again asked for guarantees of security while proceeding with their evil doing. At the same time they sent forces from Novgorod the Great by the Ilmen lake in boats against the advancing columns of the Veliki Knyaz, and fought them; but God aided the Voyevodas of the Veliki Knyaz, and 500 men of Novgorod were killed and others were captured or drowned, while others fled back to the town informing the townsmen that they had been defeated by the Voyevodas of the Veliki Knyaz. Thrown into great agita-

tion, the men of Novgorod, after deliberation, dispatched another messenger to the *Veliki Knyaz, Posadnik* Luka Klementievich, doing homage
and again asking for guarantee of security and ignoring the defeated force
which had passed down in boats, declared that as yet no men from the
town had fought with those of the *Veliki Knyaz.*

Without waiting for the return of their venturesome envoy the crafty
people conceived a great wicked design; the rebel *Posadniks* and *Tysyt-
skis,* the *Boyars,* well-to-do men, the merchants and the whole of Great
Novgorod collected together forming a fighting body of fully 30,000
men, being unaware that the sword of God was sharpened against them,
and mounting their horses, rode quickly out of the town to fall upon
the advance force of the *Veliki Knyaz* which was led by *Knyaz* Danilo
Dmitrievich and by Fedor Davidovich. Here befell what was said by
David the Prophet: "By the morning shall all the wicked of the earth
be slain; I shall destroy all the lawless of the city." When the watchers
and the scouts informed the *Voyevodas* that a large force of mounted
men was advancing from Novgorod, and that an auxiliary force was
coming in boats into the Shelon river, then the *Voyevodas* of the *Veliki
Knyaz* began to acknowledge the justice of the *Knyaz's* cause and the
perfidy of the men of Novgorod and, praying to the Lord God and to the
most pure Mother of God, and reposing their trust in God, they said
to their company: "It is our duty, brothers, to serve our sovereign the
Veliki Knyaz Ioan Vasilievich of all Russia, and were they 300,000
strong we should all the same lay down our lives in fighting for the cause
of our sovereign *Veliki Knyaz;* and God and the holy Mother of God
know that the cause of the *Veliki Knyaz* is a just cause."

Early on the morning of July 14, the day of the Apostle St. Kuld, the
entire force of the men of Novgorod was ranged on the Shelon river,
and the opposing armies faced each other across the river.

When they saw the forces of the men of Novgorod the troops of the
Veliki Knyaz precipitated themselves into the river on their horses, not
one of their horses stumbling in descending the steep bank, nor flounder-
ing in the water, and closing up they rushed upon the whole body of the
men of Novgorod and they joined in battle. And here was fulfilled what
was said by the Prophet: "Like drunken men did they stagger and fall
into confusion, and all their understanding was swallowed up"; and
again: "As in drowsiness they mounted their horses, terrible art Thou,
O Lord; who can stand against Thee?"

Thus was God's favour bestowed on the troops of the *Veliki Knyaz,*
maintaining his just cause; even as God helped Gideon against the
Midianites, and Abraham against the king *Hodologomor* of Sodom, so
did he aid the *Voyevodas* of the *Veliki Knyaz* against these unrighteous
backsliders, the men of Novgorod. Although they rebelled and arrayed
themselves against the troops of the *Veliki Knyaz,* yet they could not

raise strong hands against them, but themselves fell into confusion from the stretching of their arrowed bows, and from the weapons of their hands. Thus likewise did God in his goodness turn their faces in an hour's time, as they threw down their arms and fled back whence they had come; they ran in disgrace, casting away their armour to relieve their horses of weight, and a great number of them fell dead, for their lawlessness and for their rebellion against their sovereign the *Veliki Knyaz*. It did not appear to them that they were stricken by men's hands, but by the invisible power of the Living God and by the aid of the great *Archistrategos* Mikhail, the leader of the heavenly forces. All were in great terror and many fell dead with their faces to the earth, while others throwing themselves off their horses ran into the forests where they strayed like cattle in their separate ways—being there were no married men amongst them—but hearing on all sides the shout of "Moskva" [Moscow] from the troops of the *Veliki Knyaz*.

So did the Lord fill their wicked souls with dread that they strayed in the forests not knowing their own country. The troops of the righteous sovereign and *Veliki Knyaz* triumphing over them by God's mercy, chased the wicked men of Novgorod twenty *poprishche* [about twenty *versts*] killing many and taking others alive, while others were drowned in their boats in the Shelon river.

The troops on the field of battle proclaimed their victory by trumpet sound and kissed the sacred images, glorifying God for their victory over their presumptuous enemies.

And searching in the transport they found a writing which was the draft of an agreement between Novgorod and the king [of Poland]. This was a surprise, and it caused astonishment, and the papers were forthwith sent to the *Veliki Knyaz* Ioan Vasilievich by the hand of the *Boyar* Ivan Vasilievich Zamyatin; he was to report that a large army of Novgorod men had advanced against them with banners with the best men among them, and had fought desperately, but that God had aided the *Voyevodas* of the *Veliki Knyaz*, that the great Novgorod army was completely defeated, that many Novgorod men had fallen, and many had been captured, to the number of 1700; that here were the copies of a treaty with the King of Poland, and with these they sent a prisoner, the man who had written out the draft, to serve the *Veliki Knyaz* in his accusation of the crafty men of Novgorod.

The pious *Veliki Knyaz* was gladdened by the unspeakable mercy of God in the aid given to him from on high against his cunning enemies. Praising God and the most pure Mother of God for having frustrated their wicked design of corrupting the sacred churches of God, of causing agitations and of producing hostilities between great sovereigns to the utter discomfiture of all Orthodoxy. He found among the documents the draft of a treaty with the king, by the terms of which the men of Novgorod agreed to surrender all the towns and districts of the *Veliki Knyaz*, with his lands and waters and with all the taxes of Novgorod the Great, setting forth the names of the envoys to be sent to the king—Panfili Selifontov and Kurila Ivanov, son of Makar—and naming him "our honourable king and sovereign." It is written, that their sickness shall turn upon their heads and their untruth shall descend upon them. So may it be with them for their craftiness and evil counsels.

The pious *Veliki Knyaz* of all Russia Ioan Vasilievich, having prayed to God and to the most pure Mother of God, went forward in his great work to Novgorod the Great, with his younger brothers *Knyaz* Yuri Vasilievich and *Knyaz* Boris Vasilievich, with the [Tartar] *Tsarevich* with all his *Knyazes* and *Voyevodas* and with all the people of his lands, hastening to his *Voyevodas* and to his advance army.

When the men of Novgorod were brought before the *Veliki Knyaz*, he, the pious one, with a godly wisdom accused the crafty men of their cunning and dishonourable proceedings, of departing from the light of true worship and giving themselves up to Latinism, of surrendering themselves to the Latin king while being the patrimony of him the *Veliki Knyaz*; and of surrendering to the Latin king according to the draft of a treaty with him all the towns, districts, lands and waters which belonged to him the *Veliki Knyaz* of Moscow, together with the taxes. Having found them guilty of all this, and being thus stirred against the men of Novgorod, he ordered them to execution by the sword, the chief *Posadniks*, among whom was Dmitri the eldest son of the charming Marfa, the town *Posadnik*; and she was also to lose her life by decapitation; together with these Vasili Seleznev Guba, Kiprian Arzubiev and Iremia were also beheaded for their conspiracy and crime in seeking to take to Latinism. Many other *Posadniks*, *Tysyatskis*, *Boyars* and men of substance of Novgorod were sent away to various towns or thrown into prisons, while others were retained in the fortress under charge to bide their time.

When God's aid came down from on high, with the leader of the heavenly host, the great *Archistrategos* Mikhail, in that hour Great Novgorod trembled before the wrath of God, and the *Posadniks*, the *Tysyatskis*, the men of substance, the *Boyars*, the merchants, and all the land of Novgorod turned their hearts towards good.

So did those men of Novgorod come unanimously to one decision; taking with them the priest-hermit Feofil, nominated *Vladyka* of Novgorod the Great and of Pskov, the Archimandrites, and *Igumens*, the worthy fathers and hermits, the priests from all the seven cathedral churches, and a great number of the best men of the town, they went to the pious sovereign and *Veliki Knyaz* of all Russia Ioan Vasilievich, and all of them prostrating themselves before him, they repented them with tears and in great sorrow of their crimes, praying: "Merciful lord and *Veliki Knyaz*

of all Russia Ioan Vasilievich, for the Lord's sake pardon us guilty men
of Novgorod the Great your patrimony; grant us, Lord, your favour, withdraw your anger, hold back your sword and extinguish your fires, silence
your thunders, spare the land from ruin, be merciful and let your irre-
sponsible people see the light."

And they all came on many days to his brothers, Knyaz Yuri Vasilievich, Knyaz Andrei Vasilievich, and to Knyaz Boris Vasilievich, humbling themselves before them and praying them to plead for them to their
elder brother, the Veliki Knyaz Ioan Vasilievich; and on many days they
likewise visited the Boyars, the Knyazes and Voyevodas, beseeching them
because of the sorrows of all Great Novgorod to plead for them, before
the Veliki Knyaz. The gracious brothers of the Veliki Knyaz, Knyaz Yuri
Vasilievich, Knyaz Andrei Vasilievich, and Knyaz Boris Vasilievich,
favoured them as of their patrimony, and compassionating them, and
together with all the Knyazes and Boyars, did plead for them before their
brother the Veliki Knyaz of all Russia, praying him to have regard for
them of his patrimony and to lay aside the wrath in his heart. The
gracious and intelligent sovereign Veliki Knyaz of all Russia, Ioan Vasilievich, seeing before him such a multitude of penitent people, and
among them his own priests, the hermit priest Feofil, the Vladyka-elect
of Novgorod the Great and of Pskov, who had grieved sore many days,
as also his brothers and the Boyars and Knyazes in supplication before
him, and the righteous Veliki Knyaz being also mindful of the writing he
had received from his spiritual father Filip, Metropolitan of all Russia
in which as pastor and teacher of Christ's flock the Metropolitan entreated the Veliki Knyaz, with his blessing, to be merciful to the people
of his patrimony, those many Orthodox Christians for whose souls he
grieved, and for the sake of Christian peace to accept their petitions, and
remembering also the words which came from the mouth of our Lord:
"Be merciful even as our Father in heaven, forgive man's trespasses as
your Father will forgive yours," and again: "Blessed is the merciful," so
because of these words spoken by God, and of all these intercessions, the
Veliki Knyaz granted grace to his patrimony, to Feofil the Vladyka-elect
of Novgorod the Great and of Pskov, to the Posadniks, Tysyatskis, merchants and to the whole of Novgorod the Great: he withdrew from them
the anger of his heart, withheld his sword and his menace over the land,
and commanded that all the captives should be freed without ransom.
He put a termination to the war and to plunder; and as to taxes and
tribute, he settled them all in writing, on oath, after which the Veliki
Knyaz withdrew from his patrimonial domains of Novgorod peacefully
with his brothers, his Boyars, with the Knyazes and Voyevodas and with
all his armed forces.

From his Voyevodas operating on the Dvina the Veliki Knyaz received
communications to the effect that they had defeated Knyaz Vasili

Shuiski, the servant of Great Novgorod, who with men from the country beyond the *Volok*, from the Dvina country and from the Korel region had advanced in large numbers and had fought with them great battles from morning to night on land and on water, but that God had aided the forces of the *Veliki Knyaz* under *Voyevoda* Vasili Fedorovich and his comrades, that a large number of the men of Novgorod were slain and others captured; so were the men of Novgorod overcome with fatigue and staggered in battle that they could not move their hands or turn their heads; that their *Knyaz* was wounded by an arrow and was taken away in a boat by his men, being barely alive, and that the towns on the Dvina had been burned and demolished. Thus did God's grace and mercy descend from on high in aid of the right of our sovereign the righteous and pious *Veliki Knyaz* Ioan Vasilievich of all Russia. On receipt of this intelligence the pious *Veliki Knyaz* gave praise to God and to the most pure Mother of God for those great mercies, and returned to his throne in the God-protected city of Moscow on the 1st day of September of the new year 6980 (1472).

Having received their liberty from their sovereign Ioan Vasilievich the *Veliki Knyaz* of all Russia, the men of Novgorod at once dispersed from out of the town to their several homes. A large number of people proceeded to Russa in big vessels, and to the Volkhov river with their wives and children and possessions; their cattle and with their movable houses, going to the places of their residence by the Ilmen lake, or by way of the Russa lake, the breadth from shore to shore on all sides being sixty *poprishche* [about forty miles]. When their numerous big vessels reached the middle of the lake, a storm with a hurricane of wind broke suddenly upon them, and tore their sails; there was terrible thunder and heavy rain with hail, and waves of mountain height, and dreadful, broke up their barges and all their big vessels in the middle of that frightful lake. There was in that hour an overwhelming terror and a raging storm, with shrieking and crying, many people clinging to each other, bitterly bewailing their peril, and in their agony tearing their clothes; mothers embracing their infants, fathers their sons, while shedding many tears and praying: "Lord save us, in the hour of our destruction and of our separation from the evils of this world." Sadness and woe to those who take to evil! This was not within sight of their friends, and they got no help from them; unless it came from on high, because of the straits of the great city and the angry spirit pervading it; the while that the big vessels were being shattered and wrecked, and all the men and women with their children were perishing in the deep waters separating from each other and tumbling about at the will of the waves which left nothing living in the waters, but all drowned and put to death. It was heard afterwards that the number of drowned in the lake was 7000. Thus did God punish his people of the Novgorod country for their wicked imagin-

ings, those evil-minded men, even for relinquishing their faith and in-
clining to Latinism. When it came to the ears of Great Novgorod that
on the Dvina the Voyevodas of the Veliki Knyaz had beaten Knyaz
Vasili Shuiski and the Novgorod men, while a large multitude had been
drowned in the lake, then tears were added to tears, and wailings to
wailings, realizing that the whole of the Novgorod country was by the
wrath of the Veliki Knyaz of all Russia, Ioan Vasilievich, burned and laid
waste by war, with its best men driven out, which had never happened
to them before. But all this evil and ruin they had brought upon themselves by their cunning and faithlessness and for their going to Latinism,
having allowed themselves to be misled by cunning people and rebels;
and that civic disaster and human blood shall they be made to account
for by the Almighty God, according to the writing: "Lord! destroy the
provokers of strife; and let the consequences fall on the heads of the
traitors and on their souls in this world and in the next, amen."

22

Contarini's Impression
of Moscovy in 1476

The Italians were the first west Europeans to notice
the rising power of Moscovy. Their perception
stemmed partly from contacts they established with
Moscow following the marriage, in 1472, of Ivan III
to Sophia Paleologue (the niece of the last Byzantine Emperor), who was brought up in Florence.
Sophia attracted many Italian Renaissance artists

Reprinted with permission of the Cambridge University Press from Travels to
Tana and Persia by Josafa Barbaro and Ambrogio Contarini. Translated from
the Italian by William Thomas and S.A. Roy, and Edited, with an Introduction
by Lord Stanley of Alderly (London, Published for the Hakluyt Society, 1873),
pp. 158–166. Items in brackets are mine.

and architects to Moscow, including Aristotle Fiora-
venti, Marco Ruffo, Pietro Solario, and Marco
Bruno, who built and decorated several palaces and
cathedrals within the Kremlin walls. Italians also
sought contacts with Moscovy to establish an alliance against the growing menace of the Ottoman
Turks. In 1476, Venetian ambassador Ambrosio
Contarini (n.d.–1499) stopped in Moscow on his
journey home from Persia where he had unsuccess-
fully sought aid against the Turks. In Moscow, Contarini had an audience with Ivan III which resulted
in the following impression of Ivan and of conditions
in his state.

On the 22d September, 1476, it pleased God that we should
enter Russia. There were a few little Russian villages in the middle of
the woods, and when it was known that Marco [Russian guide] was with
the caravan, the people came forth—with great timidity, however, on
account of the Tartars—and brought him a little honey in the combs.
Of this he gave me a portion, and I was certainly in want of it, as all our
provisions were exhausted, and we were reduced to such a state that we
could scarcely mount our horses. We left here, and reached a city called
Resan [Riazan], belonging to a lord whose wife is sister to the Duke of
Muscovy, the houses, as well as the castle of which, are all of wood.
Here we obtained bread and meat in abundance, as well as their beverage of apples, by which we were much restored. After leaving here, we
travelled through extensive forests, and at night we all lodged in Russian
villages, and were able to take some repose, as by the aid of God we
appeared to have reached a place of security. We then came to another
city named Colonna [Kolomna], which is situated on a branch of the
Volga, called Mosco, over which there is a large bridge. We left here,
and I was sent in advance by Marco, as the caravan would not go so
quickly.

On the 26th, praising and thanking God, who had taken pity on us in
so many dangers and extremities, we entered Moscow, which belongs to
Duke Zuanne [Ivan III], the sovereign of Great White Russia. I should
state that, during the greater part of the time we occupied in passing the
desert, which was from the 18th of August, when we left Citracan
[Astrakhan], until we reached Moscow on the 25th of September, as we
had no wood, we cooked our food with the dung of the cattle. Having
reached here, then, in safety, Marco provided lodgings for myself and
my people, and stables for the horses, which, although small and cheer-
less, seemed to me a grand palace in comparison with what I had had to
put up with.

On the 27th, Marco entered Moscow, and came in the evening to see me, bringing with him some provisions, which are very abundant in this city, as I shall describe hereafter. He exhorted me in the name of his sovereign to be of good cheer, as I might consider myself at home; for which I thanked him as well as I was able.

On the 28th, I went to visit Marco, and, as I was desirous of returning home, I requested him to be pleased to procure me an audience of the Duke. This he did, as the Duke shortly afterwards sent for me. After the usual salutations I thanked his lordship for the good offices I had experienced at the hands of Marco, his ambassador, as I could certainly say, with truth, that by his means I had escaped many dangers. And, although I had benefited by these services personally, they might be considered as having been rendered to my Illustrious Seignory, whose ambassador I was. The Duke scarcely allowed me to finish my speech, but, with a severe look, complained of Zuan Battista Trivisano. I will not enter into this subject, as it is beside the purpose; but when, after a long conversation, I requested to be allowed to take my departure, he said that I should receive an answer on that subject at another time; and with this I was dismissed by the Duke, who was about to leave the city. It is his custom to visit the various parts of his dominions every year. He especially looks after a Tartar, in his pay, who commands, it is said, five-hundred horsemen, to guard the frontiers of his territory from the incursions of the Tartars.

Being desirous, as I have said, of leaving, I endeavoured to obtain an answer to my request, and was again summoned to the palace, before three of the Duke's principal barons. They informed me, in the Duke's name, that I was welcome, and repeated everything that the Duke himself had said, complaining at the same time about the above-mentioned Zuan Battista. In conclusion, they told me that I might go or stay, as I pleased; and with this they dismissed me.

As I was indebted to Marco for the amount of my ransom with the interest, as well as for some other expenses which he had incurred on my account, I begged him to have the goodness to allow me to leave, and that as soon as I had reached Venice I would send him all that I owed him. He would not, however, consent to this, as he said that the Tartars and Russians whom I had promised to pay, wanted the money; and, as I was unable, after various attempts, to influence either the Duke or Marco in this matter, I determined to send Stephano to Venice to advise the Illustrious Seignory of all that had occurred, that they might with their accustomed clemency and good nature provide against my ending my days in this country.

On the 7th of October, 1476, I dispatched Priest Stephano in company with a certain Nicolo da Leopoli, who was well acquainted with the road, while I remained in Moscow. I found here Maestro Trifoso, a goldsmith from Catharo, who had made, and was engaged in making, many beautiful vases and other articles for the Duke. There was also a Maestro Aristotele da Bologna, an engineer, who was building a church in the Piazza, besides many Greeks from Constantinople, who had come in the suite of Despina [Sophia], with all of whom I was on terms of great friendship. The room which Marco had given me was small and unpleasant, and made an uncomfortable dwelling-place; but, by the influence of Marco, I obtained a lodging in the house of Maestro Aristotele, which was situated close to the Duke's palace, and was very convenient. A few days afterwards, however (for what reason I never heard), I was ordered, in the Duke's name, to leave this house, and I was, with difficulty, provided with two little chambers outside the castle, where I remained until my departure, one of which I occupied myself, while the other served for my attendants.

The city of Moscow is situated on a little hill, and is built entirely of wood, as is the castle. It is traversed by a river called Moscow, on one side of which stands the castle and part of the city, and on the other the remaining portion. The river is crossed by numerous bridges. Moscow is the principal city, and the residence of the Duke. It is surrounded by forests, with which, indeed, the greater part of the country is covered. The country abounds in all kinds of corn; and when I was there, you might have bought more than ten of our *stare* of wheat for a ducat, and other corn in proportion. The meat principally eaten is that of cows and pigs, of which you can procure, I believe, more than three pounds for a soldo. They give a hundred fowls or forty ducks for a ducat, and geese are little more than three *soldi* each. A great number of hares are brought to market, but other game is very scarce, because, I imagine, they do not know how to catch them. There are small birds of all kinds, and very cheap. They do not make wine of any kind, nor have they any fruit, with the exception of a few water melons and wild apples. The climate is so excessively cold, that the people stay nine months of the year indoors. As it is difficult to travel in the summer time, on account of the thick forests and the great quantity of mud caused by the melting of the ice, they are obliged to get in all their provisions in the spring, for which purpose they use their *sani* or sledges on which they stow everything, and which are easily drawn by one horse. By the end of October the river which passes through the city is frozen over, and shops and bazaars for the sale of all sorts of things are erected on it, scarcely anything being sold in the town. They do this, as the river, from being surrounded on all sides by the city, and so protected from the wind, is less cold than anywhere else. On this frozen river may be seen, daily, numbers of cows and pigs, great quantities of corn, wood, hay, and every other necessary, nor does the supply fail during the whole winter. At the end of November, all those who have cows or pigs, kill and bring them, from time to time, to the city market. They are frozen whole, and it is curious to see so many skinned cows standing upright on their feet. The meat that you eat has sometimes been killed three months or more. Fish, fowls, and all other provisions are treated in the same way. Horses run on this river when it is frozen, and a good deal of amusement takes place. Sometimes, also a neck is broken. Both the men and women are handsome, but they are a brutal race. They have a pope of their own, appointed by their sovereign, and hold ours in little esteem, saying that we are doomed to perdition. They boast of being great drunkards, and despise those who are not. They have no wine of any kind, but drink a beverage made of honey and the leaves of the hop, which is certainly not a bad drink, especially when old. The sovereign, however, will not grant permission to every one to make it; for, if they had that permission, they would be constantly intoxicated, and would murder each other like brutes. Their custom is to remain from morning till midday in the bazaars and to spend the remainder of the day in the taverns in eating and drinking. After midday you cannot obtain any service of them whatever. A great many merchants frequent this city from Germany and Poland during the winter, for the sole purpose of buying peltries, such as the furs of young goats, foxes, ermines, squirrels, wolves, and other animals; and, although these furs are procured at places many days' journey from Moscow—towards the north-north-east, or the north-west—they are all brought here where the merchants buy them. A great many, also, go to a town called Novogardia [Novgorod], on the confines of *Francia* and Upper Germany, and eight days' journey west of Moscow. This town, although it has a republican government, is subject to the Duke, to whom it pays a yearly tribute. This prince, from what I have heard, possesses a large territory, and might raise a large army, but the men are worthless. The country is bounded by that part of Germany which belongs to the King of Poland. Towards the north-north-west there is said to be a certain nation of idolaters, without any sovereign, but who, when so inclined, pay obedience to the Duke of Muscovy. There are some who are said to adore the first thing they see, and others who sacrifice an *animal* at the foot of a tree, and afterwards worship it. Many other things are told, which I shall not repeat, as I have not witnessed them myself, nor are they credible. The Duke may be thirty-five years of age; he is tall and thin, and handsome. He has two brothers, and his mother is still alive. Besides two daughters by Despina, who is said to be *enceinte*, he has, by another woman, a son who is not in great favour, on account of his bad conduct. I might mention other things, but it would take too long. I remained in Moscow from the 25th of September until the 21st of January, and I certainly received good treatment from everyone. After visiting his dominions, the Duke returned to Moscow about the end of December. I had sent Priest Stephano for my ransom, and was certain that it would be forthcoming, yet wishing very much to hasten my return home, as the way of living of the country did not agree with me, I spoke to some gentlemen who were favourable to my desire of leaving; and a few days afterwards received an invitation to dine with the Duke. He then told me that he was willing that I should depart, and that he should be happy to serve our Illustrious Seignory, and pay whatever was due to the Tartars and Russians for my ransom. The banquet to which I was invited was certainly served in good style, not only with regard to the numerous dishes, but in every other respect. As soon as the dinner was over, according to the custom of the country, I returned to my apartments. A few days afterwards the Duke invited me to dine with him again, and he ordered his treasurer to give me what money I required to pay the Tartars and the Russians. I then went to his palace, where I was made to put on a dress of ermine (that is, the skin only), and received also a thousand squirrel skins, with which I returned home. I also, at the Duke's request, paid a visit to Despina, with whom, after the usual salutations and compliments, I had a long conversation. She treated me with great kindness and courtesy, and entreated me earnestly to recommend her to my Illustrious Seignory.

The following day I was invited to the palace to dine with the Duke. Before sitting down to table, we entered a chamber where I was received by His Highness Marco, and one of the secretaries in a most courteous manner. The Duke entreated me to signify to my Illustrious Seignory that he was their good friend, and wished to remain so; that he willingly allowed me to depart, and that if I required anything more I should have it. When the Duke spoke to me I retired from him, but he approached me with great kindness. I answered all his questions, and thanked him appropriately, and we conversed for more than an hour. He showed me, with great good nature, some of his dresses of cloth of gold, lined with ermine, which were most beautiful. We then left this chamber, and soon after sat down to table. The dinner was longer than usual; the dishes more numerous; and many of his barons were present. When the banquet was over, I rose from table and presented myself before his Highness, who, with a loud voice, that everyone might hear, took leave of me in courteous terms, and with great demonstration of good-will towards our Illustrious Seignory; and I replied in a becoming manner. I was, afterwards, presented with a large cup of silver filled with their beverage made of honey, and was told to drink the contents, and keep the cup. This custom is observed when they wish to show very great honour either to ambassadors or others. But as there appeared to me too much to drink at once, I drank about a quarter of it, and His Highness, who was aware of my habits, seeing that I could not drink more, ordered the cup to be emptied and given back to me. I kissed his Highness's hands, and took leave of him. I was accompanied to the staircase by many of his barons, who embraced me with great demonstrations of friendship. I then went home, and had prepared everything for my departure; but Marco wished that I should previously dine with him.

On the 21st of January, 1476, after partaking of a good dinner with Marco and my own people, I took leave of him, and we entered our sani and departed. These sani, which are only used on the ice, somewhat resemble little houses, and are drawn by one horse. Each person has his own. You sit inside with as much clothing as you require and drive the horse. They go very fast and are made to contain all the provisions and everything that is necessary. The Patriarch of Antioch, or Brother Ludovico, who had been detained by the Duke on the representation of Marco, was, after great efforts on my part, released, and was to have accompanied us; but, seeing that he appeared to have no desire to do so, I started alone with my people, and a man was sent by the Duke to accompany me, with orders that I should be provided with other guides from place to place throughout the whole of his territories. In the evening we lodged at a very strange village; and, although I was aware that we should have to undergo many discomforts and hardships, on account of the intense cold of those countries, and from having to travel continually through forests, I welcomed every discomfort and was intent on nothing but travelling day and night; nor had I any fear, so great was my desire to escape from those places and ways of living.

We left this village on the 22d, and travelled continually through forests, in extreme cold, until the 27th, when we reached a little town called Viesemo [Viazma]. Leaving here, we took guides from place to place, and reached another little town called Smolencho [Smolensk], from which we departed with another guide, leaving the dominions of the Duke of Muscovy to enter Lithuania, which belongs to Casimir, King of Poland. We then proceeded to a small town called Trochi, where we found His Majesty, the said King.

Be it observed that, from the 21st of January, when we left Moscovy, until the 12th of February, when we reached Trochi, we travelled continually through forests. The country was generally flat, with a few hills. Sometimes we found a village where we rested, but usually slept in the forest. At midday we took our meals at places where we found that fires had been made, and the ice had been broken to water the horses by persons who had preceded us. We then added wood to the fire, and sat around it to partake of what little provision we had with us. We certainly underwent great suffering; for when we were warm on one side, we had to turn the other to the fire, and I slept in my sano rather than on the ground. We travelled three days and slept two nights on a frozen river; and we were said to have travelled three hundred miles, which is a great distance. . . .

23

Ending
of the Mongol Yoke
in 1480

The reign of Ivan the Great (1462–1505) is remembered for such significant developments in
domestic and foreign policy as energetic annexation
of territories to Moscovy, conquest of Novgorod,
establishment of contacts with western Europe, efforts to gain an outlet on the Baltic for Moscovy,
the emergence of the concept of "Moscow, the
third Rome," and the overthrow of the Mongol
yoke, to name only a few. The last achievement, as
the following Chronicle account indicates, came in
1480. It was far from a spectacular victory, for the
once powerful Golden Horde had, by this time,
disintegrated into several independent, feuding
khanates (Kazan, Crimean, Nogai, and others),
which were incapable and unwilling to challenge the
rapidly rising might of Moscow.

In this year [1480] the Grand Prince [Ivan III] received news
that Khan Akhmat was advancing with the entire Horde, with his sons
and feudal lords and princes, in accordance with an agreement reached
with King Casimir [of Poland], whereby the King incited him against
the Grand Prince in order to destroy [Orthodox] Christianity. The
Grand Prince went to Kolomna where he remained, and sent his son,
Grand Prince Ivan, to Serpukhov, while Prince Andrei Vasilevich Men-
shoi [brother of Ivan III] was in Tarusa; the remaining princes and
voevodas were in other places on the Oka River. Khan Akhmat, upon
learning that the Grand Prince was along the [Oka] river with all his

From *Polnoe Sobranie Russkikh, Letopisei (Complete Collection of Russian
Chronicles)* (St. Petersburg, 1885), vol. 8, pp. 205–207. Translation mine. Items
in brackets are mine.

forces, advanced toward Lithuania, around the Oka River, where he expected the arrival of the King [Casimir] and his armies, but his guides led him to the ford on the Ugra River. The Grand Prince dispatched his son and his brother and *voevodas* with all of their forces to the Ugra River. Upon reaching the Ugra, their destination, they occupied the ford and ferries. The Grand Prince himself left Kolomna for Moscow to attend a council and get advice from his [spiritual] father, Metropolitan Gerontii, his mother, Grand Princess Maria, his uncle, Prince Michael Andreevich [of Mozhaisk], and his [spiritual] father, Archbishop Vassian Rostovskii, and all of his *boyars*, inasmuch as they were all in Moscow preparing for a siege. And they pleaded with the Grand Prince to remain firm against Islam on behalf of Orthodox Christianity. The Grand Prince took note of these pleas, received a blessing, and went to the Ugra where he encamped himself at Kremnets with a small group of people, sending others to Ugra. Back in Moscow, the mother of the Grand Prince, Metropolitan Gerontii, Archbishop Vassian, and the Abbot of the Troitsk Monastery, Paisii, pleaded that the Grand Prince request the help of his brothers [Andrei the Elder, and Boris, with whom Ivan III was not on speaking terms]. The Grand Prince consented to their pleas and allowed his mother to send for them, promising to reward them. The Grand Princess sent after them, instructing them to go immediately to the aid of the Grand Prince.

Khan Akhmat went to Lithuania near Mtsensk and Liubutsk and Odoev with his Tartars, and camped at Vorotinsk where he expected the royal aid. The King [of Poland], however, did not come to his aid; neither did he send any army, because he was engaged in another war [with the Crimean Tartars]. At that time Khan Mengligirei of the Crimean Tartars pillaged the royal lands of Podolie, thereby helping the Grand Prince.

Akhmat arrived at the Ugra with all of his forces, with the intent of crossing the river. When the Tartars came they began to shoot at our [forces], and our [forces] shot at them. Some Tartars advanced against Prince Andrei; others against the Grand Prince; while still others unexpectedly advanced against the *voevodas*. Our forces, using arrows and harquebusses, killed many Tartars; their arrows were falling among our forces but did not hurt anyone. They pushed the Tartars away from the river, though they tried to advance for many days; as they could not cross the river they stopped and waited until it should freeze.

The brothers Prince Andrei and Prince Boris came to Kremenets to the Grand Prince, who greeted them cordially. When the river froze, the Grand Prince, afraid of Tartar invasion, ordered his son, Grand Prince Ivan, and his brother Andrei, and his *voevodas* to join him at Kremenets with all of their forces in order to unite their forces in the struggle with the enemy. In Moscow itself everyone was afraid. When our forces left the bank of the river, then the Tartars were frightened and fled, thinking that the Russians were letting them across the river in order to fight them, while our forces thought that the Tartars had crossed the river and were pursuing them, and so they came to Kremenets.

The Grand Prince with his son and brothers and with all his *voevodas* went to Borovsk, saying that he would fight them there.

Khan [Akhmat] fled to the Horde, and Khan Ivak of the Nogai Tartars advanced against him, killed him, and took the Horde; one of the Tartar Khans wanted to occupy some frontier lands beyond the Oka River, but the Grand Prince sent his two brothers against him, and when the Tartars heard about it they fled.

O, brave and courageous Russian sons, try to defend your country, Russian land, from the Tartars! Make all necessary sacrifices in order to put an end to the burning and pillaging of your homes, the killing of your children, the abusing of your wives and your daughters—things that other great lands are now suffering from the Turks, such as Bulgaria, Serbia, Greece, Trapezund, Peloponnesus, Albania, Croatia, Bosnia, Mankup, Kafa and many other lands. They did not defend themselves courageously and were defeated, and lost the countries, lands, and states, and now they move through foreign lands poor and homeless, . . . because they were not courageous enough. Those who fled to foreign lands with wealth and gold, wives and children, have lost their soul and body and think that those who died during the initial conquest are better off than they who wander homeless through foreign lands.

24

Herberstein's Observations of Russia

> Beginning with the reign of Ivan the Great (1462–
> 1505), the military might of Moscow was elevated
> and Russia was exposed to west European travelers,
> who in turn left many interesting descriptions of the
> country and its people. The foremost of these ob-
> servations is that of Baron Sigismund von Herber-
> stein, who visited Russia in 1517 and again in 1526
> as Ambassador of the Holy Roman Empire. Herber-
> stein's observations are vital for two basic reasons:
> first, they are based upon the personal experience
> and sixteen months' residence in the country of a
> man familiar with the history and language of the
> people; and second, they represent the first authen-
> tic and detailed account of sixteenth century Mos-
> covy, the power of its rulers, the customs of its
> people, and the climate and resources of the coun-
> try.

In thus entering upon the description of Moscow, which is
the capital of Russia, and which extends its sway far and wide through
Scythia, it will be indispensable, candid reader, that I should in this work
touch upon many parts of the north, which have not been sufficiently
known either to ancient authors or those of our own day, and it will
follow that I shall sometimes be compelled to differ from the accounts
they give. And in order that my opinion in this matter may not be looked
upon with suspicion, or considered presumptuous, I assert with all honesty, that not once only, but repeatedly, while engaged as ambassador
for the Emperor Maximilian, and his grandson Ferdinand king of the

---

Reprinted with permission of the Cambridge University Press from Sigismund
von Herberstein, *Notes Upon Russia: Being a Translation of the Earliest Account of that Country, Entitled Rerum Moscoviticarum Commentarii*. Translated and edited by R. H. Major (London, Published for the Hakluyt Society,
1851), vol. 1, pp. 3–6, 24–25, 30–38, 53–59, 84–85, 91–95, 101–102, 105–
107, and vol. 2, pp. 1–7. Items in brackets are mine. Spellings of some proper
names have been modernized.

Romans, I have seen and investigated Moscow, as it were under my very eyes (as the saying is); that I made myself acquainted with the greater part of the talented and trustworthy men of the place, and did not rely upon this or that man's account, but trusted only to the unvarying statements of the many; and having the advantage of knowing the Slavonic language, which is identical with the Russian and Moscovite, I have written these things and handed them down to the memory of posterity, not only as an ear, but as an eyewitness, and that not with any disguise in my description, but openly and freely. . . .

[There follows an outline of Russian history from the Varangians to Ivan the Great and his son Vasili, 1505–1533]

This Ivan Vasilievich was so successful, that he overcame the people of Novgorod in battle at the river Scholona, and reduced them to acknowledge him as their lord and prince, on certain proposed conditions. He granted them a large sum of money and then left them, after having first appointed a representative to supply his place; then again returning after the lapse of seven years, he entered the city with the co-operation of the Archbishop Theophilus, reduced the inhabitants to the most abject servitude, and seizing the gold and the silver and all the goods of the citizens, carried off more than three hundred waggons full of booty.

He himself was only once engaged in war, when the principalities of Novgorod and Tver were taken possession of; at other times he never used to go to battle, but nevertheless always carried off the palm of victory; so that Stephen the Great Palatine of Moldavia would often say, when speaking of him at his banquets: "That he increased his dominion while sitting at home and sleeping, while he himself could scarcely defend his own boundaries by fighting every day." He even appointed and deposed the kings of Kazan at his own pleasure; sometimes he threw them into prison, but at length, in his old age, received a severe defeat at their hands. He was the first who fortified his ducal residence at Moscow with a wall, as it is seen at this day. Moreover he was so hostile to women, that if any women met him by chance, they almost always fainted with terror at the sight of him. No access was allowed to him for poor men, who were oppressed by the more powerful or unjustly treated; he generally drank so excessively at dinner as to fall asleep, and while his guests were all struck with terror and sitting in silence, he would awake, rub his eyes, and then first begin to joke and make merry with them. But although this Grand Duke was so powerful a prince, he was nevertheless compelled to acknowledge the sway of the Tartars, for when the Tartar ambassadors were approaching, he would go forth from the city to meet them, and make them be seated while he stood to receive their addresses, a circumstance which so annoyed his Greek wife, that she would daily tell him she had married a slave of the Tartars, and to induce her husband to throw off this servile habit would sometimes persuade him to feign sickness on the approach of the Tartars. There was within the citadel of Moscow a house in which the Tartars lodged for the purpose of learning what was going on at Moscow, and as this also gave great offence to his wife, she sent messengers with liberal presents to the queen of the Tartars, begging her to give up that house to her; for that she had been admonished in a dream from heaven to build a temple upon that spot; at the same time she promised to allot another house to the Tartars. The queen granted her request; the house was destroyed and a temple was built on its site, and the Tartars thus driven out of the citadel have never been able to obtain a house from any subsequent Duke. . . .

At that time also the grand duke attacked the kingdom of Kazan both with a naval and military force, but returned unsuccessful, and with the loss of a large number of his soldiers. Although, however, the Prince Vasiley is thus most unsuccessful in war, he is, nevertheless, constantly being praised by his courtiers as if he had brought things to a happy issue; and on occasions when scarcely half his army has returned home, they have told him that not a man was lost in battle. In the sway which he holds over his people, he surpasses all the monarchs of the whole world, and has carried out his father's plan of ejecting all princes and others from the garrisons and fortified places. He certainly grants no fortresses to his relations, nor even puts them in charge of any, but oppresses nearly all of them with close confinement; and whoever' receives his orders to attend at court, or to go to war, or upon any embassy, is compelled to undertake whatever it may be at his own expense, with the exception of the younger sons of nobles of slender fortune, whom he sends for every year, and maintains with a fixed but inadequate stipend. But such of these as receive six gold pieces yearly, forfeit the stipend every third year; and those who receive twelve gold pieces every year, are compelled to hold themselves in readiness, and fully equipped, for the performance of any duty, at their own expense, and with their own horses; and to the more distinguished among them, namely, such as undertake an embassy, or any office of a more weighty character, are assigned districts, or towns, or villages, which are allotted to them according to their respective dignity, or the task performed. From each of these governments, however, certain annual tributes are paid to the prince: the fines extorted from the poor who may chance to be guilty of any delinquencies, and some other perquisites, are all that these nobles receive. The Grand Duke grants tenures of this kind generally for a year and a half; but if he regards any one with unusual favor or goodwill, he adds a few months to the period, but when that time is elapsed, all favor ceases, and the service must be performed six years gratuitously. There was one Vasiley Tretyack Dolmatov, a favorite of the prince, and one of his private secretaries, who, when appointed ambassador to the Emperor Maximilian, and receiving orders to make his preparations, declared that he had not the means and appurtenances necessary for such a journey; upon which he was immediately seized in Bielosero [Beloozero], and thrown into prison for life. After his death, which was most miserable, his property, both real and personal, was seized by the prince for himself; and although he thus acquired three thousand florins in ready money, he did not give even a farthing to the brothers and heirs of the deceased. Independent of common report, one Ivan, a scribe, who was appointed by the prince to supply me with the daily necessaries of life, confessed that this was the case, and that he had him in his custody at the time that he was taken. The two brothers of Vasiley likewise, Feodore and Zacharias, who were appointed my purveyors on my return from Moscow to Smolensko [Smolensk], confirmed his statement.

Whatever articles of value ambassadors who have been sent to foreign princes bring back with them, the prince places in his own treasury, saying, that he will recompense them in some other manner, which manner is as I have described above. For when the ambassador, Prince Ivan Posetzen Yaroslavski, was sent with Semen (*i.e.*, Simeon) Trofimov as his secretary, to the court of Charles V, they were presented by the emperor with heavy torques and chains of gold, and with Spanish money, and that in gold; and also by my master, the emperor's brother Ferdinand, Archduke of Austria, with cups of silver and baskets of gold and silver, and German money in gold; but when they returned with us to Moscow, the prince immediately on their arrival took away from them the chains and cups, and the greater part of the Spanish gold pieces. When I enquired of the ambassadors respecting the truth of this matter, one of them constantly denied it, from fear of compromising his prince; the other said, that the prince had ordered the royal presents to be sent to him that he might see them: as I alluded to the matter on frequent subsequent occasions, one of them, in order to avoid falsehood on the one side if he denied, or danger on the other if he were to confess the truth, ceased to visit me. The courtiers did not deny that it was the fact, but replied, "What then, if the prince repays them in some other kind?"

He uses his authority as much over ecclesiastics as laymen, and holds unlimited control over the lives and property of all his subjects: not one of his counsellors has sufficient authority to dare to oppose him, or even differ from him on any subject. They openly confess that the will of the prince is the will of God, and that whatever the prince does he does by the will of God; on this account they call him God's key-bearer and chamberlain, and in short they believe that he is the executor of the divine will. Thus if at any time petitions are presented on behalf of any captive, or with reference to any important business, the prince himself is accustomed to reply, "when God commands, he shall be liberated." In like manner also, if any one enquires respecting some doubtful and uncertain matter, the common answer is, "God and the great prince know." It is a matter of doubt whether the brutality of the people has made the prince a tyrant, or whether the people themselves have become thus brutal and cruel through the tyranny of their prince. . . .

As Russia began, so to the present day it continues to observe the Christian faith according to the Greek ritual. The metropolitan formerly resided in Kiev, afterwards in Vladimir, but now in Moscow. It was a custom of the metropolitans to pay a visit every seven years to that part of Russia which was subject to the Lithuanians, and to return after exacting sums of money from them; but Witold* fearing that his territories would become exhausted of coin, would no longer permit this. He therefore called a convocation of bishops, and appointed a special metropolitan, who at this day holds his seat at Wilna, the metropolis of Lithuania, a city which though observing the Roman ritual, has more Russian than Roman churches in it. The Russian metropolitans hold their authority from the Patriarch of Constantinople. . . .

Metropolitans and bishops were formerly chosen at an assembly of all the archbishops, bishops, abbots, and priors of monasteries; a man remarkable for sanctity was sought for through monasteries and deserts, and was selected. But they say that it is the custom of the present prince to summon certain ecclesiastics to him, and choose one of their number acccording to his own judgment. . . .

There are also two other archbishops in the Russian monarch's dominions in Novgorod, viz., the archbishop of Magrici and of Rostov'; also, the bishops of Tver, Resan [Riazan], Smolensko, Permia [Perm], Suzdal, Columna [Kolomna], Tczernigov [Chernigov], and Sari. All these are subject to the metropolitan of Moscow; but they have certain revenues of their own out of estates and other extraordinary accidentals (as they call them); they have, however, no forts, cities, or other secular administration (as they call it). They abstain constantly from meats. I only found two abbots in Russia, but very many priors of monasteries, all of whom are chosen at the will of the prince himself, whom no one dares resist.

The mode of electing the priors is described in the letters of one Varlamus, prior of the monastery of Hutten, established in the year 7034 [1525], from which I have only selected the leading particulars. In the first place, the brothers of any monastery beseech the Grand Duke to choose a fitting prior to instruct them in divine precepts. After the election, he is compelled, before he is confirmed by the prince, to bind himself by an oath and a bond, that he will live a pious and holy

---

* Grand Duke of Lithuania (n.d.–1430)

life in that monastery, according to the appointment of the holy fathers—to appoint all officers with the consent of the elder brothers, according to the custom of their predecessors—to advance such as are faithful in performing their duties, and to give diligent attention to the welfare of the monastery—to consult three or four of the elders on important questions of business, and after deliberation to refer the matter to the whole fraternity, and to decide and settle according to their general opinion; not daintily to live in private, but constantly to be at the same table and eat in common with the monks; diligently to collect all the registers and annual returns, and deposit them faithfully in the treasury of the monastery. All these things he promises to observe under a heavy penalty, which the prince can inflict on him even to the deprivation of his office. The senior monks also bind themselves by an oath that they will observe all the aforesaid rules, and faithfully and diligently obey the prior who shall be appointed.

Those who are consecrated secular priests are for the most part such as have served a long time in the churches as deacons. But no one is consecrated deacon unless he be married, whence they are very often married and ordained deacons at the same time. But if the betrothed of any deacon is in bad repute, he is not ordained deacon: it is necessary that he should have a wife of unblemished character.

When the wife of a priest is dead he is immediately suspended from officiating, but if he lives in chastity, he may be present in the choir as a minister with the other minister of the church, at the offices and other divine engagements. Indeed it was the custom formerly for widowers who lived in chastity to administer the sacraments without blame, but now the custom is introduced that no widower be permitted to perform the sacraments, unless he enter some monastery and live according to rule. If any priest who is a widower enter on a second marriage, which he is free to do, he has nothing in common with the clergy, nor does any priest whatever dare either to administer the sacrament, to baptize, or to perform any other duty, unless a deacon be present.

Priests hold the first place in the churches, and if any one of them on any account were to do that which is contrary to religion and the priestly office, he is brought to a spiritual tribunal; but if he be accused of theft or drunkenness, or fall into any other vice of that sort, he is punished by the *secular* magistrate as they call him. I saw some drunken priests publicly whipped at Moscow, whose only complaint was, that they were beaten by slaves, and not by a gentleman. A few years ago, one of the prince's deputies caused a priest who had been caught in theft to be strangled, at which the metropolitan was very displeased, and laid the matter before the prince. When the deputy was summoned to the prince, he replied, that "according to the ancient custom of the country a thief who was not a priest was hanged"; and so he was sent away unblamed. If a priest complain before a lay judge that he has been struck by a layman (for all kinds of assaults and injuries apply to the secular law), then the judge, if he happen to learn that the layman was provoked by the priest, or previously injured in any way by him, punishes the priest.

Priests are generally maintained from the contribution of people connected with the court, and have some small tenements allotted to them with fields and meadows, whence they derive their support by their own and their families' industry, like their neighbours. They have very slender offerings. Sometimes the church money is put out at interest at ten per cent., and they give the interest to the priest from fear of being compelled to maintain him at their own expense. There are some also who live by the liberality of the princes. Certainly, not many parishes are found endowed with estates and possessions, except the bishoprics and some monasteries. No parish or priesthood is conferred on any one but a priest. In every church there is only one altar, and they do not think it right that the service should be performed more than once a day. A church is very seldom found without a priest, who is bound only to perform the services three times a week.

They wear nearly the same dress as the laity, with the addition of a small round skull cap to cover the tonsure, and a broad hat to keep off the heat and rain, or they use an oblong beaver hat of a grey colour. They all carry staves to lean upon, called Possoch [*Posokh*].

Abbots and priors, as we have said, preside over monasteries—the latter are called Igumens, the former Archimandrites. Their laws and regulations are very severe, but are gradually falling into disuse, and becoming obsolete. They dare not indulge in any sort of amusement. If any one is found to have a harp or any musical instrument, he is most severely punished. They constantly abstain from meat. They all obey, not only the commands of the prince, but all the boyars sent by the prince. I was present when my purveyor requested something at the hands of a certain prior, and finding that he persisted in refusing to comply with his request, he threatened to have him beaten, the hearing which immediately produced the desired effect. There are many who leave the monasteries and betake themselves into wildernesses and there built huts, in which they live sometimes alone and sometimes with companions. They seek their livelihood from the earth and the trees, eating roots and the fruits of the trees. These are called Stolpniki: for Stolp means a column, and their narrow little dwellings are raised up high in the air and supported on columns.

The metropolitan, the bishops, and archbishops, constantly abstain from all kinds of meat; but when they invite laymen or priests at seasons when meat is eaten, they have the prerogative of being permitted to place meat before them at their entertainment; but this is prohibited to abbots and priors.

The archbishops, bishops, and abbots, wear round black mitres; but the bishop of Novgorod alone wears a white two-horned mitre after our fashion. The daily garments of the bishops are like those of other monks, except that sometimes they have them of silk, especially the black pallium, which has three white strips waving, like the flowing of a river, from the breast in every direction, to signify that from their mouth and heart flow streams of the doctrine of faith and good works. They carry a staff in the form of a cross, on which they lean, which in the common language is called Possoch. The bishop of Novgorod wears a white pallium. The bishops confine their attention entirely to matters of divinity and to the pious promotion and advancement of religion itself, and intrust the management of both private and public affairs to their officials. . . .

The principal care of the monks is to convert all men whatsoever to their own creed. The hermit monks have already brought over to the faith of Christ a great part of those who were idolaters through daily and industriously disseminating the word of God amongst them. Even now they go to various countries in the north and east, which they can only reach by the greatest toil, at the risk of both fame and life, and without hope of the least personal advantage; nor do they seek it, for they have an eye to this one thing only, *viz.*, that they may be able to do an acceptable service to God, and to recall into the right path the souls of many who have gone astray (sometimes confirming the doctrine of Christ by death), and to bring them in as gain to Christ. . . .

The Moscovites boast that they are the only true Christians, and condemn us as deserters from the Primitive Church and from the old sacred institutions. But if any one of our religion of his own accord goes over to the Moscovites, or even flees to them against the will of his master, as though for the sake of learning and embracing their religion, they say that he ought not to be let go or restored to his master, even if he should demand him back, a fact which came to my knowledge in a certain instance. . . .

They do not contract marriages within the fourth degree of consanguinity or relationship. They think it heretical for brothers to marry their sisters. Also, no one dare take to wife the sister of his kinsman. They likewise most rigidly observe that no marriage take place between those who are connected by the spiritual relationship of baptism. If any one marry a second wife, and become a bigamist, they allow it indeed, but scarcely think it a lawful marriage. They do not permit a third marriage, except for some weighty cause; but a fourth they allow to nobody, and do not even consider it Christian. They admit divorces, and grant a writ of repudiation, but they mostly conceal it, because they know it to be contrary to religion and the statutes. . . .

They do not call it adultery unless one have the wife of another.

Love between those that are married is for the most part lukewarm, especially among the nobles and princes, because they marry girls whom they have never seen before; and being engaged in the service of the prince, they are compelled to desert them, and become corrupted with disgraceful connections with others.

The condition of the women is most miserable; for they consider no woman virtuous unless she live shut up at home, and be so closely guarded that she go out nowhere. They give a woman, I say, little credit for modesty, if she be seen by strangers or people out of doors. But shut up at home they do nothing but spin and sew, and have literally no authority or influence in the house. All the domestic work is done by the servants. Whatever is strangled by the hands of a woman, whether it be a fowl, or any other kind of animal, they abominate as unclean. The wives, however, of the poorer classes do the household work and cook. But if their husbands and the men-servants happen to be away, and they wish to strangle a fowl, they stand at the door holding the fowl, or whatever other animal it may be, and a knife, and generally beg the men that pass by to kill it. They are very seldom admitted into the churches, and still less frequently to friendly meetings, unless they be very old and free from all suspicion. On certain holidays, however, men allow their wives and daughters, as a special gratification, to meet in very pleasant meadows, where they seat themselves on a sort of wheel of fortune, and are moved alternately up and down, or they fasten a rope somewhere, with a seat to it, in which they sit, and are swung backwards and forwards; or they otherwise make merry with clapping their hands and singing songs, but they have no dances whatever.

There is at Moscow a certain German, a blacksmith, named Jordan, who married a Russian woman. After she had lived some time with her husband, she one day thus lovingly addressed him: "Why is it, my dearest husband, that you do not love me?" The husband replied, "I do love you passionately." "I have as yet," said she, "received no proofs of your love." The husband inquired what proofs she desired. Her reply was: "You have never beaten me." "Really," said the husband, "I did not think that blows were proofs of love; but, however, I will not fail even in this respect." And so not long after he beat her most cruelly; and confessed to me that after that process his wife showed much greater affection towards him. So he repeated the exercise frequently; and finally, while I was still at Moscow, cut off her head and her legs.

All confess themselves to be Chlopos [Kholops], that is, serfs of the prince. Almost all the upper classes also have serfs, who either have been taken prisoners, or purchased; and those whom they keep in free service are not at liberty to quit at their own pleasure. If any one goes away without his master's consent, no one receives him. If a master does not treat a good and useful servant well, he by some means gets a bad name amongst others, and after that he can procure no more domestics.

This people enjoy slavery more than freedom; for persons on the point of death very often manumit some of their serfs, but they immediately sell themselves for money to other families. If the father should sell the son, which is the custom, and he by any means become free or be manumitted, the father can sell him again and again, by right of his paternal authority. But after the fourth sale, the father has no more right over his son. The prince alone can inflict capital punishment on serfs or others. . . .

Justice is carried out very strictly against thieves; when they are caught, the order is, that they shall first have their heels broken, and then rest two or three days while they swell, and then while they are yet broken and swollen they make them walk again. They employ no other method of torturing malefactors to confess robberies or to inform against their accomplices. But if a man, when brought up for examination, be found to deserve death, he is hanged. Criminals are seldom punished with any other kind of punishment, unless they have committed some uncommonly heinous crime. Thefts, and even murders, unless they have been committed for the sake of gain, are seldom visited with capital punishment. If, indeed, a man catch a thief in the act and kill him, he can do so with impunity, always provided, however, that he bring the man that he has killed to the prince's palace, and explain how the matter occurred. . . .

Few magistrates have authority to inflict capital punishment. No subject dares to put another to the torture. Most malefactors are brought to Moscow or the other principal cities, but convicts are generally punished in winter time, for in summer military pursuits preclude the opportunity of attending to these matters. . . .

The testimony of one nobleman is worth more than that of a multitude of low condition. Attorneys are very seldom allowed: every one explains his own case. Although the prince is very severe, nevertheless all justice is venal, and that without much concealment. I heard of a certain counsellor who presided over the judgments being apprehended, because in a certain case he had received bribes from both parties, and had given judgment in the favor of the one who had made him the largest presents: when he was brought to the prince he did not deny the charge, but stated that the man in whose favor he had given judgment was rich, and held an honorable position in life, and therefore more to be believed than the other, who was poor and abject. The prince revoked the sentence, but at length sent him away with a laugh unpunished. It may be that poverty itself is the cause of so much avarice and injustice, and that the prince knowing his people are poor, connives at such misdeeds and dishonesty as by a predetermined concession of impunity to them.

The poor have no access to the prince, but only to the counsellors themselves; and indeed that is very difficult. Ocolnick holds the place of a praetor or judge appointed by the prince, otherwise the chief counsellor, who is always near the prince's person, is so called. Nedelsnick is the post of those who summon men to justice, seize malefactors and cast them into prison; and these are reckoned amongst the nobility.

Laborers work six days in the week for their master, but the seventh day is allowed for their private work. They have some fields and meadows of their own allowed them by their masters, from which they derive their livelihood: all the rest is their master's. They are, moreover, in a very wretched condition, for their goods are exposed to plunder from the nobility and soldiery, who call them Christians and black rascals by way of insult.

A nobleman, however poor he might be, would think it ignominious and disgraceful to labor with his own hands; but he does not think it disgraceful to pick up from the ground and eat the rind or peeling of fruits that have been thrown away by us and our servants, especially the skins of melons, garlic, and onions; but whenever occasion offers, they drink as immoderately as they eat sparingly. They are nearly all slow to anger, but proud in their poverty, whose irksome companion they consider slavery. They wear oblong dresses and white peaked hats of felt (of which we see coarse mantles made) rough from the shop.

The halls of their houses are indeed large and lofty enough, but the doors are so low, that in entering, one must stoop and bend one's self.

They who live by manual labor and work for hire, receive a deng and a half as one day's pay; a mechanic receives two dengs, but these do not work very industriously unless they are well beaten. I have heard some servants complain that they had not received their fair amount of beating from their masters. They think that they have displeased their master, and that it is a sign of his anger if they are not beaten. . . .

The city of Moscow then, the capital and metropolis of Russia, together with the province itself, and the river which flows by it, have but one and the same name, and in the vernacular language of the people are called Mosqwa [Moskva]. Which of the three gave its name to the other two is uncertain; but it is likely that the name was derived from the river. For although the city itself was not formerly the capital of the nation, yet it is evident that the name of Moscovites was not unknown to the ancients. The river Mosqwa, moreover, has its source in the province of Tver, nearly seventy *wersts* [*versts*] above Mosaisko [Mozhaisk] (a *werst* is nearly the length of an Italian mile), not far from a place called Oleskno, and measuring thence a distance of ninety *wersts*, flows down to the city of Moscow, and having received some streams into itself, flows eastward into the river Occa [Oka]. It begins, however, to be navigable six miles above Mosaisko, at which place materials for building houses and other purposes are placed on rafts and brought down to Moscow. Below the city the merchandise, *etc.*, imported by foreigners, is brought up in ships. The navigation is, however, slow and difficult on account of the numerous turnings and windings with which the river is indented, especially between Moscow and the city of Columna [Ko- lomna], situated on the bank of the river about three miles from its mouth, where, by its many long windings, it increases the length of the passage by 270 *wersts.* The river is not very abundant in fish, for indeed, with the exception of mean and common sorts, it has none at all. The province of Moscow also is not over extensive or fertile, for the sandy soil which covers it and which kills the corn with the least excess of dry- ness or moisture, is a very great obstacle to fertility. To this must be added the immoderate and excessive inclemency of the atmosphere, for as the severity of the winter overpowers the heat of the sun, the seed which is sown cannot in some places reach maturity. For the cold is sometimes so intense there that in the same manner as with us in sum- mer time the earth splits into clefts with too much heat, so with them it does so from the extreme cold, and water thrown into the air, or saliva spit from the mouth, freezes before it reaches the ground. We ourselves, when we arrived there in the year 1526, saw some boughs of fruitbearing trees that had entirely perished with the rigor of the preceding winter, which had been so severe that year, that many couriers (whom they call *gonecz*) were found frozen in their carriages. There were some men driv- ing cattle tied together with ropes from the neighboring districts to Moscow, who, overpowered by the excessive cold, perished together with the cattle. Several itinerants also, who were accustomed to wander about the country with bears taught to dance, were found dead in the roads. The bears also, stimulated by hunger, left the woods and ran about hither and thither through the neighbouring villages and rushed into the houses, while the rustic multitude, terrified at their aspect and strength, fled and perished miserably out of doors with the cold. This excess of cold is sometimes equalled by the too great heat, as in A.D. 1525, when nearly everything that had been sown was burnt up by the immoderate heat of the sun; and such a want of provision followed that drought, that what could previously be bought for three dengs, would afterwards cost twenty or thirty. A great many districts, and woods, and corn-fields, were seen burnt up by the excessive heat. The smoke of this so filled the country, that the eyes of those who walked out were severely injured by it; and besides the smoke, a certain darkness supervened, which blinded many.

It is evident from the trunks of large trees which still exist, that the whole country was not long since very woody; but although the husband- men give care and labor to the cultivation of trees, all except such as grow in the fields are brought hither from the neighbouring provinces. There is abundance of corn and common vegetables, but none of the sweeter kinds of cherries or nuts (except filberts) are found in the whole country. They have indeed the fruits of other trees, but they are insipid. They cultivate melons with particular care and industry. They put earth mixed with manure into beds of a good depth, and set the seed in them, by which plan it is equally protected against immoderate cold or heat; for if the heat should happen to be too great, they prevent it from suffocating the seed by making little spiral chinks in the earth, which has been thus mixed with manure, while in excessively cold weather the warmth of the manure itself affords protection to the buried seed.

There is no honey in the province of Moscow, nor is there any game, except hares. Their cattle are much smaller than ours, but not without horns, as a certain person has written, for I have seen there oxen, cows, goats, and rams, all horned. The city of Moscow has a very eastward position among the other cities of the north, which we easily perceived in our journey thither; for when we left Vienna, we proceeded direct to Cracow, and thence travelled nearly a hundred German miles northward; at length the road turning eastward, we reached Moscow, situated, if not in Asia, at any rate on the very extreme confines of Europe, where it joins Asia, of which circumstance I shall say more hereafter in my description of the Don.

The city itself is built of wood, and tolerably large, and at a distance appears larger than it really is, for the gardens and spacious court-yards in every house make a great addition to the size of the city, which is again greatly increased by the houses of smiths and other artificers who employ fires. These houses extend in a long row at the end of the city, interspersed with fields and meadows. Moreover, not far from the city, are some small houses, and the other side of the river some villas, where, a few years ago, the Prince Vasiley built a new city for his courtiers, called Nali (which in their language means "pour in"), because other Russians were forbidden to drink mead and beer, except on a few days in the year, and the privilege of drinking was granted by the prince to these alone; and for this reason they separated themselves from intercourse with the rest of the inhabitants to prevent their being corrupted by their mode of living. Not far from the city are some monasteries, which alone appear like a great city to persons looking from a distance. Moreover, in consequence of the great extent of the city, it is confined by no settled boundary, nor has it any useful defences in the shape of walls, fosses, or ramparts. The streets are, however, blocked up in some places by beams thrown across them, and are guarded by watchmen placed there at early nightfall, so that no one is allowed access by that way after a stated hour; and any who are taken after that by the watchmen are either beaten, stripped, or thrown into prison, unless they happen to be persons of distinction or respectability: and even these are generally accompanied home by the watchmen. Such watches are generally set wherever there is an open entrance into the city, for the

Mosqwa flows by one side of the city, and the river Jausa [Iauza], which flows into it under the city itself, has such steep banks, that it scarcely admits of being forded. In this latter river many mills have been erected for the public use of the city, which seems to be mainly defended by these rivers; with the exception of a few stone houses, churches, and monasteries, it is entirely a city of wood. The number of houses which it is said to contain is scarcely credible. For they say, that six years before my arrival at Moscow, the houses were counted by an order of the prince, and that the number exceeded 41,500. This city is so broad and spacious, and so very dirty, that bridges have been constructed here and there in the highways and streets and in the other more distinguished parts. There is a fortress in it built of burnt tiles, which on one side is washed by the Mosqwa and on the other by the River Neglima [Neglinaia]. The Neglima flows from certain marshes, but is so blocked up before the city around the upper part of the fortress, that it comes out like stagnant water, and running down thence, it fills the moats of the fortress, in which are some mills, and at length, as I have said, is joined by the Mosqwa under the fortress itself. The fortress is so large, that it not only contains the very extensive and magnificently built stone palace of the prince, but the metropolitan bishop, the brothers of the prince, the peers, and a great many others, have spacious houses of wood within it. Besides these, it contains many churches, so that from its size it might itself almost be taken for a city. This fortress was at first surrounded only by oaks, and up to the time of the Grand Duke Ivan Danielovich was small and mean in appearance. It was he, who, by the persuasion of Peter the metropolitan, first transferred the imperial residence to this place. Peter had originally selected that place from love of one Alexius, who was buried there, and who is said to have been famous for miracles; and after his death, being buried in this place, miracles were likewise done at his tomb, so that the place itself acquired such a celebrity, from a certain notion of its sacredness and religious character, that all the princes who succeeded Ivan thought that the seat of empire ought to be held there. For on the death of Ivan, his son of the same name retained his seat there; and after him, Dimitry; and after Dimitry, that Vasiley, who married the daughter of Witold, and left behind him Vasiley the Blind. Of him was born Ivan, the father of that prince, at whose court I was ambassador, and who first surrounded the fortress with a wall; and his descendants, nearly thirty years after, have brought the work to completion. The ramparts and battlements of this fortress, as well as the prince's palace, were built of brick, in the Italian style, by Italians, whom the prince had sent for from Italy with the offer of large remuneration. There are also, as I have said, many churches in it, nearly all of wood, except the two handsomest, which are built of brick. One of these is consecrated to the Blessed Virgin, the other to St. Michael. In the

church of the Blessed Virgin are buried the bodies of the two archbishops who were the cause of the prince's transferring thither the seat
of empire and the metropolis; and principally on that account they
have been enrolled among the number of the saints. The other church
is used as a burial-place for the princes. There were also many churches,
being built of stone, at the time that I was there.

The climate of the country is so wholesome, that, from the sources of
the Don, especially northwards, and a great way towards the east, no
plague has raged there in the memory of man. They sometimes, however,
have a disorder of the bowels and head, not unlike the plague, which
they call "the heat": those who are seized with it die in a few days. That
disorder was very prevalent when I was at Moscow, and took off one of
my servants; but from the people being accustomed to live in so wholesome a climate, if the plague at any time be raging in Novgorod,
Smolensko, or Plescow [Pskov], from fear of contagion they exclude from
their own country any people who come thence to them.

The people of Moscow are more cunning and deceitful than all others,
their honor being especially slack in business contracts—of which fact
they themselves are by no means ignorant, for whenever they traffic with
foreigners, they pretend, in order to attain greater credit, that they are
not men of Moscow, but strangers.

The longest day in Moscow in the summer solstice, is said to be
seventeen hours and three quarters. I could not, at that time, ascertain
from anybody the exact elevation of the pole, although one man told
me, but upon uncertain authority, that he had heard it was fifty-eight
degrees. At length I myself made a venture with the astrolabe, and on
the ninth day of June, at noon, observed that the sun was at fifty-eight
degrees. From which observation it was deduced, by the reckoning of
men skilled in these things, that the elevation of the pole was fifty
degrees, and that the longest day was seventeen hours and one quarter.

25

Ivan the Terrible's Own Account of His Early Life

The childhood of Ivan the Terrible (1530–1584) was not a pleasant one. His father, Vasili III (1505–1533), died when Ivan was three years old; his mother, Helena Glinskaia, when he was seven. The regency period was marked by the absence of a strong central government and offered Russian *boyars* an opportunity for intrigue, corruption, violence, and neglect of and lack of respect for the young Prince. During his youth Ivan concealed his feelings of revenge, but when he assumed full power in 1547, upon his formal coronation, his reign spelled the end for many *boyars*. Ivan forced some of the *boyars* into exile, but others perished during the reign of terror known as *oprichnina*. Ivan's policies strengthened the power of the Tsars at the expense of the nobility.

. . . I will prove in the greatest detail what evil I have suffered from my youth even unto the present day. For this is clear (even if you were young in those years, yet none the less this you can know): when, by the decree(s) of God, our father, the great sovereign, Vasily, having exchanged the purple for the angel's form, had left all that was perishable and the fleeting earthly kingdom and come to the heavenly [realm], to that everlasting eternity, to stand before the Tsar of Tsars and the Lord of Lords, I remained with my only (-begotten) brother Georgiy,

Reprinted with permission of the Cambridge University Press from J. L. I. Fennell, ed., *The Correspondence between Prince A. M. Kurbsky and Tsar Ivan IV of Russia 1564–1579* (Cambridge, England, Cambridge University Press, 1955), pp. 69–101, alternate. See original source for footnote references.

who has departed this life in sanctity. I was then three years old and my
brother was one, and our mother, the pious Tsaritsa Elena, was left in
such miserable widowhood—as though in the midst of flames, she suffered on all sides now unmitigated strife stirred up against her by all
peoples—by the foreign peoples encircling [our realm], Lithuanians,
Poles, Perikopians, Nadchitarkhan, and Nogais, and Kazan',—now mani-
fold misfortune(s) and suffering(s) [inflicted by] you traitors; for, like
unto you, you mad dog, Prince Semen Bel'sky and Ivan Lyatsky ran
away to Lithuania; [from there] whither did they not run like men possessed? To Tsargrad and to Crimea and to the Nogai [Tatars] and on all
sides they raised strife against the Orthodox. But they had no success.
Thanks to the intervention of God and the most pure Mother of God
and the great miracle workers, and because of the prayers and the blessing of our parents, all these things, like the counsel of Ahitophel, were
scattered. In like manner later did the traitors raise up our uncle, Prince
Andrey Ivanovich, against us, and with those traitors did he go to Novgorod, (so, these are they whom you praise! You call them our "well-
wishers" and "those that lay down their lives for us"!). And at that
time did these [traitors] secede from us and adhere to our uncle, Prince
Andrey, and at their head was your brother [i.e., cousin], Prince Ivan,
the son of Prince Semen, the son of Prince Petr Romanovich Lvov, and
many others. And likewise with the help of God did this plot miscarry
[lit. this counsel was not achieved]. Well then, is that the "well-wishing"
of those whom you praise? Thus do they "lay down their lives for us"
by wishing to destroy us and raise our uncle to the throne? But later, in
their treacherous manner, they began to hand over our patrimony to our
Lithuanian enemy—the towns of Radogoshch, Starodub, Gomel'—thus
do they "wish us well"? When there is no one in the land with whom
to wreak destruction at home [lit. from the land] and to turn glory to
deceit, then do they cast in their lot with [lit. join in love with] foreigners, only so that they may wreak destruction of which no memory
shall remain!

   Thus by God's will did it come to pass that our mother, the pious
Tsaritsa Elena, went from the earthly kingdom to the heavenly; and we
and our brother Georgiy, who has departed this life in sanctity, remained
as orphans, [having lost] our parents and receiving no human care from
any quarter; and hoping only for the mercy of God, we put our trust in
the mercy of the most pure Mother of God and the prayers of all the
Saints and the blessing of our parents. But when I had entered upon my
eighth year of life [lit. from birth] and when thus our subjects had
achieved their desire, namely to have the kingdom without a ruler, then
did they not deem us, their sovereigns, worthy of any loving care, but
themselves ran after wealth and glory, and so leapt on one another [in
conflict]. And what did they [not] do then! How many *boyars* and

well-wishers of our father and *voevodas* did they massacre! And the
courts and the villages and the possessions of our uncles did they seize
and they set themselves up in them! And [the majority of] my mother's
treasure did they transfer to the Great Treasury, furiously kicking out
[at each other] and stabbing with sharp implements; but the remainder
they shared amongst themselves. Your grandfather, Mikhailo Tuchkov,
did this. And so Prince Vasily and Prince Ivan Shuisky of their own
accord did appoint themselves my guardians and thus did they raise
themselves to the throne; and all those who had been our father's and
our mother's main traitors did they release, one after the other, from
imprisonment and win over [*lit.* reconcile] to their side. And Prince
Vasily Shuisky began to live in the court of our uncle, Prince Andrey
Ivanovich, and in that court—as it were in a Jewish synagogue—they
seized Fedor Mishurin, the private *d'yak* of our father and of us, and
having put him to shame they murdered him. And they banished Prince
Ivan Fedorovich Bel'sky and many others to various places and rose up
in arms against the Church and, deposing the Metropolitan Daniel from
the metropolitanate, they sent him into banishment; thus did they
achieve their desire in all things and themselves began to rule. But as
for us, together with our only (-begotten) brother Georgiy, who has departed this life in sanctity—they began to feed us as though we were
foreigners or the most wretched menials. What sufferings did I [not]
endure through [lack of] clothing and through hunger! For in all things
my will was not my own [*lit.* I had no will]; everything was contrary to
my will and unbefitting my tender years. I (will) recall one thing:
whilst we were playing childish games in our infancy Prince Ivan
Vasil'evich Shuisky is sitting on a bench, leaning with his elbows on
our father's bed and with his leg up on a chair; and he did not even
incline his head towards us, either in parental manner, or even as a
master—nor was there any element of servility to be found [in his attitude to us]. And who can endure such arrogance? How can I enumerate
such countless sore sufferings as I put up with in my youth? Many a
time did I eat late, not in accordance with my will. But what of the
treasures inherited by me from my father [*lit.* of my parental heritage]?
With their cunning scheming they seized it all, as though it were pay
for the *boyar* children; but from them they took it all for themselves for
their own profit, rewarding them [the *boyar* children] not according to
their service and recompensing them not according to their merits; and
they appropriated the incalculable treasure of our grandfather and of
our father; and so from this treasure did they forge for themselves golden
and silver vessels and upon them they inscribed the names of their parents as though they had been the possession of their parents. Now all
people know that during the rule of our mother Prince Ivan Shuisky
had a marten fur coat [lined] with green mohair and the skins were

shabby [*lit.* ancient]; now supposing this was a [genuinely] ancient possession of the Shuiskys, surely it would have been better, rather than to
forge those vessels [as they did], to have exchanged the fur coat and
with the surplus [money accruing from the sale of the new coat] to have
forged the vessels? But what shall I say concerning the treasure of my
uncles? They seized it all for themselves and after this they fell upon
[*lit.* jumped on] the towns and villages and thus with the bitterest
torment in divers ways did they plunder without mercy the properties
of those living there. Who can enumerate the attacks [carried out] by
them on their neighbours? All my subjects did they make as servants
unto themselves; but their own servants did they set up like grandees;
and thinking they were ruling and organizing—instead of this they
brought to pass much injustice and disorganization, making immeasur-
able profit from all and doing and saying everything for gain.

And when they had lived thus for a long time and when I was growing
up physically, I did not wish to remain in servile submission [*lit.* under
servile power] and for this reason I sent away (from myself) Prince Ivan
Vasil'evich Shuisky to service and ordered my *boyar*, Prince Ivan Fedorovich Bel'sky, to be beside me. And Prince Ivan Shuisky, having united
all the people beneath his banner and led them to the oath of allegiance
[*lit.* to the kissing of the cross], marched in arms on Moscow and his
advisers, Kubensky and others, before his arrival seized our *boyar*, Prince
Ivan Fedorovich Bel'sky, and other *boyars* and *dvoryane* one after the
other and exiled them to Beloozero and murdered them; yea, and they
drove Metropolitan Ioasaf with great indignity from the metropolitanate.
Then Prince Andrey Shuisky together with his partisans came into our
refectory and in frenzied manner having seized and put to shame before
us our *boyar*, Fedor Semenovich Vorontsov, they bore him out from our
refectory and intended to kill him. And we sent unto them Metropolitan
Makary and our *boyars*, Ivan and Vasily Grigor'evich Morozov, with our
order not to kill him, and they, barely [hearkening] unto our order,
exiled him to Kostroma; and they afflicted the metropolitan with indignity and they tore his cloak upon him to shreds together with the
istochniki and they pushed our *boyars* in the back. Well then, is that
their "well-wishing"—that they, opposing our commands, seized our
boyars and those who are pleasing to us, and murdered and tortured
them with various torments and persecutions? Is it thus that they "lay
down their lives" for their sovereigns, waging war against our state and
in a mob seizing [*boyars*] before our very eyes, and [is it right] for a
servant to have intercourse with us, [his] sovereign, or for a sovereign
to beg [favors] from his servant? Is it right to call this "faithful service"? Indeed the whole universe will mock, seeing such "faithfulness"!
And what of the persecutions inflicted by them, which occurred at that

time? From the death of our mother unto that time for six and a half years they ceased not to practice these evil things!

But when we reached the fifteenth year of our life, then did we take it upon ourselves to put our kingdom in order and thanks to the mercy of God our rule began favourably. But since human sin ever acerbates the Grace of God, it came to pass that—because of our sins and the intensification of God's wrath—a fiery flame burned the ruling city of Moscow, and our treacherous *boyars*, who are called martyrs by you (their names will I intentionally pass over), seized the moment which appeared [*lit.* as it were] favourable to their treacherous wickedness [and] incited the feeblest-witted of the people [by saying] that the mother of our mother, Princess Anna Glinsky, together with her children and her retinue extracted human hearts and with such magic set fire to Moscow and that we had knowledge of this their ,counsel; and owing to the incitement of those traitors, the people, raising a cry and having seized in frenzied manner our *boyar*, Prince Yury Vasil'evitch Glinsky in the chapel of the holy martyr Dimitry of Salonica, and having dragged him out, inhumanly slew him in the apostolic cathedral of the Assumption of the most holy Mother of God opposite the throne of the metropolitan, and filled the church with his blood; and they dragged his dead body into the porch of the church and laid him, like one condemned [to death], in the market place. And this his murder in the church is known to all, and not as you lyingly assert, you cur! (Now) while we were living in our village of Vorob'evo these traitors stirred up the people to kill us too, on the grounds that we were hiding from them the mother of Prince Yury [Glinsky], Princess Anna, and his brother Prince Mikhail. How can one help but deride such sophistries! For what reason, pray, should we ourselves be the incendiary of our own kingdom? Indeed, so many possessions—the legacy [*lit.* blessing] of our forefathers—did we lose as could not be found again in the whole universe. Who could be so insensate or wild as to destroy his own possessions when in anger with his servants? He would burn down their [houses], but would preserve himself. In everything is your currish treachery brought to light. And how could one sprinkle water to such a height as [the church of] St. John? This is indeed clear madness. And with such "well-wishing" is it befitting for our *boyars* and *voevodas* to serve us, (namely) by assembling like a pack of hounds without our knowledge and slaughtering our *boyars*—yea, and even those in blood relationship [*lit.* in blood line] with us? And thus do they lay down their lives for us, desiring at all times to despatch our soul from this world into the world to come? For us they deem the law to be sacrosanct, but themselves wish not to travel the [same] path with us! Why too in your pride do you boast, you cur, of your warlike bravery and likewise [of that] of other hounds and traitors? For our Lord Jesus Christ says [*lit.* saying. Dat.

absolute] "if a kingdom be divided against itself, that kingdom cannot stand;" and how can one conduct military operations against an enemy if the kingdom be torn by fratricidal struggles? For how can a tree flower if its roots are dry? Likewise [is] this [the case] too: if there is not good order in the kingdom beforehand, how can wars be fought with bravery? For if a commander does not sufficiently strengthen his army, then he is conquered rather than conqueror. But you, disregarding all these things, praise bravery alone; and as for what bravery consists in, this you consider of no importance and you show yourself to be a man who not only does [not] strengthen bravery, but rather destroys it, for you are [as] nought: at home a traitor, in the field—bereft of reasoning; for you wish by fratricidal strife and by wilfulness to strengthen your bravery, which is impossible.

Now at this time that cur, Aleksey, your chief, was in the court of our kingdom during our youth, and I knew not by what means he was promoted from *batozhnik*; but we, having seen such treachery on the part of our grandees, thus took him from the dung-heap and placed him together with the grandees, hoping for faithful [*lit.* straight] service from him. What honours and riches did I not heap upon him—[and] not only upon him, but also upon his family! Yet what true service did I get from him? Listen further. Afterwards, for the sake of spiritual counsel and the salvation of my soul, I took [into my service] the priest Sylvester, thinking that he, because of his ministry at the altar of the Lord, would have care for his soul; but he, having trampled under foot his priesthood vows and his ordination [and] all that [appertains] to service with the angels at the altar of the Lord, "which things the angels desire to look into," where the Lamb of God is ever sacrificed for the salvation of the world and is never consumed—he, indeed, whilst still in the flesh, was deemed worthy [to perform] the Seraphic service with his own hands; and all this he trampled down in his cunning way; yet at first it seemed as though he had begun in a righteous manner, following the Holy Scriptures; [and] when I saw in the Holy Scriptures that it is right to submit to good preceptors without any consideration, then, willingly, but through ignorance, did I obey even him for the sake of spiritual counsel. But he was carried away by power like Eli the priest [and] began to form friendships as laymen do. Then we assembled all the archbishops and the bishops and all the holy synod of the Russian metropolitanate, and as for what befell us in our youth, the disgraces inflicted by us [*lit.* our disgraces] upon you, our *boyars*, and likewise too the hostility towards us and the misdemeanours committed by you, our *boyars* —for all these things did we ourselves publicly ask forgiveness before our father and interceder, Makary, Metropolitan of All Russia. And [to] you, our *boyars*, and to all our people did I grant [forgiveness] for your misdemeanours and [decreed] that henceforth all memory of them be obliterated; and so then did we begin to treat you all as [though you were] good men.

But you did not abandon your first cunning habit[s], but returned again to your former ways and thus began to serve us with cunning counsel and false, and to do all things with scheming and not with simplicity. And so the priest Sylvester joined Aleksey too in friendship and they began to hold counsel in secret and without our knowledge, deeming us to be incapable of judgment; and thus did they begin to give worldly counsel in the place of spiritual, and thus did they begin little by little to lead all the *boyars* into contumacy, taking the splendour of our power from us and leading you into opposition, and in honour almost levelling you with us, while they made the young *boyar* children your equals in honour. And so did this evil little by little become confirmed; and he [Sylvester] began to allocate to you patrimonies and villages—such patrimonies which by the decree of our grandfather, the Grand Prince, had either been taken from you or might not be disposed of by you—even these patrimonies did he scatter in the wind in an unbefitting manner and [thus] did he destroy that decree of our grandfather and win the friendship of [*lit.* reconcile to himself] those many people. And then he admitted his confederate, Prince Dimitry Kurlyatev, into our council; and taking precedence over us in such manner by means of [*lit.* for the sake of] spiritual advice he thus acts as it were for the sake of [my] soul and not from cunning; and thus did he and that confederate of his begin to establish their evil counsel; not one position [*lit.* power] did they neglect in which they did not appoint their favourites, and so in all things did they achieve their desire. And after this did he and that confederate of his take from us the power given to us by our forefathers so that you, [who are] our *boyars* [only] by our grace [alone], might be honoured with the dignity of precedence. And all these things did they place in their hands [*lit.* power] and in your hands, as it suited you and as anyone of you desired; for that reason, then, did they strengthen [their positions] with friendships and when they had all things in their power entirely according to their will, then, without asking us aught, as though we did not exist, did they make regulations and take measures according to their will and to the desire of their advisers. Whenever we gave any good advice, they did not avail themselves of it; but if *they* were to give any refractory or corrupt advice, then were they acting for the common weal!

And so neither in external affairs nor in internal affairs, nor in the smallest and prettiest things (and [I refer to such things as] footwear and sleeping)—was anything according to my will; but everything was done according to their desire, while we remained, as it were, a child. Now is this "contrary to reason" that, I, having reached man's estate, did not desire to be a little child? Likewise afterwards this too became a habit [lit. was established]: if we had at that time to contradict even one of the most insignificant counsellors, then all these [my words] were interpreted as impious, as is written in your calumnious epistle; but if any of his most inferior advisers were in their madness to utter haughty words to us, not as to a master or as to a brother, but as to the most inferior thing, then all these things too were reckoned to be pious; and whoever provided us with a little obedience or peace, to his lot fell persecution and torment. And should anyone annoy us in aught or cause us to suffer [lit. bring to us] any oppression, to his lot fell wealth, glory and honour. And if I did not acquiesce [lit. if it were not so], then [they said,] this [would lead] to the downfall of my soul and the destruction of the kingdom! And so, while we continued to suffer such persecution and oppression, such evils increased, not from day to day, but from hour [to hour]; and all that was repugnant to us increased, while as for obedience and peace [being] afforded to us—these things decreased. Such then was the Orthodox Faith at that time! Who indeed can recount in detail both the persecutions and oppressions [I suffered] in my ways of life, in my movements and in repose, and likewise in my attendance at church and in all my manner of life? And so it was then; they imposed these things upon us in God's name, deeming that they were inflicting such persecutions upon us for the good of our soul and not through cunning.

Likewise, when by God's will we set out against the godless people of Kazan' with the banner inscribed with the Cross, the banner of all the Orthodox Christian host, to defend Orthodox Christianity, and [when] thus by the inexpressible mercy of God, who gave [us] victory over that Mussulman people, we returned home safe and sound with all the host of Orthodox Christianity—what shall I say of the "well-wishing" towards me of those who are called martyrs by you? This then [will I say]: having placed me like a prisoner on a ship they conveyed me with very few people through the godless and most unbelieving land! Had not the all-powerful right hand of the Almighty protected my humility, then in any case would I have lost my life. Such is the "well-wishing" of those men in whose defence you speak, and thus do they "lay down their lives for us" by striving to deliver our soul into the hands of foreigners!

Likewise, when we had arrived in the ruling city of Moscow God increased his mercy towards us and gave us at that time an heir, our son Dimitry. But after a short time had passed [it fell to our lot]—as indeed it falls to the lot of [all] men—to be afflicted with sickness and to be sorely ill; and then did those who are called by you "well-wishers" rise up like drunken men with the priest Sylvester and with your chief Aleksey, thinking that we were no longer alive, having forgotten our good deeds and even their own souls too, and [having forgotten] that they had kissed the Cross [in allegiance] to our father and to us, [vow-ing] to seek no other sovereign but our children. Yet they desired to raise to the throne Prince Vladimir, who is far removed from us in the line of succession [*lit.* generation]; while our infant, given to us by God, did they, like Herod, desire to destroy (and how could they fail to destroy him!), having raised Prince Vladimir to the throne. For even though it was said in the ancient secular writings, yet none the less is [the following] fitting: "Tsar does not bow down to tsar; but when one dies, the other rules." [If] then we, while still alive, enjoyed such "well-wishing" from our subjects, what will it be like after our death! But again thanks to God's mercy we recovered, and thus was this counsel scattered. But the priest Sylvester and Aleksey ceased not from that time forth to counsel all that was evil and to inflict [on me] still harsher oppression, conceiving persecutions of various kinds against our [true] well-wishers, while indulging every whim of Prince Vladimir; and likewise they stirred up great hatred against our tsaritsa Anastasia and likened her to all the impious tsaritsas; as for our children, they were not able even to call them to mind.

Likewise did that cur, that traitor, Prince Semen Rostovsky, who, because of our grace and not according to his merits, was honoured by us with [the dignity of] counsellorship, revile our counsel in his treacherous manner before the Lithuanian ambassadors, Pan Stanislas Dowojna and his suite, censuring us and our tsaritsa and our children. And when we had investigated this wickedness of his we none the less inflicted a merciful punishment upon him [*lit.* mercifully inflicted . . .]. And after that the priest Sylvester with you, his evil counsellors, began to surround that dog with every protection [*lit.* to keep him in great protection] and to help him with every [possible] favour—and not only him, but all his kin. And so from that time forth a period of prosperity fell to the lot of all traitors; while we from that time forth suffered great oppression. And even you too were at one with them: it is well known that you and Kurlyatev (the son) intended to judge the Sitsky case.

Likewise when the war began, that is, the war against the Germans—but more will be said about this in greater detail later on—the Priest Sylvester together with you, his counsellors, attacked us fiercely on this score, and as for the sickness which, because of our sins, had been visited upon us and upon our tsaritsa and upon our children—they claimed that these things happened because of them—that is, because of our disobedience to them. How shall I recall the hard [*lit.* merciless] journey to the ruling city from Mozhaisk with our ailing tsaritsa Anastasia? Owing to one single little word did she rank as worthless [in their eyes]. But as for prayers and journeys to desert places [*i.e.,* hermitages], gifts and vows to the saints [*lit.* sanctity] for the salvation of our soul, for our bodily health and for all our well-being and for that of our tsaritsa and of our children—all these things were taken completely from us by your cunning scheming. And as for medical skill, for our health's sake, there was no mention of it at that time.

And as we remained thus in such dire afflictions and as we were not able to endure such oppression as you inhumanly inflicted [upon us], for this reason did we investigate the treacherous deeds of that dog Aleksey Adashev and all his advisers, and [yet] we exercised our wrath with mercy; the death penalty we did not inflict, but we banished them to various places. But the Priest Sylvester, seeing his advisers set at naught, for this reason left of his own will; but we, having given him our blessing, did not dismiss him, not because we were ashamed [of anything], but because we did not wish to judge him here [on earth], but in the world to come, before the Lamb of God, for the evil he has done to me while ever serving me and [yet] in his cunning manner overlooking me. There will I accept judgment for as much as I have suffered, spiritually and bodily, at his hands. For this reason I have allowed his son to remain unmolested even to the present day—and only from our presence is he debarred. And should anyone like you say that it is ridiculous to give way to [*lit.* obey] a priest, [then my reply would be that,] seeing you know not thoroughly the Christian monastic rule [wherein we are told] that it is right to submit to one's teachers, and seeing you were dull of hearing, needing a teacher for the time and now you are become such as have need of milk and not of strong meat—for these reasons would [such a person like you] say these things. And for the reason I have mentioned above did I do Sylvester no harm. But as for the laymen who are under our power, with them did we deal according to their treachery; at first we punished [*lit.* touched] no one with the death penalty; but we ordered everyone—whoever had adhered to them—to keep away from them and not to adhere to them [further]; and when we had laid down this decree we confirmed it by [exacting] the oath on the Cross. But since our decree was disregarded by those whom you call martyrs and their accomplices and since they transgressed the oath on the Cross, they not only did not keep away from those traitors, but they began to help them still more and to scheme in all manner of ways in order to return them to their former dignity and to plot all the more fiercely against us; and since their malice showed itself to be unquenchable and their will [*lit.* understanding] was revealed as inflexible—for this reason the guilty ones received such a judgment according to their guilt.

26

Moscow and the Court of Ivan the Terrible in 1553

In 1553, three English ships set out to find a northern passage to China. Two of the ships were lost in the Arctic and the third, under Captain Richard Chancellor, sailed to the mouth of the Northern Dvina. Chancellor made his way to Moscow where he was well received by Ivan the Terrible, who encouraged him to return. This journey is important for two reasons: it inaugurated lively commercial relations between England and Russia, carried on by the Muscovy Company, which was organized in London for that purpose and endowed with extensive privileges by Ivan the Terrible (see Chapter 27); and it resulted in Chancellor's interesting description of Moscow and of his reception at the court of Ivan the Terrible.

The [city of] Moscow is from Iaroslav 200 miles. The country between them is very well replenished with small villages, which are so well filled with people that it is wonder to see them: the ground is well stored with corn which they carry to the city of Moscow in such abundance that it is wonder to see it. You shall meet in a morning 700 or 800 sleds coming or going thither, that carry corn, and some carry fish. You shall have some that carry corn to Moscow, and some that fetch corn from thence, that at the least dwell a thousand miles off; and

Reprinted with permission of the Cambridge University Press from Richard Hakluyt, *The Principal Navigations, Voyages, Traffiques, & Discoveries of the English Nation* (Glasgow, James MacLehose and Sons, 1903), vol. 2, pp. 225–230, 234–236. Spellings have been modernized to facilitate reading. Items in brackets are mine.

all their carriage is on sleds. Those which come so far dwell in the North parts of the Duke's dominions, where the cold will suffer no corn to grow, it is so extreme. They bring thither fish, furs, and beasts' skins. In those parts they have but small store of cattle.

The [city of] Moscow itself is great: I take the whole town to be greater than London with the suburbs: but it is very rude, and stands without all order. Their houses are all of timber, very dangerous for fire. There is a fair castle, the walls whereof are of brick, and very high: they say they are eighteen feet thick, but I do not believe it, it does not so seem, notwithstanding I do not certainly know it: for no stranger may come to view it. The one side is ditched, and on the other side runs a river called Moscow which runs into Tartary and so into the sea called Mare Caspium: and on the North side there is a base town, which has also a brick wall about it, and so it joins with the castle wall. The Emperor lies in the castle, wherein are nine fair Churches, and therein are religious men. Also there is a Metropolitan with diverse Bishops. I will not stand in description of their buildings nor of the strength thereof because we have better in all points in England. They are well furnished with ordinance of all sorts.

The Emperor's or Duke's house neither in building nor in the outward show, nor yet within the house is so sumptuous as I have seen. It is very low built in eight square, much like the old building of England, with small windows, and so in other points.

Now to declare my coming before his Majesty: After I had remained twelve days, the Secretary which has the hearing of strangers did send for me, advertizing me that the Duke's pleasure was to have me to come before his Majesty with the king's my master's letters: whereof I was right glad, and so I gave my attendance. And when the Duke was in his place appointed, the interpreter came for me into the outer chamber, where sat one hundred or more gentleman, all in cloth of gold very sumptuous, and from thence I came into the Council chamber, where sat the Duke himself with his nobles, which were a fair company: they sat round about the chamber on high, yet so that he himself sat much higher than any of his nobles in a chair gilt, and in a long garment of beaten gold, with an imperial crown upon his head, and a staff of crystal and gold in his right hand, and his other hand half leaning on his chair. The Chancellor stood up with the Secretary before the Duke. After my duty done and my letter delivered, he bade me welcome, and inquired of me the health of the King my master, and I answered that he was in good health at my departure from his court, and that my trust was that he was now in the same. Upon the which he bade me to dinner. The Chancellor presented my present unto his Grace bareheaded (for before they were all covered) and when his Grace had received my letter, I was required to depart: for I had charge not to speak to the

Duke, but when he spoke to me. So I departed unto the Secretary's chamber, where I remained two hours, and then I was sent for again unto another palace which is called the golden palace, but I saw no cause why it should be so called; for I have seen many fairer than it in all points: and so I came into the hall, which was small and not great as is the King's Majesties' of England, and the table was covered with a tablecloth; and the Marshal sat at the end of the table with a little white rod in his hand, which board was full of vessel of gold; and on the other side of the hall did stand a fair cupboard of plate. From thence I came into the dining chamber, where the Duke himself sat at his table without cloth of estate, in a gown of silver, with a crown imperial upon his head, he sat in a chair somewhat high: There sat none near him by a great way. There were long tables set round about the chamber, which were full set with such as the Duke had at dinner: they were all in white. Also the places where the tables stood were higher by two steps than the rest of the house. In the midst of the chamber stood a table or cupboard to set plate on; which stood full of cups of gold: and amongst all the rest there stood four marvelous great pots or crudences as they call them, of gold and silver: I think they were a good yard and a half high. By the cupboard stood two gentlemen with napkins on their shoulders, and in their hands each of them had a cup of gold set with pearls and precious stones, which were the Duke's own drinking cups: when he was disposed, he drunk them off at a draught. And for his service at meat it came in without order, yet it was very rich service: for all were served in gold, not only he himself, but also all the rest of us, and it was very massive: the cups also were of gold and very massive. The number that dined there that day was 200 persons, and all were served in golden vessel. The gentlemen that waited were all in cloth of gold, and they served him with their caps on their heads. Before the service came in, the Duke sent to every man a great shiver of bread, and the bearer called the party so sent to by his name aloud, and said, John Basilevich Emperor of Russia and great Duke of Moscovy does reward you with bread: then must all men stand up, and do at all times when these words are spoken. And then last of all he gave the Marshal bread, whereof he ate before the Duke's Grace, and so did reverence and departed. Then came the Duke's service of the Swans all in pieces, and every one in a different dish: which the Duke sent as he did the bread, and the bearer said the same words as he said before. And as I said before, the service of his meat is in no order, but comes in dish by dish: and then after that the Duke sends drink, with the like saying as before is told. Also before dinner he changed his crown, and in dinner time two crowns; so that I saw three different crowns upon his head in one day. And thus when his service was all come in he gave to every one of his gentlemen waiters meat with his own hand, and so likewise drink. His intent thereby is, as

I have heard, that every man shall know perfectly his servants. Thus when dinner is done he calls his nobles before him name by name, that it is wonder to hear how he could name them, having so many as he has. Thus when dinner was done I departed to my lodging, which was an hour within night. I will leave this, and speak no more of him nor his household: but I will somewhat declare of his land and people, with their nature and power in the wars. This Duke is Lord and Emperor of many countries, and his power is marvelous great. For he is able to bring into the field 200,000 or 300,000 men: he never goes into the field himself with under 200,000 men: And when he goes himself he furnishes his borders all with men of war, which are no small number. He leaves on the borders of Liefland 40,000 men, and upon the borders of Lithuania 60,000 men, and toward the Nogay Tartars 60,000, which is wonder to hear of: yet never does he take to his wars neither husbandman nor merchant. All his men are horsemen: he uses no footmen, but such as go with the ordinance and laborers, which are 30,000. The horsemen are all archers, with such bows as the Turks have, and they ride short as do the Turks. Their armor is a coat of plate, with a skull on their heads. Some of their coats are covered with velvet or cloth of gold: their desire is to be sumptuous in the field, and especially the nobles and gentlemen: as I have heard their trimming is very costly, and partly I have seen it, or else I would scarcely have believed it: but the Duke himself is richly attired above all measure: his pavilion is covered either with cloth of gold or silver, and so set with stones that it is wonderful to see it. I have seen the King's Majesties' of England and the French King's pavilions, which are fair, yet not like unto his. And when they are sent into far or foreign countries, or foreigners come to them, they are very gorgeous. Else the Duke himself goes but meanly in apparel: and when he goes between one place and another he is but reasonably apparelled over other times. In the while that I was in Moscow the Duke sent two ambassadors to the King of Poland, which had at the least 500 horses; their sumptuousness was above measure, not only in themselves, but also in their horses, as velvet, cloth of gold, and cloth of silver set with pearls and not scant. What shall I farther say? I never heard of nor saw men so sumptuous: but it is no daily guise for when they have not occasion, as I said before, all their doing is but mean. . . .

The Duke gives sentence himself upon all matters in the law. Which is very commendable, that such a Prince will take pains to see ministration of justice. Yet notwithstanding it is wonderfully abused: and thereby the Duke is much deceived. But if it fall out that the officers be espied in cloaking the truth, they have most condign punishment. And if the plaintiff can nothing prove, then the defendant must take his oath upon the Crucifix whether he is in the right or no. Then is demanded if the plaintiff be any thing able further to make proof: if he be not, then sometimes he will say, I am able to prove it by my body and hands, or by my champion's body, so requiring the contest. After the other has his oath, it is granted as well to the one as to the other. So when they go to the field, they swear upon the Crucifix, that they are both in the right, and that the one shall make the other to confess the truth before they depart forth of the field: and so they go both to the battle armed with such weapons as they use in that country: they fight all on foot, and seldom the parties themselves do fight, except they be Gentlemen, for they stand much upon their reputation, for they will not fight, but with such as are come of as good a house as themselves. So that if either party require the combat, it is granted unto them, and no champion is to serve in his place: wherein is no deceit: but otherwise by champions there is. For although they take great oaths upon them to do battle truly, yet is the contrary often seen: because the common champions have none other living. And as soon as the one party has gotten the victory, he demands the debt, and the other is carried to prison, and there is shamefully used till he take order. There is also another order in the law, that the plaintiff may swear in some causes of debt. And if the party defendant be poor, he shall be set under the Crucifix, and the party plaintiff must swear over his head, and when he has taken his oath, the Duke takes the party defendant home to his house, and uses him as his bond-man, and puts him to labor, or lets him for hire to any such as need him, until such time as his friends make provision for his redemption: or else he remains in bondage all the days of his life. Again there are many that will sell themselves to Gentlemen or Merchants to be their bond-men, to have during their life meat, drink and clothes, and at their coming to have a piece of money. Yes, and some will sell their wives and children to be bawdes and drudges to the buyer. Also they have a law for felons and pickers contrary to the laws of England. For by their law they can hang no man for his first offense; but may keep him long in prison, and oftentimes beat him with whips and other punishment: and there he shall remain until his friends are able to bail him. If he be a picker or a cut-purse, as there are very many, the second time he is taken, he has a piece of his nose cut off, and is burned in the forehead, and kept in prison till he find sureties for his good behavior. And if he be taken the third time, he is hanged. And at the first time he is extremely punished and not released, except he have very good friends, or that some Gentleman require to have him to the wars: And in so doing, he shall enter into great bonds for him: by which means the country is brought into good quietness. But they are naturally given to great deceit, except extreme beating did bridle them. They are naturally given to hard living as well in fare as in lodging. I heard a Russian say, that it was a great deal merrier living in prison than forth, but for the great beating. For they have drink and meat without any labor, and get the charity of well disposed people: But being at liberty they get nothing. The poor are very innumerable, and live most miserably: for I have seen them eat the pickle of herring and other stinking fish: nor the fish cannot be so stinking nor rotten, but they will eat it and praise it to be more wholesome than other fish or fresh meat. In my opinion there are no such people under the sun for their hardness of living.

27

First Privileges Granted by Ivan the Terrible to English Merchants, 1555

The immediate result of Chancellor's unintended voyage to Moscow was the chartering of the Muscovy Company in London in 1555 in order to establish trade relations with Moscow. Because Ivan the Terrible was interested in west European commercial and military relations, the Muscovy Company had no difficulty in acquiring many rights and privileges. Its representatives set up trading depots in many Russian cities and traveled extensively through most of the possessions of Moscovy.

Reprinted with permission of the Cambridge University Press from Richard Hakluyt, *The Principal Navigations, Voyages, Traffiques, & Discoveries of the English Nation* (Glasgow, James MacLehose and Sons, 1903), vol. 2, pp. 297–303. Spellings have been modernized to facilitate reading.

Ivan Vasilevich, by the grace of God Emperor of Russia, Great Duke of Novgorod, Moscow, etc. To all people that shall see, read, hear or understand these presents, greeting. Foreasmuch as God has planted all realms and dominions in the whole world with sundry commodities, so as the one has need of the amity and commodities of the other, and by means thereof traffick is used from one to another, and amity thereby increased: and for that as amongst men nothing is more to be desired than amity, without the which no creature being of a natural good disposition can live in quietness, so that it is as troublesome to be utterly wanting, as it is perceived to be grievous to the body to lack air, fire, or any other necessities most requisite for the conservation and maintenance thereof in health: considering also how needful merchandise is, which furnishes men of all that which is convenient for their living and nourishment, for their clothing, trimming, the satisfying of their delights, and all other things convenient and profitable for them, and that merchandise brings the same commodities from diverse quarters in so great abundance, as by means thereof nothing is lacking in any part, and that all things be in every place (where intercourse of merchandise is received and embraced) generally in such sort, as amity thereby is entered into, and planted to continue, and the enjoyers thereof be as men living in a golden world: Upon these respects and other weighty and good considerations, us hereunto moving, and chiefly upon the contemplation of the gracious letters, directed from the right high, right excellent, and right mighty Queen Mary, by the grace of God Queen of England, France, etc., in the favor of her subjects, merchants, the governor, consuls, assistants, and community of merchants, adventurers for the discovery of lands, etc.

Know ye therefore, that we of our grace special, mere motion, and certain knowledge, have given and granted, and by these presents for us, our heirs and successors, do give and grant as much as in us is and lies, unto Sebastian Cabot, Governor, Sir George Barnes, Knight, etc., Consuls: Sir John Gresham, etc., Assistants, and to the community of the aforenamed fellowship, and to their successors for ever, and to the successors of every of them, these articles, grants, immunities, franchises, liberties and privileges, and every of them hereafter following, expressed and declared. Videlicet:

1. First, we for us, our heirs and successors, do by these presents give and grant free license, faculty, authority and power unto the said Governor, Consuls, Assistants, and community of the said fellowship, and to their successors for ever, that all and singular the merchants of the same company, their agents, factors, doers of their business, attorneys, servants, and ministers, and every of them may at all times hereafter for ever more surely, freely and safely with their ships, merchandises, goods and things whatsoever sail, come and enter into all and singular our lands, countries,

dominions, cities, towns, villages, castles, ports, jurisdictions and districts
by sea, land or fresh waters, and there tarry, abide and sojourn, and buy,
sell, barter and change all kind of merchandises with all manner of
merchants and people, of whatsoever nation, rite, condition, state or
degrees they be, and with the same or other ships, wares, merchandises,
goods and things whatsoever they be, unto other empires, kingdoms,
dukedoms, parts, and to any other place or places at their pleasure and
liberty by sea, land, or fresh waters may depart, and exercise all kind of
merchandises in our empire and dominions, and every part thereof freely
and quietly without any restraint, impeachment, price exaction, pressure,
straight custom, toll, imposition, or subsidy to be demanded, taxed or
paid, or at any time hereafter to be demanded, taxed, set, levied or inferred upon them or any of them, or upon their goods, ships, wares,
merchandises and things, of, for or upon any part or parcel thereof, or
upon the goods, ships, wares, merchandises, and things of any of them,
so that they shall not need any other safe conduct or license general,
or special, of us, our heirs or successors, neither shall be bound to ask
any safe conduct or license in any of the aforesaid places subject unto us.

2. Item, we give and grant to the said merchants this power and
liberty, that they, neither any of them, nor their goods, wares, merchandises or things, nor any part thereof, shall be by any means within
our dominions, lands, countries, castles, towns, villages, or other place or
places of our jurisdiction, at any time hereafter attached, stayed, arrested
nor disturbed for any debt, duty or other thing, for the which they be
not principal debtors or sureties, nor also, for any offense or trespass
committed, or that shall be committed, but only for such as they or any
of them shall actually commit, and the same offenses (if any such happen), shall be by us only heard, and determined.

3. Item, we give and grant, that the said merchants shall and may have
free liberty, power and authority to name, choose and assign brokers,
shippers, packers, weighers, measurers, wagoners, and all other meet and
necessary laborers for to serve them in their feat of merchandises, and
minister and give unto them and every of them a corporal oath, to serve
them well and truly in their offices, and finding them or any of them
doing contrary to his or their oath, may punish and dismiss them, and
from time to time choose, swear and admit other in their place or places,
without contradiction, let, vexation or disturbance, either of us, our
heirs, or successors, or of any other of our justices, officers, ministers or
subjects whatsoever.

4. Item, we give and grant unto the said merchants and their successors, that such person as is, or shall be commended unto us, our heirs
or successors by the Governor, Consuls and Assistants of the said fellowship resident within the city of London within the realm of England, to
be their chief factor within this our empire and dominions, may and

shall have full power and authority to govern and rule all Englishmen that have had, or shall have access, or repair in or to this said Empire and jurisdictions, or any part thereof, and shall and may minister unto them, and every of them good justice in all their causes, plaints, quarrels, and disorders between them moved, and to be moved, and assemble, deliberate, consult, conclude, define, determine and make such acts, and ordinances, as he so commended with his Assistants shall think good and meet for the good order, government and rule of the said merchants, and all other Englishmen repairing to this our said empire and dominions, or any part thereof, and to set and levy upon all, and every Englishmen, offender or offenders, of such their acts and ordinances made, and to be made, penalties and mulcts by fine or imprisonment.

5. Item, if it happen that any of the said merchants, or other Englishmen, as one or more do rebel against such chief factor or factors, or his or their deputies and will not dispose him or themselves to obey them and every of them as shall appertain, if the said rebels or disobedients do come, and be found in our said empire and jurisdictions, or any part and place thereof, then we promise and grant, that all and every our officers, ministers, and subjects shall effectually aid and assist the said chief factor or factors, and their deputies, and for their power shall really work, to bring such rebel or disobedient rebels, or disobedients to due obedience: And to that intent shall lend unto the same factor or factors, and their deputies upon request therefore to be made, prisons, and instruments for punishments from time to time.

6. Item, we promise unto the said merchants, and their successors upon their request to exhibit and do unto them good, exact and favorable justice, with expedition in all their causes, and that when they or any of them shall have access, or come to or before any of our justices, for any their plaints moved, and to be moved between any of our subjects or other foreigner, and them, or any of them, that then they shall be first and forthwith heard, as soon as the party which they shall find before our justices shall be depeached, which party being heard forthwith, and as soon as may be, the said English merchants shall be rid and dispatched: And if any action shall be moved by or against any of the said merchants being absent out of our said empire and dominions, then such merchants may substitute an attorney in all and singular his causes to be followed as need shall require, and as shall seem to him expedient.

7. Item, we grant and promise to the said merchants, and to their successors, that if the same merchants or any of them shall be wounded, or (which God forbid) slain in any part or place of our empire or dominions, then good information thereof given, we and our justices and other officers shall execute due correction and punishment without delay, according to the exigence of the case: so that it shall be an example to all other not to commit the like. And if it shall chance the factors,

servants, or ministers of the said merchants or any of them to trespass or offend, whereby they or any of them shall incur the danger of death or punishment, the goods, wares, merchandises, and things of their masters shall not therefore be forfeited, confiscated, spoiled nor seized by any means by us, our heirs or successors, or by any of our officers, ministers or subjects, but shall remain to their use, frank, free, and discharged from all punishment and loss.

8. Item, we grant that if any of the English nation be arrested for any debt, he shall not be laid in prison, so far as he can put in sufficient surety and pawn: neither shall any sergeant, or officer lead them or any of them to prison, before he shall have known whether the chief factor or factors, or their deputies shall be sureties, or bring in pawn for such arrested: then the officers shall release the party, and shall set him or them at liberty.

9. Moreover, we give, grant and promise to the said merchants, that if any of their ships or other vessels shall be spoiled, robbed, or damnified in sailing, anchoring or returning to or from our said empires and dominions, or any part thereof, by any pirates, merchants, or other person, whatsoever he or they be, that then and in such case, we will do all that in us is to cause restitution, reparation, and satisfaction to be duly made to the said English merchants by our letters and otherwise, as shall stand with our honor, and be consonant to equity and justice.

10. Item, for us, our heirs and successors, we do promise and grant to perform, maintain, corroborate, authenticate, and observe all and singular the aforesaid liberties, franchises, and privileges, like as presently we firmly do intend, and will corroborate, authenticate and perform the same by all mean and way that we can, as much as may be to the commodity and profit of the said English merchants, and their successors for ever.

And to the intent that all and singular the said gifts, grants and promises, may be inviolably observed and performed, we the said Ivan Vasilevich by the grace of God Emperor of Russia, Great Duke of Novgorod, Moscow, etc., for us, our heirs and successors, by our Imperial and lordly word in stead of an oath, have and do promise by these presents, inviolably to maintain and observe, and cause to be inviolably observed and maintained all and singular the aforesaid gifts, grants and promises from time to time, and at all and every time and times hereafter. And for the more corroboration hereof have caused our seal hereunto to be put.

28

A Letter
from King Sigismund of Poland
to Elizabeth I, 1559

The establishment of commercial relations, followed
by Ivan the Terrible's search for closer ties with
England, was ill received in some European countries. At first the French feared that Ivan might be
persuaded by Mary Tudor and her husband Philip
II of Spain to join the anti-French and anti-Ottoman
struggle then in progress. When Ivan the Terrible
started his drive to establish Moscow's control in
the Baltic Sea, the Poles became chief opponents of
English rapprochement with Moscow and, through
their King, pleaded for termination of English trade
with Moscow.

Sigismund Augustus by the grace of God King of Poland, Great
Duke of Lithuania, Russia, Prussia, Masovia and Samogetia, etc. Lord
and heir etc., to the most Noble Princess Lady Elizabeth, by the same
grace of God Queen of England, France and Ireland, etc., our dear
sister and kinswoman, greeting and increase of all felicity. Whereas your
Majesty writes to us that you have received two of our letters, we have
looked that you should have answered to them both. First to the one, in
which we intreated more at large in forbidding the voyage to Narva,
which if it had been done, we had been unburdened of so often writing
of one matter: and might have answered your Majesty much better to
the purpose. Now we thus answer to your Majesty to those matters of
which you write to us the 3d of October [1559] from Windsor. First,

Reprinted with permission of the Cambridge University Press from Richard
Hakluyt, The Principal Navigations, Voyages, Traffiques, & Discoveries of the
English Nation (Glasgow, James MacLehose and Sons, 1903), vol. 2, pp. 485–
487. Spellings have been modernized to facilitate reading.

forasmuch as your Majesty at the request of our letters has discharged the arrest of merchants' goods, and of the names of the men of Denmark our subjects, which was set upon them by the commandment of Your Majesty: and also have restored the old and ancient liberty of traffic, we acknowledge great pleasure done unto us in the same: and also think it to be done according to common agreement made in times past. Neither were we ever at any time of any other opinion touching your Majesty, but that we should obtain right and reason at your hands. Forasmuch as we likewise shall at all times be ready to grant to your Majesty, making any request for your subjects, so far as shall stand with justice, yet neither will we yield anything to your Majesty in contention of love, benevolence, and mutual office, but that we judge every good turn of yours to be recompensed by us to the uttermost: and that shall we prove as occasion shall serve. Therefore we shall command the arrests, if any be made by our subjects (as it is unknown to us) of merchants' goods and English names to be discharged: and shall conserve the old liberty of traffic, and all other things which shall seem to appertain to neighborhood between us and your Majesty: so that none of the subjects of your Majesty hereafter presume to use the navigation to the Narva forbidden by us and full of danger not only to our parts, but also to the open destruction of all Christian and liberal nations. The which as we have written afore, so we now write again to your Majesty that we know and feel of a surety, the Moscovite, enemy of all liberty under the heavens, daily to grow mightier by the increase of such things as be brought to the Narva, while not only wares but also weapons heretofore unknown to him, and artifices and arts be brought unto him: by means whereof he makes himself strong to vanquish all others. Which things, as long as this voyage to Narva is used, cannot be stopped. And we perfectly know your Majesty cannot be ignorant how great the cruelty is of the said enemy, of what force he is, what tyranny he uses on his subjects, and in what servile sort they be under him. We seemed hitherto to vanquish him only in this that he was rude of arts and ignorant of policies. If so be that this navigation to the Narva continue, what shall be unknown to him? Therefore we that know best, and border upon him, do admonish other Christian princes in time, that they do not betray their dignity, liberty and life of them and their subjects to a most barbarous and cruel enemy, as we can no less do by the duty of a Christian prince. For now we do foresee, except other princes take this admonition, the Moscovite puffed up in pride with those things that be brought to the Narva, and made more perfect in warlike affairs with engines of war and ships, will make assault this way on Christendom, to slay or make bound all that shall withstand him: which God defend. With which our admonition diverse princes already content themselves and abstain from the Narva. The others that will not abstain from the said voyage shall be impeached by our navy and incur the danger of loss of life, liberty, wife and children. Now therefore if the subjects of your Majesty will forbear this voyage to Narva there shall be nothing denied to them of us. Let your Majesty well weigh and consider the reasons and occasions of our stopping of ships going to the Narva. In which stopping our subjects of Denmark be in′ no fault, as we have already written to your Majesty, neither use we their counsel in the same. In any other matter, if there be any fault in them against your Majesty or your subjects, we will gladly do justice upon them, that your Majesty may well understand that we be careful of you and your subjects. Neither think we it meet to take Hamburg, or any other place to judge the matter; for we have our council and judgment seat at Rie, where your Majesty and your subjects, or any other shall have justice administered unto them, with whom we have had ancient league and amity. And thus much we have thought good to let your Majesty understand. Fare you well. Dated the sixth of December the 39th of our reign.

Sigismund Augustus Rex

29

A Letter
from Ivan the Terrible
to Elizabeth I, 1570

Ivan the Terrible sought to establish closer ties with the English government after he granted privileges to their merchants. He sent several diplomatic mis-

From Iurii Tolstoy, ed., *Pervyia sorok let snoshenii mezhdu Rossieiu i Anglieiu. 1555–1593 (The First Forty Years of Relations between Russia and England, 1553–1593)* (St. Petersburg, 1875), pp. 110–115. Spellings have been modernized to facilitate reading.

sions and in 1567, through Anthony Jenkinson, a
representative of the Muscovy Company, he even
proposed a military alliance between England and
Moscovy "against all of our mutual enemies." British
failure to respond to Ivan's plans resulted in a sub-
stantial reduction of privileges and a series of rather
bitter letters from Ivan to Elizabeth.

For that before time certain subjects of your brother king Edward, namely Richard Chancellor and others, being sent for some occasion to all people and places and having writings to all kings, emperors,
dukes, lords, and rulers (but namely unto us not one word was written),
and those your brother's subjects, Richard and his fellows, we know not
after what sort, whether it were willingly or unwillingly, came and
anchored in our haven, by the sea side, and to our town of Dvina, and
we, as it behooved a Christian prince, showed them so much favor that
we received them with honor, and at our princely and appointed dinners,
we of our goodness sent for them; and we sent them back again unto
your brother. And after that it pleased your brother to send the said
Richard Chancellor and one Richard Gray unto us, and we in like cause
showed our goodness unto them and sent them back again. And after
that your brother sent the said Richard to us the third time, and thereupon we sent unto your brother our messenger Osip Grigorevich Nepeia.
And to your brother's merchants and to all Englishmen we gave our
letters of privilege so large as the like was given to our nation, never
thinking to have had received friendship of your brother and of you and
service of Englishmen. And in the meantime that we sent our messenger
the same time your brother died, and your sister Mary* succeeded his
place; and so married with Philip, king of Spain, the which king and
your sister received our messenger honorably, and so sent him back
again unto us; but they sent no word to us. And at that time your merchants did work much deceit against our merchants, and began to sell
their wares dear, taking for all things more than things were worth. And
since that time the Queen, your sister, died, and that the king Philip
was sent away and that you were crowned Queen of England; and we all
that time did your merchants no harm, but willed them to traffick, as
they had done before time.

And how many letters have been brought to us hither, and not one
letter that has been sealed with one seal, but every letter has had a contrary seal, which is no princely fashion, and such letters in all places be
not credited, but every prince has in his realm one proper seal; but we
did give credit to these letters, and according to your letters we wrought.

---

* Mary Tudor, 1553–1558.

And after that you sent unto us your messenger Anthony Jenkinson about the affairs of merchants, and we, thinking him to have had credit with you, we had therefore sworn him, and also your merchant Ralph Ruttar, because of interpreting for that in such weighty affairs, we stood need of true interpreting, and we sent you by word of mouth of our great and secret meaning desiring friendship of you and that you would have sent over to us some near and trusty servant of yours and Anthony to have come with him, or else Anthony alone for that we know not whether Anthony did tell you all our words or no, for we heard not of him in a year and a half after, and here came not from you neither messenger neither ambassador. And therefore we of our goodness gave unto your merchants another privilege, thinking how to have been in good credit with you and therefore our goodness was the greater to them.

And after that we had news, that a subject of yours was come to the Narva, by name Edward Goodman, which had many letters. But we sent to him to inquire of Anthony but he told us nothing of him, and [we] commanded him to be searched for letters and we found many letters; and in those letters were written words not allowable against our princely state and empire, how that in our empire were many unlawful things done, and he gave evil language to our messengers, which were sent to him, but we of our goodness caused him to be stayed honorably till such time as we should have answer from you of those affairs that we sent of to you by Anthony.

And after that there came from you a messenger to the Narva about merchants' affairs, namely George Midelton, and we sent to him to know whether Anthony were come to you or no, and when he should come from you to us. But your messenger George would tell us nothing of this matter, but did miscall our messengers and Anthony also, and we commanded him to be kept, till such time as we had and knew of the matter, that we committed to Anthony.

And not long after that we were informed that your ambassador Thomas Randall was come to our port of Dvina, and we of our goodness sent to meet him, the son of a gentleman, and we commanded the said gentleman to be his guide, and we did entreat him with great honor and we commanded our said gentleman to inquire of him whether Anthony were with him or no, but he told our gentleman nothing; for Anthony was not with him, but all his talk was of bourses and affairs of merchants. And when he was come to our empire we sent unto him many times, that he would come and confer with our counsel that we might have had knowledge of those great affairs that we sent you word of by Anthony, but he after a rude manner denied to come; but he wrote supplications against Glover and Rutter and upon affairs of merchandise he wrote, but of our princely affairs he made them of none effect and therefore your ambassador was kept the longer from our presence, and after that our city was stricken by the hand of God with the plague, so that it was not possible for us to give him presence, but so soon as it pleased God to withdraw from us the plague of sickness, we gave him presence, and all his talk was upon merchants' affairs; and then we sent unto him our counsellor and captain of Vologda Duke Athanasius Ivanovich Viazemskii, and our seal keeper Ivan Mikhailov, and our secretary Andrei Vasilev. We willed them to inquire of him if he had commission of those affairs, which we sent you word of by Anthony, and he told them that he had commission for those affairs also; thereupon we did augment our goodness unto him after that he was diverse times with us and ever he spoke about bourses and affairs of merchandise and very seldom would talk with us of our princely affairs, and at that time we had occasion for to ride to our inheritance of Vologda, and we gave commandment to our gentlemen that they should conduct him thither, and he being arrived thither we sent unto him our presaid counsellor and our secretary Peter Grigoriev, and willed them to treat with him how those affairs of amity might be between us, but the talk which your ambassador had was to establish merchants, and we willed him to talk with us of our affairs, and we talked of them and we did agree how those affairs should pass between us, and then we wrote our letters, and to our letters we set our seal and then if they had pleased you, that then you would have caused your letters to have been written and to have sent some trusty ambassador, and that Anthony Jenkinson might have been sent with him. The cause which we were so desirous to have had Anthony Jenkinson to have come, was that we would have known of him whether he did declare unto you the words which we commanded him to tell you by mouth, and to have known of him whether the words did please you, or no, and how you were minded of that matter. And so we sent in company with your ambassador our ambassador, Andrei Gregorievich Savin.

And you have sent us our ambassador back, but you have not sent your ambassador to us, and you have not ended our affairs according as your ambassador did agree upon, and your letters be not thereto agreeable, for such weighty affairs be not ended without confirmation by oath, or without ambassadors, but you have set aside those great affairs, and your counsel does deal with our ambassador about merchants affairs; and your merchants Sir William Garrard and Sir William Chester did rule all business. And we had thought that you had been ruler over your land and had sought honor to your self and profit to your country, and therefore we did pretend those weighty affairs between you and us. But now we perceive that there be other men that do rule, and not men but boursers and merchants, the which seek not the wealth and honor of our majesties, but they seek their own profit of merchandise: and you flower in your maidenly estate like a maiden. And whosoever was trusted in our affairs, and did deceive us, it were not meet that you should credit them.

And now seeing it is so, we do set aside these affairs. And those bourser merchants, that have been the occasion that the pretended wealths and honors of our majesties has not come [to] pass, but do seek their own wealth, they shall see what traffick they shall have here, for our city of Moscow, before their traffick to it, has not greatly wanted English commodities. And the privileges that we gave to your merchants and sent to you, that you would send it [to] us again, and whether it be sent or no, we will give commandment that nothing shall be done by it, and all those privileges which we have given aforetime be from this day of none effect.

Written at our honor of Moscow since the foundation of the world 7079 [1570] years, the xxiv day of October.

30

Ivan the Terrible's Punishment of Novgorod in 1570

The reign of Ivan the Terrible (1547–1584) is usually remembered for its conquest of the Volga Basin and Siberia, its establishment of commercial ties with England, its struggle with Poland for access to the Baltic Sea, and its perfection of an autocratic, brutal rule in Russia. The latter achievement, in fact, gave him the descriptive title by which he is most commonly known, "the Terrible." The validity of this description is evidenced by Ivan's utter

From *Polnoe Sobranie Russkikh Letopisei* (*Complete Collection of Russian Chronicles* (St. Petersburg, 1885), vol. 3, pp. 254–262. Translation mine. Items in brackets are mine.

devastation of Novgorod in 1570, when tens of thousands of Novgorodians were butchered in a week-long orgy because of Ivan's unfounded suspicion that Novgorod's Archbishop contemplated placing the city under Polish-Lithuanian protection.

On Monday the 2d of January, in the year 7079 [1570], after the creation of the world, the day of commemoration of the Holy Father and Roman Pope Silvester, the illustrious Tsar and Grand Prince Ivan Vasilevich, lord of All Russia, sent an advance guard of the army in forced march toward Great Novgorod. The army units consisted of *boyars*, army commanders, princes, nobles, courtiers, and an uncountable multitude of other troops.

When these troops had arrived before Great Novgorod, according to the order of the illustrious Tsar and Grand Prince Ivan Vasilevich, lord of All Russia, they established a great camp in the environs of the city, surrounded by strong posts with fortifications of every kind. They erected sentinel towers near the posts and decreed that the inhabitants of the city be closely watched in order that not one human being could escape from the city.

And other princes and nobles of the Tsar from the same advance guard rode in all directions in the area around Great Novgorod and sealed all the monasteries and money boxes of the Church. They captured the abbots, the black clergy, the deacons, and the elders from the monasteries, and took them, perhaps 500 or more persons, to Great Novgorod. They were brought to the place of execution where they were to wait until the arrival of the Tsar.

And other nobles of the Tsar from the same advance guard seized the priests and deacons of all the churches in Novgorod and also brought them to the execution site. Every ten prisoners were assigned a police officer. And these officers received orders to keep the prisoners in iron chains and to beat them mercilessly from morning to evening at the place of execution until ransom was obtained. The Tsar ordered that each prisoner pay twenty rubles in the currency of Novgorod for ransom.

And other nobles of the Tsar from the same advance guard dispersed over all streets in Great Novgorod and among all the parishes, whereupon they sealed up all the manors of the distinguished people of Great Novgorod, along with their wealth, and erected numerous guard posts for the purpose of keeping watch until the arrival of the Tsar.

By order of the monarch, other nobles of the same advance guard arrested all the administrative officials and all the important merchants of Great Novgorod and placed them under guard. They were chained, their houses were sealed up with all their wealth, and their wives and children were ordered closely watched until the arrival of the sovereign.

On January 6th of the same year, 1570, the festival of our Lord and Savior Jesus Christ's baptism, the illustrious Tsar and Grand Prince Ivan Vasilevich, lord of All Russia, arrived in Great Novgorod. He was accompanied by his son, the rightful heir to the throne, Prince Ivan Ivanovich, and an uncountable host of princes, boyars, courtiers and other troops, including 1500 *streltsi* [musketeers]. . . .

On Saturday, the day after his arrival, the illustrious Tsar and Grand Prince Ivan Vasilevich, lord of All Russia, gave the order that the abbots, clergy, and monks who had previously been brought to the place of execution should be beaten to death with clubs. After they had all been killed, he ordered that each be buried at the monastery where he had resided. . . .

On Sunday, the 8th of January, the Tsar went to the Church of St. Sophia with his troops to attend High Mass. At the great Volkhov bridge, near the Black Cross, the Tsar was welcomed, according to custom, by Pimen, the Archbishop of Great Novgorod, with crosses and miraculous ikons. When, according to old custom, Archbishop Pimen wanted to bless the Tsar and Grand Prince Ivan Vasilevich, as well as his rightful heir to the throne, Prince Ivan Ivanovich, with the crucifix, the Tsar and Grand Prince Ivan Vasilevich and his son and heir to the throne, Prince Ivan, refused to receive the Archbishop's blessing. The Tsar said to Archbishop Pimen, "You villain, you do not hold a life-giving cross in your hand, but rather a weapon. And with this weapon you want to wound the Tsar's heart, for you are malicious and you are devising plots with traitors among the inhabitants of this city. You want to give the great, holy city of Novgorod, which is a part of our inherited dominion, to the enemies, to the aliens, the Lithuanian King Sigismund Augustus. Although you call yourself the shepherd, the teacher, the ecclesiastical prince of the great apostolic cathedral of divine wisdom and of St. Sophia, you are only a wolf, a thief, a murderer, a traitor. You attempt to damage our sceptre and crown." After the Tsar had revealed his anger through such words, he ordered the Archbishop to go into the Church of St. Sophia and to perform the holy liturgy in its entirety. And the Orthodox Tsar and Grand Prince Ivan Vasilevich himself, accompanied by the rightful heir to the throne, Prince Ivan Ivanovich, and all his retinue, walked behind the holy, life-giving crucifix and the sacred, miraculous ikons, and entered the Church of St. Sophia where he heard the divine liturgy. After the divine service, the Tsar, accompanied by his courtiers, princes, and warriors, went to Archbishop Pimen's palace for dinner. The Tsar sat at the table and began to eat. Soon afterwards, he stopped and turned to his princes and boyars. As was his custom, he shouted an order in a loud voice shaking with anger. The Tsar commanded his men to plunder the Archbishop's money box, his entire court with all the neighboring buildings, cells and rooms, and to seize his courtiers and attendants and place them under guard until further orders. The Tsar ordered that the Archbishop himself be placed under close surveillance after his property had been confiscated, but the Tsar sent two *dengas* each day from the treasury for his maintenance.

The Tsar ordered his steward, Lev Andreevich Saltykov, as well as his high priest, Eustachius, together with several *boyars*, to go into the Church of St. Sophia and to confiscate the treasures in the vestry as well as costly, sacred vessels, the holy and miraculous ikons from Korsun, and paintings by Greek artists. In addition, the Tsar decreed that all holy church treasures, the holy, divine, costly, and wondrous ikons, and the chasubles used in celebrating mass, and the bells in all of Great Novgorod's churches be confiscated. . . . (The Tsar had similar confiscations carried out in the monasteries in the environs of Novgorod.)

Thereupon, the Orthodox Tsar and Grand Prince Ivan Vasilevich, lord of All Russia, and his son, the rightful heir to the throne, Prince Ivan Ivanovich, held court in the suburbs of Gorodishche where he had encamped upon his arrival. The Tsar commanded that the powerful *boyars*, the important merchants, the administrative officials, and the citizens of every rank be brought before him, together with their wives and children. The Tsar ordered that they be tortured in his presence in various spiteful, horrible, and inhuman ways. After many various unspeakable and bitter tortures, the Tsar ordered that their bodies be tormented and roasted with fire in refined ways. And the Tsar commanded his nobles to bind the hands and feet and heads of these tortured and roasted human beings with fine ropes in various ways. He ordered that each man be tied to a sled, be dragged to the Volkhov bridge behind the fast-moving sleds, and be thrown into the Volkhov River from the bridge. The Tsar ordered that their wives and children be brought to the Volkhov bridge where a high platform had been erected. He commanded that they be chained on the arms and legs and that the children be tied to their mothers and then be thrown from the platform into the waters of the Volkhov River. Meanwhile, the Tsar's men, the nobles and soldiers, moved about in small boats on the Volkhov River, armed with spears, lances, hooks, and axes. When the people, men and women of all ages, surfaced, they were stabbed by the soldiers with hooks, lances, and spears, or they were struck with axes. In a horrible manner they were submerged without mercy in the depths of the river, and abandoned to a terrible and bitter death.

Because of our sins, this unspeakable shedding of Christian blood, caused by the excessive anger of the Tsar, continued uninterrupted each day for five weeks or more. And every day perhaps a thousand human beings of all ages were thrown into the water and drowned; occasionally there were fifteen hundred, and if perchance only five or six hundred people were thrown into the water, the day in question was considered an easy day, one deserving of thanks.

After the end of the punishment, the Orthodox Tsar and Grand

Prince Ivan Vasilevich, lord of All Russia, went to the renowned and important monasteries in the environs of Great Novgorod. He decreed that the churches, the monasteries, the cells, and the buildings be plundered. He ordered that the grain in the barns and the fields be burned, and that the livestock of every kind, horses and cows, be slaughtered.

Thereupon, the Orthodox Tsar and Grand Prince Ivan Vasilevich, lord of All Russia, returned to Great Novgorod. He ordered that the merchants' stores in all the city, in the alleys and streets, be robbed of their goods and that the warehouses and shops be destroyed. Afterwards, the Orthodox Tsar and Grand Prince rode with all of his people and warriors through all of Novgorod and its suburbs, pitilessly robbing all the inhabitants, including the women, breaking windows and doors, and demolishing the houses and manors. (For several weeks similar treatment was given the region under control of Great Novgorod. The surviving citizens of Novgorod were pardoned, with the exception of those whom the Tsar had transported to Moscow and ordered beheaded.)

31

Russia at the End of the 16th Century

The establishment of commercial relations between England and Moscovy enabled many Englishmen to travel to and report on Russia. One of the most interesting of these reports is *The Russe Com-*

Reprinted with permission of the Cambridge University Press from Edward A. Bond, ed., *Russia at the Close of the Sixteenth Century. Comprising the Treatise "Of the Russe Common Wealth," by Dr. Giles Fletcher; and the Travels of Sir Jerome Horsey. . . .* (London, Published for the Hakluyt Society, 1856), pp. 26–45, 146–152. Spellings have been modernized to facilitate reading. Items in brackets are mine.

monwealth, by Dr. Giles Fletcher, who visited Russia in 1588 as an ambassador of Queen Elizabeth I. Like all European visitors, Fletcher paid special attention to the resources of the country, and customs, manners, and behavior of the people. This should not be surprising, for, to a sixteenth century European, Russia was as distant ánd mysterious as is perhaps Tibet to the western world today. Scholars regard Fletcher's work as an excellent source on Russia at the close of the sixteenth century.

The State or Form of Their Government

The manner of their government is much after the Turkish fashion: which they seem to imitate as near as the country, and reach of their capacities in politic affairs, will give them leave to do.

The state and form of their government is plain tyrannical, as applying all to the behoof of the prince, and that after a most open and barbarous manner: as may appear by the *sophismata* or secrets of their government afterwards set down, as well for the keeping of the nobility and commons in an under proportion, and far uneven balance in their several degrees, as also in their impositions and exactions, wherein they exceed all just measure, without any regard of nobility or people: farther then it gives the nobility a kind of unjust and unmeasured liberty to command and exact upon the commons and baser sort of people in all parts of the realm where so ever they come, specially in the place where their lands lie, or where they are appointed by the emperor to govern under him; also to the commons some small contentment, in that they pass over their lands by descent of inheritance to whither son they will; which commonly they do after our gavelkind; and dispose of their goods by gifts or testament without any control. Wherein notwithstanding both nobility and commons are but storers for the prince, all running in the end into the emperor's coffers: as may appear by the practice of enriching his treasury, and the manner of exactions set down in the title of his customs and revenues.

Concerning the principal points and matters of state, wherein the sovereignty consists (as the making and annulling of public laws, the making of magistrates, power to make war or league with any foreign state, to execute or to pardon life, with the right of appeal in all matters, both civil and criminal) they do so wholly and absolutely pertain to the emperor, and his counsel under him, as that he may be said to be both the sovereign commander, and the executioner of all these. For as touching any law or public order of the realm, it is ever determined of before any public assembly or parliament be summoned. Where, besides his council, he has none other to consult with him of such matters as are concluded before hand, but only a few bishops, abbots, and friars: to no other end than to make advantage of the people's superstitions, even against themselves, which think all to be holy and just, that passes with the consent of their bishops and clergy men, whatsoever it be. For which purpose the emperors are content to make much of the corrupt state of the Church, as now it is among them, and to nourish the same by extraordinary favors, and immunities to the bishops' sees, abbeys, and friaries: as knowing superstition and false religion best to agree with a tyrannical state, and to be a special means to uphold and maintain the same.

Secondly, as touching the public offices and magistracies of the realm, there is none hereditary, neither any so great nor so little in that country, but the bestowing of it is done immediately by the emperor himself. Insomuch that the very *diaks* or clerks in every head town, are for the most part assigned by himself. Notwithstanding, the emperor that now is (the better to intend his devotions) refers all such matters pertaining to the state, wholly to the ordering of his wife's brother, the L[ord] Boris Fedorovich Godunov.

Thirdly, the like is to be said of the jurisdiction concerning matters judicial, specially such as concern life and death. Wherein there is none that has any authority or public jurisdiction that goes by descent, or is held by charter, but all at the appointment and pleasure of the emperor, and the same practiced by the judges with such awe and restraint, as that they dare not determine upon any special matter, but must refer the same wholly up to Moscow to the emperor's council. To show his sovereignty over the lives of his subjects, the late emperor Ivan Vasilevich [Ivan the Terrible], in his walks or progresses, if he had misliked the face or person of any man whom he met by the way, or that looked upon him, would command his head to be struck off. Which was presently done, and the head cast before him.

Fourthly, for the sovereign appeal, and giving of pardons in criminal matters to such as are convicted, it is wholly at the pleasure and grace of the emperor. Wherein also the empress that now is, being a woman of great clemency, and withal delighting to deal in public affairs of the realm (the rather to supply the defect of her husband), does behave her self after an absolute manner, giving out pardon (specially on her birth day and other solemn times) in her own name, by open proclamation, without any mention at all of the emperor. Some there have been of late of the ancient nobility, that have held diverse provinces by right of inheritance, with an absolute authority and jurisdiction over them, to order and determine all matters within their own precinct without all appeal or control of the emperor. But this was all annulled and wrung clean from them by Ivan Vasilevich, father to this emperor. . . .

The Manner of Holding Their Parliaments

Their highest court of public consultation for matters of state is called the [*Zemskii*] *Sobor*, that is, the public assembly. The states and degrees of persons that are present at their parliaments, are these in order. (1) The emperor himself. (2) Some of his nobility, about the number of twenty, being all of his council. (3) Certain of the clergy men, etc., about the same number. As for burghers or others to represent the community, they have no place there: the people being of no better account with them than as servants or bond slaves that are to obey, not to make laws, nor to know any thing of public matters before they are concluded.

The court of parliament (called *Sobor*) is held in this manner. The emperor causes to be summoned such of his nobility as himself thinks meet, being (as was said) all of his council, together with the patriarch, who calls his clergy, to wit, the two metropolitans, the two archbishops, with such bishops, abbots, and friars as are of best account and reputation among them. When they are all assembled at the emperor's court, the day is intimated when the session shall begin. Which commonly is upon some Friday, for the religion of that day.

When the day is come, the clergy men assemble before at the time and place appointed, which is called *stol*. And when the emperor comes attended by his nobility, they arise all, and meet him in an out room, following their patriarch, who blesses the emperor with his two fore-fingers, laying them on his forehead and the sides of his face, and then kisses him on the right side of his breast. So they pass on into their parliament house, where they sit in this order. The emperor is enthroned on the one side of the chamber. In the next place, not far from him, at a small square table (that gives room to twelve persons or thereabouts), sits the patriarch with the metropolitans and bishops, and certain of the principal nobility of the emperor's council, together with two *diaks* or secretaries (called *dumnyi diaks*), that enact that which passes. The rest place themselves on benches round about the room, every man in his rank after his degree. Then is there propounded by one of the secretaries (who represents the speaker) the cause of their assembly, and the principal matters that they are to consider of. For to propound bills what every man thinks good for the public benefit (as the manner is in England), the Russian parliament knows no such custom nor liberty to subjects.

The points being opened, the patriarch with his clergy men have the prerogative to be first asked their vote, or opinion, what they think of the points propounded by the secretary. Whereto they answer in order, according to their degrees, but all in one form without any discourse: as having learned their lesson before, that serves their turns at all parliaments alike, whatsoever is propounded. Commonly it is to this effect:

That the emperor and his council are of great wisdom, and experience, touching the policies and public affairs of the realm, and far better able to judge what is profitable for the common wealth than they are, which attend upon the service of God only, and matters of religion. And therefore it may please them to proceed. That instead of their advice, they will aid them with their prayers, as their duties and vocations do require, etc.

To this or like effect having made their answers every man in his course, up stands some abbot or friar more bold than the rest (yet appointed before hand as a matter of form), and desires the emperor it would please his majesty to command to be delivered unto them what his majesty's own judgment and determinate pleasure is, as touching those matters propounded by his *diak*.

Whereto is replied by the said secretary in the emperor's name:

That his highness, with those of his noble council, upon good and sound advice have found the matters proposed to be very good and necessary for the common wealth of his realm. Notwithstanding, forasmuch as they are religious men, etc., know what is right, his majesty requires their godly opinions, yea and their censures too, for the approving or correcting of the said propositions. And therefore desires them again to speak their minds freely. And if they shall like to give their consents, that then the matters may pass to a full conclusion.

Hereunto, when the clergy men have given their consents (which they used to do without any great pausing), they take their leaves with blessing of the emperor: who brings the patriarch on his way so far as the next room, and so returns to his seat, till all be made ready for his return homeward. The acts that thus are passed by the *Sobor* or parliament, the *diaks* or secretaries draw into a form of proclamation, which they send abroad into every province and head town of the realm, to be published there by the dukes and *diaks* or secretaries of those places. The session of parliament being fully ended, the emperor invites the clergy men to a solemn dinner. And so they depart every man to his home. . . .

Of the Nobility, and by What Means It Is Kept in an Under Proportion Agreeable to That State

The degrees of persons or estates of Russia (besides the sovereign state or emperor himself), are these in their order.

1. The nobility, which is of four sorts. Whereof the chief for birth, authority, and revenue are called the *udelnye kniazia*, that is, the ex-

empted or privileged dukes. These hold sometimes a several jurisdiction, and absolute authority within their precincts, much like unto the states or nobles of Germany. . . . But the late emperor Ivan Vasilevich, father to this prince, being a man of high spirit, and subtle in his kind, meaning to reduce his government into a more strict form, began by degrees to clip off their greatness, and to bring it down to a lesser proportion: till in the end he made them not only his vassals, but his *kholops*, that is, his very villains or bondslaves. For so they term and write themselves in any public instrument or private petition which they make to the emperor. So that now they hold their authorities, lands, lives and all at the emperor's pleasure, as the rest do.

The means and practice whereby he wrought this to effect against those and other of the nobility (so well as I could note out of the report of his doings) were these, and such like. First, he cast private emulations among them about prerogatives of their titles and dignities. Wherein he used to set on the inferiors, to prefer or equal themselves to those that were accounted to be of the nobler houses. Where he made his advantage of their malice and contentions, the one against the other, by receiving devised matter, and accusations of secret practice and conspiracies to be intended against his person and state. And so having singled out the greatest of them, and cut them off with the good liking of the rest, he fell at last to open practice, by forcing of the other to yield their rights unto him.

2. He divided his subjects into two parts or factions by a general schism. The one part he called the *oprichniki* or select men. These were such of the nobility and gentry as he took to his own part, to protect and maintain them as his faithful subjects. The other he called *zemskii*, or the commons. The *zemskii* contained the base and vulgar sort, with such noblemen and gentlemen as he meant to cut off, as suspected to mislike his government, and to have a meaning to practice against him. Wherein he provided that the *oprichniki* for number and quality of valor, money, armor, etc., far exceeded the other of the *zemskii* side, whom he put (as it were) from under his protection: so that if any of them were spoiled or killed by those of the *oprichniki* (which he accounted of his own part), there was no amends to be sought for by way of public justice, or by complaint to the emperor.

The whole number of both parts was orderly registered and kept in a book: so that every man knew who was a *zemskii* man and who of the *oprichniki*. And this liberty of the one part to spoil and kill the other, without any help of magistrate or law (that continued seven years), enriched that side and the emperor's treasury, and wrought that withal which he intended by this practice, viz., to take out of the way such of the nobility as [he] himself misliked: whereof were slain within one week to the number of three hundred within the city of Moscow. This tyrannical practice of making a general schism and public division among the subjects of his whole realm, proceeded (as should seem) from an extreme doubt and desperate fear which he had conceived of most of his nobility and gentlemen of his realm, in his wars with the Poles and Crimean Tartars. What time he grew into a vehement suspicion (conceived of the ill success of his affairs), that they practiced treason with the Poles and Crimeans. Whereupon he executed some, and devised his way to be rid of the rest.

And this wicked policy and tyrannous practice (though now it be ceased) has so troubled the country, and filled it so full of grudge and mortal hatred ever since, that it will not be quenched (as it seems now) till it burn again into a civil flame.

3. Having thus pulled them, and ceased all their inheritance, lands, privileges, etc., save some very small part which he left to their name, he gave them other lands of the tenure of *pomestie* (as they call it), that are held at the emperor's pleasure, lying far off in an other country; and so removed them into other of his provinces, where they might have neither favor nor authority, not being native nor well known there. So that now these of the chief nobility (called *udelnye kniazia*) are equalled with the rest: save that in the opinion and favor of the people they are of more account, and keep still the prerogative of their place in all their public meetings.

Their practice to keep down these houses from rising again and recovering their dignities, are these and such like. First, many of their heirs are kept unmarried perforce, that the stock may die with them. Some are sent into Siberia, Kazan, and Astrakhan, under pretence of service, and there either made away or else fast clapped up. Some are put into abbeys, and shire themselves friars by pretence of a vow, to be made voluntary and of their own accord; but, indeed, forced unto it by fear, upon some pretended crime objected against them. Where they are so guarded by some of special trust, and the convent it self (upon whose head it stands that they make no escape), as that they have no hope but to end their lives there. Of this kind there are many of very great nobility. These and such like ways, begun by the emperor Ivan Vasilevich, are still practiced by the Godunovs, who, being advanced by the marriage of the empress their kinswoman, rule both the emperor and his realm (specially Boris Fedorovich Godunov, brother to the empress), and endeavor by all means to cut off or keep down all of the best and most ancient nobility. Whereof diverse already they have taken away, whom they thought likeliest to make head against them and to hinder their purpose, as *Kniaz* Andreas Petrovich Kurakin, a man of great birth and authority in the country. The like they have done with Peter Golovin [?] (whom they put into a dungeon where he ended his life), with *Kniaz* Vasili Iurievich Golitsyn, with Andrei Ivanovich Shuiskii, accounted among them for a man of a great wisdom. So this last year was killed in a monastery (whither they had thrust him) one *Kniaz* Ivan Petrovich Shuiskii, a man of great valor and service in that country: who, about five or six years since, bore out the siege of the city of Pskov, made by Stefan Batory, king of Poland, with 100,000 men, and repulsed him very valiantly, with great honor to himself and his country and disgrace to the Pole. Also Nikita Romanov, uncle to the emperor by the mother's side, was supposed to have died of poison or some like practice. . . .

The second degree of nobility is of the *boyars*. These are such as the emperor honors (besides their nobility) with the title of counsellors. The revenue of these two sorts of their nobles, that rises out of their lands assigned them by the emperor, and held at his pleasure (for of their own inheritance there is little left them, as was said before) is about a thousand marks a year: besides pension which they receive of the emperor for their service in his wars, to the sum of 700 rubles a year, and none above that sum. . . .

In the third rank are the *voevodas*, or such nobles as are or have been generals in the emperor's wars. Which deliver the honor of their title to their posterities also: who take their place above the other dukes and nobles that are not of the two former sorts, *viz.*, of the *udelnye kniazia* nor of the *boyars*.

These three degrees of their nobility, (to wit) the *udelnye kniazia*, the *boyars*, and the *voevodas*, have the addition of *vich* put unto their surname, as Boris Fedorovich, etc.: which is a note of honor that the rest may not usurp. And in case it be not added in the naming of them, they may sue the *beschest* or penalty of dishonor upon them that otherwise shall term them.

The fourth and lowest degree of nobility with them is of such as bear the name of *kniazia* or dukes, but come of the younger brothers of those chief houses, through many descents, and have no inheritance of their own, save the bare name or title of duke only. For their order is to deliver their names and titles of their dignities over to all their children alike, what so ever else they leave them. So that the sons of a *voevoda*, or general in the field, are called *voevodas* though they never saw the field, and the sons of a *kniaz* or duke are called *kniazia*, though they have not one groat of inheritance or livelihood to maintain themselves withal. Of this sort there are so many that the plenty makes them cheap: so that you shall see dukes glad to serve a mean man for five or six rubles or marks a year, and yet they will stand highly upon their *beschest* or reputation of their honors. And these are their several degrees of nobility.

The second degree of persons is of their *syni boyarskie*, or the sons of gentlemen: which all are preferred, and hold that name by their service in the emperor's wars, being soldiers by their very stock and birth.

To which order are referred their *diaks* or secretaries, that serve the emperor in every head town, being joined in commission with the dukes of that place.

The last are their commons, whom they call *muzhiks*. In which number they reckon their merchants and their common artificers. The very lowest and basest sort of this kind (which are held in no degree) are their country people, whom they call *krestiane*. . . .

Of the Government of Their Provinces and Shires

The whole country of Russia . . . is divided into four parts, which they call *chetverts* or tetrarchies. Every *chetvert* contains diverse shires, and is annexed to a severall office, whereof it takes the name. The first *chetvert* or tetrarchy bears the name of *Posolskii chetvert*, or the jurisdiction of the office of the ambassages, and at this time is under the chief secretary and officer of the ambassages, called Andrei Shuvalov [?]. The standing fee or stipend that he receives yearly of the emperor for this service, is 100 rubles or marks.

The second is called the *Rozriadnii chetvert*, because it is proper to the *rozriad* or high constable. At this time it pertains by virtue of office to Basil Shuvalov [?], brother to the chancellor, but it is executed by one Zapon Abramov. His pension is a hundred rubles yearly.

The third is the *chetvert* of *Pomestie*, as pertaining to that office. This keeps a register of all lands given by the emperor for service to his noblemen, gentlemen, and others, gives out and takes in all assurances for them. The officer at this time is called Lazar Belushkin [?]. His stipend is 500 rubles a year.

The fourth is called *Kazanskii dvorets*, as being appropriate to the office that has the jurisdiction of the kingdoms of Kazan and Astrakhan, with the other towns lying upon the Volga, now ordered by one Druzhinin Penteleev [?], a man of very special account among them, for his wisdom and promptness in matters of policy. His pension is 150 rubles a year.

From these *chetverts* or tetrarchies is exempted the emperor's inheritance or *votchina* (as they call it), for that it pertained from ancient time to the house of Belsky [?], which is the surname of the imperial blood. This stands of 36 towns with their bounds or territories. Besides diverse peculiar jurisdictions, which are likewise deducted out of those *chetverts*, as the shire of Vagha [?] (belonging to the Lord Boris Fedorovich Godunov), and such like.

These are the chief governors or officers of the provinces, not resident at their charge abroad, but attending the emperor whether soever he goes, and carrying their offices about with them, which for the most part they hold at Moscow, as the emperor's chief seat.

The parts and practice of these four offices, is to receive all complaints and actions what soever that are brought out of their several *chetverts* and quarters, and to inform them to the emperor's council. Likewise to send direction again to those that are under them in their said provinces, for all matters given in charge by the emperor and his council, to be done or put into execution within their precincts.

For the ordering of every particular province of these four *chetverts* there is appointed one of these dukes, which were reckoned before in the lowest degree of their nobility, which are resident in the head towns of the said provinces. Wherof every one has joined with him in commission a *diak* or secretary to assist him, or rather to direct him. For in the executing of their commission the *diak* does all.

The parts of their commission are these in effect. First, to hear and determine in all civil matters within their precinct. To which purpose they have under them certain officers, as *gubnii starets* or coroners, who, besides the trial of self murders, are to attach felons: and the *sudia* or under justices, who themselves also may hear and determine in all matters of the same nature, among the country people of their own wards or bailiwicks: but so that in case either party dissent, they may appeal and go farther to the duke and *diak* that reside within the head town. From whom also they may remove the matter to the higher court at Moscow of the emperor's council, where lie all appeals. They have under them also *sotskii starets*, that is, aldermen, or bailiffs of the hundreds.

Secondly, in all criminal matters, as theft, murder, treason, etc., they have authority to apprehend, to examine, and to imprison the malefactor, and so having received perfect evidence and information of the cause, they are to send it ready drawn and orderly digested up to Moscow, to the officer of the *chetvert* whereunto that province is annexed: by whom it is referred and propounded to the emperor's council. But to determine in any matter criminal, or to do execution upon the party offending, is more than their commission will allow them to do.

Thirdly, if there be any public service to be done within that province (as the publishing of any law or common order by way of proclamation, collecting of taxes and impositions for the emperor, mustering of soldiers, and sending them forth at the day and to the place assigned by the emperor or his council), all these and such like pertain to their charge.

These dukes and *diaks* are appointed to their place by the emperor himself, and are changed ordinarily at every year's end, except upon some special liking or suit the time be prorogued for a year or two more. They are men of themselves of no credit nor favor with the people where they govern, being neither born nor brought up among them, nor yet having inheritance of their own there or else where. Only of the emperor they have for that service 100 marks a year, he that has most, some fifty, some but thirty. Which makes them more suspected and odious to the people, because being so bare, and coming fresh and hungry upon them lightly every year, they rack and spoil them without all regard of justice or conscience. Which is easily tolerated by the chief officers of the *chetverts*, to the end they may rob them again, and have a better booty when they call them to account: which commonly they do at the end of their service, making an advantage by their injustice and oppression over the poor people. There are few of them but they come to the *pudki* or whip when their time is ended, which themselves for the most part do make account of. And therefore they furnish themselves with all the spoil they can for the time of their government, that they may have for both turns, as well for the emperor and lord of the *chetvert*, as to reserve some good part for themselves.

They that are appointed to govern abroad are men of this quality: save that in the four border towns that are of greatest importance, are set men of more special valor and trust, two in every town. Whereof one is ever of the emperor's privy council. These four border towns are Smolensk, Pskov, Novgorod, and Kazan, whereof three lie towards Poland and Sweden, one borders far off upon the Crimean Tartar. These have larger commission than the other dukes of the provinces that I spoke of before, and may do execution in criminal matters. Which is thought behoofull for the commonwealth: for incident occasions that may happen upon the borders that are far off, and may not stay for direction about every occurrence and particular matter from the emperor and his council. They are changed every year (except as before), and have for their stipend 700 rubles a year he that has most: some have but 400. Many of these places that are of greatest importance, and almost the whole country, is managed at this time by the Godunovs and their clients.

The city of Moscow (that is the emperor's seat) is governed altogether by the emperor's council. All matters there, both civil and criminal, are heard and determined in the several courts held by some of the said council, that reside there all the year long.

Only for their ordinary matters (as buildings, reparations, keeping of their streets decent and clean, collections, levying of taxes, impositions, and such like) are appointed two gentlemen and two *diaks* or secretaries, who hold a court together for the ordering of such matters. This is called the *zemskii* house. If any townsman suspect his servant of theft or like matter, hither he may bring him to have him examined upon the *pudki* or other torture. Besides these two gentlemen and secretaries that order the whole city, there are the *starostas* or aldermen for every several company. The alderman has his *sotskii* or constable, and the constable has certain *desiatskii* or decurions under him, which have the oversight of ten households apiece, whereby every disorder is sooner spied, and the common service has the quicker dispatch. The whole number of citizens, poor and rich, are reduced into companies. The chief officers (as the *diaks* and gentlemen) are appointed by the emperor himself, the *starosta* by the gentlemen and *diaks*, the *sotskii* by the *starosta* or alderman, and the *desiatskii* by the constables.

This manner of government of their provinces and towns, if it were as well set for the giving of justice indifferently to all sorts, as it is to prevent innovations by keeping of the nobility within order and the commons in subjection, it might seem in that kind to be no bad nor unpolitic way for the containing of so large a commonwealth, of that breadth and length as is the kingdom of Russia. But the oppression and slavery is so open and so great, that a man would marvel how the nobility and people should suffer themselves to be brought under it, while they had any means to avoid and repulse it: or being so strengthened as it is at the present, how the emperors themselves can be content to practice the same, with so open injustice and oppression of their subjects, being themselves of a Christian profession.

By this it appears how hard a matter it were to alter the state of the Russian government as now it stands. First, because they have none of the nobility able to make head. As for the lords of the four *chetverts* or tetrarchies, they are men of no nobility, but *diaks* advanced by the emperor depending on his favor, and attending only about his own person. And for the dukes that are appointed to govern under them, they are but men of a titular dignity (as was said before), of no power, authority, nor credit, save that which they have out of the office for the time they enjoy it. Which does purchase them no favor, but rather hatred of the people, for asmuch as they see that they are set over them, not so much for any care to do them right and justice, as to keep them under in a miserable subjection and to take the fleece from them, not once in the year (as the owner from his sheep), but to poll and clip them all the year long. Besides, the authority and rule which they bear is rent and divided into many small pieces, being diverse of them in every great shire, limited besides with a very short time: which gives them no scope to make any strength, nor to contrive such an enterprise, if happily they intended any matter of innovation. As for the common people (as may better appear in the description of their state and quality afterwards set down) besides their want of armor and practice of war (which they are kept from of purpose) they are robbed continually both of their hearts and money, (besides other means) sometimes by pretense of some service to be done for the common defense, sometimes without any show at all of any necessity of commonwealth or prince. So that there is no means, either for nobility or people, to attempt any innovation, so long as the military forces of the emperor (which are the number of 8000 at the least in continual pay) hold themselves fast and sure unto him and to the present state. Which needs they must do, being of the quality of soldiers, and enjoying withal that free liberty of wronging and spoiling of the commons at their pleasure, which is permitted them of purpose, and to make them have a liking of the present state. As for the agreement of the soldiers and commons, it is a thing not to be feared, being of so opposite and contrary practice much one to the other. This desperate state of things at home, makes the people for the most part to wish for some foreign invasion, which they suppose to be the only means to rid them of the heavy yoke of this tyrannous government. . . .

Of the Private Behavior, or Quality of the Russian People

The private behavior and quality of the Russian people, may partly be understood by that which has been said concerning the public state and usage of the country. As touching the natural habit of their bodies, they are for the most part of a large size and of very fleshly bodies, accounting it a grace to be somewhat gross and burly, and therefore they nourish and spread their beards to have them long and broad. But, for the most part, they are very unwieldy and unactive withal. Which may be thought to come partly of the climate, and the numbness which they get by the cold in winter, and partly of their diet, that stands most of roots, onions, garlic, cabbage, and such like things that breed gross humors, which they use to eat alone and with their other meats.

Their diet is rather much than curious. At their meals they begin commonly with a *charka*, or small cup, of *aqua vitae* (which they call Russian wine) and then drink not till towards the end of their meals, taking it in largely and all together, with kissing one another at every pledge. And therefore after dinner there is no talking with them, but every man goes to his bench to take his afternoon's sleep, which is as ordinary with them as their night's rest. When they exceed and have variety of dishes, the first are their baked meats (for roast meats they use little) and then their broths or pottage. To drink drunk, is an ordinary matter with them every day in the week. Their common drink is mead; the poorer sort use water, and thin drink called *kvas*, which is nothing else (as we say) but water turned out of his wits, with a little bran mashed with it.

This diet would breed in them many diseases, but that they use bath-stoves or hot houses in stead of all physic, commonly twice or thrice every week. All the winter time, and almost the whole summer, they heat their *peches*, which are made like the German bathstoves, and their *potlads*, like ovens, that so warm the house, that a stranger at the first shall hardly like of it. These two extremities, specially in the winter, of heat within their houses and of extreme cold without, together with their diet, makes them of a dark and sallow complexion, their skins being tanned and parched both with cold and with heat, specially the women, that for the greater part are of far worse complexions than the men. Whereof the cause I take to be, their keeping within the hot houses, and busying themselves about the heating and using of their bathstoves and *peches*.

The Russian, because that he is used to both these extremities of heat and cold, can bear them both a great deal more patiently than strangers can do. You shall see them sometimes (to season their bodies) come out of their bathstoves all on a froth, and fuming as hot almost as a pig at a spit, and presently to leap into the river stark naked, or to pour cold water all over their bodies, and that in the coldest of all the winter time. The women, to mend the bad hue of their skins, used to paint their faces with white and red colors, so visibly that every man may perceive it. Which is made no matter, because it is common and liked well by their husbands, who make their wives and daughters an ordinary allowance to buy them colors to paint their faces withal, and delight themselves much to see them of foul women to become such fair images. This parches the skin, and helps to deform them when their painting is off.

They apparel themselves after the Greek manner. The nobleman's attire is on this fashion. First, a *tafta*, or little night cap, on his head, that covers little more than his crown, commonly very rich wrought of silk and gold thread, and set with pearl and precious stone. His head he keeps shaven close to the very skin, except he be in some displeasure with the emperor. Then he suffers his hair to grow and hang down upon his shoulders, covering his face as ugly and deformedly as he can. Over the *tafta* he wears a wide cap of black fox (which they account for the best fur) with a tiara or long bonnet put within it, standing up like a Persian or Babylonian hat. About his neck (which is seen all bare) is a collar set with pearl and precious stone, about three or four fingers broad. Next over his shirt (which is curiously wrought, because he strips himself into it in the summer time while he is within the house) is a *zhupan*, or light garment of silk, made down to the knees, buttoned before; and then a *caftan*, or a close coat buttoned and girt to him with a Persian girdle, whereat he hangs his knives and spoon. This commonly is of cloth of gold, and hangs down as low as his ankles. Over that he wears a loose garment of some rich silk, furred and faced about with some gold lace, called a *ferris*. An other over that of chamlet or like stuff, called an *alkaben*, sleeved and hanging low, and the cape commonly brooched and set all with pearl. When he goes abroad he casts over all these (which are but slight, though they seem to be many) an other garment, called an *honoratka*, like to the *alkaben*, save that it is made without a collar for the neck. And this is commonly of fine cloth or camel's hair. His buskins (which he wears in stead of hose, with linen folds under them instead of boot hose) are made of a Persian leather called *saphian*, embroidered with pearl. His upper stocks commonly are of cloth of gold. When he goes abroad he mounts on horseback, though it be but to the next door, which is the manner also of the *boyars* or gentlemen.

The boyar's or gentleman's attire is of the same fashion, but differs in stuff; and yet he will have his *caftan* or undercoat sometimes of cloth of gold, the rest of cloth of silk.

The noble woman (called *chyna boyarshina*) wears on her head, first, a calotte of some soft silk (which is commonly red) and over it a frontlet, called *poviazka*, of white color. Over that, her cap (made after the coif fashion of cloth of gold) called *shapka zemskaia*, edged with some rich fur, and set with pearl and stone. Though they have of late begun to disdain embroidery with pearl about their caps, because the *diaks'* and some merchants' wives have taken up the fashion. In their ears they wear earrings (which they call *sarzha*) of two inches or more compasse, the matter of gold set with rubies, or sapphires, or some like precious stone. In summer, they go often with kerchiefs of fine white lawn or cambric fastened under the chin, with two long tassels pendant.

The kerchief spotted and set thick with rich pearl. When they ride or go abroad in rainy weather, they wear white hats with colored bands (called *shapka zemskaia*). About their necks they wear collars of three or four fingers broad, set with rich pearl and precious stone. Their upper garment is a loose gown, called *rubashka*, commonly of scarlet, with wide loose sleeves hanging down to the ground, buttoned before with great gold buttons, or, at least, silver and gilt, nigh as big as a walnut. Which has hanging over it, fastened under the cap, a large broad cape of some rich fur, that hangs down almost to the midst of their backs. Next under the *rubashka* or upper garment they wear another, called a *letnik*, that is made close before with great wide sleeves, the cuff or half sleeve up to the elbows, commonly of cloth of gold; and under that a *ferris zemskii*, which hangs loose, buttoned throughout to the very foot. On the hand wrists they wear very fair bracelets, about two fingers broad, of pearl and precious stone. They go all in buskins of white, yellow, blue, or some other colored leather, embroidered with pearl. This is the attire of the noblewoman of Russia, when she makes the best show of herself. The gentlewoman's apparel may differ in the stuff, but is all one for the making or fashion.

As for the poor *muzhik* and his wife, they go poorly clad. The man, with his *odnoratka*, or loose gown, to the small of the leg, tied together with a lace before, of coarse white or blue cloth, with some *shuba*, or long waistcoat, of fur or of sheepskin under it, and his furred cap and buskins. The poorer sort of them have their *odnoratka* or upper garment, made of cow's hair. This is their winter habit. In the summer time, commonly they wear nothing but their shirts on their backs and buskins on their legs. The woman goes in a red or blue gown when she makes the best show, and with some warm *shuba* of fur under it in the winter time. But in the summer nothing but her two shirts (for so they call them) one over the other, whether they be within doors or without. On their heads they wear caps of some colored stuff, many of velvet or of cloth of gold; but for the most part kerchiefs. Without earrings of silver or some other metal, and her cross about her neck, you shall see no Russian woman, be she wife or maid.

As touching their behavior and quality otherwise, they are of reasonable capacities, if they had those means that some other nations have to train up their wits in good nurture and learning. Which they might borrow of the Poles and other [of] their neighbors, but that they refuse it of a very self pride, as accounting their own fashions to be far the best. Partly also (as I said before) for that their manner of bringing up (void of all good learning and civil behavior) is thought by their governors most agreeable to that state and their manner of government. Which the people would hardly bear, if they were once civilled and brought to more understanding of God and good policy. This causes the emperors to keep out all means of making it better, and to be very wary for excluding of all peregrinity that might alter their fashions. Which were less to be disliked, if it set not a print into the very minds of his people. For as themselves are very hardly and cruelly dealt withal by their chief magistrates and other superiors, so are they as cruel one against an other, specially over their inferiors and such as are under them. So that the basest and wretchedest *krestianin* (as they call him) that stoops and crouches like a dog to the gentleman, and licks up the dust that lies at his feet, is in intolerable tyrant where he has the advantage. By this means the whole country is filled with rapine and murder. They make no account of the life of a man. You shall have a man robbed sometime in the very streets of their towns, if he go late in the evening, and yet no man to come forth out of his doors to rescue him, though he hear him cry out. I will not speak of the strangeness of the murders and other cruelties committed among them, that would scarcely be believed to be done among men, specially such as profess themselves Christians.

The number of their vagrant and begging poor is almost infinite, that are so pinched with famine and extreme need, as that they beg after a violent and desperate manner, with "give me and cut me, give me and kill me," and such like phrases. Whereby it may be guessed what they are towards strangers, that are so unnatural and cruel towards their own. And yet it may be doubted whither is the greater, the cruelty or intemperancy that is used in that country. I will not speak of it, because it is so foul and not to be named. The whole country overflows with all sin of that kind. And no marvel, as having no law to restrain whoredomes, adulteries, and like uncleanness of life.

As for the truth of his word, the Russian for the most part makes small regard of it, so he may gain by a lie and breach of his promise. And it may be said truly (as they know best that have traded most with them) that from the great to the small (except some few that will scarcely be found) the Russian neither believes any thing that an other man speaks, nor speaks any thing himself worthy to be believed. These qualities make them very odious to all their neighbors, specially to the Tartars, that account themselves to be honest and just in comparison of the Russian. It is supposed by some that do well consider of the state of both countries, that the offense they take at the Russian government and their manner of behavior, has been a great cause to keep the Tartar still heathenish, and to mislike (as he does) of the Christian profession.

32

Bussow's Account
of the Russian Famine
of 1601–1604

The reign of Boris Godunov (1598–1605) is noted
for its energetic policy of expansion across Siberia,
for interest in west European contacts, and above
all, for setting the stage for the chaos known as
"Time of Troubles." Many factors contributed to
Russia's troubles, however, some contemporary ob-
servers thought that famine and social unrest were
"the beginning of the calamity." The following is an
eyewitness account of the famine by a German
merchant, Konrad Bussow, who lived in Moscow
from 1584 to 1613.

In 1601 the high price of bread began, and continued until
1604. The price of a barrel of rye rose to ten to twelve florins; whereas
earlier it cost no more than twelve to fifteen groschen. The famine in the
country was more severe than the famine in besieged Jerusalem which is
described by Joseph. According to Joseph, the Jews ate dogs, cats, rats,
mice, and even leather from old saddles, shields, and boots, as well as
pigeon dung. One well-born woman, tormented by the famine, killed
her only child, cooked it, and ate it. This is one of the most depressing
situations that one finds in Joseph's account. But I swear by God that in
Moscow I saw, with my own eyes, people who rolled in the streets and,
like animals, ate grass during the summer and hay during the winter.
Some of those who died had hay as well as human excrement in their
mouths. Parents killed, prepared, and cooked many of their children;

From Konrad Bussow, *Moskovskaia Khronika, 1584–1613* (*Moscow Chronicle,
1584–1613*) (Moscow-Leningrad, Akademiia Nauk, 1961), pp. 97–98. Translation mine. Items in brackets are mine.

children did the same with their parents; hosts with visitors; and visitors with hosts. Human flesh, finely ground, baked in pies (a kind of pastry), was sold and consumed like beef. A traveler, then, was forced to be careful in his selection of an inn. When Tsar Boris [Godunov] was informed of these horrible, inhuman killings, which the famine and high cost of living brought about, and of the great number of the famine's casualties, he proposed to alleviate this poverty and God's punishment with the help of his treasury. He ordered four large enclosures to be constructed within the outside walls [of the city of Moscow] (which were about four German miles long), where every morning the poor of the city of Moscow assembled and where they received one *denga* per person. When poor peasants near Moscow heard of this mercy, they left their homes and jobs and ran to Moscow with their wives and children in order to receive money. As a result, there assembled so many people in Moscow that they were forced to distribute as much as 500,000 *dengas* daily. This [distribution of aid] continued for a long time but did not decrease the cost of living at all. Daily, on the Tsar's orders, they collected hundreds of corpses and carried them outside the city in wagons—an undertaking which was awesome to observe. Specially appointed people washed the dead, wrapped them in a white cloth, put red shoes on them, and wheeled them to the church to be buried. During those four years of the high cost of bread, as a result of the Tsar's mercy in feeding the poor, clothing them, and burying them, the state treasury was drained of many hundreds of thousands of rubles. How depleted the treasury became during this time can be easily ascertained. I have been told by trustworthy individuals—government clerks and merchants—that during the high cost of bread, in Moscow alone, more than 500,000 people whom the Tsar fed, died from hunger, and he ordered them to be buried in red shoes and wrapped in cloth. And this occurred in one city only. [No one knows] how many people in the countryside and other cities perished from starvation and diseases and were buried at the expense of the tsarist treasury. . . . Woe to a country or people subjected to God's anger. Boris, however, was embittered, blind, and did not humble before these horrible misfortunes, but hoped to ease the misery with the aid of a rich treasury. By the will of the merciful God, several ships from German seaports arrived in Narva with a cargo of wheat, which could have made possible the feeding of hundreds of thousands of people. Boris, however, did not wish this kind of humiliation, that is, buying and selling foreign food in a country rich in food. The ships were ordered to leave without selling the grain because the Russians were forbidden to buy it under threat of the death penalty. Boris ordered the food reserves of the entire country to be surveyed. They discovered large grain-stacks, one hundred or more *sazhens* [one *sazhen* equals seven feet] long, which had stood there unthreshed, for about fifty years and which were covered with weeds and other growth. Boris ordered that these be threshed and that the grain be sent to Moscow and other cities. He also ordered that his warehouses be opened in all cities, and many thousands of barrels of grain were sold daily at half price. He decreed that poor widows, orphans, and especially foreigners, receive a number of barrels of flour in their homes without charge in order to prevent their suffering.

He called upon princes, boyars, and monasteries to take notice of the country's plight and to offer their grain reserves and sell these at a low price.

Princes, boyars, and monasteries fulfilled the Tsar's will. But the devil . . . suggested to rich grain merchants of Moscow to buy the princely, boyar, and monastery grain through the poor at a low price and sell it back to the poor at a high price. With the decline of the high cost of bread, which caused the death of hundreds of thousands and drained Boris' treasury, a new punishment appeared—war and bloodshed.

33

A Letter from the False Dmitri to Boris Godunov, 1604

In Russian history, the period from 1601 to 1613 is commonly known as the "Time of Troubles." One of its basic characteristics was the appearance of several pretenders to the Russian throne, the earliest of whom was Dmitri, who claimed to be a son of

From S. M. Solovev, *Istoriia Rossii s drevneishikh vremen* (*History of Russia since Ancient Times*) (Moscow, Izdatelstvo sotsialnoekonomicheskoi literatury, 1960), vol. 8, pp. 413–414. Translation mine.

Ivan the Terrible. Dmitri made a favorable impression on many Russians, and with their support he
came to Moscow, only to be assassinated shortly
thereafter.

It grieves us that you have desecrated your soul—created in the
image of God—to such a degree, and that you are preparing its destruction through your tenacity. Do you not know that you are a mortal? You
should have been satisfied, Boris, with the position which God accorded
you; but you, our subject, have stolen our state, against the will of God
and with the help of the devil. Your sister, our brother's wife, secured
power of government over the entire state for you; and you exploited the
fact that our brother dedicated himself for the most part to the service
of God, by murdering, under various pretexts, several of the most respected princes, such as the Princes Ivan and Andrei Shuiskii, then the
best people of our capital, and partisans of the Shuiskii family. You
blinded Tsar Simeon and had his son Ivan poisoned. You have not even
spared the clergy: you banished Metropolitan Dionisius into a monastery, but you nevertheless told our brother Feodor that he had suddenly died; we know, however, that he is still alive today and that you
eased his lot after our brother's death; you have also ruined others whose
names we cannot remember, because we were still in our childhood at
that time. Although we were just a child, you will still recollect how often
we admonished you not to murder the subjects. You will recall how we
dispatched your partisan Andrei Kleshnin, whom our brother Feodor
had sent to us in Uglich. Your partisan, after delivery of the commis-
sioned message, and counting on your protection, did not show us proper
deference. You were dissatisfied with this, and we were an obstacle to
you in the path leading to the throne. After you murdered our dignitaries
you began to sharpen your knife for us also; you persuaded our official
Michael Bitiagovskii, together with twelve chamberlains, Nikita Kacha-
lov, and Osip Volokhov, to assassinate us; you thought that our physician, Simeon, was part of the plot, but thanks to his efforts we were
saved from the death which you prepared for us. You told our brother
that we had fatally wounded ourselves in a fit of epilepsy. You know
how deeply our brother mourned the news. He ordered that our body
be brought to Moscow; you, however, influenced the patriarch, who ruled
that it would be improper to place the body of a suicide victim beside
those who died in Jesus Christ. Thereupon our brother wanted to travel
personally to Uglich for the funeral; you told him, however, that a
dangerous epidemic was raging in Uglich, and at the same time you
challenged the Khan of the Crimean Tartars. You had at your disposal
an army twice as large as that of the enemy, but you pitched camp

before Moscow and forbade your troops to attack the enemy under penalty of death. For three days you lay encamped across from them, and then you let them withdraw unmolested; the Khan left our kingdom without being punished. And you returned home, and only three days later did you begin to pursue the enemy. When Andrei Klobukov apprehended the incendiaries and they explained that you had incited them to set Moscow in flames, you instructed them to accuse Klobukov of the guilt, and you had him seized and tortured to death on the rack. After the death of our brother (whose passing you hastened), you began to bribe beggars, cripples, and blind men with great sums of money, so that they loudly cried out everywhere that you should be Tsar. After you had assumed the throne, however, the families of the Romanovs, Cherkasskiis, and Shuiskiis were given the opportunity to become acquainted with your kindness. Come to your senses and do not incite us to great anger with your evil. Give back to us what is ours. And we will forgive you all your guilt and allot to you a peaceful place. It is better for you to suffer somewhat in this world than to burn eternally in hell for the sake of the numerous souls whom you have murdered.

34

Shuiskii's Decree against Runaway Peasants, March 9, 1607

The "Time of Troubles" (1601–1613) saw major political and social chaos. It witnessed the appearance of a number of pretenders to the vacant throne

From *Vosstanie Bolotnikova, Dokumenty i materiialy* (*Bolotnikov's Uprising: Documents and Sources*) (Moscow, Sotsekgis, 1959), pp. 211–214. Translation mine. Items in brackets are mine.

of Russia, invited foreign intervention, and, above all, presented the peasants with an opportunity to seek better working conditions. The nobles who disapproved of peasant flights, forced the newly elected Tsar Shuiskii (1606–1610) to issue a decree that allowed them an extended period of time to search for their runaway peasants. This decree was a significant milestone in the growth of Russian serfdom.

On March 9, 1607, Vasili Shuiskii (1606–1610), Tsar and Grand Prince of All Russia, together with Patriarch Ermogen, the Holy Sobor and the tsar's own council, heard a report of the *pomestie prikaz* [Estates Department] [prepared by] the *boyars* and clerks, which complained that peasant changes from one place of work to another created great difficulties, extremes, and violence against the weak by the strong —something that was absent during the reign of Ivan Vasilevich, when peasants had freedom of movement. At Boris Godunov's suggestion, discarding the advice of old *boyars*, Tsar Feodor Ivanovich [1584–1598] prohibited the [free] movement of peasants and forced everyone to report how many peasants he had, an action which soon thereafter led to many animosities, extremes, and litigations. When Tsar Boris Feodorovich [Godunov] saw the great commotion among the people, he set aside the law and allowed the peasants a limited freedom of movement, an action which judges did not know how to interpret in passing sentences. Consequently, now we are witnessing many quarrels and violence; many are ruined and there are many murders, banditries, and highway robberies.

As a result, with the aid of the Holy Synod and in accordance with the rule of the Holy Fathers, we have prepared [the following law:]

Those peasants who were registered in 1601 should, within the next fifteen years, return to those with whom they were originally registered; and should these peasants now be working for someone else, and if there is a search warrant for them, as well as [a complaint] against those who harbor them now, even if the litigation is incomplete, or should former owners start legal proceedings by September 1, [1607], those people who have such peasants on their estates should return them by 1616, together with their wives, children, and their livestock without any charge to those to whom they originally belonged; and whoever shall not return them by the said time as provided in this *ukaz* [decree], he will be forced to pay a fine as well as a rental. Those peasants for whom there will be no search warrant by September 1, [1607] should not be returned, but should be registered with those to whom they currently belong.

And those peasants who will henceforth leave their owners and join other [owners], regardless of whom they may be, and if [the new owners] accept them, this will be contrary to our *ukaz*. When such a peasant is found he will be returned, together with all the fruits of his labor, to the original owner from whom he fled; and if that peasant had built a home, that home should not be transferred, but a fair price must be paid for it; he should also be fined ten rubles for violating the tsar's *ukaz*; do not accept any strangers; if you do you will pay a rental of three rubles per year to the owner of the runaway peasant; annual rental for a runaway slave is also three rubles.

And should a peasant without a family come to anyone and hire himself for a seasonal summer's or winter's work or for the entire year, he who hires him for a year does not violate this *ukaz* and cannot be fined for accepting him because his real master knows where he lives.

And should a woman or a widow or a maid run away into someone's estate and marry there, the peasant who marries a strange woman should be given to the owner of the woman, with all of his livestock and [all of his] children born of this marriage; and should this peasant have children from his former wife, they are not affected; the stepmother should not take them; those under fifteen years old, however, should be allowed to go with their father.

Those individuals who have a slave girl under eighteen years old, or a widow of two years' widowhood, or a young single man under twenty, and allow them neither to marry nor be free, such maids, widows, and young men should go and complain to the state treasury; and if the treasury, upon investigating the complaint, should prove that these individuals are grown and their master does not allow them to marry, they should be set free, in Moscow by the treasury, and in other cities by a local state official and courts; and should their master then complain that these individuals had stolen or taken away something, he should not be heard nor [should] the matter [be] allowed to be brought before the court. Do not detain unmarried persons since it is contrary to the Divine law and the teachings of the Holy Fathers; moreover such practice will not cause the population to increase.

Those peasants, slave men and slave women, who will run away from their masters following the issuing of this *ukaz*, and should they be harbored by other masters, their owner has permission to search for his peasants, male slaves and women slaves, for fifteen years following their flight; after fifteen years they should neither be sought after nor punished.

In cities, *namestniks* [administrators], *voevodas* [appointed officials], judges, clerks, and all state officials should know [of all developments] in their cities and learn of all happenings in territories under their respective jurisdiction from the elders, [land] captains, and priests whether there are any newcomers; and if they be informed of their whereabouts they should apprehend them and ask to whom they belong, where they are from, from whom they ran away, how long and where they have lived. And should anyone attempt to bribe him [the official] and should he reveal it and report it, the would-be briber should be fined by the treasury and be forced to deposit a guarantee that he will transport the fugitive to his master. The treasury should collect a fine of ten rubles from him, while those who harbor fugitives more than seven days should be fined ten rubles per household for every runaway man, and three rubles for harboring a fugitive woman or a girl.

And should someone's slave, or a peasant, or a woman be accepted on the lands or villages of the Tsar and the Grand Prince, or on monastery lands, or in villages of the Patriarch, the Church, or a monastery, the responsibility for accepting these fugitives should be placed on the stewards and elders of those villages or lands. This ukaz permits searches for the fugitives in all those villages, lands, cities, and settlements.

And those *namestniks*, judges, clerks, and all other officials who will neither investigate nor inquire about the newcomers but will accept bribes, and should this be reported, then such officials should be fined twice the amount of their gain, dismissed from their position, and never accepted into the state service again.

35

Conditions
for Wladislaw's Ascension
to the Throne of Moscovy, 1610

One of the candidates for the Russian throne during the "Time of Troubles" was Prince Wladislaw, the son of an ambitious Polish King, Sigismund III.

From *Akty otnosiashchiesia k istorii Zapadnoi Rossii, sobranye i izdannye arkheograficheskoiu Kommissieiu* . . . (Documents Pertaining to the History of Western Russia, Collected and Published by the Archeographic Commission) (St. Petersburg, 1846–1853), vol. 4, pp. 314–317. Translation mine. Items in brackets are mine.

For a time it appeared that Wladislaw had a strong
chance to become tsar of Russia, but the obstinacy
of his father, who actually wanted the Russian
throne for himself, upset Wladislaw's chance. As the
following excerpts indicate, Wladislaw would have
been a "constitutional" tsar of Russia.

A reply of the most illustrious Sigismund III, by the grace of
God, King of Poland and Grand Prince of Lithuania, on articles and peti-
tions of the boyars, courtiers, nobles, officials and counsellors of the
Moscovite state.

1. You have requested: that with God's blessing the great lord, his
grace the King [of Poland] permit his son Wladislaw to become the great
Tsar and Grand Prince of the state of Moscovy and of all famed and
great Russian states; that his majesty the great Tsar and Grand Prince be
crowned on the Moscovite throne with the tsarist crown and diadem
in Moscow by the Patriarch of Moscow in accordance with ancient custom, in the same fashion as all past rulers of Moscow and of the famed
Moscovite state were crowned. To this his royal grace consents and hopes
that Providence will in time send real peace to this state [of Moscovy].

2. [You have requested] that the Holy Orthodox Greek faith and the
Holy Apostolic Church be preserved, that it retain its former beauty as
well as the content of the teachings of the apostles and the Church
fathers, and that Roman Catholic, Lutheran, and other teachers cause
no religious schism. And that those Roman Catholics who wish to attend
Greek Church service must come there in humility, as befits true Christians, and not with pride, or with their hats on, or with their dogs, or
at times when it is not appropriate. To this [request] his royal grace
would like to state the following: Roman Catholics must have their own
church, a problem which was negotiated during the reign of Boris
[Godunov], and in that Church they must have priests or Polish clergy,
and this problem will have to be negotiated with the Patriarch, the
government, and all important boyars, for there is a need for at least
one Roman Catholic church in the capital city of Moscow to serve
Poles and Lithuanians; and should a Russian happen to go to a [Roman
Catholic] church he should conduct himself in the same appropriate
manner as is done in Russian churches. Neither his grace, the King, nor
his royal grace, the son, will allow conversions from Greek to Roman
or any other faith, inasmuch as faith is God's gift and no one should be
forced to renounce his belief; a Russian should have free worship in the
Russian faith, and a Pole or a Lithuanian in the Polish faith.

3. His grace, the King, as a great Christian sovereign, with his son,
will have great respect for holy shrines and remains of the saints. The

Patriarch of Moscow, as well as metropolitans, archbishops, bishops, and all the clergy will be protected and respected [by us] similarly as we protect and respect Roman Catholic servants of God, that is, archbishops, bishops, and all priests. We will neither interfere in Church affairs nor do we wish to comment on matters relative to the teachings of the Holy Fathers and of the Apostolic Church; and his grace, the lord, will not approve as bishop anyone who does not deserve that position. . . .

5. His grace, the lord, would like to be kind to the *boyars*, courtiers, and all important government officials, as was the custom earlier, and he would also like to preserve all ancient customs; those who had grants, or monetary rewards, or owned either *pomesties* [estates of service nobles],[1] or *votchinas* [hereditary estates], will have them as of old; his grace, the lord, from his own grace and generosity and in return for service, will increase and add to their wealth.

6. In accordance with the ancient custom, his grace, the lord, will make his gracious grants to the service people, nobles [*dvorianom*] and lesser nobility early each year; and should something be acquired not from the sovereign and not according to their dignity, or should someone suffer unjustly, then his grace, the sovereign, will consult with the *boyars*, and whatever their judgment will be, his sovereign grace will approve; he will also follow the advice of the *boyars* on the means to improve devastated *pomesties* and *votchinas*; those nobles and petty nobility who receive the sovereign's grants [of tax proceeds] from cities, his grace, the lord, will continue to grant them in return for services, as was the custom earlier.

7. His grace, the lord, will pay, as of old, from the government treasury, monetary and grain salaries to the gunners and hoopers in Moscow and other cities, who were in the service of previous sovereigns.

8. Courts must be conducted by custom and in accordance with the Code of Law [*Sudebnik*]; and should anyone wish to introduce changes aimed at improving the justice of the courts, this change is reserved to the *boyars* of the whole country; and his grace, the lord, will not interfere with improvements in the court system. . . .

11. Should anyone commit a crime deserving of punishment, his grace, the lord, will punish him, regardless of his rank, on the basis of his crime, but with prior just consultation with the *boyars* and other important people; wives, children, and brothers who neither took part in the crime nor knew of it, should not be punished and may remain on their *votchinas* or *pomesties*; and no one should be punished or deprived of his honor, or imprisoned or deprived of his *pomestie* or *votchina* without first being found guilty by the court and by all the *boyars*. Individuals of high rank should not be unjustly demerited while lesser officials should be promoted according to their service only. *Votchinas* and other property should not be confiscated; property of those who die

without heirs should pass on to their next of kin. And his grace, the lord, will do all this only in consultation with the *boyars* and with agreement of influential *boyars*, and without their consent he will do nothing. His grace, the lord, will not exile anyone to prison in Lithuania or Poland. For learning purposes, citizens of Moscow are free to travel abroad in every Christian country, except pagan or Islamic, and his grace, the lord, will not confiscate their estates or properties for this. . . .

14. His grace, the lord, will collect goods and all state revenues from cities and villages, and money from taverns, and from customs as of old; that is, as was done similarly by his predecessors; his grace, the lord, will add no new taxes to the existing ones. To cities destroyed by the war, his grace, the lord, will send officials to assess the damage. Taxes from those who remained there will be collected on the basis of this assessment. And his grace, the lord, may increase the taxes in cities that were not damaged [only] with the consent of the *boyars* and other influential people.

15. Polish and Lithuanian merchants are free to trade in the Moscovite state and Russian-Moscovite merchants are free to trade in Poland and Lithuania. This freedom is applicable to all commodities. His royal grace allows Russian merchants to travel freely through Poland and Lithuania to other countries; his royal grace will collect dues from them in Moscow and in all cities of Moscovy as well as in Poland and Lithuania on the basis of the old customs, neither adding anything new to these nor collecting anything illegally.

16. His royal grace will not allow peasants to go from Russia to Lithuania or from Lithuania to Russia; while in Russia he will not permit mixing between various layers of Russian society.

17. His royal highness will allow the *boyars* to retain their slaves on the basis of the old custom so that they will serve their *boyars* or their lords as of old; and his grace will not grant them [the slaves] any freedom.

18. Should his grace, the lord, wish to station cossacks along the Volga, Don, Ural, and Terek Rivers, he may have them, upon prior consultation concerning it with *boyars* and important people. When, with God's permission, his royal grace [Wladislaw] shall reach Moscow, the Patriarch, the Holy Synod, *boyars*, nobles, and people of other social layers may petition for items not included in these articles; then his grace will approve these according to the custom of the Moscovite state with [the consent of] the Patriarch, the Holy Sobor, *boyars*, and all the country.

Written in our camp near Smolensk, February 4, 1610.

Sigismund rex.

36

Olearius' Commentaries on Moscovy in the 1630s and 1640s

Commercial, diplomatic, and cultural contacts be-
twen Moscovy and Europe attained a lively tempo
in the seventeenth century. Not only did Europeans
come to Moscow in greater numbers than ever before, but they also left more accurate accounts of
their impressions of Moscovite politics, customs,
habits, and related matters. The best of these accounts is that of Adam Olearius (1599–1671), a
German scholar who, as an official of the Duke of
Holstein, visited Moscow on four occasions—1634,
1636, 1639, and 1643. Olearius, who had studied
at the University of Leipzig, spoke Russian, mingled
with the Moscovites, and observed and recorded
their virtues and follies as no foreigner had done before. Olearius' descriptions, and sketches are considered a major work on the seventeenth century
history of Russia, and his analysis is so penetrating
and so richly rewarding for the reader that it is
presented here at considerable length.

But it is time we returned to our Moscovites, whom we shall
consider, first, in relation to their habit and stature, then to their humor
and manner of life.

They are for the most part corpulent, fat, and strong, and of the

From Adam Olearius, *Voyages and Travells of the Ambassadors Sent by Fred-
erick Duke of Holstein to the Great Duke of Muscovy and the King of Persia
. . . Containing a Complete History of Muscovy, Tartary, Persia, and Other
Adjacent Countries . . . The Second Edition Corrected.* (London, 1669), pp.
56–73, 88–98, 100–108. Spelling has been modernized to facilitate reading.
Items in brackets are mine.

same color as other Europeans. They much esteem great beards (when the mustaches hide the mouth) as also great bellies; so that those who are well furnished about the mouth, and have good fat pouches, are very considerable among them. The *gostis*, or the Great Duke's merchants, whom we found in the antechamber, when we were brought to our public audience, had been chosen particularly for those two perfections, for the greater honor of their prince.

The great lords shave their heads; persons of lower condition cut their hair, and priests and others belonging to the church, wear their hair so long, that it hangs down over their shoulders to half their backs. Those lords who are out of favor at Court, let their hair grow and hang negligently about their heads, thereby expressing their affliction; no doubt after the example of the ancient Greeks, whom the Moscovites are apt to imitate in all their actions.

The women are well proportioned; neither too big, nor too little: having possible good faces, but they paint so palpably, that if they laid it on with a brush, and had a handful of meal cast in their faces when they had done, they could not disfigure themselves as much as the paint does. But the custom is so general, that the most handsome must comply, lest they should discredit the artificial beauty of others; whereof we saw an example in the wife of Prince Ivan Borisovich Cherkasskii, who was the handsomest lady of all Moscovy, and was loath to spoil with painting what the rest of her sex took so much pains to preserve thereby: but the other women informed against her, and would not be quiet, till their husbands had forced that prince to give way that his wife might daub her face after the ordinary manner. So that painting is so common in Moscovy, that when any are to be married, the bridegroom, that is to be, sends among other presents some paint to his bride, as we shall see when we come to speak of their marriages.

Married women put up their hair within their caps or coifs, but the maids let theirs hang down their backs in two tresses, and tie it at the ends with a piece of crimson silk. Children under ten years of age, as well girls as boys, have their hair cut, all except two mustaches, which are left over the temples; so that there being no difference in their habits, that of their sex is discovered only by the two brass or silver rings, which the girls wear in their ears. . . .

If a man consider the natures and manner of life of the Moscovites, he will be forced to avow, that there cannot be anything more barbarous than that people. Their boast is that they are descended from the ancient Greeks, but, to do them no injustice, there is no more comparison between the brutality of these barbarians and the civility of the Greeks, to whom all other parts of the world are obliged for all their literature and civilization, than there is between day and night. They never learn any art or science, nor apply themselves to any kind of study:

on the contrary, they are so ignorant, as to think, a man cannot make an almanac unless he be a sorcerer, nor foretell the revolutions of the moon and eclipses, unless he have some communication with devils. Upon this account it was, that the Moscovites generally grumbled when the Great Duke would have entertained me into his service, in the quality of his astronomer and mathematician, as we returned from our voyage into Persia, and raised a report that their prince was going to bring a magician into his Court. This aversion I discovered in the Moscovites, took off that little inclination I sometime had to embrace that employment, which was offered me, not so much upon the account of my abilities in astronomy, as to engage me to continue in the country, because they knew that I had exactly observed and drawn into a map the whole course of the river Volga whereof they were unwilling that strangers should have any knowledge. When I came to Moscovy, upon the affairs of the Duke of Holstein, my master, in the year 1643, I showed them upon a wall of an obscure chamber, through a little hole I had made in the shutter of the window, by the means of a piece of glass polished and cut for optics, all that was done in the street, and men walking upon their heads: this wrought such an effect in them, that they could never after be otherwise persuaded than that I held a correspondence with the devil.

They esteem physicians, and medicine, but will not permit that people should make use of the same means as is done elsewhere to gain the perfection of that science. They will not suffer the body to be opened, so that the causes of diseases may be found out, and they have a strange aversion for skeletons. . . .

Their industry and subtlety is chiefly seen in their traffick, in which there is no craft or cheat but they make use of, rather to circumvent others, than to prevent being deceived themselves. I wondered to see them sell cloth at three Crowns and a half the ell, which they had bought of the English at four, and yet I was told they made a good profit thereby; for buying the cloth at twelve months time per payment, and selling it for ready money, though at a lower rate, they made use of the money, and employed it in other things, which brought in more profit than they would have made by selling the cloth upon time, though they sold it much dearer than it cost them. They make a conscience to retain what is paid them more than their due, and are so honest as to return what they have received by mistake: but they think it no sin, in their dealings, to surprise those who trade with them, giving this reason, that the merchant is to make his advantage of the wit and industry God has bestowed on him, or never meddle with traffick. According to this principle, a certain Dutch merchant having notoriously over-reached several Moscovites, these gentlemen were so far from being troubled at it, that they spoke of him, as of an excellent ingenious man, and desired they might go partners with him, out of a hope they conceived, that he would discover some great secrets to them.

And whereas cheating cannot be exercised without treachery, lying, and distrust, which are its constant attendants, they are marvelously well versed in these qualities as also in the features of calumny, which they commonly make use of against those on whom they would be revenged for theft, which among them is the most enormous of all crimes, and the most severely punished. To this end, they are so cunning, as to pawn at, or get secretly conveyed into their lodgings, whom they would accuse, those things which they would have believed were stolen from them, or they thrust them into their enemy's boots; for in them the Moscovites commonly carry their money and letters. To make some provisions against these abuses, the Great Duke made an edict in the year 1634, enjoining that for the future, all promises or obligations, whether for borrowing of money or pawning, though it were between father and son, should be set down in writing and signed by both parties, else the debt to be lost. Heretofore, especially in the reign of the tyrant Ivan Vasilevich, there needed no more to procure a man's death or banishment, than to accuse him of high treason, without any process, evidence, or defense allowed, all that were charged being punished, without any distinction of sex, age, or quality. Calumnies and false suggestions were so common under that prince, that many strangers, even public persons, many times fell into those misfortunes, the tyrant never regarding their character as ambassadors, nor that of the princes by whom they were sent. He banished into Siberia, the Emperor's ambassador, and caused him to be so ill-treated, that the poor man resolved at last to change his religion, hoping by his apostasy to alleviate his misery. The Great Duke Michael Feodorovich, showed no more respect for the late king of France, when he sent the Marquis of Exidueil into Siberia where, by the artifices of his colleague, James Russel, he was a prisoner three years. . . .

But now they proceed with more caution, and no man is condemned without an exact information of the crime laid to his charge. And for the utter taking away of all calumny, the accuser must be content to endure the torture first; and if, while he is in the torment, he persists in his accusation, the accused person is also put to it, nay many times he is condemned without so much as being heard. We saw an example of this in the wife of one of the Great Duke's farriers, who desirous to be rid of her husband, charged him that he would have poisoned the horses, and had he the opportunity, even the Great Duke himself. She endured the torture without varying in her accusation, and her husband was sent to prison into Siberia. We were shown this woman, who was still paid the one-half of her husband's pension. From this kind of demeanor among the Moscovites and their infidelity one to another, it may be judged what foreigners are to expect from them, and how far they are to be trusted.

They never profess their friendship, nor contract any with others, but for their own interest and advantage. The ill-education they have when young, never learning anything beyond reading and writing, and certain vulgar prayers, makes them blindly follow that which in beasts is called instinct; so that nature being in them depraved and corrupted, their whole life must needs be a constant course of viciousness. Thence it comes they are brutish, doing all things according to their unbridled passions and appetites.

The fierceness of all other nations, some islanders excepted, argues something of spirit and generosity; but the opinion the Moscovites have of themselves and their abilities, is sottish, gross, and impertinent; and the pride and vain glory of those who are even so little advanced in honors or estates, is insupportable. They dissemble it not, but all their behavior, words, and actions, discover what they really are. Upon this principle they ground the fond conceit they have of the greatness, power, and wealth of their prince, whom they prefer before all the other monarchs of Europe. Thence it is also, that they would not have other princes assume those qualities which may denote their competition with him. They sottishly and insolently command ambassadors to be uncovered first, and by force take all advantages over them, imagining it were a great injury to themselves and their prince, to treat foreigners with any civility. Private persons write and speak in unhandsome terms, but such as give the less offense, in that they bear with the same treatment from others. 'Tis true, they began to learn a little civility, since they became sensible of the advantages arising to them from the commerce they have with foreigners, and there are some who use them with discretion: but of these there are very few. . . .

They are all much given to quarrelling, insomuch that in the streets they will rail at, and abuse one another like fish-wives, and that with such animosity, that those who are not acquainted with their humor think they will not part without fighting; but they seldom come to those extremities, or if they fight, it is with their fists, or switches, and the height of their rage is kicking, as much as they can, in the belly and about the sides. 'Twas never yet known that any Moscovite fought with sword or pistol, or that they are sensible of that gallantry wherein many would unjustly place true courage. The great lords, princes, and boyars, fight on horseback, but the weapon is a good whip, and so they soon decide what differences happen between them.

When they quarrel, they forbear cursing, swearing and blaspheming, but rail at one another in such bitter and horrid expressions, as no country being able to parallel them, 'tis but discretion to forbear defiling this relation therewith. The language of fathers and mothers to their children, and of the children to them again, is such as cannot be expressed without horror, much beyond what the most debauched persons elsewhere are guilty of. Some years since the Great Duke prohibited these insolences upon pain of whipping, and the magistrate was ordered to send *streltsi* and sergeants among the people to surprise offenders and to see them immediately punished. But it was found by experience that the remedy came too late, and that the mischief was so deeply rooted, and so generally spread, that it was not only hard, but absolutely impossible to put those prohibitions into execution. So that, for the vindication of persons of high quality an order was made, that he who affronts any such, or any of the Great Duke's officers, either by word or deed, should be fined, which fine they call *beschestie*, and sometimes amounts to 2000 Crowns, according to the quality of the person injured. If an officer of the Great Duke's makes his complaint of injury done him, his reparation will be according to his relation to the Court; to a lady, 'tis doubled, to a son, 'tis augmented by a third part; to a daughter, there is an abatement of a third part: and the penalty is paid as many times as there are persons injured, though they were dead many years before. If the offender has not to pay, he is put into his adversary's hands, who disposes of him so as to make him his slave, or cause him to be whipped by the common executioner. . . .

There is nothing polite in their conversation; on the contrary, they are not ashamed to yawn, belch, and stretch themselves wherever they are, their belching being the more offensive, by reason of the abundance of onions and garlic they use in all their meat, which make their breaths strong enough without those exaltations. This they are so accustomed to, that they stick not to do it in any company, the Great Duke's presence only excepted.

They do not apply themselves to the study of any art or science, nor inquire into the affairs of other countries, and consequently never discourse of any such thing: but it were well on the other side, if they could forbear talking of their uncleannesses and brutalities, which they make their divertissement in their debauches. I speak not of the entertainments of great lords, but of the ordinary company keeping of the Moscovites, where all of their discourse is of the abominations which they themselves have done, or seen committed by others, making ostentation of crimes which here would be expiated by fire, and the memory thereof buried in their ashes. But as they are wholly given up to all licentiousness, even to sins against nature, not only with men, but also with beasts, he who can tell most stories of that kind, and set them out in most gestures, is accounted the bravest man. Their fiddlers put them into songs, and their mountebanks make public representations of them, and stick not to show their breeches, and sometimes all they have to their spectators. Those who lead bears about, jugglers, and puppet players, who erect a stage in a moment, by the means of a coverlet, which, being tied about their waist, is brought up over their heads, and within it they show their puppets, representing their brutalities and sodomies, make sport to the children, who are thereby induced to quit all sentiments of shame and honesty.

Nay these are quite discarded by the Moscovites. The posture of their dancing, and the insolence of their women, are infallible marks of their bad inclinations. We have seen at Moscow both men and women come out of the public brothel-houses stark naked, and incite some young people of our retinue to naughtiness by filthy and lascivious expressions. Idleness, which is the mother of all vices, and seems to have been bestowed on these barbarous people as their portion, is that which makes them run into these excesses, whereto their drunkenness does also contribute; inasmuch as being naturally inclined to luxury, when they are once got into their wine they mind nothing else. I have to this purpose a story, which the Great Duke's interpreter told me when we were at Novgorod: how that in the said city, there is an anniversary devotion, to which come abundance of pilgrims. He who is allowed to keep a tippling-house, gets a permission from the Metropolitan, to pitch several tents, for the accommodation of the pilgrims of both sexes, who are sure to be there betimes in the morning before service, and to take some cups of strong water. Nay some of them, instead of minding their devotions, spend the day in drinking, whence arise such strange disorders, that he told me he saw a woman so drunk there, that coming out of a tent she fell down; and fell asleep, naked as she was, in the street in the day-time. Which gave occasion to a Moscovite, who was also drunk to lie down by her, and, having made use of her, to fall also asleep in sight of many people, who having made a ring about them, only laughed at the posture they were in, till at last an old man, conceiving a horror at the spectacle, covered them with his own garment.

There is no place in the world where drunkenness is more common than in Moscovy. All, of all conditions, ecclesiastics and lay, men and women, old and young, will drink strong water at any time, before, at, and after their meals. They call it *tsarkovino*, and fail not to offer it to those who visit them. The lowest sort of people, peasants and slaves, refuse not cups which are given them by some persons of quality, but will drink of it till they lie down, and many times die in the place. Nay their great ones are not free from this vice, as for example, the Moscovite ambassador, sent to Charles, King of Sweden, in the year 1608, who, forgetting his quality and the affairs his master had entrusted him with, took so much strong water the night before he was to have audience, that the next day being found dead in his bed, they were forced to carry him to his grave, instead of conducting him to audience.

The meaner sort of people think it not enough to stay in the tippling-house till they have not a copeck left in their purses, but many times pawn their clothes there even to their shirts, which is no more than what is seen daily during our abode in Moscow. Being lodged at Lubeck-house, as I went to Novgorod, in my voyage to Moscow in 1643, I saw coming out of an ale-house not far thence, several of those drunkards, some without caps, others without shoes or stockings, some without waistcoats, and only their shirts. . . .

Being in the same city of Novgorod at the time of our second embassy, I saw a priest coming out of the tippling-house, who coming by our lodging would needs give the benediction to the *strelets*, who stood sentinel at the door, but as lifted up his hands, going to make the inclination used in that ceremony, the head, fraught with the vapors of the wine, was so heavy, that weighing down the whole body, the priest fell down in the dirt. Our *strelets* took him up with much respect, and received his daggled benediction; it being, it seems, a thing very ordinary among them.

The Great Duke Michael Feodorovich [1613–1645], who was a sober person, and hated drunkenness, considering with himself that it was impossible absolutely to prevent these excesses, made in his time several orders for the moderating of them, causing the tippling-houses to be shut up, and prohibiting the selling of strong water, or hydromel without his permission, and that those places where they were sold, should sell only by the quart and pint, and not by cups. This had some effect, in that there were no more Adamites seen in the streets, but hindered not their being strewed with drunkards, the neighbors and such of their friends, as had a design to be merry, sending to the tavern for several bottles of strong water which they would be sure to turn off ere they parted.

The women are no less given to drink than the men. I saw a pleasant example of it at Narva, in the house where I lodged, whither many Moscovite women came one day to their husbands, sat down with them, and took off their cups as smartly as they did. The men being got drunk, would have gone home, but the women thought it was not yet time to draw off, though invited thereto by a good number of boxes o' th' ear, and got their husbands to sit down again, and to drink roundly as before, till such time as that the men being fallen down asleep upon the ground, the women sat upon them, as upon benches, and drunk on till they also were forced to lie down by them. . . .

Tobacco was heretofore so common there, that it was generally taken, both in smoke and powder. To prevent the mischiefs occasioned by the use of it, which were not only that the poorer sort of people ruined themselves thereby, in as much as if they had but a penny, they would rather bestow it in tobacco than bread, but also because many times it set houses on fire and those that took it presented themselves with their stinking and infectious breaths before their images, the Great Duke and the Patriarch thought fit in the year 1634 absolutely to forbid the sale and use of it. Those who are convicted of having either taken or sold any, are very rigorously punished. They have their nostrils split or are whipped, as we have often seen done; of the manner of which punishment we shall speak when we come to treat of the administration of justice in that country.

The perverse disposition of the Moscovites, the baseness of their education, and the slavery they seem born to, cause them to be treated like beasts, rather than people endowed with reason. They are naturally so much inclined to idleness, that it were impossible to bring them to take any pains, but by the whip, and the cudgel, which yet they are not much troubled at, as being hardened to blows, by the custom which the younger sort have to meet on holidays, and to divert themselves by cuffing or fighting with staves, never being angry at what happens. Those who are free born, but poor, do so little value that advantage, that they sell themselves with their family for a small matter; nay, they are so mindless of their liberty, that they will sell themselves a second time, after they have recovered it, by the death of their master, or some other occasion.

Their submission to their superiors discovers the lowness of their spirits, and their slavery. They never come before persons of quality, but they bow down to the ground, which they touch and smite with their forehead, nay, there are some who will cast themselves at their lords' feet, to give them thanks after they have been sufficiently beaten by them. No Moscovite, what quality soever be he of, but makes his brag to be the Great Duke's *kholop* [slave], and to express their humility or abjection, even in the least things, they put their names into diminutives, and neither speak nor write to him, but instead of Ivan, they say Ivaniushka, that is the diminutive; and sign thus, *Petrushka tvoi kholop*, Peter, your slave. The Great Duke speaking to them uses the same expression, treating them in all things like slaves, as far as whips and cudgels can do it, which is but consonant to their own acknowledgment, that their persons and estates are God's and the Great Duke's. . . .

As for slaves, their number is not regulated; some lords have above a hundred of them in their country houses and farms; those they entertain for their service in the city do not diet in their houses, but have board wages, their allowance so small, that it is as much as they can do to live upon it. And this is one of the chiefest causes of the many disorders and mischiefs done at Moscow, there passing hardly a night but violences and murders are committed. Great lords and rich merchants have a guard in their courts, who watch all night, and are obliged to express their vigilance by the noise they make upon boards with a stick, much after the manner of playing upon the timbrels, which done, they give as many knocks as the clock has struck hours. But these guards watching many times more for the advantage of house breakers than of their masters, there is none used now, and no servant is taken into a house, but upon good city security for his truth.

This great number of slaves makes it unsafe to walk the streets of Moscow in the night time unarmed and without company. We had the experience of it in some of our servants upon several occasions. Our master cook, who had been employed at a person's of quality, where the ambassadors had dined, was killed as he came home in the night; which misfortune happened also to the steward belonging to the Swedish ambassador Spiring. The lieutenant, who had commanded our German and Scottish musketeers in our voyage into Persia, was in like manner killed in the night, having been with some others at the wedding of a German merchant's daughter. And as there passed no night almost without murder, so these disorders increased towards great festivals, especially on flesh days, which they call *maslenitsa*. On St. Martin's Eve, we counted fifteen dead bodies in the court of *zemskii*, a place where they are exposed that their kins and friends may know them, and take order for their burial. If no body owns them, they are dragged thence like carrion and thrown into a ditch without any ceremony.

The insolence of these villains is so great, that they stuck not to set upon the Great Duke's principal physician in the day time. They stopped him in the street as he was going home, struck him off his horse, and would have cut off his finger, on which he had a gold seal-ring, had he not been relieved by some sent to his rescue, by a prince of his acquaintance, who living near thereabouts had seen him set upon. The misery is, that no citizen will so much as look out of his window, much less come out of his house to relieve those that are affronted, so much are they afraid to come into the same misfortune they see others engaged in. Since our being there, some course has been taken herein. Watches being set, who stop those who go in the night without a torch or lantern and carry them to the *streletskii prikaz*, where they are punished the next day.

At hay making time the road between Moscow and Tver is very dangerous to travel, by reason of the great number of slaves employed in that work, making their advantage of a mountain whence they discover those that pass, whom they rob and kill, without any reparation to be expected from their masters, who, not allowing their slaves what to subsist upon, are forced to connive at their crimes.

Masters dispose of their slaves, as they do of any other movable; nay, a father may sell his son, and alienate him for his own advantage. But the Moscovites have this piece of vain glory, that not only they seldom come to those extremities, but also had rather see their children starve at home, than suffer them to go out anywhere to service. 'Tis only debt that sometimes engages them to make over their children to their creditors, the boys at ten, the girls at eight Crowns, a year, the children being no less obliged to satisfy the debt than their fathers, as also to endure that cruel treatment which desperate debtors are to expect, or to sell themselves to their creditors. . . .

The Moscovites spend not much in house keeping, nor the boyars, as well as those of a lower condition. It is not above thirty years, that their lords and chiefest merchants have built their houses of stone: for before they were no better lodged than the meaner sort, in very poor wooden buildings. Their household stuff is suitable to their lodgings, and commonly consist in three or four pots, and as many wooden or earthen dishes. Some have pewter, but very few, and unless it be some few drinking cups and goblets, there is not any of silver. They know not what scouring means, insomuch that the Great Duke's plate looks little better than the tavern pots, which are made clean but once a year. The better sort hang their rooms but with mat; and to set them out yet a little better, they have only two or three images wretchedly painted. They have few feather beds, but are content with mattresses, nay with chaff or straw, and if not that to be had, they lay upon their cloths, which in summer they lay upon a bench or table; in the winter, upon their stoves which are flat as in Livonia. In this country it is that master and mistress, men and maids, are shuffled all together into the same room; nay in some places in the country, I have seen the poultry and the pigs had ordinarily the same lodging with the master of the house. . . .

No Moscovite, what condition or quality soever he be of, but sleeps after dinner; whence it is that about noon most shops are shut up, and the merchants or their apprentices sleeping at the door: so that about that time there is no more speaking with persons of quality or merchants, than there is at midnight.

This was one sign whereby they discovered the imposture of the pretender Dmitri. We shall find in the ensuing story of him, that the imposter slept not after dinner, and that the Moscovites inferred thence that he was a foreigner; as also by his aversion to baths, which are so common in Moscovy, that there is neither town nor village, but has very many of them, both public and private. This is all they have gentle among them, as a thing they conceive necessary upon several occasions, especially at marriages, after the first coition.

At Astrakhan I had the curiosity to go unknown into one of them, which by a division of boards was contrived into two rooms. But besides that it was easier to look out of one into the other, by reason of the distance there was between the boards, both men and women went out at the same door, those of either sex who would express a greater modesty hiding what they would not have seen with a handful of leaves, which being dried in summer, they for this purpose put a-soaking into warm water; but some were stark naked, and the women were not shy to come in that posture and speak with their husbands, even while other men stood by.

'Tis almost a miracle to see how their bodies, accustomed to, and hardened by cold, can endure so intense a heat, and how that, when they are not able to endure it any longer, they come out of the stoves, naked as the back of a man's hand, both men and women, and go into the cold water, or cause it to be poured upon them, and in winter, how they wallow in the snow. Some of our young men would often walk before these public stoves, to see the several·postures of the women that came out, and diverted themselves in the water, and were so far from being ashamed, that they would talk wantonly with them, and were not troubled when any of our people came into the water to them. And this we saw not only in Moscovy, but also in Livonia, where the inhabitants, especially the Finns, who are settled there, going out of these stoves, in the coldest of the winter, run into the snow, and rub their bodies with it, as if it were soap, then return into the stoves to take advantage of a more moderate heat: and all this so as that this change of contrary qualities does not in any way prejudice their health. The reason then of it must be custom, in as much as being thus used from their childhood, and that habit being as it were converted into a second nature, they are indifferently enured to both heat and cold. . . .

The Moscovites are of a healthy and strong constitution, long lived and seldom sick; which when they are, their ordinary remedies, even in burning fevers, are only garlic and strong waters. Persons of quality make use of physicians, though but within these few years, and are persuaded that remedies may do them good.

Fornication is very common among them, and yet they permit not public stews, which diverse other Christian princes not only permit, but authorize, and have an advantage arising out of them for their protection. Marriage is thought honorable among them, and polygamy forbidden. A widower or widow may marry twice or thrice, but must not offer at a fourth marriage, which if they should, the priest that should bless them would be cast off.

They observe in their marriages the degrees of consanguinity, and do not willingly marry such as are near to them either by kindred or alliance. Nor do they permit two brothers to marry two sisters; and they observe also a spiritual alliance, not suffering that godfathers and godmothers of the same person should intermarry. The celebration of marriage among them is thus.

Young men and maids are not suffered to see one another, much less to have any discourse of marriage, or to make any promise one to another, by word or writing. But when those who have children marriageable, especially daughters, have found out a match they like, they speak to the young man's parents, and declare the desire they have to make an alliance with them. If they approve of what is proposed, and the young man desire to see the maid, yet is it absolutely denied. If she be handsome, they will be content the mother or some other woman of the kindred, should see her, and if she be no way defective, that is, neither blind nor lame, the friends on both sides treat about the marriage, and conclude all things, the intended young couple not so much as being allowed to see one another. For they bring up their daughters in very private chambers (especially persons of quality) where they keep them locked up, so as that the bridegroom does not see his bride till she is brought into his chamber. And thus it comes to pass, that he who thinks he has married a handsome maid, has some crooked piece put upon him; nay, instead of the man's daughter he was to have, some kinswoman or servant maid is thrust upon him; of which I have several examples. So that it is not to be wondered at, that matrimonial discontents are so frequent among them. . . .

As soon as the wedding is over, the women must resolve to live a retired life, and not to go out of the house but very seldom, receiving the visits of their kindred and friends oftener than they give any. The daughters of great persons, and rich merchants, as they are not much brought up to house keeping, so they trouble themselves but little with it, when they are married. Their chief employment is sewing, or embroidering handkerchiefs of white taffeta or cloth, or making little purses or some such toys. The clothes they wear within doors are made of some common stuff of little value; but when they go to the church, or that their husbands would honor a friend with their presence, they are magnificently clad, and forget not to paint their faces, necks and arms. . . .

It is not to be much wondered that they are so hardly treated by their husbands, for they have lewd tongues, are given to wine and will not let slip the opportunity to pleasure a friend. So that having all these three excellent qualities, they cannot take much unkindly the cudgellings, which they from time to time receive from their husbands: but they take comfort from the example of their friends and neighbors, who, behaving themselves after the same manner, are accordingly no better treated. Yet I cannot believe what Barclay says in his *Icon Ammorum*, that the Moscovite women are not persuaded their husbands love them, if they are not beaten by them; at least I can say this, I never met with any who were glad when they were beaten. They have the same passions and inclinations as other women have. They are sensible of good and bad usage, and it is not likely they should take the effects of anger and displeasure for expressions of kindness and friendship.

It is possible some foolish woman might tell her husband so in jest, or that one distracted might desire to be beaten, such as she of whom Petrejus in his *Chronicle of Moscovy* speaks of, who having lived many years in good correspondence with her husband (who was an Italian, as he says, though the Baron of Herberstein affirms he was a German, and by profession a black smith, named Jordan) told him one day that she could not believe he loved her, since he had not yet beaten her. The husband willing to assure her of his real affection gave her a good cudgelling, and perceiving that she took a certain pleasure in it, made use of that exercise so often, till at last she died. But were it granted that this is but a story, as it seems to be no other, yet ought we not to judge of all the Moscovite women by this particular example.

They think that adultery is not committed but when one man marries another man's wife: what ever else may be done amounts but to fornication, and when a married man is taken in it, his punishment is whipping, and some days imprisonment, or happily he is sentenced to live some time on bread and water. Then he is set at liberty, and may resent the complaints made by his wife against him upon that occasion. A husband who can convince his wife of a miscarriage of this nature, may have her shaved and put her into a monastery. Those who are weary of their wives often make use of this pretense, accuse their wives of adultery, and suborn false witnesses, upon whose depositions they are condemned without being heard. Religious women are sent to her lodgings, who put her into their habit, shave her and carry her away by force into the monastery, whence she never comes out, having once suffered the razor to come upon her head.

The most ordinary cause of divorce, at least the most plausible pretense, is devotion. They say they love God better than their wives, when the humor takes them to go into a monastery: which they do without their consent, or making any provision for the children they have had between them. And yet this kind of retiring out of this world is so much approved among them (though St. Paul says that such are worse than heathens and infidels) that if the woman marries again they make no difficulty to confer priesthood on this new proselyte, though before he had been but a tailor, or shoemaker. Barrenness is also another cause of divorce in Moscovy: for he who has no children by his wife may put her into a monastery, and marry again within six weeks. . . .

The Moscovites are extremely venereous, yet will not have to do with a woman, but they must first take off the little cross which is hanged about her neck when she is christened; nor would they do it in a place where there are any images of their saints, till they have covered them. They go not to church the day they have dealt with a woman till they have washed themselves and changed their shirts. Those that are more devout go not into it at all, but say their prayers at the door. Priests are permitted to come into the church the same day, provided they have washed themselves above and below the navel, but dare not approach the altar. The women are considered more impure than the men, and therefore they ordinarily stay at the church door all service time. He who lies with his wife in Lent may not communicate that year; and if a priest commits that offense he is suspended for a year; but if one that pretends to priesthood be so unhappy as to fall into it, he can never recover himself, but must quit his pretension.

Their remedy against this kind of uncleanness is rather bathing than repentance, which is the reason they use the former upon all occasions. Dmitri, who impersonated the son of the Great Duke Ivan Vasilevich, who had been killed long before at Uglich, never bathed himself, upon which the Moscovites suspected him to be a foreigner. For perceiving he would not make use of a bath made ready for him eight days after his marriage, they conceived a horror against him, as a heathen and profane person, sought diverse other pretenses, set upon him in the castle, and killed him the 19th day after his wedding. . . .

The politic government of Moscovy is monarchial and despotical. The Great Duke is the hereditary sovereign of it, and so absolute that no prince or lord in all his dominions but thinks it an honor to assume the quality of his majesty's *kholop*, or slave. No master has more power over his slaves than the Great Duke has over his subjects, what condition or quality soever they be of. So that Moscovy may be numbered among those states whereof Aristotle speaks when he says there is a kind of monarchy among the barbarians which comes near tyranny. For since there is no other difference between a legitimate government and tyranny than that in the one the welfare of the subjects is of greatest consideration, in the other the particular profit and advantages of the prince, we must allow that Moscovy inclines much to tyranny. We said before that the greatest lords think it is not below them to put their names in the diminutive; nor is it long since that for a small matter they were whipped like slaves, but now their lesser miscarriages are punished with two or three days imprisonment. . . .

No people in the world have a greater veneration for their prince than the Moscovites, who from their infancy are taught to speak of the Tsar as of God Himself, not only in their acts and public assemblies, but also in their entertainments and ordinary discourse. Thence proceed their submissive forms of speaking: The honor to see the brightness of the eyes of his Tsarist Majesty; only God and the Tsar know it; all they have belongs to God and the Tsar. The Great Duke Ivan Vasilevich [Ivan IV] reduced them to these submissions. . . .

When we said the state of Moscovy was monarchial we presupposed that the prince is a monarch and has alone all the prerogatives of sovereignty. He is not subject to the laws; he only makes them and all the Moscovites obey him with so great submission, that they are so far from opposing his will that they say: the justice and word of their prince is sacred and inviolable.

He only creates magistrates and deposes them, ejects them, and orders them to be punished with such absolute power that we may say of the Great Duke what the Prophet Daniel says of the king of Babylon, that he put to death whom he would and saved whom he would. He appoints governors and lieutenants for the provinces for the disposal of the ancient demesne and administration of justice, who have with them a *diak*, or secretary, and these take cognizance of all matters, give final and absolute judgment in all cases and cause their sentences to be put in execution without any appeal. . . .

He alone has the power to make war and peace with other princes. For though he takes the advice of his princes and *boyars*, yet he does not always follow it, but makes them know that notwithstanding the freedom he gives them to advise him, he reserves to himself the power of doing what he thinks fit.

He only confers honors and rewards the services that are done him with the qualities of princes, *boyars*, dukes; and whereas the Moscovites have heard that it is a mark of sovereignty in Germany to make doctors, the Great Duke meddles with that also and grants letters patents to physicians and surgeons who are foreigners. . . .

He only levies taxes and impositions and regulates them according to his pleasure, so as that he takes five in the hundred upon all merchandise upon the frontiers of his dominions, both coming and going out.

It is his prerogative to send ambassadors to the Emperor, the kings of Poland, Denmark, Sweden and other princes, his neighbors. These ministers are either *Velikii posol*, Great Ambassador, or *poslannik*, or Envoy. Heretofore, especially in the time of Ivan Vasilevich, they treated foreigners, even the public ministers of princes, with much disrespect; but now it is otherwise. Ambassadors are entertained with great civility; and their charges defrayed from the day of their entrance into the Great Duke's dominions, to that of their departure thence; they are treated at great feasts and have very rich presents bestowed upon them. Whence it comes that other European princes make no difficulty to send their ambassadors thither, nay some have their ordinary residents there, as the kings of England and Sweden. All the presents made by the Great Duke consist in furs, and he never sends any solemn embassy but it carries such as are very considerable for the prince to whom it is sent. . . .

Heretofore the Moscovites had but few laws and few customs according to which all cases were decided. They concerned only attempts against the Great Duke's person; treason against the state; adulteries; thefts; and debts between private persons. The decision of all other affairs depended on the breast of the judge. But in the year 1647, the Great Duke assembled together the most famous men of the kingdom, and caused to be set down in writing, and to be published, several laws and ordinances, whereby the judges are to regulate themselves. They were printed in folio under the title of *Sobornoe Ulozhenie*, that is to say, universal and general right for the direction of the *boyars*.

Heretofore their proceedings were thus. In those cases where the parties were not agreed as to the matter of fact, and had no evidence of either side, the judge asked the defendant whether he would take his oath, that the matter was as he alleged, or refer it to the plaintiff's oath. He who proffered to take his oath was once a week for three weeks one after another brought before the judge, who every time pressed into him the importance of an oath and the sin he would burden his conscience withal, if he swore falsely. If, notwithstanding these remonstrances, he still persisted in his readiness to take his oath, though he swore nothing but the truth, yet people looked on him as an infamous person, would spit in his face and turn him out of the church, into which he was never received afterwards, much less was he admitted to the communion, unless it were at the point of death. Now they do not proceed with so much rigor, but only bring him, who is to take his oath, before an image of one of his saints, where he is asked whether he will take his oath upon the salvation of his soul. If he persists, they give him a little Crucifix to kiss, and afterwards the saint's image, which for that purpose is taken down from the wall. If the oath be good, the party who took it is not to be admitted to the communion for three years, and though he be not treated as an infamous person, yet those of any quality will not easily suffer him in their company; but a perjured person is severely punished, first cruelly whipped, then banished. Whence it comes that the Moscovites endeavor all they can to avoid it, though upon any trivial occasion, especially in their dealings, they stick not to swear at every word, and have incessantly in their mouths their *po Khristu*, by Christ, making the sign of the cross at the same time; but there is little credit to be given to these kinds of oaths, as proceeding from deceit and passion. They permit foreigners to take their oaths according to the rules of their several religions.

No invention but they make use of to force people to confess the truth by torture. One of the most cruel, in my opinion, is the *strapado*, which is given in this manner. The malefactor, having his hands tied behind him, is wound up into the air and so hangs, having fastened to his feet a great beam upon which the executioner ever and again gets up to augment the pain and further the dislocation of the members, while the smoke and fire which are made under his feet, burns and stifles him. Sometimes they cause the malefactor's head to be shaven, and as he is so hanging they pour cold water, drop by drop, upon the crown, which is such a torment as no other comes near, not even that of whipping (which they many times give those in that condition), though they at the same time clap a red hot iron upon the stripes.

In ordinary quarrels, he who gives the first blow gets the worst. Murder committed without any necessity of defense is punished with death. The guilty person is kept six weeks in a very close prison, and fed only with bread and water, after which he receives the communion and has his head cut off.

Thieves are tortured that they may discover their accomplices, and confess their other crimes. If it be the first offense, they are whipped from the castle gate to the great market place, where the offender has an ear cut off, and is put into prison for two years. If he offends the second time, he is punished in the same manner, and is kept in prison till he has company, to be banished to Siberia. Theft is never punished with death in Moscovy; but the concealers and receivers fare no better, which is the best course that could be taken to bridle the lewd inclinations of that people.

The ordinary punishments are slitting the nostrils, whipping, and the *batovki*. The last is not always infamous and public; yet is there not any master of a family, but gives it his children and servants. He who is to receive this chastisement puts off his *kaftan*, and having only his shirt on, lays himself down upon the ground on his belly, and then two men set themselves cross upon him, one upon his neck, the other upon his feet, having each of them a little wand or switch in his hand, wherewith they beat him upon the back, much after the manner that feltmongers beat their furs to get out the worms. They ordinarily have their nostrils slit who have taken tobacco, in snuff, contrary to the Great Duke's prohibition.

Whipping, as it is given in Moscovy, is one of the most barbarous punishments that ever were heard of. September 24, 1634, I saw eight men and one woman whipped for selling of *aqua vitae* and tobacco. The executioner's man took them up one after another upon his back, being stripped down to the waist, and having their feet tied together with a cord, which passing between his legs that held them up, was held by another servant of the executioner's, so fast that they were not able to stir. The executioner stood three paces off with a bull's pizzle, having fastened to the end of it three straps or thongs of an elk's skin, not tanned, and consequently as sharp as a razor, with which he laid on their backs with all his strength, so that the blood gushed out at every lash. The men had each of them twenty-five or twenty-six till the clerk, who had in a note what number of lashes they were to receive, cried *dovolno*, that is to say, enough. The woman had but sixteen yet did she fall into a swoon. Being thus disciplined, so as that their backs were in a manner sliced and slashed all over, yet were they all tied by the arms, two and two together, those who had sold tobacco having a little horn full of it, and those who had sold *aqua vitae*, a little bottle about their necks, and whipped through the city, and after they had walked them about half a league about, they were brought back to the place of their first execution and dismissed. This is so cruel a punishment that some die of it. . . . Some after they are thus punished wrap themselves up in the skin of a sheep newly killed.

Heretofore these punishments were not infamous, and those who had passed through the executioner's hands were admitted into the best companies, as was also the executioner himself, whose profession was considered so honorable that sometimes even merchants quit theirs, to serve the magistrate at executions, and would buy the employment, and after certain years sell it again to others. The advantage of it is in this, that the executioner is not only paid by the judge, but gets money also out of the criminal to be more gently treated, though indeed the greatest profit he makes comes from the *aqua vitae*, which he sells underhand to the prisoners. But now this employment is not much courted since the Moscovites have begun to learn somewhat of civility from their neighbors. Nor is the executioner permitted to sell his office, but it must continue in his family, which failing, the butchers are obliged to recommend to the place one of their body.

All we said of the cruelty of their punishments is yet below what they inflict on such as cannot pay their debts. He who pays not at his time, mentioned in the bond, is put into a sergeant's house, having a certain further time to make satisfaction. If he fail, he is carried to prison, whence he is every day brought out to the place before the Chancery, where the common executioner beats him upon the shin-bone with a wand about the bigness of a man's little finger for a whole hour. That done, he is returned to prison, unless he can put in security to be forthcoming the next day at the same hour, to be treated in the same manner, till he has made satisfaction. And this is executed with such rigor upon all sorts of persons, what condition or quality soever they be of, subjects or foreigners, men or women, priests or lay persons. . . .

As to the religion of the Moscovites, before we enter into the discourse of it, we shall say that there have been Lutheran doctors in Sweden and Livonia, who have made it a problematical question whether the Moscovites were Christians or not. They might as well have made it disputable in their acts whether the Moscovites are men; since there is not so great a difference between their religion and that of other Christians as there is between their morality and manner of life and that of many other men; but as laughter and speech makes them men, so baptism and their external profession of the Christian religion denominates them Christians. If a man would take their word for it, they are the only true Christians in the world, since they only have been baptized, whereas others have been only sprinkled. . . .

'Tis true, their religion is full of abundance of chaffy superstitions; in that they consider the Virgin Mary, the Evangelists, the Apostles and an infinite number of other saints, not only as simple intercessors, as the most intelligent affirm, but also as causes and co-operators of their salvation. There is no Moscovite but gives his saints and their images the honor due only to God, who is so jealous thereof, that He treats the false worship as spiritual whoredom. The ignorance of the meaner sort of people is so gross that they place all religion in the honors and veneration they give their images. It is also all the instructions they give their children, who in order to devotion, learn only to stand with great respect before those images to say their prayers. Their good works (which they believe meritorious) are building of monasteries and churches, and giving alms; besides which they do nothing whereby a man might judge of their faith by their works. . . .

The Moscovites in their schools learn only to read and write in their own language, and care not for the learning of any other; but within these few years they have, with the Patriarch's consent, opened a school where Greek and Latin are taught under the direction of a native Greek, named Arsenius. It is not yet known what may be expected from it, but certain it is that there are among the Moscovites those that want neither ingenuity nor an inclination to study, and would learn anything did they but meet with any body to teach them. . . .

Those who are to profess the Moscovite religion are obliged to go for six weeks into a monastery, where the monks instruct them and teach them their prayers, the manner of honoring the saints, of doing reverence to their images, the making the sign of the cross. Then they are brought to the place where they are to be baptized, where they are obliged to abjure their former religion, to detest it as heretical and to spit as often as it is named. After their baptism they are clad in Moscovite habits, being presented with a noble vestment from the Great Duke, who also allows them a pension suitable to their quality.

There is a great number of apostates in Moscow, where many foreign soldiers, especially French, were rebaptized after the War of Smolensk, about twenty-five years since, though they were not acquainted with the language of the country, nor had any knowledge of the Moscovite religion. Which may in some measure be excusable in common soldiers who mind not what they are to expect in the other world; but my wonder is, how persons of quality, such as want neither ingenuity nor judgment, should be inclined to apostatize and embrace a contrary religion, merely for subsistence sake. . . .

Those Moscovites who change their religion in other countries, and would return to their communion, must be first rebaptized; which is the more observable in that the Greek religion, though she approves not the baptism of the Latin church, yet seems to be satisfied with the former which they might have received in their church so as not to oblige converts to rebaptization upon their change of religion. . . .

[They] have images painted with oil upon wood, wretchedly colored and ill-proportioned, about a foot in breadth, somewhat more in length. They will not meddle with them if they are not made by one of their religion, though they came from the best painter's hand in Europe. At Moscow there is a particular market place for images where nothing else is sold, though they call that kind of commerce bartering or trucking with money, out of a belief they have that the names of buying and selling carry not enough respect in them for sacred things. Heretofore they obliged foreigners to have of them in their houses that their Moscovite servants might be thereby excited to the exercise of their devotion; but the present Patriarch permits not, they should be profaned by the Germans; insomuch that Charles du Moulin, having bought a stone house, the seller scraped the wall where an image had been painted and carried away what he had scraped off. The peasants would not permit us to touch them, not to turn our feet toward them when we lay down. Nay, some were at the charge of incense to purify them after we had left their houses.

The walls of their churches are full of them, and they represent for the most part our Saviour, the Virgin Mary, St. Nicholas, Patron of Moscow, or the particular saints they make choice of for the principal object of their devotions. Those who commit sins deserving excommunication are obliged to cause their saint to be taken away, who is not to be suffered in their churches no more than their persons. Great persons and rich merchants adorn their images with pearls and other precious stones. All Moscovites look upon them as things so necessary as that without images they could not say their prayers, which whenever they do they always set wax candles before their saint and look very steadfastly upon him as long as the devotion lasts. . . .

The Moscovites respect their images as if there were somewhat of divinity in them, and they attribute unto them the virtue of miracles, whereof we had this example in the year 1643, that an old image began to change color and to turn a little reddish, they immediately cried out a miracle. The Great Duke and the Patriarch were frightened thereat, as if that red color presaged some misfortune to either the Prince or the people; nay they sent out orders for extraordinary fasts and public prayers to be made all over the kingdom, if the painters who were sent for to have their advice in this affair had not all assured them that there was nothing they should be troubled at, since there was nothing extraordinary, but that time, having consumed and eaten out the paint, had only discovered the first color of the wood, which was red.

Their monks and priests have nevertheless the art to make them do miracles, or to observe such things in them as oblige the people to extraordinary devotions, which must not want their offerings, that the priest may not want his advantage. The city of Archangel furnishes us with a good example to this purpose, of two priests there, who, having got together a vast sum of money by their impostures, must needs fall out at the parting of it, and upbraid one another of their cheats so loudly that the magistrate coming to hear of it, they had thirty lashes apiece with the executioner's good will, after the manner we have before described their whipping. These jugglers put the people into continuous frights, and besought them with so strange a veneration for their images that in their greatest dangers their recourse is only to them. . . .

As to their churches, we said, there were about 2000 churches and chapels in the city and suburbs of Moscow. Those which are of stone are round and vaulted, because God's houses ought to represent heaven, which is his throne. They have neither seats nor benches, by reason none sit down, but all say their prayers either standing or kneeling. The late Great Duke, who was much given to devotion, lay all along upon the ground when he said his prayers. They have no organs or other musical instruments in their churches, not using any out of this persuasion, that things inanimate cannot glorify God; that they were allowed in the pedagogy of the Law, but that under the New Testament, they were no more to be used than any other of the Jewish ceremonies. The Patriarch that now is has shown his enmity to music, yet greater, in prohibiting the use of all those musical instruments which the Moscovites were wont to make use of at their merry meetings. Some four or five years ago, he caused all private houses to be searched for instruments, and having loaded five wagons with them, he sent them over the River of Moscow, where they were all burnt. Only the Germans kept theirs, nor could the Patriarch, with all his authority, oblige the boyar Boris Nikita Ivanovich Romanov to put away his musicians. . . They hold they [churches] are profaned by foreigners, such as are not of their communion; upon which account it was that, when at the beginning of our travels, we entered into them, they came out and thrust us out, and many times they swept after us. If it chance a dog gets in, they think it not enough to sweep the church, but they also incense it, and purify it with holy water. They also have much respect for their church yards, and suffer not that any should make their water in them. . . .

The ecclesiastical government consists of a Patriarch, several Metropolitans, Archbishops, Bishops, Arch-deacons, Protopops, and Priests. The Patriarch among them has the same authority as the Pope has in the Latin Church. The Patriarch at Constantinople had heretofore the nomination of him. In time he came to have only the confirmation of him; but now of late he has lost both. Filàret Nikitich, the late Great Duke's father was the last that desired confirmation from the Patriarch of Constantinople. At present the Patriarch of Moscovy is chosen by the other prelates who meet in the great church within the castle, called *sobor*, and name two or three prelates of the most eminent for learning and good life and present them to the Great Duke, who, after some conference with the prelates, proceeds jointly with them to the election; unless those that are named be all of such eminency that they are at a loss which to make choice of, and so forced to it by lot, which course they took at the election of this last Patriarch. He was a prelate of the second order, and had been named with two other Metropolitans, upon the reputation of his good life. The lot falling upon him, all those of the first order were discontented thereat, so that they put it to the lot a second time, in which also it fell again to him: but the ambition of the other competitors appearing still in their countenances, the Great Duke was pleased to comply with them and to put it to the lot a third time, which fell in like manner to the same person, upon which all acquiesced. His name is Nikon, and he had been before Metropolitan of Rostov and Iaroslav, and is now about forty-five years of age. He lives within the palace, where he has built him a house of stone. He keeps a good table, and is a person of so pleasant a disposition that he discovers it in those actions that require the greatest gravity. For a handsome gentlewoman being presented to him for his benediction after she had been rebaptized with several others of her friends, he told her that he was in some doubt whether he should begin with the kiss, which is given to proselytes after their baptism, or with the benediction.

The Patriarch's authority is so great that he in manner divides the sovereignty with the Great Duke. He is the supreme judge of all the ecclesiastical cases, and absolutely disposes of whatever concerns religion, with such power that in things relating to the political government, he reforms what he conceives prejudicial to Christian simplicity and good manners without giving the Great Duke any account of it, who, without any contestation commands the orders made by the Patriarch to be executed. . . .

They have a great number of monasteries, both for men and women, as well in cities as up and down the country, and they all in a manner follow the rule of Great St. Basil. Indigence, age, infirmities, domestic discontents, and violence fill their convents, rather than devotion. When any embrace that kind of life of their own accord, if they are of ability, they are permitted to carry some part of their estates along with them into the monastery, but are obliged to leave the remainder to their heirs. Heretofore, the more superstitious sort made over all they had, and the extravagance had so far prevailed on many, that in time, the monks would have been masters of the best part of Moscovy, if a course had not been taken to prevent it. They have set hours for their service, and they say most of their prayers by beads. Their austerity of life is very great in as much as they live only on salted fish, honey, milk, cheese, herbs, and pulse, especially cucumbers, fresh and pickled, which they mince very small and eat with a spoon in some of their kvas. They have this common with all the other Moscovites, that they can hardly write and read. Not one in ten can say the Lord's Prayer, much fewer that are acquainted with the Creed and the Ten Commandments. These monks live not so re-tired a life, but that they are seen in great numbers, both in cities and all over the country, where their employment is the same with that of the peasants from whom they are distinguished only by their habit. It is also true there are abundance of anchorets, who build chapels upon the highways, and live in woods like hermits, subsisting only by the alms given them by travellers. . . .

Their interments are accompanied by abundance of ceremonies, as

indeed are all their public actions. As soon as the sick person is departed, they send for all his kindred and friends, who being come into
the house stand about the body, excite one another to bemoan him, as
it were to heighten the lamentations of the women, and ask the deceased why he would die. Whether his affairs were in good condition?
Whether he wanted meat and drink? Whether his wife were not handsome and young enough? Whether she had been unconstant to him?
etc. Then they send a present of beer, *aqua vitae* and hydromel to the
priest, that he may pray for the soul of the deceased party. The body is
well washed, and after they have put a clean shirt or a shroud about him,
they put on his feet a pair of new shoes of a very thin Russian leather,
and so they lay him into the coffin with his arms across the breast. Their
coffins are made of the trunk of a tree and are to be sold everywhere. It
is covered with a cloth, or haply with some coat of the deceased, and
carried to the church. If it be a rich man, and that the season of the year
permit it, he is not buried so soon, but kept above ground eight or
ten days during which the priest comes to incense the corpse and cast
holy water on it every day.

The funeral solemnity is after this manner. First there goes a priest,
carrying the image of the saint which had been assigned the deceased at
his baptism for his patron. Next go four virgins of the next of kin to the
deceased, who are to go as mourners, and who fill the air with their
horrid cries and lamentations, keeping such exact time, that they both
give over and then begin all together. Then follows the body carried by
six men upon their shoulders; and if it be a monk or a nun, some of their
own profession do them that office. The priests go all about the body,
and incense it all the way to keep off evil spirits, and withal sing certain
psalms. The kindred and friends follow the body, but without any order,
having every one a wax candle in his hand.

Being come to the grave, the coffin is uncovered, and the image of the
deceased party's saint is held over him, while the priest says certain
prayers, in which there come often these words: Lord look upon this soul
in righteousness, as also some passages of their liturgy, during which the
widow continues her lamentations, and makes the same questions she
had done before. Then the kindred and friends take leave of the deceased, kissing either him or the coffin, and at last the priest comes up
to him, and puts between his fingers a piece of paper, which is a kind
of testimonial of his behavior in this world, signed by the Patriarch, or
the Metropolitan of the place, and the confessor, who sell those papers
dear or cheap, according to their abilities who buy them. This testimonial,
which is a kind of pass for his admittance into the other world, runs
thus: We whose names are hereunto subscribed, the Patriarch, or Metropolitan, and Priest of the city of _____, do make known and certify,
by these presents, that the bearer of these our letters has always lived
among us like a good Christian, professing the Greek religion; and

though he has committed some sins, yet that he has confessed the same, and that thereupon he has received absolution, and taken the communion, for the remission of his sins: That he has honored God and his saints; that he has said his prayers, and that he has fasted on the hours and days appointed by the church, and that he has carried himself so well toward me, who am his confessor, that I have no reason to complain of him, nor to deny him the absolution of his sins. In witness whereof, we have given him the present testimonial to the end that upon sight thereof, St. Peter may open unto him the gate of eternal bliss. As soon as he has this passport given him, the coffin is shut up and put into the grave, with the face of the deceased turned toward the East. Those who accompanied him thither do their devotion to the images, and return to the house of the deceased, where they find dinner ready, and where many times they drown their affliction with all other sentiments of mortality in hydromel and aqua vitae. Their mourning lasts forty days, during which they make three feasts for the kindred and friends of the deceased, to wit, the 3d, the 9th, and the 20th day after the burial. . . .

Some build huts over their graves which they cover with mats for the convenience of the priest, who, morning and evening for the space of six weeks, is to make prayers there for the deceased. For though the Moscovites do not believe there is any purgatory, yet they say there are two several places to which the souls retire after their departure out of the body, where they expect the day of judgment; some in a pleasant and delightful place, having conversation with angels; others in a sad and dark valley, having the society of devils. That the souls being yet in their way, may be diverted out of the evil way by the prayers of priests and monks, nay, that these have so great an interest with God as to obtain a certain ease and alleviation of their misery, for those souls which are with the devils, and to appease him against the day of judgment. Such as are of ability give alms daily during the six weeks; which may indeed be ordinary among the Moscovites who made no difficulty to enrich themselves any way, and believe that sin is to be expiated by alms. Whence it comes that no Moscovite almost, but, as he goes to church, or about his occasions, buys bread, which he afterwards distributes among the poor, who, though very numerous, yet get so much, that being not able to consume all themselves, they dry up the rest in an oven and make it a kind of biscuit, which they call sukhar and sell it in the market to travelers.

The Moscovites tolerate all sorts of religions and suffer all nations to live among them, as Calvinists, Lutherans, Armenians, Tartars, Turks, and Persians, excepting none, but Jews and Roman Catholics. There is a great number of Protestants all over Moscovy, and in the city of Moscow itself there are about a thousand who have the free exercise of their religion. Those of the Reformed religion and the Lutherans had their churches heretofore in the quarter of Tsargorod; but it is about twenty

years since that the Lutherans lost theirs by the imprudence of their
wives; because those of merchants would not give place to the officers'
wives, who indeed for the most part were but servant-maids, dressed up
a little finer than they had gone before. The contest grew so high that
they came from words to blows in the very church, with so much scandal
that the Patriarch, then accidentally passing by, having understood the
occasion of their falling out, commanded the church to be demolished,
which was immediately done. But they were permitted to build another
in the quarter *Bolshoi gorod*. They took away their church from those of
the Reformed religion because, not content with the wooden chapel
which had been given them within the white wall, they would needs
build there an edifice of stone, which was in a manner finished, when the
Patriarch, who had not given his consent for the doing of it, caused both
to be pulled down. Now foreigners have neither church nor houses
within the city. For the Germans, finding themselves exposed to the
decisions of the Moscovites, after the Patriarch had ordered them to go
in a habit distinct from that of the inhabitants of the country, to free
themselves out of that persecution, petitioned the Tsar to protect them
against the outrages and affronts they daily received. On the other side
the priests complained that foreigners built on their foundations, and
lessened the revenue of the livings; so that the Great Duke, to please
both sides, assigned them without the city, near the gate called *Pokrovi*,
a place big enough to contain all the houses of foreigners who immediately demolished those they had in the city, and in a short time made
up that part of the suburbs, which is called *Novaia innozemskaia sloboda*
[New Foreign Quarter], where the Lutherans have two churches, and
those of the Reformation two more, one for the Dutch and the other
for the English; and where they have this further satisfaction that they
converse but little with the Moscovites, and are out of all danger of those
frequent fires which commonly begin in the houses of those barbarous
Christians.

The Lutherans, and those of the Reformed religion live very quietly
together, and the Moscovites trade indifferently with either; but they
have so great an aversion for the Roman Catholics that they would never
grant them a toleration of their religion in Moscovy. In the year 1627,
the late king of France proposed, by Louis des Hayes, a treaty for the
regulation of commerce with the French, and at the same time for a
church where they might have Mass said, but it was denied. And in the
first war of Smolensk, they would not entertain Catholic soldiers. Nay
in the treaty they made with us for our passage into Persia, it is an
express article that we should not take any Roman Catholics into our
retinue. So that it is much to be admired that they should call to the
crown Wladislaw, Prince of Poland and Sweden; though that election
came to nothing, for reasons into which it is beside the subject of our

relation to inquire, as it is also into those which may be given of the animosity of the Moscovites against the Roman Catholics, whereof the grounds are to be searched for in ecclesiastical history, which has nothing common with the relation of our travels. . . .

37

The Code of Law of 1649

One of the most important documents of seventeenth century Russia is the *Ulozhenie*, or *Code of Law*, of 1649. Prepared by a landed assembly (*zemskii sobor*), the *Ulozhenie* represents the first serious Russian attempt at codification. It consists of 968 articles grouped into twenty-five chapters of unequal length. The complete Table of Contents and Chapters I, II, IV, V, and VI are included here.

The *Ulozhenie*, among other things, legalized the complete enserfment of the peasantry, granted the nobles broad privileges, furthered the consolidation of absolutism, and prohibited the further expansion of church and monastery estates. The *Ulozhenie*, in other words, provided the direction for Russia's development, and many of its basic provisions remained in force until 1833. This fact, however, should not be interpreted as a testimonial to the *Ulozhenie's* merits, but rather, in the words of historian V. O. Kliuchevskii, as an indication that "Russia could do without a decent collection of laws."

From M. N. Tikhomirov and P. P. Epifanov, eds., *Sobornoe Ulozhenie 1649 g.* (*The Code of Law of the 1649 Assembly*) (Moscow, Izdatelstvo Moskovskogo Universiteta, 1961), pp 70–75, 78–81. Translation mine. Items in brackets are mine.

CHAPTER

Chapter I

Blasphemers and Heretics

1. If a member of another faith, regardless of which faith, or a Russian, should blaspheme our Lord and Saviour Jesus Christ, or His mother the Holy Queen, Mary, the Virgin Mother of God, or the honorable cross, or its holy servants, each such case should be investigated thoroughly, using all possible means. An inquiry about it should be organized, and the blasphemer of God should be burned at the stake.

2. And should some scoundrel come into God's church during the

holy liturgy and should he in some way try to prevent its completion, he should be seized, his action investigated, and he should be condemned to death without mercy.

3. And should someone, upon entering God's church during the holy liturgy or during church singing, start directing insults against Patriarch, or Metropolitan, or Archbishop, or Bishop, or Archimandrite, or Igumen, or the ecclesiastical order [in general], and thereby disrupt holy singing in that church, the Sovereign should be informed of this, an investigation should be inaugurated, and for his action the scoundrel should be whipped at the market place.

4. And should anyone, upon entering God's church, start a fight with another person and kill that person, the murderer should be sentenced to death.

5. And should he only wound and not kill, he [the guilty one] should be mercilessly whipped at the market place, put in prison for a month, and made to compensate the injured person twice for the insult.

6. And if a scoundrel should strike anyone in God's church but inflict no wound, he should be whipped with a cane for this insult and [be] made to compensate the injured person.

7. If someone should insult another person verbally but should not harm him [bodily], the guilty person should be put into prison for a month. And whoever was insulted should be compensated in order to prevent the occurrence of any outrages in God's churches in the future.

8. In church during the singing, no one can present a personal petition to the Sovereign Tsar and Grand Prince Aleksei Mikhailovich of All Russia, nor to the Great Lord, His Eminence Joseph, Patriarch of Moscow and of All Russia, nor to Metropolitans, Archbishops, and Bishops, in order to prevent confusion in the church during the church singing, because God's church was created for prayer [not for business]. All Orthodox Christians should stand and pray in God's churches with fear and should not think of worldly matters.

9. And whoever should forget the fear of God and disregard the Tsar's decree and petition either the Sovereign, or the Patriarch, or other officials about a personal matter in God's church during church singing, such petitioner should be thrown into prison for a term to be determined by the Sovereign.

Chapter II

The Sovereign's Honor, and How To Guard His Health

1. Should anyone think maliciously about the Sovereign's health, and should another person report him concerning this malicious thought, there should be made an inquiry into his malicious thought and in-

tended action against his Tsarist Majesty, and such person, upon investigation, should be executed.

2. Likewise, should a member of his Tsarist Majesty's government wish to seize control of the Moscovite state and become Sovereign, and should he, to attain this evil goal, organize an army or conspire with the enemies of his Tsarist Majesty, issue out charters, or aid them in any way, in order to seize control of the Moscovite state or do some other foolish thing with the aid of those enemies of the Sovereign, and should someone report him, there should be organized a proper inquiry into his treason, and such traitor should be sentenced to death.

3. And should anyone give away a city of his Tsarist Majesty to an enemy through treason, or accept foreigners into cities of his Tsarist Majesty for treasonous purposes, and then investigation be conducted into it, such traitors should be executed.

4. And should anyone consciously and treacherously burn either a city or manors, and then be apprehended during his act or afterwards, and an inquiry be conducted into his evil act, such person should be burned mercilessly.

5. Service estates, hereditary estates, and livestock of all traitors should be transferred to the possession of the Sovereign.

6. Wives and children of traitors, if they were aware of their treasons, should be executed.

7. If a wife knew nothing of the treason of her husband, or children of the treason of their father, and if this be verified by an investigation, such persons should be neither executed nor punished; the Sovereign will determine how much of the service and hereditary estates they should be allowed to retain for their livelihood.

8. If a traitor had children, but they, prior to his treason, were separated from him, did not live with him, and hence knew nothing of his treason, and if they had their own livestock and their own hereditary estates, from such children neither livestock nor hereditary estates should be confiscated.

9. And if someone should commit treason and leave [as survivors] in the Moscovite state either his father, or his mother, or his brothers, or his cousins, or his uncles, or any other member of his family, and if he lived with them and they jointly owned their livestock and their hereditary estates, such traitor should be thoroughly investigated in order to determine whether his father, or his mother, or his relatives knew of his treason. Should an investigation determine that they knew of his treason, they should be executed and their livestock and hereditary and service estates transferred to the Sovereign.

10. If, however, an investigation should determine that they knew nothing of the treason of the traitor, they should not be executed and their livestock and their service and hereditary estates should not be confiscated.

11. If a traitor should return from a foreign country to the Moscovite state, and if the Sovereign should pardon him and forgive his guilty action, and then if he should obtain a new service estate through service, the Sovereign may return his old hereditary estate to him, but he cannot grant him his old service estate.

12. If someone should report that another person has revealed a great state secret, but he does not have witnesses to substantiate his report, does not convince anyone [with his arguments], and no evidence exists to aid in the investigation into the revelation of state secrets, a decree should be issued on this problem, following an inquiry, as the Sovereign should direct.

13. And if someone should reveal the state of the Sovereign's health, or if they should disclose information about people whom they serve, or, if they be peasants, to whom they belong, and if such reports are not convincing, they should not be believed. After they have been severely punished for spreading lies, through merciless whipping with a knout, such individuals should then be returned to those persons to whom they belong. Such informers should not be believed or listened to in the future on anything except matters of great importance.

14. And should anyone, regardless of his status, say that he is a government official, and then should it be determined that he is not, such person should be knouted for impersonating a government official, and afterwards he should be returned to those persons to whom he belongs.

15. And if someone apprehends a traitor on the road, and either kills him or captures him and returns him to the Sovereign, that traitor should [in the latter case] be executed, and the person who apprehended or killed him should be given the livestock of the traitor as the Sovereign should decree.

16. And whoever should report that another person had revealed state secrets or was about to commit treason, and the person who had been reported on is absent at the time, that person must be found and he must confront the accuser face to face. If a thorough investigation should verify the validity of the charges, a decree should be issued as stipulated above.

17. If a person should report that another is about to reveal state secrets or to commit treason, and then fail to prove it, and if an investigation should determine that he fabricated his evidence, such informer should be punished in the same manner that the person who had been reported upon would have been punished if he had been found guilty.

18. Should a person in the Moscovite state, regardless of his social status, learn of the existence of mass discontent, or conspiracy, or any other evil design, [in Moscow] the existence of such plots should be reported either to Aleksei Mikhailovich, the Sovereign Tsar and Grand Prince of All Russia, or to his boyars or his high assistants, or [in the provinces], to local voevodas or other officials of the central government.

19. If someone should know or hear of the existence of mass discontent or a conspiracy or any other evil design against his Tsarist Majesty, but fails to report it either to the Sovereign, or his *boyars*, or his high assistants, or *voevodas*, or other officials of the central government in provincial cities, and then the Sovereign should find out that that person was aware of the existence of such action but failed to report it, and an inquiry be conducted into it, such persons should be sentenced to death without mercy.

20. During an insurrection, mass discontent, or conspiracy, no one should break into, or rob, or inflict bodily harm on his Tsarist Majesty, his *boyars*, his high assistants, members of the *boyarskaia duma* [Council of Notables], his advisers, his *voevodas* in regiments, and other officials in provincial cities.

21. Whoever should initiate mass discontent or a conspiracy against his Tsarist Majesty or his *boyars*, or his high assistants, or members of the *boyarskaia duma* or his advisers, or *voevodas* in regiments, or other officials of the central government in provincial cities, and pillage or inflict bodily harm on them, those persons who initiate it should be condemned to death without mercy.

22. Should *voevodas* of regiments or officials of the central government in provincial cities inform the Sovereign that either service people or people of other classes had approached them in numbers resembling mass discontent or a conspiracy and threatened to kill them, and if those people who had been reported on should petition the Sovereign to investigate those *voevodas* and officials of the central government and deny that they had approached them with any mass discontent or a conspiracy and say that they came only in small numbers to petition them, upon such petition of the Sovereign a thorough investigation should be conducted of those city officials and, in the regiments, of the military personnel. If this investigation in cities and regiments should determine that these people really came to the *voevodas* and to the officials of the central government with genuine petitions and not for robbery purposes [as it had been reported], such people should not be sentenced to death. Those *voevodas* and officials of the central government who erroneously reported to the Tsar should be severely punished as the Tsar should determine. . . .

Chapter IV

Forgers of Documents, Signatures, and Seals

1. If someone should forge a charter of the Sovereign, or the Sovereign's signature on a charter, or if he should alter anything on an official document without the Sovereign's authorization, or the approval of either the *boyars*, or members of the *boyarskaia duma*, or of lesser

officials, and forge the signature of a clerk, or if someone should make for himself a seal similar to the Sovereign's seal, such individual, upon investigation, should be executed for such crimes.

2. If someone should steal the Sovereign's seal from the Sovereign's charters or other official documents and attach these seals to forged documents, or if he should write illegal documents and then attach such seals to them without the Sovereign's permission, such individuals should be executed and their forged documents invalidated.

3. If a person should forge some documents and then die, and after his death these documents should be discovered by members of his family or his officials, and if either members of his family or his officials should petition the Sovereign on the basis of these documents, such petitions should be investigated to determine how they obtained these documents, where they found them, and whether they were aware that these documents were forged. If, in the course of the investigation, these persons should acknowledge their complicity or knowledge that these documents were forged and that they held them for personal gains, such individuals should be sentenced to death.

4. But if the investigation should determine that they held those forged documents without being aware that they were forged, such people should not be sentenced to death; the documents must be invalidated and no one should stand trial.

Chapter V

Mint Masters Who May Counterfeit Money

1. If mint masters should make either copper, or tin, or economical money [i.e., adulterated money], or if they should add copper, tin or lead to silver and thereby cause harm to the Sovereign's treasury, such mint masters should be executed by pouring [molten matter down their throats].

2. And if gold or silver masters accept someone's gold or silver work and start adding either copper, or tin, or lead to the silver or gold, upon discovery of this [alteration] they should be knouted. And those people who were hurt by this action, that is, by [the mint master's] alteration of gold and silver through copper, tin, or lead, should be compensated for the loss suffered.

Chapter VI

Permits to Travel into Other Countries

1. And should someone wish to travel for trade purposes or other private matters from the Moscovite state into a foreign country which is on peaceful terms with the Moscovite state, such person in Moscow

must petition the Tsar, and in [other] cities [petitions are to be addressed to the local] voevodas for a travel permit. Without a travel permit no person should travel. Voevodas in cities must issue travel permits without delays.

2. If a voevoda should delay issuing a travel permit and thereby cause delay and a loss, and then if a petition of grievance be submitted about it [to the Tsar], and then an inquiry be held about it, those voevodas will incur the Tsar's great anger. And if they cause a loss they must pay it double, and this [the fine] should go to the petitioner.

3. And if someone should travel into another country without a travel permit, and having been in another state then return to the Moscovite state, and then be reported by someone that he had travelled without a travel permit for treasonous purposes or for some other foolishness, such reports about illegal travels into foreign countries without the Sovereign's permits should be thoroughly investigated. And if an investigation should establish that a person travelled into another country without a travel permit for treasonous purposes or other evil matter, such person, upon investigation, should be sentenced to death.

4. And should investigation establish that a person travelled into another country without a travel permit for trade purposes and not for treason, he should be penalized by knouting, so that others, seeing it, might learn that they should not do the same [i.e., travel abroad without travel permits].

5. And in those border cities and districts where villages of the Sovereign and villages of state peasants, and hereditary and service estates join Lithuanian or German border lands, and where the Sovereign's lands thrust into the Lithuanian or German side or where Lithuanian or German lands thrust into the Sovereign's side, in such cases free people and peasants living in the Sovereign's villages, or in villages of state peasants, or on hereditary and service estates, are permitted to travel through those Lithuanian or German border lands without permits from one city to another; they are also allowed to meet Lithuanian or German people; it should not be held against them that they live adjacent to those Lithuanians or Germans who live in border areas.

6. Should service or hereditary nobles of border areas hear that some of their own people or their peasants are trying to commit treason or some other foolishness, they should notify the Sovereign, and in cities they should also provide appropriate information to local voevodas and bring such people or peasants before them. The voevodas should thoroughly interrogate and investigate such suspects who had been reported upon, using all possible means, and then should report their findings to the Sovereign. Such people should be held in prison until the Sovereign decides what to do with them.

38

Provisions of Russian Protectorate over Ukraine in 1654

In 1654 the Russian Tsar Aleksei (1645–1672) and the Ukrainian Cossacks, who were the leaders of the Zaporozhie Host, signed an agreement which temporarily formed the basis of Ukrainian–Russian relations. Because of its vagueness, the agreement of 1654 caused the development of various conflicting views in historical literature. Some scholars have called it a personal union, others an incorporation, and still others a vassalage, a military alliance, and a treaty between two independent sovereigns. Regardless of its interpretations, the 1654 agreement placed Russia in control of a rich and strategically vital area, thereby strengthening her position *vis-à-vis* Poland and the Ottoman Empire.

A Petition of Ukrainian Cossacks to the Tsar Alexei with the Resolutions of the Tsar on Each Point, March 31, 1654

To the Great Sovereign, Tsar and Grand Duke Alexei Mikhailovich, the Autocrat of all the Great and Little Russia, [i.e., Ukraine] and the Ruler and Possessor of many States

His Tsarist Majesty's subjects, Bohdan Khmelnitsky, the Hetman of the Zaporozhie Host, as well as the whole Zaporozhie Host and the whole Christian Russian world, most respectfully beg that His Tsarist Majesty grant them what their envoys, [Samiilo Zarudny and Pavlo Teteria] are to petition, and they will serve His Tsarist Majesty, according to his orders, forever.

[Note] His Tsarist Majesty's resolutions concerning each article follow after each one.

Reprinted by permission of the publisher from George Vernadsky, *Bohdan: Hetman of the Ukraine* (New Haven, Yale University Press, 1941), pp. 131–140.

[The Kozaks Ask]

Article 1

That in [Ukrainian] towns the officeholders will be chosen among the natives who are worthy of it; they shall rule the subjects of His Tsarist Majesty and collect taxes for the Tsarist treasury honestly. [Such an arrangement is recommended] for the reason that in case a governor appointed by His Tsarist Majesty should come [to a Ukrainian town] and begin to violate the natives' rights and make new ordinances, it would be a great annoyance to them; and if the natives themselves should be officeholders, they would rule in accordance with their rights.

[The Tsar's Resolution]

And concerning this article His Tsarist Majesty graciously ordered that the article stand according their petition. There shall be [elected] office-holders in [Ukrainian] towns, *videlicet* mayors, burgomasters, counselors, assessors, and they shall collect for His Tsarist Majesty sundry taxes in money and in grain, and shall pass them over to his sovereign treasury, [handing them] to His Tsarist Majesty's agents; and the agents sent by His Tsarist Majesty for receiving the tax moneys shall supervise the [town] collectors, that the latter act honestly.

Article 2

That, through the kindness of His Tsarist Majesty, the Secretary-General of the Host will receive [yearly] appropriation of 1000 Polish zloty [gold coins] for the clerks of his office; and of 300 Polish zloty for the Justices of the Host; and of 100 Polish zloty for the secretary of the Host Court; and of fifty zloty for the secretary of each regiment as well as for the standard bearer of each regiment; and of thirty zloty for the standard bearer of each hundred; and of fifty zloty for the master of Hetman's insignia.

[Resolution]

His Tsarist Majesty has graciously ordered according to their petition; and that the money be appropriated from the local income.

Article 3

That a mill be assigned for the sustenance of each [of the following officeholders]: the Secretary of the Host; the two Justices of the Host;

the Colonels; the Asauls of the Host and those of each regiment, because they have great expenditure.

[Resolution]

His Tsarist Majesty has graciously ordered according to their petition.

Article 4

That concerning the artillery of the Host His Tsarist Majesty would graciously provide for the winter quarters and food of the cannoneers and all the artillery workers; also [to appropriate yearly] 400 gold coins to the quartermaster of the artillery, and fifty gold coins to the master of the artillery standards.

[Resolution]

His Tsarist Majesty has graciously ordered that the amount should be appropriated from local income.

Article 5

That the Hetman and the Zaporozhie Host should be free to 'receive envoys who since long ago have come to the Zaporozhie Host, in case they mean well; and only in case there shall be [about these embassies] something wrong with regard His Tsarist Majesty the Host should notify His Tsarist Majesty.

[Resolution]

Concerning this article His Tsarist Majesty has ordered that [the Host] shall receive and dismiss the bona fide envoys, and write truly and immediately to His Tsarist Majesty [to inform the Tsar] on what business they came and with what [instructions] they were dismissed. With regard to envoys sent by some [foreign power] on business detrimental to [the interests of] His Tsarist Majesty, those ambassadors and envoys should be detained by the Host, and [the Host] should write about them immediately to His Tsarist Majesty for his ukase; and they should not be dismissed without His Tsarist Majesty's ukase. And there should be no exchange of envoys [between the Host on the one hand and] the Turkish Sultan and the King of Poland [on the other hand], without a ukase of His Tsarist Majesty.

Article 6

[An abstract.] Concerning the Metropolitan of Kiev the envoys had no written instruction; and in their speeches they begged that His Tsarist Majesty graciously grant his patent conferring to the metropolitan bishop his possessions.

[Resolution]

His Tsarist Majesty graciously granted his patent confirming to the metropolitan bishop [of Kiev] and all [Ukrainian] clergy their estates they now possess.

Article 7

That His Tsarist Majesty deign to send his army to Smolensk at once without any delay in order that the enemy [i.e., the Poles] should not [have time to] prepare themselves and be joined by other [reënforcements, taking into account] that now the [Polish] troops are in bad estate. [The Tsar] should not believe any Polish insinuations in case they make recourse to such.

[Resolution]

His Tsarist Majesty has already decided to set forth personally against his enemy the King of Poland and likewise to send his boyars and generals with ample troops as soon as the roads will be dry [after the thawing of the snow] and there will be forage for horses.

Article 8

That soldiers be hired, about 3000 or even more, at His Tsarist Majesty's will, to be stationed on the [Ukrainian-Polish] frontier to protect Ukraine [from the Poles], and that they should be stationed permanently.

[Resolution]

His Tsarist Majesty's soldiers are always available for the protection of Ukraine's frontiers and will be stationed permanently [to that purpose].

Article 9

The custom used to exist for the Zaporozhie Host to receive a salary [i.e., from the King of Poland]. And now they beg His Tsarist Majesty that he should appropriate [annually] to the colonels 100 thalers [each];

the regimental Asauls, 200 gold coins; the Host Asauls, 400 gold coins; the centurions, 100 gold coins; the [registered] Kozaks, thirty Polish zloty [each].

[The Boyars' Resolution]

More than once in previous years Hetman Bohdan Khmelnitsky and all the Zaporozhie Host had sent envoys and begged that His Tsarist Majesty show them graciousness for the sake of the Orthodox Christian Faith and the holy churches of God and intervene in their favor and accept them under the [protection of his] exalted arm and should help them against their enemies. And in that time our great sovereign, His Tsarist Majesty, was not able to accept you under his protection, since there was a permanent peace between His Tsarist Majesty, and the King of Poland and the Grand Duke of Lithuania. And whereas on the part of the King many insults and offenses were committed with regard to the father of His Tsarist Majesty, the Great Sovereign Tsar and Grand Duke Michael Fedorovich, autocrat of all Russia and ruler and possessor of many states, of blessed memory; and [with regard] to our sovereign's grand-father, the Great Sovereign and holy Patriarch of Moscow and all Russia Filaret Nikitich, of blessed memory; and [with regard] to our Great Sovereign, the Tsar and Grand Duke Alexei Mikhailovich, autocrat of all Russia, [because of all that] His Tsarist Majesty expected apologies [from the King of Poland] for all [the above-mentioned] offenses in accordance with the King's notes, and the Diet's resolutions and constitutions, and the Polish [-Russian] treaties; and His Tsarist Majesty also desired, through his ambassadors extraordinary, to reconcile the Hetman Bohdan Khmelnitsky and all the Zaporozhie Host with the King of Poland in the following way: in case the King Jan Kazimierz should make peace with the Kozaks according to the provisions of the Zborov treaty, and would not persecute the Orthodox Christian Faith, and would remove the Uniates, in that case His Tsarist Majesty was ready to grant amnesty to those [Poles] who by insulting his sovereign honor deserved capital punishment. And with this offer [our Tsarist Majesty] sent to the King Jan Kazimierz his great and plenipotentiary state ambassadors, the boyar and Lord-Lieutenant of the Great Perm, Prince Boris Alexandrovich Repnin-Obolensky with associates; and those great plenipotentiary ambassadors of His Majesty spake to the King and his Lords in Council about that peace and action offering various methods [of settlement]; and the King Jan Kazimierz and his Lords in Council did not agree with any proposal and thus brought this great thing to naught, and dismissed those great and plenipotentiary ambassadors of His Tsarist Majesty without any result. And our great sovereign, His Tsarist Majesty, in view of such numerous [cases of] incorrectness and rudeness and falsehood on the part of the King, and because of his desire to protect the Orthodox Christian Faith and all the Orthodox Christians from the Roman persecutors aiming at the destruction of God's churches and the annihilation of the Christian faith, has accepted you under [the protection of] his exalted arm. And it is for your protection that our great sovereign, His Tsarist Majesty, having raised numerous Russian and Tatar and German troops, is personally setting forth against the enemies of [Orthodox] Christianity, and is sending his boyars and generals with many troops as well. And for the organization of these armies, according to his sovereign ukase, large sums have been distributed; therefore they, the envoys [of the Kozak Host], taking into consideration such munificence of His Tsarist Majesty for the sake of their protection, should not now mention the matter of payment of the salary to the Zaporozhie Host. And when the sovereign privy boyar and Lord-Lieutenant of Tver, Vasili Vasilevich Buturlin did visit the Hetman, Bohdan Khmelnitsky, the latter talked with him concerning the quota of the Zaporozhie Host, and suggested that it be set at 60,000; and [the Hetman suggested] that even if there should be more Kozaks registered than this quota, it would not be detrimental to the sovereign since they would not ask for pay. And they, Samiilo [Zarudny] and Pavlo [Teteria] and other men who at that time were with the Hetman, should know about it. [Besides] His Tsarist Majesty is not aware of what the revenues are from the cities and towns of Little Russia [i.e., Ukraine]; our great sovereign, His Tsarist Majesty is sending his squires [to Ukraine] to tabulate the revenues; only after those His Majesty's squires have tabulated and computed various revenues, a ukase will be promulgated as considered by His Tsarist Majesty concerning the salary of the Zaporozhie Host. And [even] now His Tsarist Majesty, showing his favor to the Hetman and all the Zaporozhie Host, doth intend, according to the old customs of his ancestors, the great sovereigns, tsars, and grand dukes of Russia, to send [some] salary to the Hetman and all the Zaporozhie Host, [to be paid] in gold coins.

Article 10

In case [the Tatars of] the Crimean Horde should attack, it would be necessary to oppose them, starting from the Astrakhan and Kazan; likewise the Don Kozaks should be ready [for a campaign against the Tatars]; however, the peace now with them should not yet be discontinued, and they should not be provoked.

[Resolution]

His Tsarist Majesty's ukase and command has already been sent to the Don Kozaks, to wit: in case the Crimean people are not stirred up, [the

Kozaks] are not allowed to provoke them or attack them; in case, however, the Crimean people should be stirred up, His Tsarist Majesty would
then issue orders for a campaign against them.

Article 11

Whereas the Hetman permanently keeps a [Kozak] garrison of 400 men,
providing them with everything, in the fortress of Kodak, on the Crimean
frontier, [the Kozaks ask] that His Tsarist Majesty would now graciously
supply to the fortress food [for the men] and powder for the guns; that
likewise, His Tsarist Majesty would graciously provide for those [Kozaks]
who guard the Kozaks' Headquarters (*Kosh*) beyond the cataracts, since
men have to be kept there.

[Resolution]

With regard to this article His Tsarist Majesty's gracious ukase will be
issued in the future after it is established what quantities of what supplies used to be sent to these localities, and how much revenue will be
collected by His Tsarist Majesty [in Ukraine].

[Concluding Remarks]

And concerning [the matter] which has been mentioned [in connection
with the Article 9 of] your petition: as soon as our great sovereign, His
Tsarist Majesty will grant to the Hetman Bohdan Khmelnitsky and all
the Zaporozhie Host his sovereign charter of your liberties, you must
muster your men [and determine] who will be [registered] as a Kozak
and who will be [counted as] a peasant. And with regard to the 60,000
quota for the Zaporozhie Host, our Great Sovereign, His Tsarist Majesty
has accepted and decreed it. As soon as you envoys come back to the
Hetman Bohdan Khmelnitsky, you are to inform him that he is to
muster the Kozaks and make the lists of their registration and send the
lists certified by his signature to His Tsarist Majesty immediately.

The Charter of the Zaporozhie Host, April 6, 1654

By the grace of God We the Great Sovereign, Tsar, and Grand Duke
Alexei Mikhailovich, Autocrat of all the Great and Little Russia, have
granted [this Charter to] Our Majesty's subjects Bohdan Khmelnitsky,
Hetman of the Zaporozhie Host, and the Secretary Ivan Vyhovsky, and
the Justices of the Host, and the Colonels, and the Asauls, and the Centurions, and to all the Zaporozhie Host. In this year A.M. 7162 [= A.D.
1654], by the grace of God he, the Hetman Bohdan Khmelnitsky and

all the Zaporozhie Host have come under [the protection of] our exalted
sovereign arm and have sworn an oath of everlasting allegiance to Us, the
Great Sovereign, and to our sovereign children and successors. And in
March [of this year] he the Hetman Bohdan Khmelnitsky and all the
Zaporozhie Host sent their envoys, the Justice of the Host Samiilo
Bohdanov [Zarudny], and the Colonel of Pereyaslav [regiment] Pavlo
Teteria; and in their note to Us the Great Sovereign, to Our Tsarist
Majesty, the Hetman and the envoys have most humbly begged that We
the Great Sovereign grant [our favor to] him the Hetman Bohdan
Khmelnitsky and to the whole Zaporozhie Host and confirm all their
former rights and the liberties of the Host, which had been established
from ancient times under the Grand Dukes of [Lithuania and] Russia
and the Kings of Poland; also [that we the Tsar guarantee] their liberties
and property rights with regard to the courts; that they be judged by
their elders and that no one [from the outside] interfere with their
Courts of the Host; and that [we the Tsar] not violate their former rights
which had been granted to both clergy and laymen on the part of the
Grand Dukes of [Lithuania and] Russia and the Kings of Poland, and
[that we] grant them a charter of confirmation of [those] rights
[stamped] with our sovereign seal; and that the quota of registered
Kozaks be fixed at 60,000, and that it always be filled up. And that in
case the Hetman by God's judgment should die, We the Great Sovereign
allow the Zaporozhie Host, according to their old custom, to elect the
Hetman among themselves and by themselves, and to notify Us as to
who shall have been elected; and that, since the Chihirin district with
all appurtenances had been assigned to the Hetman's mace, We the
Great Sovereign grant it, accordingly, to be attached to the [Hetman's]
mace; that [We] order that the Kozak estates and the lands which they
use for their sustenance not be taken from them; also that the children
keep the rights of their grandfathers and fathers on the legacy left by
Kozak widows. Therefore We the Great Sovereign, Our Tsarist Majesty,
have graciously commanded our subject, Bohdan Khmelnitsky, the
Hetman of Zaporozhie Host, and all Our Tsarist Majesty's Zaporozhie
Host, to be under [the protection] of Our Tsarist Majesty's exalted arm,
according to their former rights and privileges which have been granted
to them by the Kings of Poland and the Grand Dukes of Lithuania; and
We have ordered that these their rights and privileges be not violated
by any means, and commanded that they be tried by their elders according to their former rights; and we have decreed that the quota of the
Zaporozhie Host, according to their own request, be fixed at 60,000 to
be always filled up. And in case, by God's judgment, the Hetman should
die, We the Great Sovereign have allowed the Zaporozhie Host to elect
a [new] Hetman, according their former customs, by themselves and
among themselves, and to notify Us the Great Sovereign as to who shall

have been elected Hetman; and the newly elected Hetman shall swear his oath of loyalty and allegiance to Us, the Great Sovereign, before [our deputy] whom We the Great Sovereign shall appoint. And We have decreed that the district of Chihirin with all its appurtenances which had been attached to it before be assigned to the Hetman's mace as before. We also have forbidden [anyone] to deprive the Kozaks, their widows, and their children of their estates and their lands which they use for their sustenance, and [have decreed] that [such estates and lands] be [registered] with them, as before. And when ambassadors come from any of the neighboring countries to the Zaporozhie Host, to the Hetman Bohdan Khmelnitsky, on business concerning food, We the Great Sovereign have allowed the Hetman to receive and to dismiss those ambassadors. And the Hetman shall immediately notify Us the Great Sovereign from what states and on what business those ambassadors came and with what [instructions] they were dismissed. And in case ambassadors shall be sent [to the Zaporozhie Host] by any [power] on some business detrimental with regard to Us the Great Sovereign, such ambassadors must be detained in the Host, and notice must be sent to Us the Great Sovereign at once, and without Our Tsarist Majesty's decree [such ambassadors] should not be permitted to go back. And [the hetman] shall not maintain relations with either the Turkish Sultan or the King of Poland without Our Tsarist Majesty's decree.

And through Our Tsarist Majesty's graciousness let Our Tsarist Majesty's subjects, the Hetman of the Zaporozhie Host Bohdan Khmelnitsky and all Our Tsarist Majesty's Zaporozhie Host be under [the protection of] Our Tsarist Majesty's exalted arm, according to their former rights and privileges and all the articles which have been written above; and let them serve Us the Great Sovereign and our son the sovereign Tsarevich Alexei Alexeivich and our successors, and be loyal [to Us] and wish everything good [to Us] and, whenever our sovereign order will be issued, to set forth against our enemies and fight them, and to be in every circumstance obedient to Our Sovereign will forever.

And concerning those other articles which the above mentioned envoys Samiilo and Pavlo in the name of Bohdan Khmelnitsky, the Hetman of the Zaporozhie Host, and of all Our Tsarist Majesty's Zaporozhie Host, presented to Us the Great Sovereign, to Our Tsarist Majesty, and the articles they submitted to the privy boyars, of Our Tsarist Majesty, [to wit] the boyar and Lord-Lieutenant of Kazan, Prince Alexei Nikitich Trubetskoy, the boyar and Lord-Lieutenant of Tver, Vasili Vasilievich Buturlin, and to the okolnichi and Lord-Lieutenant of Kashira, Peter Petrovich Golovin, and to the state-secretary of the privy council, Almaz Ivanov, We the Great Sovereign have listened to those articles with favor, and ordered to write under each of those articles what we have decreed with regard to each, and have commanded to deliver [the copy

of] those articles with Our Tsarist Majesty's decree, to the same envoys
Samiilo and Pavlo, and it is our desire to keep the Hetman Bohdan
Khmelnitsky and all the Zaporozhie Host in Our Tsarist Majesty's
gracious favor, and they shall trust in Our Sovereign favor.

This Our Tsarist Majesty's charter has been issued [and stamped] by
our State Seal, in our reigning city of Moscow, in the year A.M. 7162
.[= A.D. 1654], on March 27 [Julian calendar]. By the grace of God, the
Great Sovereign, Tsar, and Grand Duke Alexei Mikhailovich, Autocrat
of all the Great and Little Russia. (Seal.)

39

A Decree
on Runaway Peasants, 1661

Following the issuing of restrictions on free movement of the peasantry in the middle of the fifteenth
century (see Chapter 20), conditions of Russian
peasants deteriorated rapidly. By the early seventeenth century the majority had become serfs of one
kind or another, and to keep them in that status
the nobles obtained governmental permission to
search for and reclaim those who might have
escaped (see Chapter 34). By the middle of the
seventeenth century, serfdom, with its inhuman
conditions, was firmly and almost universally entrenched. Conditions were so inhuman that many
serfs, indeed whole villages, fled their native places

From *Polnoe Sobranie Zakonov Russkoi Imperii . . . 1649–1913* (*Complete Collection of the Laws of the Russian Empire . . . 1649–1913*) (St. Petersburg,
1830), vol. 1, No. 307, pp. 556–558. Translation mine. Items in brackets are
mine.

to escape a slow death. Some of them joined various cossack bands and others sought shelter with perhaps kinder nobles. This practice became so common that in 1661 the government issued a new decree that prohibited the harboring of runaway peasants and specified penalties for violators.

If alien runaway peasants are found in the possession of a lord of a manor . . . and it is established that they have been taken in by the administrator of the manor without the knowledge of the lord . . . this administrator should be lashed mercilessly with the knout, so that from this time on others will have no desire to take in alien runaway persons and peasants.

And the fugitives should be returned to the plaintiff, along with wives and children, their goods and their grain. And they should be sent back to their old domiciles, to the *pomestie* estates, or to the hereditary estates of the lords from whom they fled, in wagons belonging to those people who [illegally] took them in. And compensation should be extracted from the people who took the fugitives in as possessions, covering the time during which they used the fugitives, according to a tsar's decree [of 1642].

If, however, the owners of the hereditary or of the *pomestie* estates possess written confirmation from Moscow that the administrator of the manor had permission to retain runaway persons and peasants, or if it can be established that the owners of the hereditary or of the *pomestie* estates themselves took in the fugitives, the administrators in these cases should not be lashed with the knout. And the great sovereign and the *boyars* have decided that from each [guilty] lord on whose *pomestie* or on whose hereditary estate a runaway peasant is found, an additional serf shall be taken, together with wife, children, goods, and grain, in addition, of course, to the compensation covering the years the runaway spent there. All these should be given to the manorial lord who formerly owned the runaway. And if more than just one runaway is found working for a lord, then one should take not only all the runaways but also one of his own peasants for each of the runaways, in order that no one else from this time on will want to harbor and use alien peasants.

40

Avvakum's Account
of His Sufferings

In the middle of the seventeenth century a significant religious revival, aimed at breathing new life
into Russian Orthodoxy, developed in that country.
Although, initially, the revival received support from
the state and the Church authorities, a conflict soon
developed between the proponents of the reform led
by Patriarch Nikon (1606–1681) and the opponents of innovation led by Archpriest Avvakum
(1620–1682). Avvakum and his followers insisted
that old rituals be preserved and that lower clergy
and their parishioners be given a greater voice in
Church affairs. These demands were intolerable to
Nikon, and Avvakum and his followers were subjected to inhuman treatment, exile, and even execution. The following are excerpts from Avvakum's
own account of his sufferings between 1640 and
1667.

I was born in the district of Nizhnii Novgorod, beyond the
Kudma River, in the village of Grigorovo. My father, Peter, was a priest;
my mother's name was Maria, or Marfa. My father liked to drink; my
mother, however, was dedicated to fasting and prayer, and always instructed me in the fear of God. Once I saw a neighbor's livestock die,
and that night I rose and wept for my soul before an icon, for a long
time, pondering mortality and how I too must die; from that time on it
became my habit to pray every night. Then my mother was widowed and
I became a young orphan, and we were driven away by our relatives. My
mother resolved that I should marry. I prayed to the Holy Mother of
God to give me a wife who would help me to gain salvation. And in that
village was a maiden, also an orphan, who constantly went to church,

From Zhitie protopopa Avvakuma im samim napisanoe i drugie ego sochineniia
(The Life of Protopop Avvakum Written by Him and Other of His Works),
(Moscow: Gosizdat, 1960), pp. 59–64, 66–75, 77–78, 85–88, 92–95, 101–104.
Translation mine. Items in brackets are mine.

and whose name was Anastasia. Her father, Marko, was a blacksmith, and a well-to-do man, but when he died all of his wealth was squandered. Therefore, she lived in poverty, praying to God to make it possible for her to marry me; and by God's will this happened. Later my mother died and went to God in great glory. Because of persecution I moved to another place. At twenty I was ordained as a deacon, and two years later I became a priest; I was a priest for eight years and then was elevated to archpriest by Orthodox bishops. This happened twenty years ago; I have then been in Holy Orders thirty years.

When I was a priest I had many parishioners, perhaps five or six hundred souls. . . . Once, in those days, a young woman came to me burdened with many sins, including idolatry and other sins of the flesh; weeping, she began to acquaint me with her sins, in detail, in the church before the gospel. And I, thrice-accursed doctor, fell sick myself, burning inwardly with a feeling of guilt, and that moment was a very unpleasant one for me. I lit three candles, fixed them to the lectern, placed my right hand on the flame and held it there until my evil passion died; when I had dismissed the young woman, I laid away my vestments, prayed, and went home greatly disturbed. When I reached my house, about midnight, I wept before an icon until my eyes swelled, and prayed diligently that God remove me from my parishioners because the burden was too heavy for me. . . .

Shortly thereafter . . . an official abducted a daughter of a widow, and I pleaded with him to return the orphan to her mother; he scorned our prayer, became angry, and came to the church with his followers, who beat me unconscious. I lay there unconscious for about half an hour or more and was revived by God's sign of the hand. And he, frightened, gave up the girl for my sake. But then the devil incited him: he came to the church, beat me, and dragged me on the floor by my legs in my vestments, while I prayed all the time.

On another occasion, another official became very angry with me, came to my home, beat me, and like a dog, gnawed the finger of my hand with his teeth. And when his throat was full of blood, then he loosened his teeth from my hand, pushed me aside, and went away. Thanking God, I wrapped up my hand in a cloth and started for vespers. On the way he jumped on me again with two small pistols, and from a close distance he fired at me; by God's will the powder exploded in the pan and the pistol did not fire. He threw it on the ground and fired from the other and it too did not fire. As befits, I prayed to God, and walking away I blessed him [the official] and bowed before him. He, however, cursed me, but I said to him: "Ivan Rodionovich, let blessings proceed out of your mouth!" Later he seized my homestead, beat me, took everything away from me, and gave me no food for the road.

During that time my son Prokopei was born, who now, with his mother, is buried. I took my belongings, my wife, the unbaptized infant, and we set off on our journey, whither God would lead us, and on the way we baptized our son. . . . When I reached Moscow I went to Arch-priests Stefan and Neronov and Ivan; they informed the Tsar about me, and henceforth he knew about me. The reverend fathers gave me a charter from the Tsar and sent me back to my previous place; I dragged myself home to find the walls of my home pulled down. I again estab-lished myself, and the devil again raised a storm against me. There came to my village dancing bears with drums and lutes; I, a sinner in Christ's service, drove them away, destroyed the masks and the drums in a field outside the village, and took away two great bears. I beat one bear sense-less, but he revived; I let the other free in the open field. For this Vasili Petrovich Sheremetev, who sailed on the Volga to the Kazan *voevoda*-office, took me on board, reprimanded me strongly, and ordered that I bless his son, Matfei, who had a shaven face. When I saw the image of shame, I would not bless him. As a result the *boyar* became very angry and ordered that I be thrown into the Volga, and they beat me very much. But later they were nice to me; we were reconciled in the Tsar's antechamber, and my younger brother was a confessor to *boyar* Vasili's wife. . . .

Shortly thereafter I was again driven out of that place. I went to Moscow, and the Tsar, by God's will, appointed me archpriest in Iurevets on the Volga. I stayed there only about eight weeks; the devil incited priests, peasants, and women; they came to the patriarch's office, where I attended to church affairs, and dragged me out—there were about 1500 of them—to the street and whipped me and trampled me; women beat me with hand-spikes. Because of my sins they beat me un-conscious and threw me into the corner of a house. A *voevoda* came with his musketeers, took me on their horses, and rushed me to my little home; the *voevoda* stationed his men around my house. The people came to the house and raised a great storm throughout the town. The most belligerent were priests and women whom I tried to lead away from sin; they cried: "Kill the thief, the son of a bitch, and throw his body into a ditch for the dogs." On the third day, without any rest, leaving my wife and children, I left for Moscow by way of the Volga. I came to Kostroma, but there too they drove away Archpriest Daniel . . . When I reached Moscow I reported to Stefan, the Tsar's chaplain, but he repri-manded me: "Why did you leave your church?" There was more trouble awaiting me. In the evening the Tsar came to his chaplain to receive his blessing; he saw me there and asked why I had deserted my city. And my wife, children, and household of some twenty souls, who had stayed in Iurevets, represented another concern for me, as I did not know whether they were alive or dead. . . .

While I was celebrating vespers, I was arrested by Boris Neledinskii with his *streltsi*; they arrested about sixty people with me; they sent all the others to prison while they put me in chains in the patriarch's court. Early on Sunday morning they placed me in a cart, stretched out my arms, and drove me from the patriarch's court to the Androniev Monastery where they chained me again, threw me into a dark dungeon dug in the ground, and where I stayed for three days without any food or drink; chained in that darkness I did not know where was East or West. No one visited me except mice and black beetles; the crickets chirped plenty and fleas were abundant. . . . In the morning [the fourth day] the archimandrite came with the brothers and led me away; they scolded me for not yielding to the patriarch, but I replied to them from the Scriptures. They took off the big chain and put on a small one. They gave me to a monk with instruction to bring me to a church. In the church they pulled my hair, poked my ribs, pulled my chains, and spat in my eyes. May God forgive them in this and the next world. . . . I remained there for four weeks. . . .

They sent me later to Siberia with my wife and children. The journey was full of misery and only a small portion can be told here. My wife bore a child and while she was sick in a cart we drove to Tobolsk; it took us thirteen weeks to complete our journey of 3000 versts, half of it by cart and water, half by sled.

The archbishop gave me a church in Tobolsk. Here, in this church, great misery pursued me; in a year and one half I was accused of conspiracy against the Tsar five times. . . .

Then [in 1655] a decree came ordering that I be taken from Tobolsk to Lena because of my condemnation of Nikon and my accusation that he was a heretic. . . . So once again I got into my boat . . . and sailed toward Lena. When I reached Eniseisk, a second decree came ordering me to proceed to Dauria [near Lake Baikal] over 20,000 versts from Moscow. They assigned me to the regiment of Afanasii Pashkov, who had some 600 men under him; because of my sins he was a fierce man: he constantly burned, tortured and beat his people. Many times I tried to persuade him to stop it, and now I fell into his hands. Nikon informed him from Moscow to torture me.

Following our departure from Eniseisk on the Great Tunguska River, a storm sank my raft: the raft was in mid-stream, full of water; the sail was torn and only the deck remained above the water. My wife somehow managed to drag the children out of the water on the deck. I just looked to heaven and cried: "Lord save us! Lord help us!" By God's will we reached the shore. . . . From another raft, two men were washed away and drowned. Later we made necessary repairs on the bank of the river and sailed away.

When we reached the Shaman Rapids, some people came to meet us; two widows were with them, one age sixty, the other older; both were sailing to a nunnery. Pashkov tried to stop them as he wanted to marry them off. I told him that it was against canon law to marry off these

women. Instead of listening to me and letting the widows free, he became
angry and began to devise tortures for me. In another rapids, called the
Long Rapids, he set out to push me out of the raft. "You don't know
how to navigate the raft, you heretic! Why don't you go to the mountains! Don't come along with the Cossacks!" I was disturbed. Mountains
there were high, the ravines impassable, and a stone crag stood there like a
wall—you would break your neck if you tried to see its top. These
mountains were full of great snakes, geese, red ducks, black crows, gray
jack daws, eagles, hawks, gerfalcons, guinea fowl, pelicans, swans, and
other wild birds. Many wild beasts wandered at liberty in these mountains:
wild goats, deer, bison, elk, boars, wolves, and wild sheep—seen everywhere
but difficult to catch. Pashkov wanted me to live in these mountains with
beasts, snakes, and birds. . . . Some fifty men rushed toward me, seized my
raft and pulled it to him [Pashkov], who waited about three versts away. . . .
They tied the raft and the executioner brought me before him. He stood
with a drawn sword and in a rage. He asked me whether I was a priest or
not. I replied that "I am Avvakum, the archpriest; what do you want?"
He roared like a wild beast and struck me on one cheek and then on the
other, and then on my head; and having knocked me off my feet he
struck me thrice with a strap on the back and gave me some seventy
blows on my naked back with a knout. . . . At each stroke I said a prayer,
but in the middle of this flogging I screamed: "You have beaten me
enough!" He stopped. And I asked him: "Do you know why you beat
me?" And he ordered them to beat me again on the ribs; and then they
stopped. I was shaking all over and then fell. He ordered them to carry
me to an official raft; they tied my hands and feet and threw me on the
deck. It was autumn; rain fell and I lay in the rain all night. . . .

In the morning they threw me onto a small boat and took me away.
Then we reached the great rapids of Padun, where the river is about
one versta broad with three reefs stretching across. If you should miss the
passage between them you will be shattered to pieces. They brought me
to the rapids. It was raining and snowing. They put a little coat on my
shoulders; water flowed over my belly and spine, and I felt miserable.
They took me out of the boat and, skirting the rapids, they dragged me
over the stones. . . .

Then they brought me to the Bratsk fortress where they threw me
into a dungeon on the straw. I was there in the cold tower until Advent;
winter reigns there during this time, but God kept me warm without
clothes. I lay on the straw like a poor dog; sometimes they fed me and
sometimes they did not. There were many mice and I would hit them
with my cap because the fools would not give me a stick. All the time
I lay on my belly because my back was sore. There were many fleas and
lice. I wanted to ask forgiveness from Pashkov, but God's will ordained
that I endure. Then he moved me into a warm hut where I stayed
through the winter with hostages and dogs. My wife and children were

exiled to a place about twenty *versts* away. Her woman servant, Xenia, tormented her the entire winter with complaints and tantrums. My son, Ivan, still a boy, visited me after Christmas, and Pashkov ordered that he be thrown in the cold dungeon with me where the dearest one almost froze to death. In the morning he ordered him back to his mother. I never saw him again. He came to his mother with frostbite on his hands and feet.

In the spring we moved forward. We had but scant provisions, as everything had been stolen; books and clothes had been taken but other items remained. I almost drowned on Lake Baikal. I was ordered to pull a towing rope on the Khilok River; it was a very difficult task and there was no time for eating or sleeping. I suffered the entire summer. People were dying from the hardship of water travel, and my feet and belly were blue. For two summers we journeyed by water, and during the winters we crossed portages. On the Khilka River I almost drowned for the third time. The current sucked me and my boat from the shore while others remained. My wife and children remained on shore; only I and the steersman were in the boat. The swirling water tossed and pitched the boat; I climbed on the boat and cried out: "Blessed Virgin help us! Our Hope, don't let us drown!" At times my feet were in the water, at times I would climb on top. The boat was carried away for about a *versta* or more and then the people overtook it. Everything was shattered to pieces. . . .

Then we reached the Lake of Irgen. There was a portage and we carried our belongings through the winter. He [Pashkov] took my workmen away and would not allow me to hire others. The children were small, there were many mouths to feed but no one to work; one archpriest built a sleigh and hauled things through the entire winter. When spring came we sailed down the Ingod River. It was my fourth summer of travel since Tobolsk. They were cutting timber there for houses and cities. Food became scarce and people began to die from hunger and continuous work in water. The river was shallow, the rafts heavy, the wardens merciless, the sticks big, the cudgels gnarled, the knouts cutting, and the suffering cruel—fire and rack; people were hungry. . . . Oh what a time! I do not know how he [Pashkov] went mad. My wife had one gown left from Moscow which had not rotted; its value was about fifteen rubles, but more here. He gave us four sacks of rye for it, and we managed, with it and eating grass, to live on the Nercha River for another year. He starved many people, would not allow anyone to hunt, gave them a very small space, and they were forced to wander over the steppes and fields, to cut grass and dig roots; we were with them. In the winter they would eat pine cones. Sometimes God would lead us to a mare's flesh or to bones of wild beasts which the wolves had left and which we would finish. And some would eat frozen wolves or foxes— really everything. A mare foaled, and secretly the starving people devoured the foal together with the caul. When Pashkov learned about it, he tortured them to death. And when another mare died, they all became desperate because they had pulled the foal out of her; the moment they saw the head they pulled it out, and ate the blood that came out with it. Oh, what a time! Two of my little boys died during these sufferings; with others, naked and barefoot, I roamed over the hills and sharp rocks, living on grass and roots. What did I not endure?

We suffered thusly in the Dauria land about six or seven years. Some of these were not too bad. Afanasii always slandered me and ceaselessly sought my death. . . . From the Nercha River we returned to Rus. For five weeks we travelled on ice in sleighs. He [Pashkov] gave us two small ponieş for our children and belongings, so my wife and I were forced to walk, stumbling over ice. The country was barbarous and the natives were hostile. We could not afford to be separated from the horses; neither could we keep up with them because we were hungry and tired people. My poor wife trampled along and then she collapsed. Later when she fell again another tired soul fell on her; they both cried but were unable to get up. The man said: "Forgive me, lady!", and she said, "Are you trying to crush me?" Then I came and the poor soul began to complain, asking: "How long, archpriest, are these sufferings to last?" And I replied: "Markovna, till our death."   And with a sigh she said: "Well, Petrovich, let us go." . . .

After we left Dauria our food became scarce; we all prayed and Christ gave us a roebuck, a huge beast which provided us with food till we reached Lake Baikal. Near the lake we came across a Russian settlement of sable hunters and fishermen. They were pleased to see us and we were glad to see them. . . . They gave us as much food as we needed; they gave us some forty fresh-water sturgeons, saying: "Here, Father, God sent them into our fishery for you. Take them all!" I thanked them, blessed the fish, and asked them to take it back with them, saying, "What would I do with it?" They entertained me there, gave me needed provisions, and after we repaired our boat we set out across the lake. . . .

I wintered in Eniseisk, and after a summer sailing I again wintered in Tobolsk. On my way to Moscow, in all cities and villages, in churches and at fairs, I preached the word of God, taught, and exposed godless flattery. And so I arrived in Moscow after a three-year journey from Dauria; it took us five years travelling there upstream; going east we journeyed through native tribes and settlements. Much could be said about that. The natives captured me too. On the great Ob River, before my very eyes, they killed twenty Christians; they also wanted to kill me, but for some reason they let me go. Or, again on the Irtysh River, a group of natives was waiting to ambush our men from Berezov. I did not know about it and approached them at the bank, and they immediately surrounded us with their bows. I went forward and embraced them as if they were monks. . . . And they treated me kindly and they brought their wives to my wife. My wife flattered them, which they enjoyed; their women were kind. We know that if women are good then everything under Christ is well. The men hid their bows and arrows and began to bargain with me. I bought some bear meat from them and they let me free. . . .

And so I came to Moscow where the Tsar and *boyars* received me gladly, as if I were an angel. I went to see Feodor Rtishchev; he met me, I blessed him and we spoke about many things; he would not let me go for three days and three nights and later he informed the Tsar about me. The Tsar immediately ordered that I come to him and he spoke kindly to me. . . .

When they saw that I was not agreeing with them, the Tsar asked Rodion Streshnev to persuade me to hold my peace. I agreed, because the Tsar was appointed by God, at the moment he was kindly disposed toward me, and I hoped he would slowly change. They promised, on Simeon's Day, to place me at the Printing Office to correct books; I was very pleased because this sounded much better than being the Tsar's confessor. . . . After about half a year [after my return], I saw that religious matters had no success, but on the contrary rumors prevailed; and so I grumbled, wrote the Tsar pleading that he earnestly seek the old piety, defend our common mother—the Holy Church—from heresy, and place an Orthodox shepherd in the patriarchal office in place of Nikon, who was wolf, heretic, and thief. . . . From that moment on the Tsar was critical of me. He did not like [the fact] that I had started to speak again. They [bishops] would have liked to silence me, but that was impossible. And the authorities, like goats, began to leap up against me, began to plot my banishment from Moscow because those Christians who understood the truth came to me and stopped coming to their service. And I received a statement from the Tsar: "Bishops complain to me against you; they say that you have emptied their churches; go again into banishment." Thus spoke *boyar* Peter Mikhailovich Saltykov. And they took me to Mezen. . . .

After half a year of suffering they brought me back to Moscow with my two sons, Ivan and Prokopei. My wife and the others remained at Mezen. In Moscow they took us first to the Pafnutiev Monastery. Here a letter awaited us which stated as follows: "How long are you going to torture us? Join us dear Avvakum!" But since I refused as if they were devils, they flew in my face! . . .

They held me in chains in Pafnutiev for ten weeks and then they took me back to Moscow, to the room of the Cross, where the bishops argued with me. They led me to the cathedral where they cut off my hair and that of Deacon Feodor, and then they cursed us and I cursed them.

And after they held us at the patriarchal court for a while they trans-

ported us to Ugresha at night, to the Monastery of St. Nicholas. Here
God's enemies shaved my beard. . . They were like wolves who have no
pity for the sheep; they tore my hair like dogs and left only one forelock, such as the Poles wear on their foreheads. They took me to the
monastery, not via the usual road, but through marshes and mud so that
people would not see me. They could see that they behaved like fools,
but still they did not wish to terminate their folly. . . .

They kept me at Nicholas', in a cold room, for seventeen weeks. . . .
Then they brought me again to the Pafnutiev Monastery, where they
locked me up in a dark room, and, chained, kept me there for almost a
year. . . . When they brought me to Moscow from the Pafnutiev Monastery they placed me in a guesthouse, and, after many trips to the
Miracle Monastery, they brought me before the patriarchs of the entire
Christendom [in 1667] where our [Russian] bishops sat there like foxes.
I spoke a great deal with the patriarchs about the Holy Scriptures. God
opened my sinful mouth and Christ put them to shame. The last word
they spoke to me was this: "Why are you so stubborn? Our Palestine
is everywhere—Serbs, Albanians, Wallachians, Romans, Poles—they all
make the sign of the cross with three fingers; you are alone in your
obstinacy and make the sign of the cross with five fingers; this is unseemly!" I replied to them the following about Christ: "Teachers of
Christendom! Rome fell long ago and lies prostrate; the Poles fell with
it because to the end they were enemies of Christians. Your orthodoxy is
diluted because of Turkish Mohammedan oppression; you are weak. In
the future you come to us to learn. By God's decree we have autocracy
here. Until the time of Nikon, the apostate, under our pious princes and
Tsars we had pure orthodoxy in Russia and a non-seditious church.
Nikon, the wolf, decreed with the devil that men should make the sign
of the cross with three fingers; but our early shepherds made the sign of
the cross with five fingers, and they also blessed people with five fingers
according to the tradition of our Holy Fathers, Meletina of Antioch,
Theodore the Blessed, bishop of Cyrene, Peter of Damascus, and Maxim
the Greek. Our own *sobor*, held during the reign of Tsar Ivan [IV],
approved the usage of five fingers in the making of the sign of the cross
and in blessing, as was also taught by such early fathers as Meletii and
others. Likewise, at the *sobor* of the reign of Tsar Ivan, Gurii and Var-
sonofii, distinguished miracle makers of Kazan, and Philipp, the abbot
of Solovki were present." The patriarchs then began to think; but our
[Russian] wolves began to howl and belch out words against their own
fathers. They said: "Our Russian holy men were ignorant, and because
they were illiterate, understood nothing. How can one believe them?
They could not read!" . . . I tried to defend them as much as I could,
and my last words were: "I am pure and I shake the dust off my feet
before you for as it is written: 'better one who would execute God's will

than a multitude of godless.' " Then they cried out against me: "Take him away! Take him away! He has insulted us all." And they began to push me and to beat me; and the patriarchs themselves, about forty men, threw themselves at me. It was a great anti-Christ gathering. Ivan Uvarov seized me and dragged me. I cried aloud: "Stop! Do not beat me!" And they all sprang back. . . .

Then the Tsar sent an officer with *streltsi* and they took me to the Vorobiev hills. . . .

Then from the Vorobiev hills they transferred us to the guesthouse of the Andreevskii [Monastery] and then to the Savin *sloboda*. They treated us as criminals and military guards followed us everywhere, even when we went to relieve ourselves; it was a laughable and sorrowful spectacle. . . .

Then they brought us back to Moscow again, to the guesthouse of the Nikolskii [Monastery], where they demanded from us, anew, a statement of the true faith. . . .

Following the execution of my friends, but not me, they banished me to Pustozerie [in 1667 where Avvakum was burned at the stake in 1682].

41

The Treaty of Nerchinsk, August 27, 1689

The Russians encountered no difficulties in their expansion across northern Asia because the territories they conquered were inhabited by primitive people. When, in the middle of the seventeenth

From *Sbornik dogovorov Rossii s Kitaem 1689–1881* (A Collection of Treaties between Russia and China, 1689–1881) (St. Petersburg, 1889), pp. 1–6. Translation mine. Items in brackets are mine.

century, they reached the Amur Basin, they met the strong power of China. For quite some time the Chinese viewed the Russians with suspicion, forced their withdrawal from the Amur Basin, and were unwilling to enter into relations with them. In 1689, however, the two countries signed a treaty at Nerchinsk which, until the middle of the nineteenth century, was one of the basic documents governing their relations.

Article 1

A river called Gorbitsa, which near the Amur River joins the Shilka River from the left side, shall form a boundary for both states. This boundary shall then proceed from the headwaters of the Gorbitsa River along the peaks of the Kamennyi Mountains, which begin at the headwaters of said river, and which extend all the way to the Sea [of Okhotsk]. All rivers, be they big or small, which flow south from these mountains and empty into the Amur River, shall be under the suzerainty of the Chinese state; all rivers which flow the opposite direction from these mountains shall be under the suzerainty of the Russian state.

All other rivers which are between the River Udi and said mountains and are under Russian suzerainty, and those rivers which are close to the Amur and flow to the Sea [of Okhotsk] and are under Chinese suzerainty, as well as all territories which lie between the said River Udi and the mountains, shall continue undecided because the great plenipotentiary ambassadors are not empowered to settle their disposition; this condition will remain so until the plenipotentiary ambassadors of both China and Russia, upon their return home, shall receive from their sovereigns proper instructions to solve this problem through ambassadors or through correspondence.

Then the fate of these undecided territories will be decided in a peaceful, dignified manner either by letters or ambassadors.

Article 2

Moreover, the River Argun, which empties into the Amur, shall form a boundary [between China and Russia]. All lands which are on its left bank, all the way to the mountains, shall be under Chinese suzerainty. The right bank with all its territories will be part of the Russian state. [The Russians] are to transfer all of their buildings from the southern bank of the Argun River to its northern side.

Article 3

The city of Albazin, which the Russians built, should be destroyed completely, and all the people who now dwell there, with all the military and other provisions, should be transferred to Russian territory. They should leave behind neither property nor any of their small possessions.

Article 4

All Russian fugitives, who at the conclusion of this peace treaty are in China, and all Chinese fugitives who are in Russia, shall remain where they are. Those fugitives who, following the signing of this treaty, shall flee, each side shall return promptly to frontier officials.

Article 5

On the basis of the present treaty of friendship, all persons, regardless of their position, may come and go reciprocally, with full liberty, provided they have passports and buy and sell whatever they need.

Article 6

All former discords that have occurred between frontier inhabitants [of both states] prior to the signing of this peace treaty, shall be forgotten and shall not be avenged. And should, following the signing of this peace, some hunters come and pillage or kill, such people, when apprehended, should be handed over to border officials of their native country. And such individuals should be punished severely. And should pillages [or other crimes] be committed by a group of individuals, those willful individuals, when apprehended, should be handed over to border officials to be executed for their crimes. Neither side will either declare a war or shed blood on account of the actions of its frontier population. Each side will make a report of such discords to the respective governments, and such disagreements should be resolved peacefully through diplomatic correspondence.

Chinese authorities reserve for themselves the right to install along the frontiers, which have been outlined in the present treaty, markings of their choice in order to know the exact position [of the frontier].

GLOSSARY

altyn- A monetary unit in medieval Russia. One *altyn* equalled six *dengas*, or three *copecks*.

arshin- A linear measure equal to about twenty-eight inches.

barshchina- An obligation of a serf to work on his master's estate, often with this own stock and implements.

boyar- A member of the medieval Russian aristocracy, as distinguished from the service noble (*pomeshchik*). Boyars received their titles from the Tsars, headed important offices, and participated in the deliberations of the *boyarskaia duma*.

boyarskaia duma- An advisory council to the Russian Grand Princes and Tsars, consisting of important boyars, nobles, and high church dignitaries.

chelobytnaia- Literally "beating one's forehead"; a petition.

chetvert- A fourth; a quarter; a grain measure of about eight bushels; also a land measure.

chin- Occupation or profession of a group of people.

denga (pl. *dengi*)- A medieval Russian monetary unit, borrowed from the Tartars, which ceased to circulate after the seventeenth century. One *denga* equalled one-half *copeck*. In modern Russian *dengi* denotes "money."

deti boyarskie- Petty nobles, especially service nobles. There were different categories of *deti boyarskie* in Moscovy.

diak- A secretary; a clerk in an office of the central government in Moscow or in the provinces.

druzhina- The retinue of Kievan princes which helped them to trade, fight, and rule.

dukhovnaia gramota- A will; a testament.

dumnyi diak- Chief secretary or clerk who had the right to attend meetings of the *boyarskaia duma*.

dvorianin- A nobleman; a courtier; a member of the Russian nobility (*dvorianstvo*).

gost (pl. *gosti*)- A member of the highest ranking merchants in Moscow, appointed by the Tsar to handle his domestic and foreign trade in monopolized goods. *Gosti* could buy land and were exempt from certain taxes.

gostinnaia sotnia- A merchants' association (guild) of lower rank merchants in Moscow in the sixteenth and seventeenth centuries. The membership of the association varied from 100 to 350 members, who, though influential, did not enjoy the same rights and privileges as did the *gosti*.

gostinnyi dvor- A market place in Moscow where foreign or outside merchants could display their goods.

gramota- Any written document.

grivna- A monetary unit in medieval Russia consisting of ten copecks or twenty *dengas*, or twenty *nogatas*, or twenty-five *kunas*, or fifty *rezanas*. Originally, *grivna* meant a circular ingot of silver.

gubernia- An administrative unit in Russia introduced by Peter I and abolished by the Soviet government in 1923.

hetman (from German *Hauptmann*)- Commander-in-chief of the army in Poland, Lithuania, and among the Zaporozhie, or Dnieper Cossacks.

igumen- An abbot; head of a monastery; Father Superior.

izgoi- A feudal serf, bound to the owner and to the soil.

kabala- A form of servitude in medieval Russia under which an individual accepted an obligation to work for a definite and agreed period of time.

kholop- A captive, a personal slave of the prince, the boyar, or the monastery; a dependent individual, and next to the peasant, the most numerous in Russia. There were various categories of *kholops* in medieval Russia.

kholopstvo- Captivity; slavery; a surrender of freedom because of economic necessity.

Kitai gorod- A section of Moscow on the east side of the Kremlin.

kniaz- A prince.

kormlenie- A system of local administration prevalent from the fourteenth through the sixteenth centuries in Moscow, under which local administrators, who were appointed by the Tsar, received payments in kind from the local population.

kormlenshchik- A recipient of the *kormlenie*; a local administrator and tax collector, and, as a rule, a member of the nobility.

krestianin- A peasant. In medieval Russia there were different varieties of peasants according to whom they belonged (Tsar, boyars, church, monasteries, and so forth).

krestnoe tselovanie- An oath affirmed by the kissing of the cross.

kuna- A marten; also a monetary unit in Kiev and Novgorod.

mestnichestvo- An elaborate code in Moscovy regulating the quantity and quality of service which the aristocracy rendered to the prince; a "trade union" founded upon genealogical principles.

namestnichestvo- A large administrative unit in medieval Russia.

namestnik- An administrator of a *namestnichestvo*, usually a high-born nobleman appointed by the Tsar.

nemets- In a broad sense any foreigner; in a narrow sense any west European (German, Englishman, Dutchman, and so forth).

nogata- A monetary unit in Novgorod and Kiev. One *nogata* equalled $\frac{1}{20}$ of a *grivna*.

oblast- An administrative unit in Russia; a province; a region.

obrok-   Quit-rent; payment in kind or money of a serf's obligations or dues to the nobleman.

obshchina-   Russian peasant village commune; also known as *mir*.

okolnichi-   A courtier, and next to *boyars* the most important member of medieval Russian nobility.

okrug-   An administrative unit in Russia; district; region.

oprichnik-   A member of the *oprichnina*.

oprichnina-   A terrorist system employed by Ivan the Terrible (1547–1584) to crush feudal aristocracy and thus to strengthen his autocratic rule.

poltina-   A monetary unit in medieval Russia; one *poltina* equalled one-half *ruble*, or fifty *copecks*.

pomeshchik-   A recipient, and later an owner, of an estate; a nobleman.

pomestie-   An estate granted to a nobleman by a prince in return for service, usually of a military nature.

posada-   A suburb inhabited by taxpayers.

posadnik-   An elected city official in Novgorod; city mayor.

prikaz-   A department of Moscovy's government headed by either a *boyar* or an *okolnichi* and run by a *diak*. These departments were numerous.

prikazchik-   An official of the central government in cities or provinces.

pud-   A unit of weight equal to 36.113 lbs.

raba-   A female slave.

rezana-   A monetary unit in medieval Russia. One *rezana* equalled $\frac{1}{50}$ of a *grivna*.

ruble-   A monetary unit in Russia. In the fifteenth century a *ruble* was a bar of silver weighing about ¼ lb. and equal to 200 *dengas*, or 100 *copecks*.

sazhen-   A linear measure of three *arshins*, or seven feet.

sloboda-   A section of town inhabited by taxpayers, or free people.

smerd-   A free peasant in Kievan Rus who subsequently became obligated either to the prince or to a noble.

sobor-   An assembly, usually of high church dignitaries.

starosta-   A title of an elected official of a village, a *volost*, or a section of town.

stolnik-   A courtier who attended the Tsar during receptions for foreign dignitaries.

strelets (pl. *streltsi*)-   Musketeers in Moscow and other cities who received land and other privileges in return for military service.

sukonnaia sotnia-   An association of Moscow's lower-rank textile merchants in the sixteenth and seventeenth centuries.

tiaglo-   A tax or an obligation in kind or money, or both, paid by city inhabitants and peasants.

tselovalnik- A sworn man; a person who has kissed the cross; officials of local or central government in Moscovy.

tysiatsky- Commander of the city militia in Novgorod who was elected by the *veche* and who acted as commander-in-chief in the absence of the prince.

uezd- An administrative unit in Russia comprising several *volosts*.

ukaz- An edict; a statute; an administrative decree.

veche- A village or city assembly in medieval Russia which theoretically determined the domestic and foreign policy of the town, elected officials, and discharged certain judicial functions.

velikii kniaz- A Grand Prince.

versta- A linear measure; a unit of distance equal to 0.6629 miles, or about 3500 feet.

vladyka- Title of the high clergy (bishop, archbishop) of the Russian Orthodox Church.

voevoda- A military as well as administrative leader of medieval Russia, usually a high-born member of the nobility; also the Tsar's appointed official in a city or a district.

voevodstvo- An administrative unit in medieval Russia, presided over by a *voevoda*.

volost- An administrative unit in rural Russia comprising several villages.

votchina- A hereditary form of landowning in medieval Russia.

votchinnik- An owner of a *votchina*.

zakon- A legislative measure; a fundamental law.

zemskii sobor- A landed assembly in sixteenth and seventeenth century Russia, composed of free landholders having authority to deal with such major issues as war, peace, and the election of a new Tsar.

Table 1: Russian Rulers. 862-1125

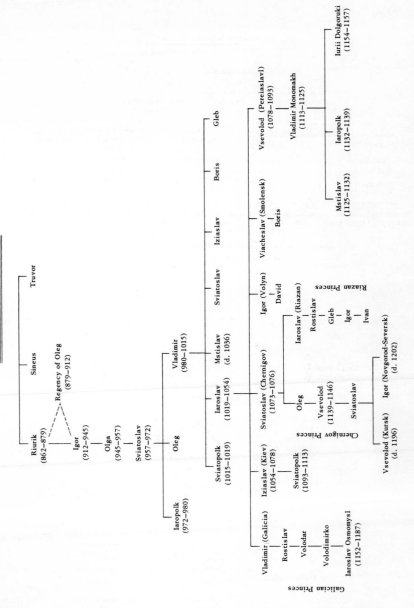

Table 2: Russian Rulers, 1125–1613

Table 3: Russian Rulers, 1613–1917

```
                            Michael Romanov
                              (1613–1645)
                                   |
        (1) Maria Miloslavskaia    m.    Aleksei    m.    Natalia Naryshkina (2)
                                       (1645–1676)
                                            |
  ┌──────────────┬──────────────┐              ┌──────────────────────────┐
Sophia         Feodor         Ivan V      (1) Eudoxia    m.    Peter I    m.    Martha Skavronskaia (2)
(Regent,     (1676–1682)   (Co-Tsar,         Lopukhina                        (Catherine I, 1725–1727)
1682–1689)                 1682–1696)             |
                                |              Aleksei            ┌─────────────────────┐
Catherine m. Charles Leopold,  Anna m. Frederick,  (d. 1718)   Anna m. Charles Frederick,   Elizabeth
           Duke of Mecklenburg    Duke of Courland     |          Duke of Holstein-        (1741–1762)
                                 (1730–1740)         Peter II        Gottorp
                                                    (1727–1730)         |
Anna m. Anthony Ulrich,                                          Peter III m. Sophie of Anhalt-Zerbst
        Duke of Brunswick-                                        (1762)      (Catherine II, 1762–1796)
        Bevern-Luneburg                                                  |
             |                                                        Paul I
          Ivan VI                                                   (1796–1801)
        (1740–1741)                                                      |
                                                         ┌──────────────┴──────────────┐
                                                     Nicholas I                     Constantine    Alexander I
                                                    (1825–1855)                                   (1801–1825)
                                                         |
                                                    Alexander II
                                                    (1855–1881)
                                                         |
                                                    Alexander III
                                                    (1881–1894)
                                                         |
                                                    Nicholas II
                                                    (1894–1917)
```

CHRONOLOGICAL TABLE

860	First Varangian expedition against Constantinople.
862	Traditional date of the establishment of Riurik Dynasty in Novgorod.
882	Transfer of the capital to Kiev.
907	First agreement between Oleg and the Greeks.
911	Second agreement between Oleg and the Greeks.
941–944	Igor's expedition against Constantinople.
945	Igor's death.
945–957	Olga's rule.
964–966	Sviatoslav's defeat of the Khazars on the Volga.
967–972	Sviatoslav's expedition in the Balkans.
968	Kiev attacked by the Pechenegs.
973	Sviatoslav's death.
973–978	Iaropolk's rule.
978–1015	Vladimir's rule.
988	Traditional date of Vladimir's conversion to Christianity.
1015–1019	Struggle for power among Vladimir's sons.
1019–1054	Iaroslav's rule.
1025	Traditional date of the founding of Iaroslavl.
1034	Iaroslav's victory over the Pechenegs.
1037	St. Sophia, Kiev, begun.
1045–1052	Building of St. Sophia, Novgorod.
1054	First appearance of the Polovtsians at Kievan frontiers.
1054–1073	*Russkaia Pravda* (Russian Justice) prepared.
1068	Invasion of the Kievan state by the Polovtsians; an uprising in Kiev against Prince Iziaslav.
1095	First election of a prince in Novgorod.
1097	Partition of Kievan Rus into patrimonial estates at Liubech Conference.
1108	Traditional date of the founding of Vladimir.
1113	Monk Nestor ends the writing of the *Primary Chronicle*.
1113–1125	The rule of Vladimir Monomakh.
1126	First election of *posadnik* (Mayor) by Novgorod *veche* (assembly).
1147	First recorded mention of Moscow.
1156	First election of a bishop in Novgorod.
1167	Destruction of Kiev by Andrei Bogoliubskii, Prince of Vladimir-Suzdal.
1169	Transfer of the capital from Kiev to Suzdal.
1185	Unfortunate expedition of Prince Igor of Novgorod-Seversk against Polovtsians.

1195	Novgorod concludes the first treaty with German cities and Gottland.
1209	First reference to Tver.
1221	Founding of Nizhnii-Novgorod (now Gorky).
1223	First invasion of Rus by the Mongols and the battle on the Kalka River.
1227	Death of Ghenghis Khan.
1237–1241	Invasion and conquest of Rus by Batu Khan.
1240	Alexander Nevskii's victory over the Swedes on the Neva River.
1242	Alexander Nevskii's victory over the Teutonic Order at Lake Peipus.
1243	Formation of the Golden Horde.
1246	First census of the population by the Mongols in the Kiev and Chernigov territories.
1245–1247	Journey of John of Pian de Carpine to Mongolia.
1252	Emergence of Moscow as an independent hereditary principality.
1253–1255	Journey of William of Rubruck to Mongolia.
1252–1263	Rule of Alexander Nevskii.
1270	Novgorod negotiates a treaty with the Hanseatic League.
1300	Transfer of Metropolitan Office from Kiev to Vladimir.
1302	Moscow annexes Pereiaslavl, Kolomna, and Mozhaisk.
1318	Prince Iurii of Moscow acquires the Charter (*iarlik*) of Grand Prince from the Mongols.
1322	Charter (*iarlik*) of Grand Prince passes to Dmitri of Tver.
1325–1340	Rule of Ivan Kalita in Moscow.
1328	Ivan Kalita gets the *iarlik* of Grand Prince.
1340	St. Sergius founds the Trinity Monastery.
1352	Black Death visits Novgorod and Moscow.
1359–1389	Rule of Dmitri Donskoi.
1360–1362	Struggle between Moscow and Suzdal for the title of Grand Princedom.
1367–1368	First stone fortifications of the Moscow Kremlin.
1371–1375	Heresy of *Strigolniks* (Shearers) in Novgorod.
1375	Tver acknowledges Moscow as Grand Principality.
1380	Dmitri Donskoi defeats Khan Mamai at Kulikovo.
1382	Moscow taken by Khan Tokhtamysh; first mention of firearms in Moscow; first coining of money in Moscow.
1392	Moscow absorbs Suzdal and Nizhnii-Novgorod.
1395	Defeat of the Golden Horde by Tamerlane.
1389–1425	Rule of Vasili I in Moscow.
1425–1462	Rule of Vasili II, the Blind.
1427	Formation of the Crimean Khanate.

1430–1466	Disintegration of the Golden Horde.
1436	Foundation of Solovetskii Monastery.
1437	Formation of the Kazan Khanate.
1439	Council of Florence attempts to reunite eastern and western Churches.
1441	Metropolitan Isidore deposed in Moscow for acceptance of Council of Florence.
1448	Church of Moscow declared autocephalous.
1453	Ottoman Turks capture Constantinople.
1458	Kievan Metropolitan assumes independence from Moscow.
1459	Formation of the Astrakhan Khanate.
1462–1505	Rule of Ivan III, the Great.
1463	Moscow annexes the principality of Iaroslavl; Moscow conquers the Mari Lands.
1463–1468	First limitations upon freedom of peasant movement.
1470	The Judaizer Heresy spreads throughout Novgorod.
1472	Moscow annexes the principality of Perm; Ivan III marries Sophia Paleologue, niece of last Byzantine Emperor.
1474	Moscow annexes Rostov.
1476	Ambrosio Contarini, the first Westerner, visits and writes about Moscow.
1478	Moscow annexes Novgorod.
1475–1479	Building of the Uspenskii Sobor (Cathedral of Assumption) in the Moscow Kremlin.
1480	Ivan III terminates the "Mongol Yoke."
1485–1516	Building of the new Kremlin in Moscow.
1489	Moscow annexes Viatka.
1497	Ivan III issues *Sudebnik* (Code of Laws).
1503	Church Council condemns the heresy of Judaizers.
1505–1533	Rule of Vasili III.
1510	Moscow annexes Pskov.
1514	Moscow annexes territories of Smolensk.
1517, 1526	Baron Heberstein's missions to Moscow.
1525	Maxim the Greek condemned by Church Council.
1533–1584	Rule of Ivan IV, the Terrible.
1547	Ivan IV assumes the title "Tsar."
1549	First meeting of the *Zemskii Sobor* (Landed Assembly).
1550	Organization of the *streltsi*; *Sudebnik* (Code of Laws) of Ivan IV.
1552	Moscow captures Kazan.
1553	Opening of the northern sea route to Russia by the English (Richard Chancellor).

1555	Formation of the "Muscovy Company" in London and the extension of privileges to it for trade throughout the Moscow State.
1556	Conquest of Astrakhan.
1558–1583	The Livonian War of Ivan IV.
1564	First book printed in Moscow by Ivan Fedorov.
1565–1584	Ivan IV's reign of terror.
1570	Ivan IV's punishment of Novgorod.
1571–1572	Crimean Tartars raid and burn Moscow.
1577	Establishment of commercial ties with Holland.
1582	Yermak conquers the Khanate of Sibir.
1584	Founding of Archangel.
1584–1598	Rule of Tsar Feodor Ivanovich.
1587–1598	Boris Godunov acts as Regent.
1588	Giles Fletcher visits Moscow.
1589	Formation of the Office of Patriarch in Moscow.
1596	Creation of Uniat Church in Poland-Lithuania.
1597	An *ukaz* grants nobles five years to claim their fugitive peasants.
1598	End of the Riurik Dynasty.
1598–1605	Rule of Tsar Boris Godunov.
1601–1604	Years of famine.
1604–1613	Time of Troubles.
1605–1606	Rule of the First False Dmitri.
1606–1607	Bolotnikov's revolt.
1607–1610	Second False Dmitri.
1610–1612	Poles occupy Moscow.
1611–1612	National uprising against Poles.
1611–1617	Swedes occupy Novgorod.
1613	*Zemskii Sobor* elects Michael Romanov as Tsar.
1613–1645	Rule of Tsar Michael Romanov.
1631	Peter Mogila, Metropolitan of Kiev, founds Kiev Academy.
1634–1643	Adam Olearius makes four visits to Moscow.
1637	Don Cossacks conquer Azov; first mission from Moscow to China.
1643–1646	Peiarkov reaches the Sea of Okhotsk.
1645–1676	Rule of Tsar Aleksei.
1648	Ukrainian Cossack uprising against Poland.
1648–1649	*Zemskii Sobor* issues *Sobornoe Ulozhenie* (Code of Laws).
1649	Trading privileges of the Muscovy Company abolished.
1652	Foundation of the German settlement in Moscow; founding of Irkutsk.
1652–1666	Nikon, Patriarch of Moscow.
1653	Last full meeting of the *Zemskii Sobor*.

1654	Ukrainian Cossacks swear allegiance to the Tsar of Moscow; Church Council adopts Nikon's reforms thereby causing a schism.
1654–1667	Russo-Polish War over the Ukraine.
1662	"Copper riots" in Moscow.
1664	Russian official, Grigorii Kotoshikhin, flees to Sweden.
1666	Establishment of postal service in Russia; Church Council deposes Patriarch Nikon.
1667	Poland cedes Kiev and Smolensk to Russia in the Peace of Andrusovo; *Novotorgovyi ustav* (New Commercial Code) promulgated; Church Council condemns Old Believers.
1667–1676	Revolt of Solovetskii Monastery against church reforms.
1670–1671	Revolt of Stenka Razin.
1672	Russians send embassies to all major European States.
1676–1682	Rule of Tsar Feodor Alekseevich.
1682	Execution of Archpriest Avvakum.
1682–1689	Regency of Sophia.
1684	Institution of formal persecution of Old Believers.
1689	Peter I deposes Sophia; Treaty of Nerchinsk with China signed.

SELECTED BIBLIOGRAPHY

Medieval Russian history, which is recorded in Church Slavonic, has not been examined as intensively in English as has modern Russian history because of the obvious language barrier. In spite of this, an impressive amount of literature in English has accumulated on the subject, and the following bibliography is an example of this growing interest. The items were chosen so that readers who are unfamiliar with the language can pursue problems that have been touched on either in this collection or in more basic texts. The selected literature is divided into three parts: (1) General works and basic texts that are currently in use or were in use in the recent past; (2) Monographic literature (except works cited in this collection); and (3) Periodical literature. The growing number of doctoral dissertations that have been completed since the end of World War II, and works in foreign languages have not been listed.

General Works and Basic Texts

Billington, James H., *The Icon and the Axe: An Interpretative History of Russian Culture*, New York: Knopf, 1965.

Blum, Jerome, *Lord and Peasant in Russia from the Ninth to the Nineteenth Century*, Princeton: Princeton University Press, 1961.

Clarkson, Jesse D., *A History of Russia*, New York: Random House, 1961.

Ellison, Herbert J., *History of Russia*, New York: Holt, Rinehart and Winston, 1964.

Florinsky, Michael T., *Russia: A History and an Interpretation*, New York: Macmillan, 1953, 2 vols.

——, *Russia: A Short History*, New York: Macmillan, 1964.

Harcave, Sidney S., *Russia: A History*, 5th ed., Philadelphia: Lippincott, 1964.

—— ed., *Readings in Russian History*, New York: Crowell, 1962, 2 vols.

Johnson, W. H. E., *Russia's Educational Heritage*, Pittsburg: Carnegie Press, 1950.

Kerner, Robert J., *The Urge to the Sea: The Course of Russian History*, Berkeley: University of California Press, 1942.

Kliuchevskii, Vasili O., *A History of Russia*, New York: Russell and Russell, 1960, 5 vols.

Leroy-Beaulieu, A., *The Empire of the Tsars*, New York: Putnam, 1893–1896, 3 vols.

Letiche, John M., ed., *A History of Russian Economic Thought: Ninth through the Eighteenth Centuries*, translated with the collaboration of Basil Dmytryshyn and Richard A. Pierce, Berkeley: University of California Press, 1964.

Lossky, N. O., *History of Russian Philosophy*, New York: International Universities Press, 1952.

Lyashchenko, P. I., *History of the National Economy of Russia to the 1917 Revolution*, New York: Macmillan, 1949.

Masaryk, Thomas G., *The Spirit of Russia: Studies in History, Literature, and Philosophy*, 2d ed., New York: Macmillan, 1955.

Mavor, James, *An Economic History of Russia*, New York: Dutton, 1925, 2 vols.

Mazour, Anatole G., *Russia: Tsarist and Communist*, New York: Van Nostrand, 1961.

Miliukov, P., *Outlines of Russian Culture*, Philadelphia: University of Pennsylvania Press, 1942, 3 vols.

Mirskii, Dmitri P., *A History of Russian Literature*, Edited and Abridged by Francis J. Whitfield, New York: Knopf, 1949.

——, *Russia: A Social History*, London: Cresset Press, 1931.

Pares, Sir Bernard, *A History of Russia*, Definitive edition, New York: Knopf, 1953.

Platonov, Sergei F., *History of Russia*, New York: Macmillan, 1925.

Pokrovskii, Mikhail, *History of Russia from the Earliest Times to the Rise of Commercial Capitalism*, New York: International Publishers, 1931.

Rambaud, A. N., *History of Russia from the Earliest Times to 1877*, New York: Collier, 1900, 2 vols.

Riasanovsky, Nicholas V., A History of Russia, New York: Oxford University Press, 1963.

Rice, Tamara T., A Concise History of Russian Art, New York: Praeger, 1963.

Riha, Thomas, ed., Readings in Russian Civilization, Chicago: University of Chicago Press, 1964, 3 vols.

Spector, Ivar, An Introduction to Russian History and Culture, New York: Van Nostrand, 1961.

Strakhovsky, Leonid I., ed., A Handbook of Slavic Studies, Cambridge: Harvard University Press, 1949.

Sumner, Benedict H., A Short History of Russia, New York: Reynal & Hitchcock, 1943.

Tompkins, Stuart R., Russia through the Ages, from the Scythians to the Soviets, New York: Prentice-Hall, 1940.

Vernadsky, George, A History of Russia, New Haven: Yale University Press, 1961.

——, Political and Diplomatic History of Russia, Boston: Little, Brown, 1936.

Vucinich, Alexander S., Science in Russian Culture: A History to 1860, Stanford: Stanford University Press, 1963.

Wallace, D. M., Russia, New York: Holt, Rinehart and Winston, 1905.

Walsh, Warren B., Russia and the Soviet Union, Ann Arbor: University of Michigan Press, 1958.

—— ed., Readings in Russian History, 4th ed., Syracuse: Syracuse University Press, 1963, 3 vols.

Wren, Melvin C., The Course of Russian History, 2d ed., New York: Macmillan, 1962.

Monographic Literature

Anderson, Matthew S., Britain's Discovery of Russia, 1553–1815, New York: St. Martin's Press, 1958.

Backus, Oswald P., Motives of West Russian Nobles in Deserting Lithuania for Moscow, 1377–1514, Lawrence: University of Kansas Press, 1957.

Bain, Robert N., Slavonic Europe: A Political History of Poland and Russia from 1447 to 1796, London: Cambridge, 1908.

Chadwick, Nora, The Beginnings of Russian History: An Inquiry into Sources, London: Cambridge, 1946.

Concevicius, Joseph B., Russia's Attitude Toward Union with Rome (9th–16th Centuries), Washington, D.C.: Catholic University of America, 1927.

Cross, Samuel H., Medieval Russian Churches, Cambridge, Mass.: Medieval Academy of America, 1949.

——, Slavic Civilization through the Ages, Cambridge, Mass.: Harvard University Press, 1948.

Curtin, Jeremiah, The Mongols in Russia, Boston: Little, Brown, 1908.

Dawson, Christopher, ed., The Mongol Mission, New York: Sheed and Ward, 1955.

Fedotov, Georgii P., *The Russian Religious Mind*, Cambridge, Mass.: Harvard University Press, 1946.

Fennell, John L. I., *Ivan the Great of Moscow*, New York: St. Martin's Press, 1961.

Fisher, Raymond H., *The Russian Fur Trade, 1550–1700*, Berkeley: University of California Press, 1943.

Graham, Stephen, *Boris Godunov*, New Haven: Yale University Press, 1933.

———, *Ivan the Terrible: Life of Ivan IV of Russia*, New Haven: Yale University Press, 1933.

Grekov, Boris D., *Kiev Rus*, Moscow: Foreign Languages Publishing House, 1959.

Gudzii, Nikolai K., *History of Early Russian Literature*, translated from the second Russian edition by Susan Wilbur Jones with an introduction by Gleb Struve, New York: Macmillan, 1949.

Howe, Sonia E., *The False Dmitri: A Russian Romance and Tragedy Described by British Eye-Witnesses, 1604–1612*, New York: Stokes, 1916.

Lamb, Harold, *The March of Muscovy: Ivan the Terrible and the Growth of the Russian Empire, 1400–1648*, Garden City, N.Y.: Doubleday, 1948.

Lantzeff, George V., *Siberia in the Seventeenth Century: A Study of Colonial Administration*, Berkeley: University of California Press, 1943.

Medlin, William K., *Moscow and East Rome: A Political Study of the Relations of Church and State in Muscovite Russia*, Geneva: Droz, 1952.

Minns, E. H., *Scythians and Greeks*, London: Cambridge, 1913.

Nabokov, Vladimir, *The Song of Igor's Campaign*, New York: Vintage Books, 1960.

Nowak, Frank, *Medieval Slavdom and the Rise of Russia*, New York: Holt, Rinehart and Winston, 1930.

O'Brien, Carl Bickford, *Muscovy and the Ukraine: From the Pereiaslavl Agreement to the Truce of Andrusovo, 1654–1667*, Berkeley: University of California Press, 1963.

———, *Russia Under Two Tsars, 1682–1689: The Regency of Sophia Alekseevna*, Berkeley: University of California Press, 1952.

Palmer, William, *The Patriarch and the Tsar*, London: Trübner, 1871–1876, 6 vols.

Paszkiewicz, Henryk, *The Making of the Russian Nation*, London: Darton, Longman & Todd, 1963.

———, *The Origin of Russia*, London: Allen & Unwin, 1954.

Rostovtsev, Mikhail I., *Iranians and Greeks in South Russia*, Oxford: Clarendon Press, 1922.

Sebes, Joseph, *The Jesuits and the Sino-Russian Treaty of Nerchinsk (1689): The Diary of Thomas Pereira*, Rome: Institutum Historicum, 1961.

Simmons, Ernest J., *English Literature and Culture in Russia (1553–1840)*, Cambridge, Mass.: Harvard University Press, 1935.

Thomsen, Vilhelm L., *Relations between Ancient Russia and Scandinavia and the Origins of the Russian State*, Oxford: Parker and Co., 1877.

Tikhomirov, Mikhail N., *The Towns of Ancient Rus*, Moscow: Foreign Languages Publishing House, 1959.

Vernadsky, George, *Ancient Russia*, New Haven: Yale University Press, 1943.
——, *Kievan Russia*, New Haven: Yale University Press, 1948.
——, *Medieval Russian Laws*, New York: Columbia University Press, 1947.
——, *The Mongols and Russia*, New Haven: Yale University Press, 1953. ◢
——, *The Origins of Russia*, Oxford: Clarendon Press, 1959.
——, *Russia at the Dawn of the Modern Age*, New Haven: Yale University Press, 1959.
Waliszewski, K., *Ivan the Terrible*, Translated by Lady Mary Loyd. Philadelphia: Lippincott, 1904.
Willan, Thomas S., *Early History of the Russia Company, 1553–1603*, Manchester, Engl., Manchester University Press, 1955.
Zenkovsky, Serge, ed., *Medieval Russian Epics, Chronicles, and Tales*, New York: Dutton, 1962.
Zernov, Nicolas, *Moscow: The Third Rome*, New York: Macmillan, 1937.
——, *St. Sergius: Builder of Russia*, New York: Macmillan, 1939.

Periodical Literature

Alef, Gustave, "Muscovy and the Council of Florence," *Slavic Review*, vol. 20, no. 3 (October 1961), pp. 389–401.
——, "The Political Significance of the Inscriptions on Muscovite Coinage in the Reign of Vasili II," *Speculum*, vol. 34, no. 1 (January 1959), pp. 1–19.
Andreyev, N., "Filofey and his Epistle to Ivan Vasil'yevich," *Slavonic Review*, vol. 38, no. 90 (December 1959), pp. 1–31.
——, "Kurbsky's Letters to Vas'yan Muromtsev," *Slavonic Review*, vol. 33, no. 81 (June 1955), pp. 414–436.
——, "The Pskov Pechery Monastery in the 16th Century," *Slavonic Review*, vol. 32, no. 79 (June 1954), pp. 318–343.
Backus, Oswald P. III, "Was Muscovite Russia Imperialistic?," *The American Slavic and East European Review*, vol. 13, no. 4 (December 1954), pp. 522–534.
Baikalov, Anatole V., "The Conquest and Colonisation of Siberia," *Slavonic Review*, vol. 10, no. 30 (April 1932), pp. 557–571.
Beazley, Raymond C., "The Russian Expansion Towards Asia and the Arctic in the Middle Ages (to 1500)," *American Historical Review*, vol. 13, no. 4 (July 1908), pp. 731–741.
Blum, Jerome, "The Beginnings of Large-Scale Private Landownership in Russia," *Speculum*, vol. 28, no. 4 (October 1953), pp. 776–790.
——, "The Rise of Serfdom in Eastern Europe," *American Historical Review*, vol. 62, no. 4 (July 1957), pp. 807–836.
——, "The Smerd in Kievan Russia," *The American Slavic and East European Review*, vol. 12, no. 1 (February 1953), pp. 122–130.
Brutzkus, J., "The Khazar Origin of Ancient Kiev," *The American Slavic and East European Review*, vol. 3, no. 1 (May 1944), pp. 108–124.
Cherniavsky, Michael, "Holy Russia: A Study in the History of an Idea," *American Historical Review*, vol. 63, no. 3 (April 1958), pp. 617–637.
Cheshire, Harold T., "The Great Tartar Invasion of Europe," *Slavonic Review*, vol. 5, no. 13 (June 1926), pp. 89–105.

Coleman, Arthur P., "The Lithuanian-White Russian Folk of the Upper Nieman," *Journal of Central European Affairs*, vol. 1, no. 4 (January 1942), pp. 399–416.

Conant, K. J., "Novgorod, Constantinople, and Kiev in Old Russian Church Architecture," *The American Slavic and East European Review*, vol. 3, no. 2 (August 1944), pp. 75–92.

Cross, S. H., "Mediaeval Russian Contacts with the West," *Speculum*, vol. 10, no. 2 (April 1935), pp. 137–144.

———, "The Scandinavian Infiltration into Early Russia," *Speculum*, vol. 21, no. 4 (October 1946), pp. 505–514.

Cross, S. H., and K. J. Conant, "The Earliest Mediaeval Churches of Kiev," *Speculum*, vol. 11, no 4 (October 1936), pp. 477–499.

Dewey, Horace W., "The 1550 Sudebnik as an Instrument of Reform," *Jahrbücher Für Geschichte Osteuropas*, New Series, vol. 10, no. 2 (July 1962), pp. 161–180.

———, "The 1497 Sudebnik—Muscovite Russia's First National Law Code," *The American Slavic and East European Review*, vol. 15, no. 3, (October 1956), pp. 325–338.

———, "Immunities in Old Russia," *Slavic Review*, vol. 23, no. 4 (December 1964), pp. 643–659.

———, "The White Lake Charter: A Mediaeval Russian Administrative Statute," *Speculum*, vol. 32, no. 1 (January 1957), pp. 74–83.

Drew, R. F., "The Siberian Fair, 1660–1750," *Slavonic Review*, vol. 39, no. 93 (June 1961), pp. 423–439.

Fennell, J. L. I., "The Attitude of the Josephians and the Trans-Volga Elders to the Heresy of the Judaisers," *Slavonic Review*, vol. 29, no. 73 (June 1951), pp. 486–509.

———, "The Dynastic Crisis, 1497–1502," *Slavonic Review*, vol. 39, no. 92 (December 1960), pp. 1–23.

Fisher, Raymond H., "Mangazeia: A Boom Town of Seventeenth Century Siberia," *Russian Review*, vol. 4, no. 1 (Autumn 1944), pp. 89–99.

Florovsky, Georges, "The Problem of Old Russian Culture," *Slavic Review*, vol. 21, no. 1 (March 1962), pp. 1–15.

Forbes, Nevil, "The Composition of the Earlier Russian Chronicles," *Slavonic Review*, vol. 1, no. 1 (June 1922), pp. 73–85.

Graham, Hugh F., "Peter Mogila: Metropolitan of Kiev," *Russian Review*, vol. 14, no. 4 (October 1955), pp. 345–356.

Jenkins, R. J. H., "The Supposed Russian Attack on Constantinople in 907: Evidence of the Pseudo-Symeon," *Speculum*, vol. 24, no. 3 (July 1949), pp. 403–406.

Kaplan, Frederick I., "The Decline of the Khazars and the Rise of the Varangians," *The American Slavic and East European Review*, vol. 13, no. 1 (February 1954), pp. 1–10.

Karpovieh, Michael, "Church and State in Russian History," *Russian Review*, vol. 3, no. 2 (Spring 1944), pp. 10–20.

Keep, J. L. H., "Bandits and the Law in Muscovy," *Slavonic Review*, vol. 35, no. 84 (December 1956), pp. 201–222.

——, "The Decline of the Zemsky Sobor," *Slavonic Review*, vol. 36, no. 86 (December 1957), pp. 100–122.

——, "The Regime of Filaret (1619–1633)," *Slavonic Review*, vol. 38, no. 91 (June 1960), pp. 334–360.

Kirchner, Walther, "The Danish-Russian Treaty of 1562," *The American Slavic and East European Review*, vol. 3, no. 2 (August 1944), pp. 39–48.

——, "The Russo-Livonian Crisis, 1555: Extracts from Joachim Burwitz' Report of February 19, 1555," *Journal of Modern History*, vol. 19, no. 2 (June 1947), pp. 142–151.

——, "The Voyage of Athanasius Nikitin to India, 1466–1472," *The American Slavic and East European Review*, vol. 5, no. 14–15 (November 1946), pp. 46–54.

Lantzeff, George V., "Russian Eastward Expansion Before the Mongol Invasion," *The American Slavic and East European Review*, vol. 6, no. 18–19 (December 1947), pp. 1–10.

Lewitter, L. R., "Poland, the Ukraine, and Russia in the 17th Century," *Slavonic Review*, vol. 27, no. 68 (December 1948), pp. 157–171, no. 69 (May 1949), pp. 414–429.

Likhachev, D. S., "Further Remarks on the Problem of Old Russian Culture," *Slavic Review*, vol. 22, no. 1 (March 1963), pp. 115–120.

Loewenson, Leo, "The Moscow Rising of 1648," *Slavonic Review*, vol. 27, no. 68 (December 1948), pp. 146–156.

Lubimenko, Inna, "England's Part in the Discovery of Russia," *Slavonic Review*, vol. 6, no. 16 (June 1927), pp. 104–118.

Meyendorff, A. F., "Anglo-Russian Trade in the 16th Century," *Slavonic Review*, vol. 25, no. 64 (November 1946), pp. 109–121.

Miller, Alexander, "Feudalism in England and Russia," *Slavonic Review*, vol. 14, no. 42 (April 1936), pp. 585–600.

Mirtchuk, J., "The Ukrainian Uniat Church," *Slavonic Review*, vol. 10, no. 29 (December 1931), pp. 377–385.

Nikolaieff, A. M., "Boris Godunov and the Ouglich Tragedy," *Russian Review*, vol. 9, no. 4 (October 1950), pp. 275–285.

O'Brien, C. Bickford, "Russia and Turkey, 1677–1681: The Treaty of Bakhchisarai," *Russian Review*, vol. 13, no. 4 (October 1953), pp. 259–268.

Polyevktov, M., "The Ways of Communication between Russia and Georgia in the Sixteenth and Seventeenth Centuries," *Journal of Modern History*, vol. 2, no. 3 (September 1930), pp. 367–377.

Raeff, Marc, "An Early Theorist of Absolutism: Joseph of Valokolamsk," *The American Slavic and East European Review*, vol. 8, no. 2 (April 1949), pp. 77–89.

Rapaport, Semen, "Mohammedan Writers on Slavs and Russians," *Slavonic Review*, vol. 8, no. 22 (June 1929), pp. 80–98.

Riasanovsky, Alexander V. "The Embassy of 838 Revisited: Some Comments in Connection with a Normanist Source on Early Russian History," *Jahrbücher Für Geschichte Osteuropas*, New Series, vol. 10, no. 1 (April 1962), pp. 1–12.

Riasanovsky, Nicholas V., "Old Russia, The Soviet Union, and Eastern Europe,"

The American Slavic and East European Review, vol. 11, no. 3 (October 1952), pp. 171–188.

Review, vol. 7, no. 1 (Autumn 1947), pp. 96–110.

———, "The Norman Theory of the Origin of the Russian State," *Russian*

Rostovtsev, Mikhail, "South Russia in the Prehistoric and Classical Period," *American Historical Review,* vol. 26, no. 1 (October 1920), pp. 203–224.

Shulgin, Basil, "Kiev: Mother of Russian Towns," *Slavonic Review, Slavonic Yearbook,* vol. 19, (1939–1940), pp. 62–82.

Spinka, Matthew, "Patriarch Nikon and the Subjection of the Russian Church to the State," *Church History,* vol. 10 (December 1941), pp. 347–366.

Stammler, Heinrich, "Russia Between Byzantium and Utopia," *Russian Review,* vol. 17, no. 2 (April 1958), pp. 94–103.

Stokes, A. D., "The Status of the Russian Church, 988–1037," *Slavonic Review,* vol. 37, no. 89 (June 1959), pp. 430–442.

———, "Tmutarakan," *Slavonic Review,* vol. 38, no. 91 (June 1960), pp. 499–514.

Stremooukhoff, Dimitri, "Moscow, the Third Rome: Sources of the Doctrine," *Speculum,* vol. 28, no. 1 (January 1953), pp. 84–101.

Tschebotarioff-Bill, Valentine, "Circular Frontier of Muscovy," *Russian Review,* vol. 9, no. 1 (January 1950), pp. 45–52.

———, "National Feudalism in Muscovy," *Russian Review,* vol. 9, no. 3 (July 1950), pp. 209–218.

Vakar, Nicholas P., "The Name 'White Russia,'" *The American Slavic and East European Review,* vol. 8, no. 3 (October 1949), pp. 201–213.

Vasiliev, A. A., "Was Old Russia a Vassal State of Byzantium?," *Speculum,* vol. 7, no. 3 (July 1932), pp. 350–360.

Vernadsky, George, "Feudalism in Russia," *Speculum,* vol. 14, no. 3 (July 1939), pp. 300–323.

———, "The Heresy of the Judaizers and Ivan III," *Speculum,* vol. 8, no. 4 (October 1933), pp. 436–454.

———, "Notes on the Social History of Kievan Russia," *The American Slavic and East European Review,* vol. 3, no. 4 (December 1944), pp. 81–92.

———, "On Feudalism in Kievan Russia," *The American Slavic and East European Review,* vol. 7, no. 1 (February 1948), pp. 3–14.

———, "The Problem of Early Russian Campaigns in the Black Sea Area," *The American Slavic and East European Review,* vol. 8, no. 1 (February 1949), pp. 1–9.

———, "The Royal Serfs (*Servi Regales*) of the 'Ruthenian Law' and Their Origin," *Speculum,* vol. 26, no. 2 (April 1951), pp. 255–264.

———, "The Status of the Russian Church During the First Half-Century Following Vladimir's Conversion," *The American Slavic and East European Review,* vol. 1 (1941), pp. 294–314.

Vucinich, Alexander, "The First Russian State: An Appraisal of the Soviet Theory," *Speculum,* vol. 28, no. 2 (April 1953), pp. 324–334.

———, "Soviet Theory of Social Development in the Early Middle Ages," *Speculum,* vol. 26, no. 2 (April 1951), pp. 243–254.

Ward, Grace Faulkner, "The English Danegeld and the Russian Dan," *The*

American Slavic and East European Review, vol. 13, no. 3 (October 1954), pp. 299–318.

William, T. S., "The Russia Company and Narva, 1558–1581," Slavonic Review, vol. 31, no. 77 (June 1953), pp. 405–419.

Yakobson, S., "Early Anglo-Russian Relations," Slavonic Review, vol. 13, no. 39 (April 1935), pp. 597–610.

Zenkovsky, Serge, "The Russian Church Schism: Its Background and Repercussions," Russian Review, vol. 16, no. 4 (October 1957), pp. 37–58.

Zenkovsky, Vasily V., "The Spirit of Russian Orthodoxy," Russian Review, vol. 22, no. 1 (January 1963), pp. 38–55.

Zernov, Nicholas, "Vladimir and the Origin of the Russian Church," Slavonic Review, vol. 28, no. 70 (November 1949), pp. 123–138, no. 71 (April 1950), pp. 425–438.